Dilemmas of World Politics

# DILEMMAS OF WORLD POLITICS

*International Issues in a Changing World*

Edited by John Baylis and N. J. Rengger

CLARENDON PRESS · OXFORD
1992

Oxford University Press, Walton Street, Oxford OX2 6DP
Oxford New York Toronto
Delhi Bombay Calcutta Madras Karachi
Petaling Jaya Singapore Hong Kong Tokyo
Nairobi Dar es Salaam Cape Town
Melbourne Auckland
and associated companies in
Berlin Ibadan

Oxford is a trade mark of Oxford University Press

Published in the United States
by Oxford University Press, New York

British Library Cataloguing in Publication Data
Data available

Library of Congress Cataloging in Publication Data
Dilemmas of world politics: international issues in a changing world
/ edited by John Baylis and N. J. Rengger.
p. cm.
Includes bibliographical references (p.   ) and index.
1. World politics—1989–   . I. Baylis, John. II. Rengger, N. J.
(Nicholas J.)
D860.D55 1992
327'.09'04—dc20      92–864
ISBN 0–19–827351–7 (cloth)
ISBN 0–19–827350–9 (paper)

Typeset by Hope Services (Abingdon) Ltd
Printed and bound in
Great Britain by Biddles Ltd,
Guildford & King's Lynn

*This book is dedicated to
the memory of
R. J. Vincent*

# PREFACE

This book was born out of our experience in trying to teach general courses in international relations and world politics. We decided that, while there were many good books that covered what we would call the traditional agenda of international relations, there were few, if any, that had as their principal focus the burgeoning debates over that agenda and how far it still reflected the nature of world politics. Moreover, we wanted to try and capture something of the excitement and intellectual ferment that characterizes the study of world politics especially at a time of such rapid change. The idea was to produce a book of a slightly different kind. Rather than attempt to cover virtually all relevant aspects of world politics, we would focus on certain especially important issues that affected world politics as a system and would do so in a way that would allow students or that great unknown, the general reader, to acquaint themselves with a vast and often formidably difficult literature and to realize its diversity, range, and intellectual interest. From a rather more parochial perspective we hoped to produce a book that could be useful for general seminar discussion.

Such a book would clearly have to be a collective endeavour and so we asked a number of our colleagues if they would be interested in trying to put something together with these ends in mind. The response was positive and so we began to think about the project in more detail. Inevitably, the project mushroomed, as academic projects do, until it involved sixteen chapters and scholars from nine universities on both sides of the Atlantic.

During this project we have incurred many debts. Our first vote of thanks must go to our contributors who put up with our written and oral reminders of rapidly shrinking deadlines and who produced their chapters despite being ferociously busy doing many other things. We are truly grateful both for their perseverance and their patience. We must secondly thank Oxford University Press, in the persons first of Henry Hardy and then of Tim Barton (when Henry disappeared into the dreaming spires), who showed faith in the project by contracting us to do it and who have supported us splendidly throughout.

Individual members of our authorial team have been of great help at various points in the process. Eric Herring has been involved in discussing the project from the outset and has made many contributions to it, not least in helping Nicholas Rengger design an undergraduate course at Bristol which reflects the book. Professors John Garnett and Ken Booth have provided much encouragement and good advice at various stages, particularly when the vagaries of academic scheduling or the national or international postal service reduced one or both of the editors to near barking lunacy.

Other people who have helped in various ways along the way and who we would like to acknowledge are, in no particular order: Stephen Kennedy, Geoff Berridge, Steve Smith, Richard Little, Caroline Kennedy, Vernon Hewitt, Michael Lee, and Jack Spence. None of them, of course, is responsible for the result. We are also very grateful to Alan Macmillan for his very thorough preparation of the index for the book.

There is one special debt that we would both like to mention. John Vincent, who died in November 1990, was one of the first authors we signed up for the book. As with everything else he did, he set about the project with great enthusiasm and vigour. His tragically early death meant that we never got his completed chapter. It would, without doubt, have been a superbly written contribution, elegant, humane, and exciting as John's contributions always were. He was, in the best and rarest sense, irreplaceable. We hope that, in some small measure, this book can stand as a tribute to him and to the respect and affection in which he was held.

JB
NJR

*Bristol and Aberystwyth*
*April 1991*

# CONTENTS

# NOTES ON THE CONTRIBUTORS

JOHN BAYLIS is a Reader in the International Politics Department and Dean of the Faculty of Economic and Social Studies at the University of Wales, Aberystwyth.

KEN BOOTH is a Professor in the International Politics Department at the University of Wales, Aberystwyth.

JOHN C. GARNETT is Woodrow Wilson Professor in the International Politics Department and Vice-Principal at the University of Wales, Aberystwyth.

ERIC HERRING is a Lecturer in International Security in the Politics Department at Bristol University.

MARK HOFFMAN is a Lecturer in the International Relations Department at the London School of Economics.

MARC IMBER is a Lecturer in the International Relations Department at the University of St Andrews.

COLIN MCINNES is a Lecturer in the International Politics Department at the University of Wales, Aberystwyth.

ROWLAND MADDOCK is a Senior Lecturer in the International Politics Department at the University of Wales, Aberystwyth.

JAMES PISCATORI is a Lecturer in the International Politics Department at the University of Wales, Aberystwyth.

NICHOLAS RENGGER is a Lecturer in Political Theory and International Relations in the Politics Department at Bristol University.

IAN H. ROWLANDS is a Lecturer in the Development Studies Institute at the London School of Economics.

PETER SAVIGEAR was formerly a Senior Lecturer in the Politics Department at Leicester University and is now a free-lance writer.

GERALD SEGAL is a Senior Fellow at the International Institute for Strategic Studies.

ADAM WATSON was formerly a Professor in the Department of Government and Foreign Affairs at the University of Virginia and a member of the British Diplomatic Service.

NICHOLAS J. WHEELER is a Lecturer in the Department of Politics at Hull University.

PAUL WILKINSON is Professor of International Relations at the University of St Andrews.

PHIL WILLIAMS is a Professor in the Graduate School of Public and International Affairs at the University of Pittsburgh.

# Introduction: Theories, Methods, and Dilemmas in World Politics

*John Baylis and N. J. Rengger*

No serious observer can have failed to be astonished at how much the international landscape has changed recently. World politics has experienced more change in the last two years than in the previous fifty. What is disputed, however, is the significance of these changes. The international system faces a whole series of questions, many of them new ones, to which we have to attempt to find satisfactory answers. These questions thus pose serious and potentially intractable dilemmas for the states, organizations, and individuals that constitute that system. This book considers these dilemmas from a wide range of differing perspectives.

The book attempts to focus then, on a series of key questions in world politics and to discuss them in a way that is accessible to students and the general reader as well as also giving those with rather more experience or knowledge something to chew on. We do not suppose that everyone will agree with the authors, indeed we confidently expect that many will not. The intention is to inform but also, and at least in equal part, to provoke discussion.

## I. Dilemmas and World Politics

Let us start, in good academic fashion, by defining some terms. For the purposes of this book we use the term dilemmas to refer to those questions about contemporary world politics where there are choices between equally plausible and usually unwelcome alternatives. In some cases this will mean that there are a number of proffered solutions or programmes on offer that defy simple adjudication; each of them, in other words, might be the best way forward. In other cases there might only be a choice among evils. Obviously, there are many dilemmas in this sense that are relevant to world politics and no single book could discuss them all. Ethical dilemmas, for example, have recently occupied a good deal of space in learned journals and books. We have chosen, however, to focus on those dilemmas whose primary locus is *systemic*. By this we mean that they are likely to have radical effects on the structure and nature of the international system itself, however they are resolved (and however temporarily). By the international system, we simply mean the set of procedures, methods, processes, and institutions that characterize the interactions that constitute contemporary world politics, including that hotly disputed notion international society, discussed in a number of chapters but most specifically in Chapter 3.

Generically we use the term 'world politics' throughout the book to emphasize the changed and changing nature of contemporary international relations. It is not that we think that 'international politics' or 'international relations' (the two most common terms for our subject) are not perfectly good terms in themselves but they have tended to be used in specific senses in the past. One of the debates running through the book concerns the extent to which 'world politics' is still 'inter-national' in the sense of primarily being about states. Without prejudging this question, it is clear that the system is now global in reach and reference and so we thought it sensible to use the term 'world politics' from the start.

In this sense, we believe that all of the key systemic 'dilemmas' of 'world politics' are present in the book. This does not mean, of course, that all the key *issues* for contemporary world politics are included. There are clearly issues that are of enormous importance which we discuss tangentially or fleetingly as part of one of the chapters. The question of refugees, for example, has clearly become increasingly important as a topic of concern in world politics over the last few years (for example the Palestinians and more recently the Kurds, Serbs, and Croats) and it clearly involves dilemmas, in our sense. Wanting to help the Kurds but not wanting to interfere in the internal affairs of another state or get bogged down in a civil war is clearly a choice between unpleasant alternatives. Why, then is there no chapter on refugees? This is because we believe that while the question of refugees is a *problem* for world politics it is not, properly speaking a *systemic dilemma*. The problem of refugees becomes part of a number of other questions if we are seeking a guide to its importance for the system as a whole. Does the existence of the refugees' question imply the further erosion of the sovereign nation state? (the type of issue considered in Chapters 2, 5, and 6, for example). Are the claims that are made on behalf of the ethical status of refugees indicative of an embryonic world community sentiment? (something like this is discussed in Chapters 1 and 3) and so on.

This conception of our focus influenced our decisions as to how to lay out the book and what issues we wanted to cover. We wanted to include all the issues—theoretical, institutional, and practical—that give rise to systemic dilemmas in our sense. Thus, we had to examine a number of issues that feature prominently in the traditional agenda of world politics (such as the security dilemma, war, nuclear weapons, etc.), as these are clearly of great importance for the future of the international system. Equally, however, we needed to address issues that are much more recent or have had a much less prominent place in the literature (for example, culture, Islam, the environment, and the changes that are allegedly reshaping key regions or states).

We came to the conclusion that, effectively, the dilemmas that concerned us could be divided into three groups. The first looks at three theoretical dilemmas that have come to occupy a prominent place among contemporary discussions of world politics. Thus the first chapter considers the traditional model of the 'security dilemma' and asks how resilient it might be to the changes just discussed. The second assesses the significance of the phenomenon of interdependence for world politics. The third asks how important conceptions of culture, society, and order are for the contemporary international system. There are obviously a large number of issues raised in these chapters but the overriding ones focus on whether or to what extent the international system is characterized by 'international anarchy' and how important ameliative or radical notions such as society might be for world politics.

The second section of this book is entitled 'Institutions'. We derive this term from the work of Martin Wight who famously suggested that 'international society' has five 'institutions': diplomacy, alliances, guarantees, war, and neutrality.[1] However, as will be obvious, we have adapted this usage. We suggest that the contemporary international system, whether or not it has societal elements (a topic at the centre of the discussion in Chapter 3), has certain 'institutions' in the sense that there are certain practices or organizations that set the parameters, as it were, for world politics. These 'institutions' generate dilemmas in our sense. They include war, the diplomatic system and its correlates, the nature, type, and roles of international organizations, and, arguably the most significant aspect of contemporary world politics, the international economy.

The final part of the book is the largest. It considers ten contemporary issues that constitute systemic dilemmas. These are subdivided into two types: issue-oriented dilemmas and regional- or state-centred dilemmas. Among the issues are the environment, nuclear weapons and their implications, terrorism, the resurgence of Islam, and mediation and the resolution of conflicts. Among the region- or state-centred dilemmas are the decline of the Soviet Union and the United States as the unchallenged great powers of the post-1945 era, the changes in contemporary Europe initiated by the end of the Cold War and their implications, and the claim that the rise of 'trading states'[2] such as Japan and the four 'little Dragons' of the Pacific rim (Hong Kong, Taiwan, South Korea, and Singapore) has set in motion a process that will result in a change in the axis of world power from the Atlantic, where it has rested for the last 500 years, to the Pacific; the rise of the so-called 'Pacific century'.

It is, of course, true that we have left out key regions of the world from this list. Do not the problems of Africa and Latin America deserve inclusion, to say nothing of the Middle East? If this book was designed to consider the most important regions or issues then certainly not to have chapters on these parts of the world would be remiss indeed, but our book is not about that. As with the case of refugees, these cases pose enormous problems for world politics but are not productive of systemic dilemmas. The problems of debt in Latin America, for example, are part of the wider problems of the international political economy (Chapter 4) as well as of the domestic politics of the states in these particular regions. Disease, hunger, and poverty in Africa are parts of the wider problem of development, in its turn a function of dilemmas created by the interaction between the problems of the international economy (Chapter 4 again), the traditional pattern of international relations (Chapter 1), and cultural or societal change (Chapter 3). The Middle East poses great questions of high policy both for states within the region and for outside powers but they are relatively familiar questions in themselves arising out of, for example, the security dilemma (Chapter 1), war (Chapter 5), terrorism (Chapter 10), or the rise of revolutionary interpretations of Islam (Chapter 9). In contrast, the possible changes in the status of the United States and the Soviet Union (Chapters 13 and 14), the actual changes in Europe (Chapter 15), and the rise to world power (at least in some senses) of Japan and China (Chapter 16) all pose genuine dilemmas for the structure of world politics that these other issues, important as they are, do not.

As we have said, we believe that all these dilemmas have a number of possible solutions and that there is no easy way of determining between them. One filter that is often tried, however, is a general theoretical or conceptual orientation towards world politics. Before we move on to consider our group theoretical issues, therefore, we should outline the main general interpretations governing the literature of world politics.

## II. Approaches to World Politics in the Twentieth Century

Relations between political communities have, of course, excited intellectual curiosity from the earliest period of human reflection upon politics. The ancient Greeks, for example, although they did not have a formal concept of international relations,[3] clearly discussed the relations between their city states and had a very well-developed states-system.[4] One of the most famous of all texts on international relations is Thucydides' *History of the Peloponnesian War*.

However, as a formal academic subject of study, politics and its sub-field international politics, have expanded exponentially in the twentieth century. As one might expect, therefore, a wide variety of differing approaches have been used to study it.[5] For the purposes of this book, therefore, we shall concentrate on the twentieth-century study of international (and now world) politics and we shall suggest that the best way to see this variety is to imagine two axes marked methodological and conceptual/ normative. Let us deal with each in turn.

## Methodological Debates

Essentially, the methodological axis runs from an extreme positivism on the one hand to a clear hermeneutic, interpretive point on the other. These are sometimes referred to as the positivistic school and the historical school.[6] Positivism here should be understood as a predilection to see the social sciences as analogous to the natural sciences. On this understanding, one is supposed to erect 'theory' on the basis of close observation and the framing of testable hypotheses. It will usually involve a great deal of quantitative work and empirical support, although there are a number of different branches of this approach, of course (see below).

'Hermeneutic', on the other hand, should be understood as assuming that political and social phenomena cannot be understood as equivalent to the data of the natural sciences. As a result, events must be understood not as discrete examples of general patterns or 'laws' (as some positivist writers would say[7]), but as historically unique, however much resemblance and/or similarity there might be between them. For this reason some writers who favour this view, for example Martin Wight, have suggested that 'international theory' is an inevitably limited subject.[8] Others regard this as rather negative and suggest that there still are interesting theoretical generalizations to be made or topics to pursue, but that they must be pursued in a manner appropriate to social enquiry, i.e., not by a 'simple' positivism.[9]

The chronological aspect of this debate need not detain us very long in a book of this sort. In essence, it was initiated by developments in the United States. After the Second World War, various techniques with their origins in science or mathematics (game theory and operational or systems analysis, for example[10]) began to be used with increasing frequency in the study of social phenomena such as politics and economics. Many writers, for example, Stanley Hoffmann in the United States and Steve Smith in Britain have also pointed out that 'international relations', as an institutionalized university subject, is largely an American invention.[11] Inevitably, therefore, as the techniques became more sophisticated and the results achieved more impressive, the claims made on behalf of these methods became correspondingly greater until some began to suggest that with the arrival of these techniques more traditional methods of examining politics or international relations, rooted in the humanities, should simply be dropped. This was the so-called 'behavioural revolution' in social science, although behaviouralism itself was in fact only a small part of it and many of the techniques that have emerged out of it (rational choice theory, for example) have little or nothing to do with behaviouralism properly so-called.

Such an approach tended to stress in its original form that the social sciences were, in fact, little different from the natural sciences in terms of the appropriate methods needed and it therefore emphasized the careful framing of testable hypotheses and the accumulation of such hypotheses into what it called 'theory', meaning generalized and generalizable propositions about the nature of international politics.[12] Leading proponents of this view have been or are Morton Kaplan and Quincy Wright at the University of Chicago, J. David Singer at Michigan, Bruce Russet at Yale, and Kenneth Waltz of the University of California, Berkeley.[13] It remains enormously influential in the study of international relations.

These assumptions gained great influence in the late 1950s and early 1960s in the United States. Simply because of the country's size and the consequent number of scholars, universities, research institutes, and think-tanks, this set of approaches rapidly came to be dominant in the emerging schools of political science and international relations. A secondary reason was that its methods of working also tended to be taken up by those in government service and by think-tanks such as the RAND (Research and Development) Corporation, the US airforce think-tank, in which pioneering work on nuclear strategy was done. Its tenets also became prominent in much European political science (especially in Scandinavia, Holland, and Germany) but had only a fragmented and attenuated influence in France, Spain, Italy, and Britain.[14]

In the latter case, however, an older tradition drawing on history, law, and philosophy remained far more common than elsewhere even after the impact of the new methods began to make themselves felt in the 1960s and early 1970s. The assumptions of writers sympathetic to this approach were that international politics was best understood as a discrete phenomenon where generalization was difficult at best and 'theory' as defined by positivists (i.e., after the manner of the natural sciences) was impossible. This did not mean, of course, that 'normative', or philosophical, reflection on international politics was impossible, though as we remarked earlier, Martin Wight, for example, had his doubts about the subject[15] and strongly influenced others of the so-called 'classical' or 'English' school in this direction. Advocates of this approach to international politics included Herbert Butter-field, Regius Professor of History at Cambridge, Hedley Bull, prior to his tragically early death in 1985 Montague Burton Professor of International Relations at Oxford, and, most significantly and influentially of all, Martin Wight, who had worked and taught at the LSE and at Sussex.[16]

This methodological division has continued down to the present. It is to be found in various forms in most of the chapters in this book. However, it is better, we think, to see it as a methodological continuum with most scholars (and, if it comes to that, practitioners) somewhere either side of the mid-point. The two poles are not necessarily opposed, however, and there have been healthy signs of late that the two camps are coming to understand the benefits each might bring to the other. There has also been a widening of methodological focus. Rational choice theory, for example, long influential in the field of economics has become increasingly popular in political science and international relations in recent years. For rational choice theorists, human beings are rational egoists; rational in the sense that they used rationality instrumentally to attain ends already given; egoists in the sense that they are utility maximizers who attempt to maximize their benefits and minimize their costs. As we have said, rational choice has only recently been regularly used as an analytical technique in international relations[17] but it is on the increase. Some uses of it are found, for example, in Chapters 1, 4, 6, and 8 of the present volume. Other ways of broadening and combining elements of both these methodological approaches can be found in some critical and radical interpretivist work (see below).

These methodological debates are thus still very much part of discussions of world politics. They have an important effect on the way world politics is perceived and analysed and, to this extent, are important for an understanding of various solutions that have been offered to the dilemmas that it is the main purpose of this book to examine.

## Conceptual and Normative Approaches

By conceptual and normative we mean to imply approaches that are concerned with *what* is explained and what might be recommended rather than *how* things are to be explained and whether they might be recommended. The conceptual and normative approaches on the second axis tend not to be dominated by one or other of the above methodological views, however. Rather they are broad churches in which a range of methodological views can apply. Speaking very generally there are three major poles around which debates in this second axis are gathered.

## Realism

The realist approach has been the dominant normative view of international relations for most of the twentieth century. Essentially, it conceives of international relations as a struggle for power and security between discrete political communities, at present primarily nation-states. These states exist in the absence of an overall sovereign power constraining them—a condition usually termed international anarchy—which has led to what John Herz famously called the 'security dilemma'.[18] This implies that the search for security on the part of state A leads to insecurity for state B which therefore takes steps to increase its security leading in its turn to increased insecurity for state A and so on (see Chapter 1 for a full discussion of this). Most realists assume that the result of this feature of international life is that the international system is a system characterized by a high degree of instability and in which states will attempt to balance against other powers that threaten them. This tendency has given rise to the most enduring aspects of realist theory, the concentration on issues of war and peace and the notion of the balance of power.[19]

For realists, the notion of 'the balance of power' has been and remains crucial to the operation of the international system. In any given system some, perhaps most, states will be 'satisfied' or 'status quo' powers. That is to say they are states who benefit from, at least to some degree, the current state of things. However, there will also usually be unsatisfied or 'revisionist powers'. In the Europe of 1914, for example, the leading status quo power was Britain, which with its vast empire and enormous trading and financial resources was the greatest power of its day. The leading revisionist power was Imperial Germany, who felt that Britain, amongst others, was denying Germany its 'rightful' place as a major power. In such circumstances it was inevitable that Britain and Germany would clash (though it was by no means inevitable that the clash would take the form that it eventually did). Equally, fear of German 'revisionist' designs spurred France into making alliances with Russia and then Britain, which in turn (in a classic 'security dilemma') increased German fear about being 'encircled' and prompted the formation of the triple alliance of Germany, Austria-Hungary, and Italy.

In more recent times perhaps the greatest advocate of the balance of power has been Henry Kissinger.[20] Kissinger is doubly interesting because (as we shall see below) he was one of the early theorists of realism but also one who got the chance to put his theories into practice as it were. He became National Security Adviser to President Nixon in 1969 and Secretary of State in 1973. It was Kissinger's enthusiasm for this principle of realist theory that was in part responsible for his support for Nixon's opening to China in 1971–2. For Kissinger, the most workable and legitimate international system is one where all parties to it (or at least all great powers) recognize it as 'legitimate' thus effectively all becoming status quo powers. Such a situation, he thinks, existed in Europe after the Congress of Vienna in 1815 roughly until 1850. Such a system depends upon the possibility of effective 'balancing' lest any of the great powers involved become restive.[21] In the Cold War period such a system did not in reality exist, in part because of the absence of such a sense of legitimacy and in part because effective balancing requires more than two players and, of course, there were only two 'great powers'—the Superpowers. Thus in bringing in China and making the 'bipolar world' a 'Great Power triangle'[22] Kissinger believed he was establishing the first component of a stable international system—the possibility of effective balancing. As Geoff Berridge has rightly said, 'in the balance of power, revolutionary power is met and checked by the decentralised organisation of preponderant counter power. This means alliance necessarily and war possibly. In a system of sovereign states there is no other way of preserving the independence of its members: the balance of power derives from the logic of the system.'[23] Issues related to these questions (order, legitimacy, and so on) are discussed in the present book in chapters by Ken Booth and Nick Wheeler, John Garnett, N. J. Rengger, Peter Savigear, John Baylis, and Gerald Segal.

Let us now look briefly at the origins and development of realism. Writers most chiefly associated with the emergence of realism in international relations have been academics, diplomats, journalists, and other commentators and include Reinhold Niebuhr, Hans Morgenthau, Nicholas Spykeman, George Kennan, Walter Lippman, Arnold Wolfers, and Henry Kissinger in the United States, E. H. Carr, Georg Schwarzenberger, and Martin Wight in Britain, and Raymond Aron in France.[24] Of course, a large variety of assumptions are made by realist writers and they do not always agree with one another. Some believe that the international system is as it is because human nature is by definition appetitive and prone to violence (Niebuhr, Morgenthau, and Wight, for example), others that it is so because of the actions of particularly malign individuals or states like Hitler or Nazi Germany. A third group see the anarchical nature of the international system as the primary cause of conflict (Waltz, Gilpin).[25]

A number of past writers are usually said to have been influential proponents of this view (for example, Thucydides, Machiavelli, and Hobbes) but in the twentieth century it arose in the 1930s and 1940s largely as a result of reflection about the political events of those years, both the policies that led up to the outbreak of the Second World War and events immediately thereafter. The differences within realism are perhaps as significant as the similarities. Writers like Carr, for example, were brilliant polemicists and his *The Twenty Years Crisis* was more responsible than any other single book for discrediting the alleged 'idealism' of the inter-war period (of which more in a moment). Morgenthau, on the other hand, was the realist who first attempted to build up realism as a systematic approach to international politics as a whole rather than (as was the case with Lippman and Kennan, for example) as a specific response to particular circumstances such as the US–Soviet rivalry and the emergent Cold War (a term that was coined, in fact, by Walter Lippman). Indeed, the Cold War proved extremely fortuitous for realists in that it appeared that their geo-political, rationalistic, balance-of-power-oriented reasoning was precisely what was required in the global competition between the forces of the West and those of the East.

In recent years a variant of realism has become extremely fashionable. Often called neo-realism, it agrees with the basic assumptions of traditional realism (that states compete for power and security) but has developed what it believes is a much more sophisticated analysis of the international system that supports this normative case through the use of positivistic methodologies which earlier generations of realists did not use. Neo-realism's presiding genius is Kenneth Waltz of the University of California, Berkeley. His *Theory of International Politics*[26] was the first and remains the most thorough presentation of the neo-realist argument, though subsequent writers (for example, John Mearsheimer, Robert Art, Stephen Krasner, and Stephen Walt in the United States and Barry Buzan and Steve Smith in Britain[27]) have also done much to elaborate and modify it. The essential neo-realist claim is that the structure of the international system determines the actions of actors within it. It does not determine specific actions, of course, but it does define the types of actions. Thus, states exist in an anarchic, self-help system where their functions are undifferentiated, however efficient (or not) they may be at achieving them. From this structural analysis of the nature of the international system, neo-realists deduce a whole range of propositions about contemporary international politics. (John Garnett's chapter addresses many of these issues in more detail.)

## Institutionalism

The second central locus of the conceptual and normative axis is the widest. In its original form it grew out of the dissatisfaction of many observers with the international system that encouraged (many believed) the outbreak of the First World War. As a result of this dissatisfaction many writers and scholars in the interwar period emphasized collective decision-making, the rule of international law and collective security achieved through the newly created League of Nations to resolve or mitigate disputes. Critics of the tendency (such as E. H. Carr) labelled it 'idealism' and the name has stuck.[28] However, the writers who articulated this view in the 1920s and 1930s were very far from being starry-eyed idealists if by that term is meant a wilful refusal to face unpleasant realities. Rather they asserted that the reality was that certain forms of international behaviour had led to the outbreak of the most horrific war in human history (the First World War) and therefore they must be changed. These writers included Alfred Zimmern, the very first Professor of International Politics (at the University Of Wales College at Aberystwyth[29]), David Davies, the liberal philanthropist who established the Chair, Philip Noel-Baker, and, in the United States, James Shotwell.[30]

Their critique focused on their belief that the system of international relations that had permitted the outbreak of the First World War could be changed into something better. They believed in collective security, for example, rather than the balance of power as the best guarantee of peace. Their hope was that the League of Nations, established after the war, could provide a forum where threats to the stability of the system could be resolved or that, on the occasions when they were not so resolved then the international community itself as a whole would act to prevent or to repel aggression. The failure of the League in the 1930s over Manchuria, Spain, and Abyssinia weakened their case, and provided fertile ground for realist critics like Carr, but even so elements of this view remained in the Charter of the United Nations, the League's successor body after the Second World War. The debates between idealism and realism are discussed in the present volume in Chapters 1–3 and also in John Baylis's chapter on Europe.

The predominance of realism in the 1940s and 1950s led to little work of this sort being done but during the 1950s and 1960s a number of writers began to question the realist perspective although they did not initially approach it from the same perspectives as the 'idealists' of the inter-war period. These included Ernst Haas at the University of California, Berkeley who drawing on earlier work by David Mitrany developed what was termed a 'functionalist' account of international relations which stressed co-operation and the need for international institutions.[31] Criticisms of realism emerged from other quarters also, John Burton, a former diplomat turned academic, suggested that realism's perception of the world as akin to a billiard table with states simply cannoning into one another ignored increasing evidence of interdependence and the importance of non-state actors in international relations.[32] World Politics was, he suggested, better seen as a 'cobweb' where pressure at one point would ripple out to many others. A third direction of criticism came from sociologists such as Immanuel Wallerstein,[33] who suggested that the international system was dependent upon the world economic system. This divided the world into a core of dominant economic powers (essentially the industrialized states of the west) and an exploited periphery and semi-periphery.

One of the common themes around which all these criticisms converged was the central importance of the modern world economy and the changes it was helping to initiate. To be sure, economics had not been ignored by realists. E. H. Carr, for example, has stressed the importance of relating politics to economics and more recent realists, Robert Gilpin, for example, have developed a powerfully articulated realist view of the international political economy.[34] However, it has tended in many other realist writers to be played down in favour of military/security issues and, in any case, it was the argument of realism's critics that the international economy was changing the way in which international politics worked and that this was ignored in realist writing. This form of critique reached its apogee in the work of Robert Keohane and Joseph Nye of Harvard University. In two path-breaking books, *Transnationalism and World Politics* (which they jointly edited) and, especially, *Power and Interdependence* (which they co-authored), they provided both a brilliant synthesis of much previous work on interdependence and evolved a complex argument of their own about the transition it was bringing about in international politics as a whole.[35] In this book these issues are central to John Garnett's chapter and are also dealt with to some extent in N. J. Rengger's, Rowland Maddock's, and Marc Imber's.

While they have both worked on rather different areas of contemporary world politics (Keohane primarily on economic and theoretical issues whilst Nye has concentrated on military/security issues), Keohane has provided a useful name for the general approach in a subsequent book.[36] He terms it an 'institutionalist' approach as its main focus is on the existence of, need for, and methods of understanding and creating, institutions in world politics. By this term he means not just formal institutions (such as the United Nations) but informal understandings and 'regimes' that govern relations between states on particular issue areas.

What links the writings of all these very disparate groups together is their concern with, and dissent from, the realist view of the state and of the system. In different ways and to different degrees they tend to argue that state-centric approaches produce a distorted view of world politics by focusing so exclusively on inter-state relations. It is not that they necessarily ignore or disparage interstate relations themselves. The 'idealists' most certainly did not; nor do Wallerstein or Keohane and Nye. They merely point out that there are other aspects to world politics (non-state actors, growing interdependence of states, societies, and economies, etc.) which the realists ignore or de-emphasize at the cost of producing an oversimplified vision of world politics. As John Garnett discusses in Chapter 2, the issue remains a very lively one today.

This approach, then, emphasizes the changes that are observable in contemporary world politics, especially those associated with economic, political, and social interdependence, a term that should here be taken to imply 'situations characterized by reciprocal effects among countries or among actors in different countries'.[37] The very different interpretations that scholars have given to this phenomenon, however, has ensured that this second approach is very broad indeed and contains within it a good deal of variety, ranging from writers very close to realism on the one hand (Lawrence Freedman, for example[38]) to those who, both methodologically and conceptually are closer to the third general group, the critical perspective (to which we shall turn in a moment). A good example here, represented in the present book, might be Ken Booth.[39]

## Critical Perspectives

The third set of perspectives have emerged primarily in the 1980s and mainly (though not exclusively) among younger scholars. Again there is a very broad range of opinions here but what unites them are criticisms both of what they see as the prevailing *methodology* of neo-realism and institutionalism, the two dominant theoretical approaches at the beginning of the 1990s (i.e., a general if 'soft' positivism), and of at least some of the normative conclusions that are said to follow from these two approaches. Most of the work of these writers has to date been primarily concerned with methodological and/or ethical issues though there were signs at the end of the 1980s that their focus had begun to shift to wider issues.[40]

This approach can roughly be subdivided in two. These have elsewhere been termed critical interpretive theory and radical interpretivism.[41] Critical interpretive theory adopts a broadly historical approach, in some ways akin to the work of people like Martin Wight and Herbert Butterfield but adds to it theoretical perspectives taken from hermeneutic political and social theory.[42] It usually has a very powerful ethical component to it as well and derives from this a critique of the contemporary international system as 'unjust' or 'exploitative' (in various ways and to various degrees). It also tends to stress the emancipatory capacities inherent in human life which, for various reasons, the international system inhibits or suppresses. Writers who offer different versions of this view are Andrew Linklater[43] and Mark Hoffman[44] (both of whom are influenced by the German social philosopher Jurgen Habermas), Mervyn Frost,[45] and Robert Cox[46] (who is strongly influenced by Marxist writing especially Gramsci). In the present volume it is chiefly discussed in N. J. Rengger's chapter and to a lesser extent in those of Mark Hoffman and Ken Booth and Nick Wheeler. It has some affinities in its normative thrust to the writings of some institutionalists and idealists, though it can take many different forms.

The second view, radical interpretivism, is strongly influenced by certain French thinkers, the so-called post-structuralists such as Foucault and Derrida. It is methodologically more radical in the sense of often abandoning all familiar touchstones of mainstream thought and tends to express itself in the language of paradox or irony. As such it has been often criticized by the mainstream for obscurantism or simply irrelevance. Even writers sympathetic to critical perspectives, such as Ken Booth, have made this charge.[47] However, holders of this view often say that their task is to open closed debates and give space for marginalized voices. In the words of two of their leading spokesmen: they attempt to 'speak the language of exile'.[48] As far as world politics is concerned this tends to mean an emphasis on 'hidden' or 'masked' aspects of mainstream concerns (such as deterrence theory, arms control, etc.), a concern with the deconstruction of the language of international relations and a stress on single issues or organized interest groups or social movements caught up in the web of world politics, such as feminist movements, green groups like Greenpeace, and so on. They also tend to emphasize those aspects of contemporary world politics that are exponentially radicalizing the environment within which world politics is experienced and understood. Thus, they examine the effects of such things as computer simulations or the information technology revolution on how we see international relations and/or world politics. Writers who provide readings of world politics from this perspective include Richard Ashley, R. B. J. Walker, James Der Derian,[49] Michael Shapiro,[50] Ole Waever, Bradley Klein, David Campbell, and Hayward Alker.[51]

Both these tendencies share a good deal. Each, in turn, is critical of both methodological and normative aspects of mainstream work while drawing on aspects of it. Each shares a commitment to historically sensitive, interpretive methodologies. They are also, however, engaged in a debate between themselves as well as a wider one within political and social studies more generally and they are still at a relatively early stage in terms of elaborating accounts, theories, or readings of world politics. Again, N. J. Rengger's chapter discusses some of their assumptions in more detail.

## Explanation or Prescription

A related question emerges from this discussion of methodology and conceptual/normative approaches. It continues to be one that divides those working in the field. It asks what the primary purpose of the study of world politics should be. After all, world politics is rather different from the study of Ancient Greek poetry or Cosmology in that it inevitably deals with real world events and processes that have a marked impact on the way people live their lives. Surely, then, we cannot see this study simply as an academic pursuit.

In part, of course, it rather depends on how one defines the notion of an academic pursuit. In universities, the western tradition suggests that knowledge of whatever sort is primarily pursued for its own sake and only secondarily or incidentally for any relevance it might have to current problems or issues. There is, however, in the study of world politics a great temptation to embark on what is sometimes called 'policy relevant' work (i.e., work that addresses a particular issue of especial concern or importance by way of advocating, in Lenin's famous phrase 'What is to be done'). Hardliners on this issue suggest that in universities at least such work should be regarded with suspicion. Others would point to the fact that there are plenty of other organizations, research institutes, and so on whose job is to do work of this sort and that those who wish to pursue it would be better off doing so in the Royal Institute of International Affairs, the International Institute for Strategic Studies, the Brookings Institution, or other similar institutes with a heavy emphasis on policy work.

Much contemporary theory of all the various sorts discussed above is of this supposedly 'policy-relevant' sort—i.e., it attempts to suggest guidelines for action or policy. Such a view is no respecter of theoretical boundaries. It can be found in dyed-in-the-wool realists but just as often among critical theorists or radical interpretivists. A useful distinction that might help to resolve this problem is between 'policy relevant' and 'policy acceptable'.[52] The critics of the 'policy-oriented' approach tend to be criticizing the notion that in following it people skew research to what is acceptable in 'policy circles' (principally, that is to say, governments and related agencies). Thus it might be better to concentrate critical fire on work that makes too much effort to be acceptable to policy-makers (policy acceptable) rather than simply relevant to them (policy relevant). After all, almost any work on politics is 'policy relevant' in the sense that it *might* have implications for policy, but this is not what is usually at stake for the critics.

However, it is also true that most of the theoretical approaches (both conceptual and methodological) purport both to explain and to prescribe and in this sense even the most obviously academic studies might have prescriptive force. Realism and neo-realism, for example, are seen by their advocates as explanatory frameworks of analysis which focus on a particular interpretation of human nature and/or the structure of the international system. They describe the world 'as it is', based on these assumptions and argue that this is the proper function of such research. However, such descriptions also work as a guide for prescription i.e. to demonstrate why proposals as to how the world might be improved (or why it might deteriorate) will (or will not) work. This, after all, was the nub of many of the realist criticisms of 'idealism'.

Many of the critics of realism argue that the realists are being wholly disingenuous when they claim that they are merely 'explaining the world as it is'. Realists, they say, smuggle certain disputed values into their supposedly 'objective' research through selectivity of the information they choose to deal with and by their implicit acceptance of the status quo. A criticism of this sort is implicit in Robert Cox's division of the subject into what he calls 'problem-solving theory' and 'critical theory'.[53] Realists do 'problem-solving theory', Cox suggests, because, however much they strive for scholarly objectivity, they always accept the givens of the system and try to suggest ways in which it might work more effectively. For them it cannot be changed into something else. Critical Theory, on the other hand, examines this question too and as such openly admits the values and assumptions it makes in its attempt to interpret the world.

In fact there is a further division that is worth bearing in mind here. Realists have often been accused of saying that ethics do not have the place (or, at the very least, they have a very different place) in international politics than they do in domestic politics. Some have indeed said this or something similar to it but it is more accurate, we suggest, to see the realist position as asserting that the facts of the world impose constraints on international action. Those who would ignore or repudiate these constraints do so at their peril for the likely result will be disaster. Thus it is not that realists deny that prescription is possible—on the contrary many of them engage in it with alacrity—rather they argue that it must be prescription of a particular sort; prescription grounded in the facts of the world as they are, not as how some would like them to be. Realism's critics on this point suggest that, in fact, the failure to imagine what alternatives might exist is to abandon any hope of achieving them; it is to give up the journey before setting out.

This division runs very deep in the study of world politics. It is not the business of this introductory chapter to come down on one side or the other. In the chapters that follow readers will doubtless be able to tell in many cases where individual authors stand. As with the earlier methodological and conceptual differences, however, the debate has a significant impact on the way that the dilemmas of world politics are dealt with.

## III. Conclusion

Of course, these various approaches do not necessitate any particular approach to world politics in terms of the dilemmas we are about to discuss. As will be seen, however, adopting a particular combination of methodologies and conceptual approaches will usually give different sets of criteria by which to make judgements when confronted with a particular dilemma.

In the chapters that follow, there is, of course, no particular line or set of views either methodologically or conceptually. There are representatives of most major approaches or schools of thought in the book and the general arguments of their chapters will, of course, reflect that. We wanted chapters that argue a case rather than simply rehearsing conventional wisdoms. Equally, it is our view as editors that understanding the dilemmas of world politics requires understanding the various ways in which the many possible approaches to the subject operate when considering particular issues and the chapters reflect this.

For these reasons, therefore, there is no 'conclusion' to this book. The dilemmas we examine are dynamic ones whose significance, character, and implications will be debated for many years. The conclusions are for our readers to draw. If we have conveyed both the intellectual excitement and importance and the political significance and difficulty of these dilemmas then our purpose in this book will have been amply fulfilled.

### Notes

1. See Martin Wight, *Power Politics* (Harmondsworth: Pelican, 1979), 111.
2. This phrase is Richard Rosecrance's. See his *The Rise of the Trading State* (New York: Basic Books, 1986).
3. A term that really owes currency to the coining of the term 'international law' by Jeremy Bentham in the 18th century. See his *Principles of Morals and Legislation* (New York: Haffner, 1948), 326.

4. For a discussion of this see Wight, *Systems of States* (Leicester: Leicester University Press, 1977) and R. Purnell, *The Society of States* (London: Weidenfeld & Nicolson, 1973), chap. 2.

5. There are many different ways to break down the theoretical variety that has characterized international relations. Perhaps best known are Martin Wight and Hedley Bull's three approaches: realist, rationalist, and revolutionist. They traced these three different views as historical traditions going back to the Renaissance. Good versions are found in Hedley Bull, *The Anarchical Society* (London: Macmillan, 1977) and Martin Wight's essay, 'Western Values in International Relations', in H. Butterfield and Martin Wight (eds.) *Diplomatic Investigations* (London: George Allen & Unwin, 1966). Almost equally well known is Michael Banks's suggestion of an 'inter-paradigm debate' between realists, structuralists, and pluralists. See Banks, 'The Evolution of International Relations Theory', in *Conflict in World Society* (Brighton Harvester Wheatsheaf, 1984). Other divisions have included those of Michael Donelan, who favours five traditions in *Elements of International Political Theory* (Oxford: Clarendon Press, 1990) and Chris Brown who suggests the emergence of two dominant traditions (other than realism) in contemporary thought: 'cosmopolitan' and 'communitarian'. See his forthcoming *New Normative Theory in International Relations*. Most of these divisions have some merits. We, however, are discussing only international relations theory in the twentieth century and suggest that for now the five categories we sketch on two axes can provide a framework on which all of these categorizations can be put.

6. Or the 'scientific' school and 'classical' school. See, for example, Morton Kaplan's article in praise of the scientific approach and Hedley Bull's reply 'International Theory: The Case for a Classical Approach', both in *World Politics*, xviii/3 and xix/7 (1966). See also: Roy Jones, 'The English School of International Relations: A Case for Closure', *Review of International Studies*, 7/1 (1981); Sheila Grader, 'The English School of International Relations: Evidence and Evaluation', *Review of International Studies*, 14 (1988); N. J. Rengger, 'Serpents and Doves in Classical International Theory', *Millennium: Journal of International Studies* (1988); Peter Wilson, 'The English School of International Relations: A Reply to Sheila Grader', *Review of International Studies*, 15 (1989).

7. See Kenneth Waltz, *Theory of International Politics* (Reading, Mass.: Addison Wesley, 1979), for example.

8. See Wight, 'Why is there no International Theory', in Butterfield and Wight, *Diplomatic Investigations*.

9. Most critical and/or radical interpretivist theorists would fall into this second camp, for example.

10. Game Theory is a method for understanding human behaviour that is predicated upon the assumption that individuals are rational egoists and seek to maximize expected benefits and minimize expected losses. Operational/Systems Analysis was pioneered by intelligence organizations (such as the Office of Strategic Services or OSS) during the Second World War.

11. See Stanley Hoffman, 'An American Social Science: International Relations', *Daedalus* (1977). Steve Smith, 'Paradigm Dominance in International Relations: The Development of International Relations as a Social Science', in H. C. Dyer and L. Mangasamain (eds.), *The Study of International Relations: The State of the Art* (London: Macmillan, 1989).

12. See Waltz, *Theory of International Politics.*

13. See ibid.; Singer, *Models, Methods and Progress in World Politics* (London: Westview, 1989); Kaplan, *System and Process in International Politics* (New York: John Wiley, 1957); Wright *A Study of War* (Chicago: University of Chicago Press, 1944); and Russett, 'The Calculus of Deterrence', *Journal of Conflict Resolution*, 3/2 (1963).

14. For an assessment of the development of European work in political science in general and international studies in particular see the papers of the *European Consortium for Political Research* workshops, Paris, 1989 (The Workshop on International Studies in Europe directed by A. J. R. Groom.)

15. See his essay 'Why is there no international theory?', in Butterfield and Wight, *Diplomatic Investigations.*

16. See ibid.; Bull, *The Anarchical Society*; Bull and Watson, *The Expansion of International Society* (Oxford: Clarendon Press, 1984).

17. See, for example, the opening two chapters in Kenneth A. Oye (ed.), *Co-operation under Anarchy* (Princeton, NJ: Princeton University Press, 1985).

18. See his article, 'Idealist Internationalism and the Security Dilemma', *World Politics* (1950).

19. For recent very good treatments of the balance of power see 'The Balance of Power', special issue of *Review of International Studies*, 15/2 (1989), ed. Moorhead Wright, and Stephen Walt, *The Origins of Alliances* (Ithaca, NY: Cornell University Press, 1986).

20. For general assessments of Henry Kissinger's diplomacy, see Roger Morris, *Uncertain Greatness* (New York: Harper and Row, 1977); George Ball, *Diplomacy for a Crowded World* (Boston: Little Brown, 1976); Stanley Hoffman, *Primacy or World Order: American Foreign Policy since the Cold War* (New York: McGraw-Hill, 1978) and, for his own account, Henry Kissinger, *White House Years* (Boston: Little Brown, 1980) and *Years of Upheaval* (Boston: Little Brown, 1982).

21. For this view of Kissinger's, see *A World Restored* (New York: Grosset and Dunlap, 1964).

22. See Gerald Segal, *The Great Power Triangle* (London: Macmillan, 1982).

23. Geoff Berridge, *International Politics: States, Power and Conflict since 1945* (Brighton: Harvester, 1987), 151.

24. See for good general treatments of these writers, Hedley Bull, 'The Theory of International Politics 1919–69' in B. Porter (ed.), *The Aberystwyth Papers* (Oxford: Oxford University Press, 1972). The most famous realists texts are: E. H. Carr *The Twenty Years Crisis* (London: Macmillan, 1939); Hans Morgenthau, *Politics among Nations* (New York: Alfred A. Knopf, 1948 and subsequent editions); George Kennan, *American Diplomacy 1900–1950* (Chicago: University of Chicago Press, 1951); Reinhold Niebuhr, *Moral Man and Immoral Society* (New York: Charles Scribners Sons, 1932); Arnold Wolfers, *Discord and Collaboration* (Baltimore: John Hopkins University Press, 1962); Henry Kissinger, *A World Restored*; Martin Wight, *Power Politics* (Harmondsworth: Penguin, 1979); and Raymond Aron, *Paix et guerre* (Paris: Calmann-Levy, 1962).

25. For an elaboration of these three views from the realist perspective, see Kenneth Waltz, *Man, the State and War* (New York: Columbia University Press, 1954).

26. Waltz, *Theory of International Politics*.

27. See John Mearsheimer, 'Back To The Future: Instability in the New Europe', *International Security* (Summer 1990); Robert Art, 'A Defensible Defence: America's Grand Strategy After the Cold War', ibid. (Spring 1991); Stephen Krasner, *Structural Conflict* (Berkeley: University of California Press, 1985); Stephen Walt, *The Origins of Alliances* (Ithaca, NY: Cornell University Press, 1986); Barry Buzan, *People, States and Fear*, 2nd edn. (London: Harvester, 1991); Steve Smith and Martin Hollis, *Explaining and Understanding International Relations* (Oxford: Clarendon Press, 1990). See also Barry Buzan, Charles Jones, and Richard Little, *The Logic of Anarchy* (forthcoming).

28. For an excellent overview of the thinkers of the 1920s and 1930s, see David Long and Peter Wilson (ed.), *Thinkers of the Twenty Years Crisis* (forthcoming).

29. The Woodrow Wilson Professorship of International Politics, named after the then President of the United States, was established in 1919 at Aberystwyth through an endowment by the Welsh philanthropist and liberal activist Lord David Davies explicitly to study international politics and prevent the outbreak of another Great War.

30. See Bull, 'The Theory of International Politics'.

31. See, for example, Ernest B. Haas, *Beyond the Nation State* (Stanford, Calif.: Stanford University Press, 1964).

32. See Burton, *A Theory of World Society* (Cambridge: Cambridge University Press, 1968).

33. See Wallerstein, *The Modern World System* (3 vols., Cambridge: Cambridge University Press, 1970, 1974).

34. See, for example, Robert Gilpin, *The Political Economy of International Relations* (Princeton, NJ: Princeton University Press, 1987).

35. Robert Keohane and Joseph Nye (eds.), *Transnationalism and World Politics* (Boston: Little Brown, 1971), ed., *Power and Interdependence: World Politics in Transition* 2nd edn. (Boston: Little Brown 1989).

36. *After Hegemony* (Princeton, NJ: Princeton University Press, 1984).

37. Keohane and Nye, *Power and Interdependence*, 8.

38. For a good statement of Freedman's current position and why he can be characterized in this way, see his 'Escalators and Quagmires: Expectations and the Use of Force', *International Affairs*, 67/1 (1991).

39. See his new edited collection, *New Thinking about Strategy and International Security* (London: Harper Collins, 1991).

40. See, for example, the chapters on War, Spies, Pressure groups, etc. in James Der Derian and Michael Shapiro (eds.), *International/Intertextual Relations* (New York: Lexington Books, 1989).

41. See N. J. Rengger and Mark Hoffman 'Modernity, Postmodernism and International Relations', in Jo Doherty, *et al.* (ed.), *Postmodernism and the Social Sciences* (London: Macmillan, 1991).

42. Hermeneutic, in this context should be understood as an approach which believes that truth is always interpretive truth and so it is usually negatively disposed to positivistic modes of reasoning which assumes that truth is clear and unambiguous and rationality instrumental, concerned with means-ends reasoning.

43. See his *Men and Citizens in International Theory* (London: Macmillan, 1980, 1990), and *Beyond Realism and Marxism* (London: Macmillan, 1990).

44. See his 'Critical Theory and the Inter-Paradigm Debate', *Millennium: Journal of International Studies*, 16/3 (1987).

45. Frost, *Towards a Normative Theory of International Relations* (London: Macmillan, 1986).

46. See his 'Social Forces, States and World Orders: Beyond International Relations Theory', in R. O. Keohane (ed.), *Neo-Realism and its Critics* (New York: Columbia University Press, 1984).

47. See his Plenary Lecture at the British International Studies Association Conference in Newcastle, in Dec. 1990.

48. See 'Speaking the Language of Exile', introduction to the special issue of *International Studies Quarterly*, ed. R. B. J. Walker and Richard Ashley (Sept. 1990).

49. See his *On Diplomacy* (Oxford: Basil Blackwell, 1987).

50. See his edited collection with Der Derian, *International/Intertextual Relations*.

51. Most of these writers are included in the Der Derian/Shapiro collection mentioned above, and/or in the *International Studies Quarterly* special issue. The Debate between the two views is the primary theme of N. J. Rengger and Mark Hoffman (eds.), *Critical Theory and International Relations* (Hemel Hempstead: Harvester, 1991).

52. We owe this distinction to Eric Herring.

53. See Robert Cox, 'Social Forces, States and World Orders: Beyond International Relations Theory', in R. O. Keohane (ed.), *Neo-Realism and its Critics* (New York: Columbia University Press, 1984).

# PART I. THEORIES

# ONE

# The Security Dilemma

*Nicholas J. Wheeler and Ken Booth*

Of all the dilemmas in world politics, the security dilemma is quintessential. It goes right to the heart of the theory and practice of international politics. Fundamental questions about philosophy and policy have to be asked and at least partly answered when considering whether the security dilemma can be mitigated or even transcended, or whether it has simply and tragically to be suffered.

## I What is the Security Dilemma?

A dilemma, by definition, is worse than a problem. A problem in international politics is a situation involving two or more parties which is difficult to deal with or overcome. A dilemma poses a different degree of difficulty: it is a situation necessitating a choice between two equal, especially equally undesirable, alternatives. In this sense a dilemma is a problem which seems incapable of a satisfactory solution.

Security is widely considered to be the transcendent value in world politics. It refers to the objective and subjective freedom from threats of individuals and groups (states have usually been thought to be of primary importance). Of paramount concern to international theory has been freedom from the threat of war. The provision of security has traditionally been recognized as the first obligation of governments.

In an ordinary sense, a security dilemma would seem simply to refer to situations which present governments, on matters affecting their security, with a choice between two equal and undesirable alternatives. In the literature on international politics, however, the term has come to have a special meaning. The phenomenon which has come to be labelled the 'security dilemma' is thought to be one of the most significant and pervasive features of relations between states.

Security dilemmas arise from a perennial problem in interstate relations, namely the inherent ambiguity of some military postures and some foreign policy intentions. The dilemmas are the direct result of the difficulty governments have of unambiguously determining what is 'defensive' and what is not. Consequently, our working definition is as follows:

A security dilemma exists when the military preparations of one state create an unresolvable uncertainty in the mind of another as to whether those preparations are for 'defensive' purposes only (to enhance its security in an uncertain world) or whether they are for offensive purposes (to change the status quo to its advantage).

As just defined, a security dilemma can be the product of two different dynamics, though the literature on the subject does not clearly distinguish between them. We will call the two types inadvertent and deliberate security dilemmas.

### Inadvertent Security Dilemmas

In this case a dilemma is created in a government's mind by the inadvertent actions of another state; that is, the latter's failure to act carefully on security matters; its behaving in ways which give unintended signals; and its insensitivity to the security needs of others. As a result of such inadvertent behaviour, the defensive military preparations of one government to enhance its security in an uncertain world (but with no intention of overthrowing the military status quo) may increase the sense of insecurity felt in another state. If the latter perceives the 'defensive' preparations of the other as potentially threatening and offensive, an inadvertent security dilemma will have arisen. This is the original conception of the security dilemma and it is believed to arise out of the very nature of the states-system.

*Deliberate Security Dilemmas*

In this case a dilemma is created in a government's mind as a result of the deliberate actions of another state. These deliberate actions themselves may be of two types. First, they may be from a militarily status quo state which adopts deliberately 'offensive' strategies in order to deter another, because it sees itself in an adversarial relationship with it. The other state (what we will call the target state) may be thrown into a dilemma as a result of the apparent contradiction between the other's declared defensive intentions and its (threatening) military capabilities. The second deliberate security dilemma may result from a revisionist or revolutionary state (wishing to change the status quo or completely overthrow the existing international political order) which adopts a posture designed to lull the target state into a false sense of security. Again, the target state may be thrown into a dilemma as a result of the apparent contradiction between the other's declared policy (reassuring) and its actual capabilities and behaviour (threatening). Deliberate security dilemmas of the two types just described arise not so much from the inherent pressures of the states-system, but from the policies of particular states.

If the threat posed by one state to another, be it inadvertent or deliberate, is accurately perceived by the potential or actual target state, then the situation cannot be classified as a security 'dilemma'. It is simply a security 'problem', albeit perhaps a difficult one. Whatever the actual intentions of the state engaging in the military preparations, it is the unresolvable uncertainty in the mind of the potential or actual target state about the meaning of the other's intentions and capabilities which creates the 'dilemma'.

From the preceding discussion it is evident that security dilemmas of whatever variety are comprised of *dilemmas of interpretation* (are the other's preparations defensive or offensive?) and then *dilemmas of response* (should the other's military preparations be matched and so risk an arms race and the further build-up of mistrust, danger, and cost, or should a wait-and-see policy be adopted thereby risking exposure to coercion or attack as a result of relative weakness?).

## II. Is the Security Dilemma Inherent in International Anarchy?

Within legitimate states security is provided by a system of law-governed relationships, with laws being made by a sovereign authority such as a Parliament, and carried out by its agents. Above the states which make up the international system, however, there is no global sovereign authority (world government) to make and execute laws which might provide security for all. In this sense the international system can be described as 'anarchical': it is ungoverned. Interstate anarchy is a condition which historically has tended to promote 'self-help' behaviour; since states cannot look to any higher authority to provide their security, they have to look after themselves. Governments may prefer to co-operate with those of other states, but because they cannot fully know the intentions of others, even when engaged in mutual co-operation, there is a tendency towards mistrust, and hence insecurity. If the mistrust is mutual, a dynamic 'action-reaction' cycle may well result, which will take the fears of both parties to higher levels. This interacting dynamic, with insecurity breeding insecurity, is the security dilemma.

The philosopher most associated with the idea of politics being a struggle for security in a hostile environment is the seventeenth-century English writer Thomas Hobbes. The adjective 'Hobbesian' is used in international politics to indicate the idea that the international system is analogous to the 'state of nature'. The latter, according to Hobbes, is a pre-society, with no authoritative legal or moral rules. In such a condition the drive for security becomes the dominant preoccupation. The Hobbesian state of nature is a state of war where life is 'nasty, brutish, and short'. Fighting is not necessarily continual, but the expectation of it is. A long tradition of international relations theorists have argued that politics between sovereign states, searching for security in an anarchical world of scarce resources, is akin to the Hobbesian state of nature. There is a significant difference, however: whereas Hobbes saw man escaping the state of nature within states through the social contract and the formation of the 'Leviathan' (government), those who apply the Hobbesian analogy to international politics do not see a similar escape possible for states.

Despite their very different philosophical starting-points, Rousseau agreed with Hobbes that a social contract was not possible between states. Rousseau considered the prospects for states developing co-operation and he recognized that it would have been perfectly rational and enlightened for the Europe of his day to form a federation (thereby abolishing the condition of anarchy). However, as Clark points out, he believed that humans would always follow their 'apparent' (myopic) self-interest as against their 'real' (long-term, enlightened) interest. He wrote: 'If, in spite of all this [the compulsion of long-term enlightened interests], the project remains unrealised, that is not because it is utopian; it is because men are crazy, and because to be sane in a world of madmen is in itself a kind of madness'. Rousseau here is pointing to the central role of trust in international relations and the problem of how to achieve it in a condition of anarchy.[1]

It is Rousseau who has provided students of international relations with the parable of the stag-hunt; it is widely regarded as expressing the essential predicament of relations between states. Rousseau describes five hungry men co-operating to hunt for a stag. The hunger of each would be satisfied by the fifth portion of a stag, but the hunger of one would be satisfied by a hare. When one of the men spies a hare within reach he leaves the group to grab it, so allowing the stag to escape. His own hunger is satisfied, but his defection and the collapse of co-operation this causes leaves his fellows hungry. The fundamental problem in such a self-help situation is that none of the hunters knows whether the others will defect and chase the hare; because of this uncertainty and lack of trust, it is understandable that each hunter will assume the worst and pursue his 'apparent' interest at the expense of his 'real' interest. Thus, even if each hunter prefers co-operation in chasing stags for all, rather than trying to help himself to a hare, the fear that one or all the others might defect as soon as the first hare comes within grasp, leads to a sub-optimal outcome for all the players. To paraphrase Rousseau's earlier quotation: to pursue 'real' interests in a world pursuing 'apparent' interests is a kind of irrationality.

Together, fear and mistrust in relations between states destroy the prospects for co-operation and increase the pressures for confrontation and even conflict. It is the structure and dynamics of the situation which magnify the problem. In a world of interstate anarchy, insecurities are created in peoples' minds which then take on a new reality: subjective insecurity becomes, in a sense, objective. These pressures are particularly intense on security questions. Herbert Butterfield has written:

> It is the peculiar characteristic of the situation I am describing—the situation of what I should call Hobbesian fear—that you yourself may vividly feel the terrible fear that you have of the other party, but you cannot enter into the other man's counter-fear, or even understand why he should be particularly nervous. For you know that you yourself mean him no harm, and that you want nothing from him save guarantees for your own safety; and it is never possible for you to realize or remember properly that since he cannot see the inside of your mind, he can never have the same assurance of your intentions that you have. As this operates on both sides the Chinese puzzle is complete in all its interlockings—and neither party sees the nature of the predicament he is in, for each only imagines that the other party is being hostile and unreasonable. It is even possible for each to feel that the other is wilfully withholding the guarantees that would have enabled him to have a sense of security.[2]

Butterfield's phrase 'Hobbesian fear' is a useful shorthand for the dynamic driving security dilemmas.

Even from this brief account it should be evident why the security dilemma is usually seen as the central problematic in the interaction of states in a condition of anarchy. Not surprisingly, when people think about the possibilities for developing co-operation and community in relations between nations, the security dilemma is often seen as a major obstacle. This has been the consensus among most mainstream writers about international politics over the years ('the realists'), but it is not a universal view. Others have argued that the security dilemma is not inescapable; like all ideas, it is said to be open to new interpretations in the light of new knowledge, different circumstances, and a changing conception of interests and values. In short, some believe that the potentiality exists, even in a condition of anarchy, for security dilemmas to be mitigated or even transcended. The security dilemma is seen to be embedded in our heads rather than in the allegedly inescapable logic of anarchy.

## III. What were the Origins of the Concept?

The insecurity dynamics implied by the notion of the security dilemma have been understood since at least Greek times. In his classic book on the Peloponnesian wars, Thucydides argued that whatever the immediate causes of the wars between Athens and Sparta, the underlying cause was the mistrust and fear about the growing power of an adversary. The most quoted sentence in the whole book points to the security dilemma. 'The growth of the power of Athens, and the alarm which this inspired in Lacedaemon, made war inevitable.'[3] In the opinion of Thucydides, 'men are motivated by honor, greed, and above all fear'.[4]

The actual term 'security dilemma' did not gain widespread usage until the 1950s, with the writings of Herbert Butterfield and John Herz. Butterfield's understanding of the insecurity dynamic focused on the inadvertent but invariable consequences of 'Hobbesian fear'. Butterfield suggested that international politics was shaped by a 'condition of absolute predicament or irreducible dilemma' which lay 'in the very geometry of human conflict'.[5] Butterfield considered that this 'irreducible dilemma' was 'at the basis of all the tensions of the present day . . . the hard nut that we still have to crack'. Running through his words is Butterfield's sense of the tragedy in international relations: 'Behind the great conflicts of mankind', he wrote, 'is a terrible human predicament which lies at the heart of the story.'

Butterfield explains the prevalence of 'Hobbesian fear' in terms of the 'universal sin' of humanity. Explaining politics among nations primarily as an outcome of a flawed human nature was one of the defining characteristics of the realists who dominated the subject in the late 1940s and 1950s. This was pre-eminently the case with Reinhold Niebuhr, who George Kennan described as the 'father' of all realists.[6] The 'will to power', according to Niebuhr, is the result of a desire for security beyond the limits of 'human finiteness'; it is a manifestation of the 'pride which Christianity regards as a sin in its quintessential form'.[7] Security is desired, but can never be achieved. Power is sought to guarantee it, but the more it is sought, the greater the problems of maintaining whatever levels of power or security are desired.

Working along similar lines to Butterfield and Niebuhr, but without the same emphasis on a flawed human nature, John Herz argued that the 'security dilemma' always existed in a situation where there was interaction between men and groups in the absence of a higher political authority. In such a condition of anarchy Herz concluded that

> there has arisen what may be called the 'security dilemma' of men, or groups, or their leaders. Groups or individuals living in such a constellation must be, and usually are, concerned about their security from being attacked, subjected, dominated, or annihilated by other groups and individuals. Striving to attain security from such attack, they are driven to acquire more and more power in order to escape the impact of the power of others. This, in turn, renders the others more insecure and compels them to prepare for the worst. Since none can ever feel entirely secure in such a world of competing units, power competition ensues, and the vicious circle of security and power accumulation is on.[8]

Writing about the security dilemma in 1959, Herz indicated that he had been unaware of Butterfield's writings on the subject when he had first claimed 'primary importance for the security dilemma'.[9] Furthermore, Herz indicated that he wished to distance himself from Butterfield's claim that the 'dilemma' was the basis of all past and present conflict. Herz suggested that there was a difference 'between "security policies" and policies motivated by interests that go beyond security proper'. By this he meant that all states pursue security, but some pursue security plus ambition. Here, Herz pointed as an example to Hitler's behaviour in the 1930s, arguing that 'it can hardly be maintained that it was a German security dilemma which lay at the heart of that conflict, but rather one man's, or one regime's amibition to master the world.' Despite differences of emphasis between Herz and Butterfield, it is evident that both writers believed that the search for security through military power tends to provoke insecurity in others. Herz put it bluntly: 'ultimately, somewhere, conflicts caused by the security dilemma are bound to emerge among political units of power'.[10]

Herz's emphasis on the self-help character of the international system rather than on the sin of humanity links directly with the book *Man, the State and War* in which Kenneth Waltz categorized and analysed the causes of war. This book, published in 1959, laid the groundwork for an approach which twenty years later became labelled as 'neo-realism'. The thrust of the latter was already evident in the way Waltz stressed Rousseau's argument that co-operation for mutual gain was probably doomed in a setting of anarchy. It was Waltz who made familiar to every student of international politics Rousseau's parable of the stag-hunt. Waltz is quite clear, like Rousseau, that the impediment to co-operation is not necessarily the character of the immediate intentions of either party: 'Instead, the condition of insecurity—at the very least the uncertainty of each about the other's future intentions and actions—works again their co-operation.'[11] In short, according to Waltz's influential analysis, the security dilemma is a structural problem in the international system.

Following the human nature pessimists like Butterfield and the embryonic neo-realists like Waltz, the third line of enquiry in the 1950s which helped to clarify the dynamics of insecurity was game theory. Here the writing of Thomas Schelling was influential. In *The Strategy of Conflict*, he discussed the dynamics of mutual distrust, the 'compounding of each person's fear of what the other fears', as he put it.[12] Discussing the fear of surprise attack—the security dilemma at its most intense—he vividly describes the 'multiplier' effect of 'compound expectations'. He illustrates what he calls the 'nervousness model' by giving the analogy of a householder's discovery of a burglar downstairs. Both men have guns (this is, after all, the United States):

Even if he prefers just to leave quietly, and I wish him to, there is danger that he might think I want to shoot, and shoot first. Worse, there is danger that he may think that I think he means to shoot. Or he may think that I think he thinks I want to shoot. And so on. 'Self-defence' is ambiguous, when one is only trying to preclude being shot in self-defence.

By such dynamics, irrational outcomes (mutual destruction) can arise 'through a rational calculation of probabilities or a rational choice of strategy, by two players who appreciate the nature of their predicament'.

Schelling clarified the way rational decisions could produce irrational outcomes in the 'nervousness model' of interstate relations. What determines the intensity of the nervousness of the participants and the manner in which nerves are handled brings in issues of cognition and decision-making. Further light was thrown on these dimensions of the security dilemma in the 1970s. According to mainstream international relations theory, anarchy has been seen as inevitably creating a sense of insecurity for governments. In practice, however, it is evident that the security problems that arise can be defined in different ways by different policy-makers.

Responses to the common predicaments of anarchy may reflect, for example, the peculiar security cultures of different states. Unique political, cultural, historical, and geographical factors tend to produce varied cognitive dynamics on the central issue of security. There is not one homogeneous security culture, as is implied by the structuralist argument. This is exemplified, for example, in the different attitudes to alliances shown by successive governments in Sweden and Norway. Both countries share similar geopolitical positions and Nordic cultures, yet Norway joined and has remained a loyal member of NATO, while Sweden has maintained a forthright position of armed neutrality.

The logic of anarchy tells us something about the pressures and constraints which have shaped the policies of states over time but it does not allow us to predict how particular states will manage their security situation. It does not tell us whether a Czechoslovakia will bow before *force majeure* or whether a Poland will fight a lost cause. This point highlights Waltz's neglect of the scope for choice as governments confront their individual security dilemmas. While Waltz accepts that there is some scope for action within the constraints of the system, the implication of his argument seems to be that states cannot really choose how they define their security problems—this is determined by the pressures of the system.

A more sophisticated analysis of the interplay between the behaviour of the units in the interstate system and the pressures created by the structure of the system can be seen in the writings of Robert Jervis. After Herz and Butterfield, Jervis has done most both to elaborate and to develop the concept of the security dilemma.

Jervis has employed the term security dilemma in both its deliberate and inadvertent senses. Mostly, he talks about the security dilemma as a situation where 'one state's gain in security often inadvertently threatens others'.[13] Thus, a state may not have aggressive designs on other states, but the interplay of fear and mistrust leads to an increase in mutual suspicion and hostility. In consequence, an action–reaction process between states would be stimulated, in which the interplay of armaments competition and worst-case forecasting about each others' intentions would promote even higher levels of mutual insecurity. Elsewhere in his writings, Jervis talks about the security dilemma 'not as the unintended consequence of policy but rather as its object'.[14] Here he is referring to the deliberate security dilemma, where one state believes it can only be secure if others are insecure.

Jervis argued that although it is difficult to draw inferences about a state's intentions from its military posture and capabilities, states do in fact draw such inferences, even when they are unwarranted. He suggested that governments believe that other governments see them as they see themselves (that is, they find it difficult to see themselves as a threat). John Foster Dulles is used to illustrate the point. Dulles said, 'Khrushchev does not need to be convinced of our good intentions. He knows we are not aggressors and do not threaten the security of the Soviet Union.'[15] The history of international relations, in contrast, shows that governments are not readily accepted by foreign governments in their own terms, and that reassurance is not easily achieved. There are many pressures predisposing those responsible for the security of states towards mistrust.

Reassurance is not easy between mistrustful governments. Even the old adage about 'actions speaking louder than words' is not completely helpful, since so many actions in international politics—particularly those of a military nature—are inherently ambiguous. Lord Grey, Britain's Foreign Secretary at the eve of the First World War, later reflected on this problem:

The distinction between preparations made with the intention of going to war and precautions against attack is a true distinction, clear and definite in the minds of those who build up armaments. But it is a distinction that is not obvious or certain to others. Each Government, therefore, while resenting any suggestion that its own measures are anything more than for defence, regards similar measures of another Government as preparation to attack.[16]

This is a perfect expression, with the benefit of hindsight, of the inadvertent type of security dilemma.

As should be evident from the preceding discussion, cognitive dynamics impact on the security dilemma in crucial ways. Butterfield seems to have been the first to capture the way they can intensify it. He wrote, for example, about conflicts being 'hot with moral indignation—one self-righteousness encountering another . . . the contemporary historians on each side . . . locked in the combative views of his own nation'.[17] During the 1970s and 1980s a range of literature elaborated the cognitive dynamics that led governments to overestimate the hostile intentions of others.

The cognitive dynamics interfering with accurate threat perception between governments, and so intensifying security dilemmas include the following:[18] *ethnocentrism*, which magnifies misperception, stereotyping, and nationalistic rivalries; *'doctrinal realism'*, which exaggerates the conflictual character of interstate relations; *ideological fundamentalism*, which heightens 'us' and 'them' attitudes; *strategic reductionism*, which takes the politics out of interstate relations and reduces it to questions of military balance or imbalance; *worst-case forecasting*, which can magnify mutual fears; *secrecy*, which increases suspicion and the difficulty of accurate threat assessment; *zero-sum thinking*, which promotes alarmism and rules out significant co-operation; and *implicit enemy imaging*, which leads to particular states being suspected by others whatever the character of their actions or non-actions. Such considerations as these, which degrade accurate threat perception and assessment, might be called 'the permanent aggravating factors' in the security dilemma. In their varying susceptibility to these aggravating factors, some national élites will be more prone than others to intensify security dilemmas.

Those explanations of international conflict which emphasize interlocking security fears have been called 'spiral theories' by Jervis.[19] Once a cycle of mutual suspicion is set in motion, the security dilemma works to escalate confrontation to higher and higher levels of hostility. The prescription from those who view the dynamics of conflict in this way is for governments to try and mitigate their security dilemma by a policy of reassurance. It is argued that policies aimed at building up military power in such circumstances, if only for deterrence, are likely to aggravate a conflict. A parallel increase in unilateral threats and strength will intensify rather than mitigate a security dilemma.

If both governments view their confrontation in 'spiral' terms (that is, they are mutually sensitive to security dilemma dangers), policies of mutual reassurance might ameliorate their confrontation. However, as Butterfield points out, one problem is that two governments locked in confrontation might not view the situation in the same way. And even if they did, neither can be completely confident of the other's real intentions. One may believe, for example, that the other is trying to lure it into a false sense of security which may later be exploited. What is more, even if governments believe others do not have aggressive designs against them, what assurance can there be that such designs will not develop in the future? Butterfield, Herz, and Jervis all recognize this fundamental problem that governments can never fully know the minds of others.[20]

Some conflicts are not the result of the interlocking fears of the classical inadvertent security dilemma exacerbated by negative psychological dynamics. Conflict is not only produced by misperception, and Jervis himself warned of the danger of 'over-psychologizing' in international relations. He argued that although an understanding of psychological dynamics is important in understanding how the security dilemma becomes reinforced through mutual misunderstanding, the 'costs of these insights is the slighting of the role of the [anarchical] system in inducing conflict and a tendency to assume that the desire for security, rather than expansion, is the prime goal for states.'[21] Here Jervis echoes Herz's criticism of Butterfield: it would be a mistake to assume that the security dilemma lies at the root of all interstate conflict. Sheer political ambition can also play a part.

If a state faces a government which is intent on aggression, then reassurance or even concessionary policies on its part may simply whet the aggressor's appetite for more expansion. This is what happened in the 1930s with the attempted appeasement of Hitler. When confronted by an unappeasable challenge, it is usually argued that states require credible policies of military deterrence to contain the aggressor. Jervis labels this type of confrontation the 'deterrence' model. But the effectiveness of deterrence is not as clear-cut as Jervis implies. In the case of Hitler and Nazi Germany, for example, the question arises as to whether deterrence by the Western powers would have worked. If appeasement can whet an aggressor's appetite, the attempt through deterrence to make permanent an unacceptable status quo might equally inflame powerful ambition.

Within the simple typology presented by Jervis, the problem for individual governments is to decide whether they are in a 'spiral' or 'deterrent' situation, and then adopt the appropriate security policies. Because of the complex cognitive problems mentioned earlier, however, identifying the situation accurately might be difficult. A government which objectively is in a 'spiral' situation, for example, may misperceive it, and as a result choose to emphasize a 'deterrent' response. The latter might include offensive weapons and doctrine. In this case the result might be to exacerbate tension further, by placing the target government under intolerable strain because of the putative threat to its own 'defence' forces. Despite the dangers of exacerbating tension in this way, by assuming hostility rather than benevolence, realists would still underline the validity of making pessimistic assumptions about others. If governments act this way, they argue, they do not risk mistaking an enemy for a friend; this was the trap into which Little Red Riding Hood fell. Her lack of any sense of danger led her to see benevolence in threatening signals.

If both parties in a 'spiral' situation emphasize deterrent postures as a result of making worst-case assumptions about each other's intentions, the outcome will be arms-racing, more fear and arms-racing, and less security for all at progressively higher levels of cost and destructive power. Worst-case forecasting has a propensity for being self-fulfilling. As George Kennan noted, those one treats as enemies tend to behave like enemies.[22] The counter-moral to the story of Little Red Riding Hood can be drawn from the tale of King Arthur's last battle. At a peace conference one of the knights drew his sword. He intended to kill a snake, but his action was misinterpreted. Others sprung to their own defence, and in a contagion of fear the knights fell upon each other, causing virtual annihilation.[23] Those who live by the worst-case forecast may die by the worse-case forecast.

Jervis's spiral/deterrence typology is therefore simple in theory, but in practice involves complexities. Another problem is the difficulty which he himself recognizes of drawing a distinction between the goal of security and that of expansion; that is, some states may believe that they can only be secure if they engage in expansionist behaviour, or if they have military superiority.

Israel, for example, continues to believe that it can only be secure if it dominates some of the territories occupied since the 1967 war. In this sense Israeli 'expansionist' behaviour might be argued to be 'defensive' in nature. The Israeli case also raises the possibility that some states might only feel secure if others are made to feel insecure. The traditional power political approach adopted by the Soviet Union until the Gorbachev revolution is one example. As typically exemplified by Stalin, this approach reflected the traditional Russian belief that fear bred respect. Jervis himself has suggested that France's policy towards Germany in the inter-war period was predicated on the premiss that French security depended on German insecurity. He notes that France believed that Germany could not be conciliated or reassured, and that as a result, the French determined that military superiority was necessary to deter German power.[24] In cases such as those just mentioned the security dilemma is not of the inadvertent type—a by-product of mutual efforts to enhance security. Instead, it seems to have resulted from the deliberate choices of particular governments. The outbreak of the First World War reveals that both the deliberate and inadvertent types of the security dilemma were at work; it also highlights the perennial problem of the interplay between defensive and offensive weapons and doctrines.[25]

From the discussion so far the prospects for achieving security in an anarchic states-system appear bleak. The security dilemma would seem to be the inevitable consequence of the structure of world politics. But not all writers agree. The remaining sections will address ideas which have been put forward arguing that the security dilemma can be mitigated or even transcended.

## IV. Can Security Regimes and Common Security Mitigate the Security Dilemma?

Realism has always been a broad church, and even some of its exponents while starting with the premiss that anarchy gives rise to the security dilemma, nevertheless go on to argue that the effects of the latter can be dampened. In Robert Jervis's words, 'The security dilemma cannot be abolished, it can only be ameliorated.'[26] This version of realism moves beyond pure power-politics by seeking to set normative limits to the struggle for power among nations. States might, for example, form 'security regimes', in which they accept rules, norms, and principles which allow for an interstate politics of reciprocity and restraint. In such a regime the existence of rules and norms and decision-making procedures can encourage the amelioration of the security dilemma at both the level of threat perceptions of individual states and at the level of the international system.

The formation of 'security regimes', according to Jervis, can be related to the dynamics of the offence–defence balance. He suggests that if offence and defence are not distinguishable, or if the offence is dominant, the need for a regime to moderate behaviour will be high, but the possibility of achieving one low. In contrast, if the individual pursuit of security is possible through defensive policies, a regime might be easy to form, though not very necessary. Jervis suggests that the best conditions for regime formation occur not only when offence and defence are distinguishable, but also when the offence is more costly than the defence. This, he believes, provides an incentive for co-operative behaviour.[27] A further prerequisite for security regime formation is that states place a common value on mutual security and co-operation (with no government believing that its security depends on the insecurity of others).[28] Persuading governments that others will reciprocate and not exploit conciliatory behaviour can be difficult if the costs of being exploited by others could be loss of territory or national independence.

The Concert of Europe which existed between 1815 and 1823 (and in a weaker form until the Crimean War) was a security regime in that it institutionalized reciprocity and restraint among the five great European powers. Governments took a long-term view of their predicament. They believed that short-run sacrifices would yield lasting gains and that others would not exploit their restraint for immediate ends. Self-interest was still the key motivator of the governments concerned, but each believed that its long-term self-interest required co-operation. In the case of the statesmen who came together in 1815 there was a determination to try and construct a framework for regulating their behaviour in a way which would prevent a recurrence of the wars between the great powers which had characterized the preceding generation.

Underpinning the idea of a security regime is the assumption that an agreed set of principles, norms, rules, and decision-making procedures might lead governments to change their understanding of their interests and of the benefits of co-operation. Henry Kissinger, for example, argued that lasting international security depends upon the creation of a legitimate international order which requires 'an international agreement . . . about the permissible aims and methods of foreign policy . . . at least to the extent that no state is so dissatisfied that, like Germany after the Treaty of

Versailles, it expresses its dissatisfaction in a revolutionary foreign policy'.[29] A 'revolutionary' power was not defined as one which was insecure, since this condition was seen as inherent in a states-system, but one which could not be reassured.

In addition to security regimes, with their emphasis on political norms, reassurance is also possible through the restructuring of military postures. To have maximum effect, regime creation and strategic reform will be carried forward in concert. Jervis recognized early that in situations where defensive policies are 'cheap, safe and effective', states may increase their security without decreasing the security of others, and that this would make possible a loosening of the security dilemma.[30] In the 1980s an 'alternative security' school developed around such ideas in Europe, not as a result of academic theorizing, however, but in response to a new phase of East–West confrontation. Alternative security thinking was largely a reaction to the INF controversy; its exponents included retired officials and military personnel, some research institutes in Western Europe and North America, and members of peace movements. Politically, these ideas were supported by several opposition parties in the West. Eventually the ideas spread to Moscow, where they were placed on the superpower agenda by President Gorbachev.

According to the alternative security school of the 1980s one of the most important lessons of the post-war period was that Western security was intimately related to that of the Soviet Union, and vice versa; modern weaponry had created an objective security interdependence. This meant that it was necessary for the West, for example, to recognize the fact that increases in Soviet insecurity did not necessarily improve Western security. The same was true in reverse. This apparently simple but rather radical notion slowly gained support under the banner of 'common security'. In contrast to the prevailing self-help security-through-strength beliefs of the early Reagan presidency, the Palme Commission Report of 1982 gave political backing to common security; the Commission argued that states can no longer obtain security at each other's expense, but only through co-operative efforts.[31]

A major implication of the common security approach was the argument that Western policy-makers needed to appreciate how and to what extent Western strategic policy itself represented a 'threat' to others. At the same time a comparable realization was developing more quickly in Soviet official circles. As Michael MccGwire has suggested, Soviet policy-makers by the early 1980s had come to appreciate that Soviet planning for the remote contingency of world war had been counter-productive; by increasing East–West tension, massive Soviet military postures over the years had in fact made more likely the possibility they had been designed to deter.[32] Common security thinking was developing in Moscow before Gorbachev came to power, and a line of influence can be traced back to alternative Western security thinking.

The body of ideas going under the umbrella terms 'common security' and 'alternative defence' crystallized in the early 1980s, though some of the doctrine and theoretical assumptions go back much further. In essence, the common security approach seeks to escape from the old trap of the security dilemma to provide a rational response to the new condition of security interdependence. Common security thinkers do not accept that the security dilemma is a necessary condition between states, and that in the case of the East–West confrontation, the countries of the northern hemisphere are not bound to live with high and permanent levels of insecurity. Choice is possible. Instead of attempting to rely indefinitely on an order based upon nuclear fear, alternative defence schemes in the 1980s sought to maintain a level of deterrence against aggression but to do so in such a way that the arms race would be reversed, crisis stability would be increased, and arms reduction would be encouraged. As a result it was hoped that political stability would evolve and gradually the security dilemma would be wound down; there would be more safety for all at less cost. These ideas developed in the first half of the 1980s against the background of the second Cold War, and in face of strong criticism by the Reagan and Thatcher governments.

By the mid-1980s the alternative security school had developed a rich menu of ideas about strategies, tactics, and weapons to ameliorate the NATO–WTO confrontation. The schemes ranged from reformist to radical, but two elements were common. The first was denuclearization, either in whole or in part, since offensive weapons of mass destruction (those developed and deployed as part of a nuclear war-fighting strategy) were thought by their nature to have a deleterious effect on the security dilemma. The second element was the objective of achieving non-provocative military postures. This was the idea that states and alliances would retain defensive forces to raise the entry price of aggression (making the benefits of occupation not worth the cost) but that offensive strategies and weaponry would be ruled out as far as possible. Security would be based on 'defensive deterrence' (what West German writers called a 'structural non-aggression capability') together with political reassurance.

Alternative security ideas are simple in theory but more complex when it comes to practice. In particular, agreeing upon the boundary between what is unambiguously defensive and potentially offensive is contentious. Both NATO and the WTO have always claimed to be 'defensive', but their doctrines and weapons have contained dangerous escalatory elements, especially when seen through the eyes of each other's defence planners. If neither side wanted war, alternative security thinkers argued that it should be possible to wind down the security dilemma by addressing the fears of each party by a process of defensive military restructuring. Mutual 'defensive supremacy' (when the defence of each side is more powerful than its opponent's offensive forces) would become the basis for stability rather than a balance of terror based on offensive power.

In the second half of the 1980s some of the ideas of common security began to see political light, largely because of President Gorbachev. The Soviet leader gave prominence to ideas about denuclearization, defensive emphasis, security interdependence, and reassurance. He backed up his words with actions, and progress was made in various arms control negotiations and in political meetings between leaders of East and West. After some suspicion on the part of NATO, both alliances began to address each other's fears, notably in the discussion of CSBMs (Confidence and Security Building Measures) in the context of the Helsinki process and in the CFE negotiations in Vienna. By the late 1980s the political revolutions throughout the communist world changed the strategic map of Europe almost overnight. Consequently, it was not possible to see the full implementation of non-provocative defence dynamics between 'defensive' alliances in confrontation; by its nature non-provocative defence can only be a slow-fix strategy to the nagging problem of the security dilemma.

In the view of realist sceptics it is not possible to mitigate the security dilemma to any serious degree, let alone escape it altogether as implied by alternative security thinking. For the realists, any mitigation that does take place can only be self-interested and embedded in power-politics. For Waltz, the idea of norms and rules regulating behaviour in a self-help system is a myth; he believes it is erroneous to deduce the existence of so-called rules and norms from observed patterns of behaviour at the international level. Waltz, following Rousseau, considers that restraints in international politics do not derive from a sense of common interest, but from a self-interested calculation of what is prudent and expedient in furthering a state's interests *vis-à-vis* others in the game of nations.

Rousseau's position has been described as a 'tradition of despair', believing that the social contract which achieves civil society within states cannot be replicated in relations between states.[33] Rousseau's solution to this problem is to propose the abandonment of international relations through a retreat into self-sufficiency by states. Since this is even more unrealistic today than it was in Rousseau's own time, he can be seen, like Waltz and the others who have followed him, as offering no relief from the trap of the security dilemma in an anarchic system of states. Those holding such views argue that the collapse of security regimes throughout history amply vindicates their viewpoint.

The Concert of Europe shows that security regimes are possible, but it did not last. According to Jervis, the regime decayed because 'by controlling the risk of war and yet not becoming institutionalized and developing supranational loyalties, the Concert may have contained the seeds of its own destruction'.[34] By making world politics seem safer, the Concert encouraged states to play fast and loose with the rules, and in the end this led to a collapse of the co-operative edifice. Security regimes can set normative limits to the struggle for power but in establishing co-operative behaviour they can also lead states to adopt a false sense of security. They may therefore believe that they can pursue their narrow self-interests without endangering the structure of co-operative arrangements.

Given his emphasis on cognitive dynamics, Jervis is strangely pessimistic about the suggestion that a better understanding of the security dilemma would appreciably improve the long-term prospects for co-operation in a condition of anarchy.[35] The impact of Gorbachev on East–West relations prompts a different conclusion. Here is a leader whose 'new political thinking' showed a novel sensitivity to the counter-productive character of military over-insurance. He recognized that it only tightened the security dilemma. He backed his words with actions, and the result within five years was a general acceptance of the end of the Cold War. Furthermore, in an interdependent, massively armed world, it is actually more difficult now to contemplate a 'Hitler' or a 'Napoleon' who might opt for what Jervis called 'unrestrained policies'. Co-operation between some states might be improbable in particular circumstances, but global conquest is impossible. The heavy defeat of Saddam Hussein suggests that even regional powers may not be able to get away with war as readily as hitherto.

Nuclear weapons helped accelerate historic trends against total war by changing the calculations about ends and means in war. During the Cold War nuclear weapons created a shared interest between the Soviet Union and United States in each other's survival. Jervis argues that nuclear weapons forced the US and Soviet Union to set limits to their competition for power; he suggests that because it was narrow self-interest that gave rise to the patterns of restraint in the US–Soviet relationship, it should not be thought that a security regime was regulating it.[36] Each country's security depended upon the restraint of the other, but this acceptance of mutual vulnerability did not lead to an escape from the security dilemma. Nuclear weapons created mutual interests between the superpowers, but they also intensified the security dilemma. This is not surprising. They exist, and therefore threaten to destroy homelands. Periodically, policy-makers in both superpowers have believed (or believed that the other believed) that strategic superiority was the key to national security. If both adversaries believe that their security depends upon escalation dominance at all levels of military conflict, there is a clear security dilemma, with both sides defining their security in zero-sum terms. Defining security in zero-sum terms is not structurally ordained; instead it arises from the definition of national security at the level of national decision-making and strategic culture. In the US–Soviet case, each saw the problem in the nature of the adversary's state, and also believed that their adversary attached significance to nuclear strength in determining each other's risk-taking propensities. All this led to each side pursuing nuclear policies which tightened the dilemma.

One notable and comprehensive attempt to build a US–Soviet security regime was conceived by Henry Kissinger, President Nixon's National Security Adviser. Kissinger hoped to build a twentieth-century 'legitimate international order' or security regime for the nuclear age in the great tradition of the nineteenth-century Concert of Europe. In the event, the design and implementation of his strategy was badly flawed. The USA failed to recognize the Soviet Union as both a political and military equal. Soviet leaders understood this, and had their own ideas about the meaning of *détente*. Moscow soon came to believe that it was largely bearing the cost of *détente*. This and other misunderstandings and basic ambiguities in what constituted the limits of permissible Superpower behaviour led to acrimony and resentment. This led to the eventual demise of the *détente* experiment of the 1970s.

The failure of *détente* could be seen as further confirmation of the thesis that security regimes contain the seeds of their own destruction. Alternatively, it might be argued that the collapse of *détente* in the 1970s lay in the failure of the USA and Soviet Union to establish consensus at the level of rules and norms, and their failure to institutionalize the relationship, rather than in the inevitable collapse of co-operation in an anarchic setting. Among the obstacles to *détente* was the 'inherent bad faith model' held by both sets of policy-makers, which led them to mistrust each other's words and actions in all circumstances. In addition, they failed to take into account each other's legitimate security interests, and instead pursued unilateral advantage when the opportunity presented itself. Without such attitudes, they might have established an enduring security regime. What happens to future US–Soviet relations, as a result of the revolution in East–West affairs marked by the collapse of Communism in Eastern Europe in 1989, will offer another fascinating experiment in the problems of building a legitimate international order. Can lasting trust grow after three quarters of a century of ideological rivalry?

## V.  Can the Security Dilemma be Escaped?

To Waltzian neo-realists, the question posed by this subheading is misbegotten, since they believe that chronic insecurity is structurally related to anarchy. And while neo-realists like Jervis allow in their theories for the formation of security regimes, Jervis himself is sceptical that the security dilemma can be progressively ameliorated. Nevertheless, neo-realist speculation on the possibilities for security regimes can be likened to the search by classical realists for normative limits on the struggle for power among states. Some of the best-known classical realists, notably E. H. Carr, Hans J. Morgenthau, Arnold Wolfers, Henry Kissinger, and John Herz, start with the assumptions of realism, criticizing utopianism for over-emphasizing the role of morality; but they were dissatisfied with a theory of international relations which accorded no role to ideals. The search for ways of transcending the security dilemma through the development of norms and principles might be characterized as 'idealist' or 'utopian', but it has consumed a good deal of theoretical and also practical effort. The key concepts are 'society' and 'community'.

Co-operative interactions between states not only prove mutually beneficial, they also create norms of behaviour. It is interesting in this regard that Jervis in his most recent work suggests that theorists of security co-operation might do well to pay greater attention to concepts of morality and obligation in explaining international co-operation.[37] Jervis is not saying that self-interest is not the key part of any co-operative strategy between governments, but he does suggest that 'without the power of at least some shared values, without some identification with the other, without norms that carry moral force, co-operation may be difficult to sustain'. It is the idea that a society can exist amidst anarchy which is at the root of some of the most important speculation about international relations.

For Hedley Bull the nature and potentialities of international society shape the character of order in interstate relations. Bull commented:

A society of *states* (or international society) exists when a group of states, conscious of certain common interests and common values, form a society in the sense that they conceive themselves to be bound by a common set of rules in their relations with each other, and share in the working of common institutions.[38]

Yet while Bull argues that the element of society between states has never ceased to exert an influence on international relations, he equally accepts that the Hobbesian 'state of war' is also a regular element.[39] Although Bull does not discuss the 'security dilemma' as such in *The Anarchical Society*, it is clear that international society is believed to constrain the worst excesses of 'Hobbesian fear'. At the same time, 'Hobbesian fear' (the security dilemma) itself is a basic obstacle to the growth of international society. In an important study of security from a neo-realist perspective, Barry Buzan agrees with Bull that 'anarchy may not be as bad as it sometimes seems'. According to Buzan, 'Although we did not choose to make the anarchy we have, once conscious of it, we can choose to mould it into more—or less—mature forms.'[40] Unlike the rigid neo-realism of Waltz, which rules out the idea of the security dilemma being mitigated, let alone escaped, Buzan suggests that the impact of the security dilemma can be minimized through 'improved anarchies'.[41] Such a 'mature anarchy', to use Buzan's usual formulation, is a society composed of 'large, politically strong, relatively self-reliant, relatively tolerant, and relatively evenly powered units'.

According to the arguments just described, governments have the choice of strengthening or weakening the element of society between them. This would be achieved through sets of practices aimed at the extension of common rules and norms furthering shared values. Deepening obligations further, the possibility arises of the growth of a global political community. In discussing this, Bull's writing exhibits a strong Kantian element which is much weaker in the thinking of 'classical' realists. This Kantian element involves the potential transcendence of the society of states by the community of humankind.

The idea of a world community (involving what is usually called a 'cosmopolitanist morality') should be distinguished from the 'morality of states'. Whereas a cosmopolitanist morality is predicated on the idea that humanity has rights and duties that transcend state borders, the 'statist' morality looks to the state as the principal bearer of rights and duties.[42] If a cosmopolitan morality were eventually to become established across the globe, with general agreement on the principles of justice, trust would be widespread and the security dilemma would disappear.

In the 1980s, the need for global ethics to meet the problems of a smaller planet became accepted by growing numbers of people. John Herz, who had done much to establish the concept of the security dilemma, had already pre-empted these views. In 1959 he concluded that the advent of nuclear weapons and the growing planetary crisis had to give rise to what he called an attitude of 'universalism' if humankind was not to destroy itself.[43] Reflecting on his work thirty years later, Herz argued that 'universalism, as I conceive it, is based on universal *interests*, such as global survival interests, not on unselfish moral principle'.[44] For Herz and others, enlightened self-interest led in the direction of the establishment of new global political arrangements. Herz speculated that human society in pursuing common solutions to common problems might at the same time be setting out a code of 'minimum ethics of human survival'. Such a set of ethics would emancipate humankind from its major security problems.

While looking towards the prospect of more universalist perspectives, Herz is sceptical that mankind will follow its real (long-term enlightened) interests over its apparent (short-term) ones, despite the threat of global catastrophe.[45] Bull, similarly, for all his talk of new global imperatives, recognized that states remained 'notoriously self-serving'.[46] Thus, while both writers produced theories looking towards escape from the more pernicious consequences of anarchy, both were sceptical about how much long-term change is possible.

For those less sceptical about the possibilities for change, the project of harmonizing interests and building allegiance to a world community is actually at work in international relations. This school of thought, which can be called neo-Kantian, received a boost from actual developments in international affairs in the late 1980s. For Kant, himself, writing at the end of the eighteenth century, republican governments held the key to the creation of an international security community because he considered that people would not wish to participate in the horrors of war when they could satisfy their welfare and interests through trade and peaceful exchange. It is not that Kant believed man to be basically good and sociable, rather he saw moral learning as crucial to the achievement of perpetual peace.[47] Moral learning will lead individuals, according to Kant, to develop a sense of cosmopolitanist morality, or in the words of contemporary critical theorists, to an enlargement of the sense of moral and political community.[48]

Kant's project did not materialize during his lifetime, but Michael Doyle is only one writer who suggests that it is now being realized in the peaceful relations of liberal-democratic states. Doyle's thesis emphasizes three contributory factors: democratic control of foreign policy; the sharing of liberal values; and a common interest in peace as a result of commercial inter-dependence.[49] The empirical evidence of the post-war years would seem to bear out his case. The most startling example of this has been the way the traditional 'state of war' between France and Germany has been transformed through common practices and institutions into a community. Among the liberal-democratic states there are still differences of outlook and interest, but the idea of resolving them by force has been de-legitimized.

A situation such as that just described was defined by Karl Deutsch and his co-workers in the 1950s as a 'security community'. In such a community peace is predictable; the security dilemma has been escaped. The means of escape are integration and community. In Deutsch's words a security community is

a group of people which has become 'integrated'. By integration we mean the attainment, within a territory, of a sense of 'a sense of community' and of institutions and practices strong enough and widespread enough to assure . . . dependable expectations of 'peaceful change' among its population. By sense of community we mean a belief . . . that common social problems must and can be resolved by processes of 'peaceful change'.[50]

Even more so than when Deutsch and his co-workers developed the concept, the existing security communities have learned to harmonize their interests, compromise their differences, and reap mutual rewards. In Western Europe, for example, 'international politics' still takes place, but issues are no longer determined by the quality and disposition of forces deployed against each other.

Communication theory is the essence of Deutsch's concept; it is communication which creates communities. The group of states studied by Deutsch was marked by a variety of distinctive characteristics: mutual compatibility of values; strong economic ties and expectations of more; multi-faceted social, political, and cultural transactions; a growing degree of institutionalized relationships; mutual responsiveness; and mutual predictability of behaviour. The defining test of whether a 'security community' exists is whether the participants target each other with their armed forces. Together, the theory of security communities and the practice of international politics among the liberal-democratic states suggests that the security dilemma can be escaped, even in a setting of sovereign states.

Some realist critics have challenged the idea that liberal-democratic states do not fight each other. It has been suggested, for example, that Germany was a liberal-democracy in 1914. Clearly, the definition of 'liberal-democracy' is crucial. Doyle himself has reasonably concluded that Germany was not a liberal-democratic state in 1914.[51] Another challenge from the realist school is the argument that Western Europe has been able to form a security community since 1945 largely because it faced a major external threat in the shape of the Soviet Union; this in turn required a security protector in the form of the United States. The latter's hegemony in the face of Soviet power eradicated Western Europe's traditional security dilemmas.[52] The conclusion of this argument is that if the US commitment were reduced or withdrawn, and the Soviet threat disappeared, then Europe might well return to its traditional condition of national competitiveness.[53] In addition, some critics of the neo-Kantian school conclude that whereas liberal democracy seems to be a sure recipe for warlessness while the community is relatively small; they wonder whether it would be possible to be confident if the number of liberal-democratic states became a hundred or so, and spread across all the world's traditionally contentious regions?

There can be little doubt that the looming Soviet threat in the 1940s and 1950s helped to stimulate West-European unity, and then helped give it coherence. With the disappearance of that threat, the reassessment of US involvement and the unification of the two Germanys, Western Europe has to face the question whether it is capable of continuing as a security community. For liberal theorists, the memories of two world wars, the strong interest in co-operation, and all the processes of economic and social integration through the EC have created a firm basis for a lasting security community. Who could now imagine Germany and France targeting each other, or deploying divisions of tanks, in order to further foreign policy?

Even if Western (and potentially Eastern) Europe have created a permanent security community on their own continent, is it possible to conceive similar patterns elsewhere? And if progress does not take place elsewhere, is it not likely that security dilemmas will be provoked and will involve Europe regardless of the character of the relationships within the European security system? Will anarchy, in short, exact its historic toll on the prospects for stable world order? Furthermore, if Western Europe is moving towards a federated political structure, will the EC just become a super-state in the global arena—perpetuating the sovereign states-system and the security dilemma—rather than a model for a post-sovereign world? Must security always be at someone else's expense, or can we achieve a global security community characterized by non-violent conflict-resolution?

The 1980s saw the spread through the study of International Relations of theories which were critical of the dominant realist paradigm. The subject became, in the words of one authoritative judge, *The Dividing Discipline*.[54] One school already mentioned— the alternative security school—grew out of the perceived need for a more effective practice of security. Another school—appropriately called Critical Theory—was rooted in a distinct philosophical tradition which challenged established outlooks. What is important about Critical Theory, philosophically, is the idea that all politics, including international politics, is open-ended and based in ethics.[55] This stands in sharp contrast to the limited horizons and claimed objectivity of Realism. Characteristically, Richard Ashley attacked Waltzian neo-realism as a statist ideology and value system masquerading as the objective laws of international relations.[56]

The highest value of Critical Theory is emancipation. The latter will lead to significantly different policies from those associated with power and order (the two values most identified, respectively, with pure realism and the International Society approach of Bull). As yet the practical dimension of emancipation —'strategies of transition'—are little developed, but they do seem logically to converge with the ideas of the alternative security school mentioned earlier. As explained by Linklater, the aim is to undertake political action to extend the moral communities with which individuals identify in the modern world. There are 'unrealized possibilities' in this regard. In the years ahead we can expect—despite, indeed because of, the Gulf War—to see renewed efforts to move the theory and practice of security out of the traditional realist grip into the different philosophical and operational camp of Critical Theory. The latter does not see the security dilemma as a necessary feature of the predicament of world politics.

## VI. Conclusion: Beyond the Security Dilemma

The concept of the security dilemma is a contested one: it is more complex than it appears at first sight; there are problems of definition and usage; and a range of philosophical standpoints exist on its significance and possible overcoming. The student of the subject can choose between three broad positions on the security dilemma:

(a) The belief that the security dilemma is inescapable because of the character of human nature and/or the structure of the international system. This is the view identified with the realist approach, either of the pessimistic human nature or neo-realist variety.

(b) The belief that although the logic of anarchy is powerful, and cannot be ultimately transcended, it can be mitigated by the development of a mature society of states. This is the view identified with the International Society approach, which might be seen as including sophisticated neo-realists.

(c) The belief that what is possible in world politics is expandable, so even though the security dilemma has been a regular feature of interstate relations in the past, the expansion of community between peoples can provide an escape from its grip. This is the view identified with a variety of alternative approaches, such as World Order and World Society thinking, and Critical Theory.

Significantly, with the exception of the most doctrinaire realists, all others accept that humans have some choice on the matter of the security dilemma.

While the evidence of history has regularly justified the pessimistic prognostications of the realists—the prevalence of war and crises, the breakdown of co-operation, and so on—trends in world politics in recent decades have begun to point in a different direction. World politics have become characterized by an increasingly complex and dense interaction at all levels (business, non-governmental organizations, individuals, and so on, and not just states). Added to this, war has become less rational between major powers, as the costs have risen and the benefits declined. All this means that the idea that the agenda of world politics is objectively set by the logic of anarchy is less tenable than in the past. It is too soon to say that the security dilemma is a historical anachronism: equally it is too soon to say that it is an 'inescapable reality'.

## Notes

1. See I. Clark, *The Hierarchy of States: Reform and Resistance in the International Order* (Cambridge: Cambridge University Press, 1989), 75.
2. H. Butterfield, *History and Human Relations* (London: Collins, 1951), 21.
3. Quoted in R. Keohane, 'Realism, Neo-Realism and the Study of World Politics', in id. (ed.), *Neo-Realism and its Critics* (New York: Columbia University Press, 1986), 7.
4. Quoted in R. Gilpin, 'The Richness of the Tradition of Political Realism', ibid. 304.
5. Butterfield, *History and Human Relations*, 20.
6. Quoted in M. J. Smith, *Realist Thought from Weber to Kissinger* (Baton Rouge, La.: Louisiana State University Press, 1986), 99.
7. Quoted, ibid. 104.
8. See J. Herz, 'Idealist Internationalism and the Security Dilemma', *World Politics*, 2/2 (1950), 157. Also, see id., *Political Realism and Political Idealism* (Chicago: University of Chicago Press, 1951).
9. Id., *International Politics in the Atomic Age* (New York: Columbia University Press, 1959), 234.
10. Id., 'Idealist Internationalism', 158.
11. K. N. Waltz, *Theory of International Politics* (Reading, Mass.: Addison-Wesley, 1979), 105. For Waltz's earlier discussion see his *Man, the State and War* (New York: Columbia University Press, 1954), 167–71.
12. T. C. Schelling, *The Strategy of Conflict* (Cambridge; Mass.: Harvard University Press, 1960), 207–8.
13. R. Jervis, 'Cooperation under the Security Dilemma', *World Politics*, 30/2 (1978), 170.
14. Id., 'Security Regimes', *International Organization*, 36/2 (1982), 177.

15. Id., *Perception and Misperception in International Politics* (Princeton, NJ: Princeton University Press, 1976), 68.
16. Ibid. 69.
17. Butterfield, *History and Human Relations*, 22.
18. This list is based on K. Booth, 'US perceptions of the Soviet Threat: Prudence and Paranoia', in C. G. Jacobsen, *Strategic Power USA/ USSR* (London: Macmillan, 1990), 63–8.
19. Jervis, *Perception* and *Misperception*, 58–113.
20. See Butterfield, *History and Human Relations*, 24; Herz, *International Politics*, 235; and Jervis, 'Cooperation under the Security Dilemma', 168.
21. Jervis, *Perception and Misperception*, 75.
22. G. F. Kennan, ('X'), 'The Sources of Soviet Conduct', *Foreign Affairs* (1947), reprinted in his *American Diplomacy 1900–1950* (London: Secker and Warburg, 1953), 111.
23. The illustration is suggested by J. C. Garnett, 'Disarmament and Arms Control', in L. Martin (ed.), *Strategic Thought in the Nuclear Age* (Baltimore: Johns Hopkins University Press, 1979), 204.
24. Jervis, 'Security Regimes', 177.
25. Id., *Perception and Misperception*, 82.
26. Id., 'Security Regimes', 178.
27. Ibid. 176–7.
28. Ibid. 178–84.
29. H. Kissinger, *A World Restored* (New York: Grosset and Dunlap, 1964), 1.
30. Jervis, 'Security Regimes', 178.
31. Palme Commission, *Common Security: A Programme for Disarmament* (London: Pan Books, 1982).
32. M. K. MccGwire, *Military Objectives in Soviet Foreign Policy* (Washington, DC: Brookings Institution, 1987), 232–334.
33. Clark, *The Hierarchy of States*, 67–89.
34. Jervis, 'Security Regimes', 184.
35. Ibid. 176.
36. Ibid. 187.
37. Jervis, 'Realism, Game Theory, and Cooperation', *World Politics*, 40/ 3 (1988), 317–49.
38. Hedley Bull, *The Anarchical Society* (London: Macmillan, 1977), 13.
39. Ibid. 24–5 and 40–1.
40. B. Buzan, *People, States and Fear*, 1st edn. (Brighton: Wheatsheaf Books, 1983), 122. For Buzan's later development of these ideas, see his 'Is International Security Possible?' in K. Booth (ed.), *New Thinking about Strategy and International Security* (London: Unwin Hyman, 1991), 31–53.

41. Buzan, *People, States and Fear*, 208.
42. See J. Vincent, *Human Rights and International Relations* (Cambridge: RIIA, 1986), 111–28.
43. Herz, *International Politics in the Atomic Age*, 300–57.
44. See Herz's comments on Richard Ashley in *International Studies Quarterly*, 25/2 (1981), 238.
45. Ibid. 240–1.
46. Bull, *Justice in International Relations*, The 1983–4 Hagey Lectures (University of Waterloo, Ontario, Oct. 1984).
47. See A. Hurrell, 'Kant and the Kantian Paradigm in International Relations', *Review of International Studies*, 16/3 (1990), 183–207.
48. See A. Linklater, *Beyond Realism and Marxism: A Critical Theory of International Relations* (London: Macmillan, 1990).
49. M. W. Doyle, 'Kant, Liberal Legacies and Foreign Affairs', *Philosophy and Public Affairs*, 12/3 (1983), 205–35.
50. See K. Deutsch, *et al.*, *Political Community and the North-Atlantic Area* (Princeton, NJ: Princeton University Press, 1957), 5.
51. Doyle, 'Kant, Liberal Legacies and Foreign Affairs', 222.
52. See J. Joffe, 'Europe's American Pacifier', *Survival*, 26/4 (1984), 174–81.
53. This argument became fashionable in some circles in 1990 as a result of the publicity attending the writings of John Mearsheimer. See his 'Back to the Future: Instability in Europe after the Cold-War', *International Security*, 15/1 (1990), 5–56.
54. K. J. Holsti, *The Dividing Discipline* (Boston: Unwin Hyman, 1985).
55. The clearest introductions to critical theory and international politics are M. Hoffman, 'Critical Theory and the Inter-paradigm Debate', *Millennium*, 16/2 (1987), 231–49, and Linklater, *Beyond Realism and Marxism*.
56. R. K. Ashley, 'The Poverty of Neo-Realism', *International Organization*, 38/2 (1984), 225–61.

# TWO

# States, State-Centric Perspectives, and Interdependence Theory

*John C. Garnett*

## I. Why have States Survived for so Long?

Since sovereign states have been around for a long time, it is easy to see how students unfamiliar with history might be led to believe that they are a permanent and unchanging feature of the international landscape. In fact, of course, for most of its history the human race has not been organized into states. In the words of Oran Young, 'Over the bulk of recorded history, man has organised himself for political purposes on bases other than those now subsumed under the concepts "state" and "nation state".'[1] Only with the break-up of medieval Christendom and the Holy Roman empire did a system of states slowly emerge, and even then these new political entities were confined to a relatively small area of the world—Europe.

It is generally agreed that the sovereign state-system formally came into existence with the Peace of Westphalia in 1648, a twin agreement which brought to an end the Thirty Years War, and signified both the secularization of politics and the rise of new independent political units called states (but not yet nation-states). In practice what the Peace did was to redraw the map of Europe into a society of legally equal states each of which exercised sovereignty within fairly well-defined frontiers and acknowledged no authority above itself. Traditional ideas of universal, horizontally structured societies or empires were relegated to the periphery of politics in favour of a division of humanity into vertically organized separate states.

Although Westphalia saw the birth of the 'state-centric' model for thinking about international relations it would be quite misleading to think that it was a rationally planned alternative to the rather ramshackle empire which preceded it. No one sat down at Westphalia and said 'Look, chaps, we've been playing medieval Christendom for the last five hundred years or so; let's change the rules and play sovereign states for a bit.' The reasons which led to the break-up of medieval Christendom are many and complex—a combination of political, technical, and economic forces prompting a 'system' change of enormous significance. Though Westphalia registered these ongoing trends it did not initiate them.[2]

Nevertheless, the classical system of statecraft which came into existence with Westphalia has provided the basic paradigm for understanding the international politics of the last three hundred and fifty years. The essential features of the paradigm are that it emphasizes the sovereign equality of the member states under international law, the significance of 'power' and 'interest' as guides to state policy, and the comparative nature of the political arena in which the 'balance of power' is the major regulating mechanism. Until the twentieth century the Westphalia system was largely confined to Europe, though the acquisition of empires by the British, the French, the Dutch, the Spanish, the Belgians, the Portuguese and the Russians meant that the system had an impact in all of the world's continents.

Since the beginning of the twentieth century, and particularly after the post-1945 decolonization process, the world has witnessed a spectacular enlargement of the Westphalia system to encompass virtually the whole world. Today, almost every inch of the planet's land mass is covered with sovereign states—over 170 of them—and what started as a purely European arrangement has now become a global system. Arguably, the expansion of international society is not yet over since the collapse of the Soviet empire has produced a further increase in the number of sovereign states.

On the face of it at least, the evolution and development of the sovereign state-system is surely one of the great success stories of all time. Despite its rather fumbling beginnings in the seventeenth century, 'the state' captured peoples' imagination and, reinforced by the ideology of nationalism in the nineteenth and twentieth centuries, has now become the major unit of political organization throughout the world, an organization to which millions of people owe allegiance and for which many are prepared to die.

One of the reasons for the power of the sovereign state— particularly when it is also a nation-state—is that no other political unit inspires such devotion and enthusiasm. *Within* the state most citizens feel some sentiment for the area in which they were born or the place where they live. And *beyond* the state people can see some value in larger groupings like NATO or the European Community. But it is difficult to see these lesser or greater allegiances providing the same sort of psychological 'high' as belonging to a nation-state. There is something peculiarly satisfying about belonging to a particular nation-state.

Apart from its continuing psychological appeal, there is a very pragmatic reason why the state survives. Politically speaking, states enjoy decisive advantages over all other organizations in domestic and international affairs. Consider, for a moment, the influence of 'Wales' both within the UK and in the wider world, and compare it with the influence of a small sovereign state of comparable size—say Belgium. Wales is undoubtedly a nation, but it is not a sovereign state. Its status is that of a principality within the United Kingdom. As such its fortunes are determined in Westminster rather than Cardiff. The Welsh cannot raise armies, make laws, or raise taxes. On the international stage Wales has no status and exercises no influence. She has no foreign policy, no embassies, no power to negotiate treaties, no right to sit in the United Nations, no authority to make war. She cannot do any of the things that Belgium can do as of right. Why not? Because Wales is not a sovereign state.

This example makes it quite clear why nations and tribes often seek to become states despite the difficulties which are put in their way. On the principle that the only clubs that are worth joining are exclusive, sovereign states jealously guard their advantages by trying to prevent secessionist groups from becoming states, and by seeking to deny any status to non-state actors. Thus, only sovereign states can join the UN; only sovereign states can conduct foreign policy; only states are subject to international law. Recognition of statehood is given sparingly and reluctantly, yet without it potential players of the game of international politics are permanently relegated to the touchline.

Given the power and importance of sovereign states it is not surprising that scholarly reflection about international politics has frequently assumed a 'state-centric' perspective. Scholars have emphasized, first, that the focus of the subject is *interstate* relations; second, that the main actors are states which are distinct, unitary, and independent entities; third, that these states are all equal in terms of their constitutional status and subject to no higher authority than themselves; fourth, that states are fairly homogenous 'billiard-ball' entities; fifth, that they exercise a monopoly of legal authority within their territory and of the use of military force both within and beyond their territory. These commonly held state-centric propositions or assumptions have been encapsulated within that theory of political behaviour known as 'realism'.

## II.  What is Realism?

Although realism is a state-centric tradition which accepts a world divided into independent sovereign states as being the normal, if not the permanent, condition of international society, it is much more than that. It is a profound philosophical approach to the study of international politics which can be traced back at least as far as Machiavelli but which, largely as a reaction to the 'idealism' of the 1920s and 1930s, dominated the study of the subject in the post-war years.[3]

It is impossible to summarize 'realism' because, even among the self-professed realists, there are important differences. But the general flavour of the realist perspective is unmistakable. Realists tend to be conservative in their views; that is to say, they see virtue in evolutionary change that is sufficiently slow for that which is best in international society to be preserved, and they are cautious both in their estimate of what can be done, and what ought to be done, to ameliorate international relationships. Realists want to make the present Westphalia system work, rather than overturn it in favour of a radical restructuring of world society. They consider *'realpolitik'* an inescapable feature of the international environment. They are sceptical about the possibilities of permanent peace and suspicious of all grandiose schemes of revolutionary change. Ideas for world government, general and comprehensive disarmament, and collective security are carefully scrutinized and rejected as impractical, perhaps even undesirable, solutions to the world's ailments. As far as their contribution to peace and international security is concerned, even the activities of the United Nations and its subsidiary organs are regarded with some scepticism.

The realists, disillusioned with nineteenth-century ideas of inevitable progress in international relations, are incapable of pointing, with any degree of confidence, in the direction in which progress lies. Many of them would sympathize with M. Oakeshott when he says, in that justly celebrated inaugural lecture of his:

in political activity then, men sail a boundless and bottomless sea; there is neither harbour for shelter nor floor for anchorage, neither starting-place nor appointed destination. The enterprise is to keep afloat on an even keel; the sea is both friend and enemy; and the seamanship consists in using the resources of a traditional manner of behaviour in order to make a friend of every hostile occasion.[4]

Perhaps the main reasons why the realists entertain minimal expectations of state behaviour are to be found in their conceptions of human nature and international society. Men are seen to be inherently destructive, selfish, competitive, and aggressive, and the international system one torn by conflict and full of uncertainty and disorder. Reinhold Niebuhr, a founding father of the realist school and one of its most brilliant exponents, speaks of man's 'stubborn pride', his 'egotism', 'will to power', 'brute inheritance', and his 'original sin'. For the realists there is an element of tragedy in human relations. In the words of Herbert Butterfield, 'Behind the great conflicts of mankind is a terrible human predicament which lies at the heart of the story.' George Kennan captured much of the pessimism in realist thought with his description of statesmen as 'actors in a tragedy beyond their making or repair'.[5]

Realists are quick to point out the limitations of international law and to emphasize the disintegrating, anarchic influences at work in an intractable international system. It is not really surprising that Thomas Hobbes is one of the realists' favourite philosophers, since his conception of the 'state of nature' resembled their conception of international society, and they share similar views of human nature. It was Hobbes who described the human condition as 'a restless struggle for power which ceaseth only in death'.[6] The realists also emphasize the ubiquity of the power struggle, and their literature is dominated by the concepts of national power and interest. Conflict is regarded as an inescapable condition of international life. Indeed this simple assumption is the starting-point of realism. Words like *harmony* and *co-operation* do not come easily to realist lips, and the realists are not much given to moralizing about international politics.

In short, the realists take exception to those who put too much faith in human reason, to those idealists who refuse to recognize the world as it is and who talk in pious platitudes about the world as it ought to be. In the words of one writer, 'Realism is a clear recognition of the limits of morality and reason in politics: the acceptance of the fact that political realities are power realities and that power must be countered with power; that self-interest is the primary datum in the action of all groups and nations.'[7]

Realism, with its state-centric emphasis, has provided an illuminating map of the world for successive generations of students trying to find their way through the complexities of world politics. Indeed, one of the weaknesses of those reared on Hans Morgenthau and his disciples is that they were almost too persuasive. Given the crude concepts of 'power' and 'interest' many students felt they had been given the keys to the universe. But the realist perspective has always had its critics among those who have found it gloomy and psychologically unpalatable. The realist view of reality is most definitely not one which lifts the spirit. In defence of the realists it must be admitted that they do not approve of the hard, ruthless world they describe. They simply regard it as a given; something that must be accepted before any progress can be made. In the words of Hans Morgenthau, 'The world, imperfect as it is from a rational point of view, is the result of forces inherent in human nature. To improve the world one must work with these forces not against them.'[8] Nevertheless, critics can be forgiven for seeing pessimism, even cynicism, in much realist writing, and detached observers might detect a note of quiet satisfaction at the predicament of mankind. Realists do seem to enjoy rubbing our noses in it, and it is hard to forgive them for that.

In recent years the realists have met renewed criticism, particularly since the end of the Cold War and the dawn of a softer climate in East–West relations. Critics have pointed out, with some justification, that the validity of the realist perspective has been eroded by a series of developments which challenge the state-centric paradigm and which have revolutionized the contemporary international scene. Taken together, they believe these changes have caused a 'paradigm shift', a 'system change' of such proportions that it is now necessary to abandon the traditional 'state-centric' perspective which has dominated the study of the subject since Westphalia in favour of a 'global politics' paradigm.

## III. Why is the State under Pressure?

Essentially, the critics of realism argue that in the modern world states are much less important than they used to be, and that the growing web of transnational relations has invalidated traditional 'billiard-ball' ideas of autonomous units constantly clashing in an eternal competition for power and security.

John Herz was one of the first scholars to point out that the strength and resilience of the state has traditionally resided in its capacity to perform two major functions. First, to defend those citizens who live within its borders, and, second, to promote their economic well-being.[9] And Herz also observed that the secret of the state's success in these areas lay in its 'impermeability' and its 'autonomy'. It was the invulnerability of 'hard-shell' units enhanced by a large measure of self-sufficiency which accounted for the success of states as political organizations. Unfortunately, modern weapon technology, particularly in the form of nuclear-tipped missiles, has meant that all states are now exceedingly permeable in the sense of being vulnerable to attack. There is no reliable defence against a nuclear-armed ballistic missile, and in much the same way that castles and city states declined when their walls could be breached by cannon and gunpowder, so modern states are being rendered obsolescent by new weapons.

The 'security' function of the state is also undermined by the fact that, in the contemporary world, security issues have slipped down the policy agendas of many states. Many of the problems which now beset us seem to have little to do with the 'high-policy' issues of peace and war, conquest and domination. These issues have been replaced by more mundane 'low-policy' problems to do with trade, welfare, and economics. In the words of E. Morse, even for Superpowers 'there is a broadening of the spectrum of policy goals, so that goals of wealth and welfare become as important as those of power and international position.'[10] For lesser states 'older ideal patterns tend to be almost completely over-shadowed by the growth in significance of low policies'.[11] The fact that military power, the ownership of which is almost a defining attribute of a state, has become virtually irrelevant in the pursuit of so many objectives, has, it is argued, further diminished the significance of the state as an actor on the international stage.

The inability of the modern state to satisfy the security requirements of its citizens and the diminished significance of security issues anyway, is matched by its growing inability to provide economic prosperity for those within its borders. The decline in 'autarky' and self-sufficiency produced by a trading world and a complex world economic order has meant that the prosperity of particular states is to a large extent now determined by events and developments beyond their borders rather than by any decisions taken by their governments.

For example, in seeking to right an ailing economy, the British government has pursued monetarist policies, promoted an 'enterprise' culture, encouraged exports, and curtailed the power of the trade unions. But at the end of the day the economic success of the United Kingdom probably depends on decisions taken by OPEC or the EEC, the Uruguay round of GATT, exchange rates, and, above all, a peaceful trading environment. Most of these matters are quite beyond the control of the British government, and recognition of this fact of life has further diminished the status of 'the state'. Kindleberger has gone so far as to argue that 'the nation state is just about through as an economic unit'.[12]

Those who believe that the state is in permanent decline bolster their arguments about its functional defectiveness with complaints about its inability to handle the whole range of new 'planet earth' problems which now confront us. For example, we are in the middle of an enormous population explosion. On current estimates the world population is growing at an annual rate of about 3.6 per cent.

According to some estimates it took two million years for the earth to have one billion inhabitants (1820). It took only a hundred more years for the second billion to be added (1920). The third billion came in forty years (1960). The fourth billion arrived in fourteen years (1974). Two more billion are expected—unless the trends begin to shift dramatically—by 1999.[13]

From a resource and environmental perspective the world is already over-populated and any increase of the size projected represents a time-bomb of unimaginable consequences and one with a short fuse.

Already the pressures of over-population have created environmental problems of massive proportions. We are now threatened by atmospheric and oceanic pollution, by 'global warming', and by the irreversible depletion of scarce minerals, including fossil fuels. In the last hundred years we have done more damage to our planet than our ancestors did in the previous ten thousand years.

Unfortunately, as Richard Falk has repeatedly explained, 'a world system composed of sovereign states cannot deal effectively or equitably with the problems facing humankind'.[14] A state's action to control acid raid within its borders is futile if its neighbours continue to pour industrial waste into the atmosphere. Unilateral attempts to limit over-fishing are doomed to failure if others refuse to behave equally responsibly. A government attempt to build 'safe' nuclear weapons and reactors is of no value if its citizens are affected by fall-out from nuclear accidents beyond its borders.

Essentially, the environmentalist argument is that vertically structured sovereign states are poorly equipped for handling issues which simply did not exist when the state system developed in the seventeenth and eighteenth centuries. What is more, the governments of these states are crippled by a traditional 'mind-set' which either keeps these global issues off the agenda altogether, or allocates a low priority to them. Sovereign states are much more comfortable when they are contending with familiar power political issues than they are with global problems. Dealing with Saddam Hussein is a more manageable problem than solving the problem of global warming.

One of the reasons for this is that governments are not much interested in long-term chronic illnesses even when they may prove terminal. Since they are usually overwhelmed by a succession of acute crises demanding immediate attention, they rarely give much thought to the shape of things to come. Harold Wilson's comment that 'a week is a long time in politics' is a pardonable exaggeration, but it emphasizes the limited horizons of those who rarely think ahead and never beyond the next election.

Perhaps it is not surprising that sovereign states which have found difficulty in adjusting to the new agenda of world politics have also found it difficult to accommodate many of the new global and humanitarian values which now preoccupy thinking people. Human rights, famine, 'common' security, wealth-sharing, world poverty, global resource management, are subjects which traditional statesmen from Metternich to Kissinger would hardly have spent a moment of their professional lives in thinking about. But these matters are now forcing themselves on to the agenda despite the inability of states to deal effectively with them.

One of the most common criticisms of the 'state-centric' approach to international politics is that it seriously undervalues the significance of the numerous non-state actors that have emerged on the international stage. These fall into a variety of categories. First, there are international organizations, or inter-state governmental actors (IGOs) as they are sometimes called. NATO, the EEC, and the UN fall into this category. Second, there are interstate non-governmental actors (INGOs) which reside within sovereign states but are independent of their governments. This group of non-state actors is very diverse in character and includes religious movements, multinational companies, terrorist organizations, the Red Cross, etc. Third, there are individual citizens who, for one reason or another, are sufficiently important to be regarded as actors on the world stage. Andrew Carnegie, the American philanthropist, and, more recently, Terry Waite, the Churchman, are examples of individuals who have played a role, albeit a small one, in international politics. Finally, there is a rather peculiar class of international actors which, though part of state governments, sometimes act independently of them. The CIA, for example, has occasionally devised and executed policies without either the knowledge or approval of the US Administration.

Of course there have always been non-state actors on the scene. Richard Mansbach *et al.* have described the international role of 'Jacobitism' in the seventeenth and eighteenth centuries,[15] and one could make an equally plausible case for the international significance of the East India Company in the seventeenth century. But there is no doubt that the explosion of non-state actors did not really occur until the second half of the twentieth century. Since 1945 the number of these enterprises has more than trebled, and it is now estimated that there are many thousands of non-state actors on the world stage. Perhaps part of the explanation for the mushrooming growth of these non-state actors lies in the failure of sovereign states to satisfy human needs, but one of the most important reasons is surely the twentieth-century revolution in communications and transport which has facilitated easy international intercourse below the official governmental level.

The relative power of at least one variety of these new actors, namely multinational companies, is suggested by a comparison of their dollar values with the gross domestic products of some sovereign states. Out of the 160-odd members of the UN, only twenty-four are richer than General Motors, only twenty-nine richer than Exxon, thirty-one richer than Ford and the Royal Dutch Shell Group, and thirty-six richer than IBM and Mobil.[16] Since wealth is power, these footloose giants can rival and threaten the power of states. This they do in two ways. First, by intervening—sometimes massively—in the domestic economies of states, and second, by creating an alternative powerful network of international relationships.

Because multinational corporations are private economic organisations, chains of command leading outside the state may multiply without ostensible loss of political sovereignty. Yet, national autonomy, the ability of a nation-state as a collectivity to make decisions which shape its political and economic future, has been diminished.[17]

Now that the British car industry has been so deeply penetrated by American and Japanese capital it is perfectly possible for large numbers of car workers in Luton or the Midlands to be thrown out of work as a result of decisions taken in Detroit or Tokyo. An important part of the British economy has slipped out of British control, and, short of nationalization, there is not much the British government can do about it.

Essentially, the argument here is that these new enterprises, many of which are beyond government control, signify the fragmentation of world politics, and suggest that other relationships are becoming as important as government-to-government relationships. By studying the behaviour of homogenous 'billiard-ball' states, realists have ignored an increasingly important category of actors and have neglected an increasingly significant amount of international activity. Richard Mansbach *et al.* have estimated that over one-third of all international activity now takes place exclusively among non-state actors. 'Further, well over fifty percent of all international activity involves interactions among non-state actors and nation states.'[18]

The thrust of the argument so far is to suggest that states have become 'dysfunctional', incapable of serving the interests either of their citizens or the world at large. In the words of Richard Falk, 'many among us are now convinced that most governments today are, in the main, not disposed to act as the guardians of human wellbeing'.[19] In addition, states are being increasingly displaced by the rise of new actors.

The conclusion which critics of the state-centric realist model draw from their analysis is that the model must either be radically amended or completely abandoned. From a 'scholarly' perspective it must be abandoned or amended because it no longer provides an accurate picture of a world which has moved on since Westphalia. That, essentially, is the position of Mansbach and his colleagues. They argue that 'the state-centric model is at best an historical anomaly and at worst a serious distortion of past and present global politics. It lacks both the descriptive and explanatory power to serve as the basis for meaningful research.'[20] From a 'survival' perspective the realist model must be amended or jettisoned because it is downright dangerous. 'The policy consequences of realist norms and prescriptions were increasingly judged to be deplorable.'[21] Realism, so the argument runs, has become a recipe for disaster because it perpetuates habits of thought which threaten to destroy us.

## IV. What is Interdependence?

Those critics who reject the pessimism and state-centric assumptions of realism have encouraged the development of a new perspective on international relations which is encapsulated in the word 'interdependence'. The starting-point of interdependence theory is the widespread recognition that today, in particular, 'no man is an island'; as human beings our futures are inextricably entwined as never before. Interdependence theorists believe that the myriad of interconnections between governments, IGOs, INGOs, and individuals which now characterizes the modern world have been neglected by realists whose obsession with the behaviour of unitary state actors has blinded them to the significance of this thickening web of criss-crossing transnational relations. They argue that once the state-centric model is abandoned it becomes possible to see international politics as—to use John Burton's suggestive metaphor—a 'cobweb' of super-imposed and intermeshing networks between governments and a whole variety of non-state actors.[22] This is a complicated model, and one of the criticisms that has been levelled at it is that a world in which there are literally thousands of players is infinitely less intellectually manageable than one dominated by sovereign states. Nevertheless, according to its supporters, it reflects contemporary reality much more closely than its state-centric alternative.

According to Robert O. Keohane and Joseph S. Nye, whose pioneering book *Power and Interdependence*[23] is a classic in the field, a world characterized by complex interdependence will display three basic features. First there will be 'multiple channels of communication'[24] between societies. These will include formal and informal links between the various actors, both official and unofficial. Second, there will be 'an absence of hierarchy among issues'.[25] What this means is that foreign policy questions are not arranged in a clear and consistent hierarchy with security issues taking priority. In the contemporary world, foreign policy issues are now so diverse—dealing with such matters as population control, energy resources, the use of space, the management of the environment, etc., as well as traditional security issues, that they cannot be hierarchically organized into a coherent foreign policy with tidy priorities. Third, there will be a diminished role for military force[26] because between interdependent states military force is an inappropriate and costly instrument. It is highly unlikely, for example, that many of the economic and welfare issues which have supplanted security on the foreign policy agendas of interdependent states will be resolved by the use of force.

The trouble with the interdependence model is that, like realism, it cannot easily be reduced to a few propositions without doing serious injustice to it. Part of the problem is that there is no general agreement on what precisely interdependence means, although, as with realism, its flavour is unmistakable. At its simplest, interdependence refers to the fact that modern states have become increasingly interlinked, their destinies intertwined in ever more complicated ways. According to G. Goodwin, interdependence refers to 'a widely shared sense of belonging to an incipient world community and a high degree of responsiveness between the state members of that community'.[27]

'Responsiveness', of course, has both positive and negative connotations. It can suggest mutual support among friends, but it can also suggest mutual antagonism between enemies. The arms race, for example, has been a symptom of the interdependence of the two Superpowers. On the whole, however, growing interdependence is regarded as a virtuous phenomenon because it suggests collaboration and co-operation, a definite improvement on the normally suspicious relationships we associate with an ungoverned 'anarchic' world. But it is worth pointing out that states which have little contact with each other are often at peace. The chances of war between China and Peru, for example, are minimal. Perhaps a world of 'autarkic' states with virtually no connections between them would be a peaceful world. Perhaps talk about 'energy independence', 'isolationism', and 'fortress America' is an intuitive reaction to the dangers of interdependence. Increasing interdependence may imply increasing co-operation and increasing prosperity, but it also contains the potential for increasing conflict. As R. Rosecrance has emphasized, 'the interdependent economic system . . . did not prevent political and military conflict as World War I showed only too well. Nor did the closer entwining of economic interests of Western states prevent the Great Depression.'[28]

When we talk about interdependence we are not simply registering the transactions and interconnections between states. We all recognize that the twentieth-century revolution in communications technology has stimulated a massive increase in the number of transactions between states at all levels. This may be a *prerequisite* for interdependence but it is not the same as interdependence. Interdependence is a description of the *quality* (not the quantity) of the relationships between states in terms of *mutual dependency*. Whether an increasing number of transactions between states produces greater interdependence will depend entirely on the nature of the transactions.

International transactions, for example, which merely involve exchanges of information between governments have hardly any implications for interdependence, but trade transactions have greater potential. Even here though, we have to be careful, since some sorts of trade relationship have a minimal effect on interdependence. For example, a country which imports luxury goods does not become nearly so interdependent with its supplier as a country which imports energy resources necessary for its industrial survival. Perhaps we can say that genuine interdependence implies a relationship which is *costly to break*.

And it is also worth pointing out that even mutual trade in vitally important strategic materials does not imply interdependence if the trading partners can easily obtain those materials from other sources. What this suggests is that, properly understood, interdependence has something to do with increased 'sensitivity' or 'vulnerability' on the part of states to developments beyond their borders.[29] When the price of oil shot up in the early 1970s as a result of the energy crisis, Japan and the United States were both 'sensitive' to the price rise, though Japan was more sensitive because she had no domestic supplies of oil to help cushion the blow. Not only was Japan more immediately *sensitive* than the United States to a rise in the price of oil, but she was also made more *vulnerable* in the longer term because of her difficulty in finding alternative sources of supply. Sensitivity and vulnerability are implied by the notion of interdependence, and it is worth noting that these concepts are not confined to *economic* interdependence. States can also be made vulnerable and sensitive by socio-political relationships and environmental problems that may develop.

A final point that is worth stressing in this conceptual clarification of interdependence is that it is very different from 'dependence'. Interdependence means *mutual* or reciprocated dependence.[30] A 'one-way' dependency in goods or services contributes nothing to interdependence. On the other hand, no theorists have insisted that interdependence means *evenly balanced* mutual dependence. *Asymmetrical* mutual dependence is usually regarded as a sufficient criterion for interdependence, although *highly* asymmetrical mutual dependence is much closer to 'dependence' than interdependence. That is why it can be misleading to regard the relationship between the developed and developing world as one of interdependence.

In the interdependence paradigm, the success of states in co-operating in an interdependent world is connected to two things—their power and bargaining skill, and the existence of favourable international regimes.

Now 'power', according to R. Keohane and J. Nye 'derives from patterns of asymmetrical interdependence between actors in the issue areas in which they are involved with each other'.[31] What this means is that A has power over B with respect to a particular issue to the extent that B is asymmetrically vulnerable to A. That is not the whole story, of course, because it takes no account of the fact that although B may be weaker than A, it may be more determined and have superior bargaining skills which may make it more powerful than A in terms of political effectiveness. North Vietnam was much weaker than the United States but it triumphed in the end.

Nevertheless, asymmetrical interdependence 'provides a first approximation of initial bargaining advantage available to either side'.[32] Traditionally 'power' has been thought of as a relatively simple commodity which states or other actors have more or less of. We talk about 'Superpowers' having more power than 'great powers' which, in turn, have more power than 'lesser powers'. What is interesting in the interdependence paradigm is the connection of power with asymmetrical vulnerability, and the idea that an actor's power will vary according to the issue under consideration. At a given moment A could exercise power over B with respect to one set of issues, but B could exercise power over A in respect of other sets of issues.

'Regimes' have been defined both tightly and loosely, but one of the most quoted definitions is that of S. Krasner. According to him, a regime exists when there are 'implicit or explicit principles, norms, rules and decision-making procedures around which actors' expectations converge in a given area of international relations'.[33] In the sense that almost every aspect of international life—economic, legal, military, or political—is conducted in a stable environment in which there are predictable and restraining patterns of behaviour, international society is criss-crossed by regimes, both explicit and implicit. In contemporary international society we have, amongst others, regimes dealing with trade, monetary affairs, arms control, conservation, transport, fishing, and the exploitation of space and natural resources. The existence of these multiple regimes, built up over hundreds of years, makes it nonsensical to describe the international system as 'anarchic' or disorderly or chaotic. Only if we use the term 'anarchy' in the special sense of meaning 'ungoverned' can it be applied to international society.

The significance of regimes in the interdependence paradigm is that, by mitigating disorder and applying rules to so many areas of both state and non-state actor behaviour, they facilitate and encourage the development of co-operative and interdependent relationships. The existence of a regime relating to a particular issue creates expectations about mutual restraint which enable actors to do business on that issue more easily. Clearly then, both the pattern and extent of interdependence is vitally affected by the existence of international regimes, and 'regime change' is bound to alter state behaviour and the levels of interdependence achieved by states.

## V. Realism or Interdependence or Both?

Those critics of realism who merely seek to modify or amend the state-centric paradigm have sought 'to integrate Realist and Liberal traditions'. In the words of Nye and Keohane—at least in their cautious later work—

We do not argue . . . that complex interdependence faithfully reflects world political reality. Quite the contrary: both it and the realist portrait are ideal types. Most situations will fall somewhere between these two extremes. Sometimes, realist assumptions will be accurate, or largely accurate, but frequently complex interdependence will provide a better portrayal of reality.[34]

For example, it could perhaps be argued that those seeking to make sense of the Iraqi invasion of Kuwait in August 1990 would glean more insights from the realist paradigm, but those grappling with European Community issues might find 'interdependence theory' more useful.

Those critics who have drawn the more radical conclusion that 'realism' must be *replaced* by 'interdependence' argue that a marriage between the two is really a marriage of incompatibles. It is very difficult to weld together a model which emphasizes the significance of states with one which stresses the importance of non-state actors. That is why at least one writer has gone so far as to favour a manner of thinking about international politics which is so sympathetic to the theory of interdependence that it *completely ignores* states. 'Only by theorizing about international systems with an appropriate language, which does not include states as political actors, can we appreciate the full theoretical impact of interdependence.'[35]

To talk about international politics without reference to sovereign states may be an interesting intellectual exercise but, frankly, there is an element of absurdity about it. States *exist*— not empirically or physically of course— but *notionally*, in the mind so to speak, in much the same way that banks, universities, churches, football clubs, and all other collective organizations exist in the mind. The state is, in reality, only an *idea*, to be found in that highly imagined world of political ideas, a world of ideas which has so deeply permeated our culture that its constructs are often assumed to be as real and tangible as physical matter itself. In most people's minds the state is no less real than the local supermarket.

Putting it slightly differently, human beings have invented abstractions called states, imagined a sort of game in which these abstractions have relations with each other, and now behave in the real world as if those things that they have imagined are actually real. In a very important sense, of course, they *are* real. For the social scientist the beliefs, myths, and ideas which give meaning to human behaviour are the very stuff of his subject. They are the 'facts' of social life, as real to him as inanimate matter is to the physical scientist. To denigrate the state on the grounds that it is not real is to miss the point. The state is a socially prevalent idea which has captured the imagination of millions of people and provides a context in which their behaviour is meaningful. No social scientist can ignore it.

Of course, empirically, as Robert Gilpin has pointed out,[36] only individuals exist and only individuals can behave. But to discuss any collective social structure only by reference to the individual behaviour of its members would be very odd indeed. Imagine a discussion at the Highbury soccer ground which considered the directors, manager, trainer, players, and groundsmen, without mentioning 'Arsenal'. Imagine a football commentary which described the moves of the players without reference to the team or club. The centre forward may put the ball into the net, but it is 'Arsenal' which is deemed to have scored the goal. Similarly, in international politics, though foreign secretaries may sign treaties, it is sovereign states that are bound by them. In truth, much human activity only makes sense in terms of the holistic organizations to which people belong. That is why it is misleading to favour an approach to international politics which ignores states and concentrates on the behaviour of individual actors within them.

The relative persuasiveness of the realist and interdependence paradigms depends to some extent on what scholars and students of international politics are interested in. Traditionally—and almost by definition—most of them have sought to understand the external behaviour of states and to appreciate the reasons why states behave as they do in international society. Why did Britain declare war on Germany in 1939; join the UN in 1945; help in the creation of NATO in 1949; relinquish her colonies in the post-war years; join the EEC in 1973; and wage war against Egypt over Suez, Argentina over the Falklands, and Iraq over Kuwait?

In examining these kinds of questions scholars have found it necessary to interest themselves in the nature of international society, the role of international law and morality, the status and significance of human rights, the causes of war, the functions of international organizations, the importance of ideology, the techniques of diplomacy, and so on. These subjects—including 'interdependence'—are not studied for their own sake, but because of the light which they throw on the behaviour of the most politically important organizations in the world—sovereign states. Without a proper appreciation of the phenomenon of interdependence, for example, political scientists would find it impossible to understand the extent to which a state's behaviour is now modified by the network of relations in which it, and the units within it, are enmeshed.

Of course, not everyone is interested in simply understanding the behaviour of states. Many contemporary students and scholars loosely attached to the field of 'International Studies' are now more interested in such problems as 'world poverty', 'over-population', 'environmental pollution', 'resource management', 'justice', etc. *'Global Issues'* is an interesting and important subject, but it is not the same as *'International Politics'* even when its subject-matter overlaps that discipline. Those who study it often have overtly normative motives, and many of them prefer to cut the cake along 'interdependence' lines because if they have any interest at all in state behaviour, it is peripheral rather than central.

Critics of realism usually begin by explaining in a few sentences what they think the 'essence' of it is. The realist attitude of mind is reduced to a few bald propositions, e.g., 'states as coherent units are the dominant actors in international politics'; 'force is a usable and effective instrument of policy'; 'questions of military security take precedence over economic and social affairs'.[37]

My objection to this approach is that a rich and sophisticated tradition of thought with a very long pedigree cannot be boiled down in this way without gross distortion. The image of realism held by many of those who are opposed to it is little more than a crude caricature. It bears as much resemblance to the subtle thoughts of writers like E. H. Carr, Reinhold Niebuhr, George Kennan, Hans Morgenthau, Hedley Bull, and Henry Kissinger as the puppets of 'Spitting Image' do to their real world counterparts.

It is all too easy to set up straw men in order to knock them down. Contrary to what is suggested by the caricature, no sophisticated realist has ever believed that states are the only actors on the world stage; nor have they ever regarded states as unitary 'billiard-ball' type structures. Most realists have a thorough understanding of 'bureaucratic politics' and the complexity of organizational decision-making. Realists have always been aware of the significance of economic affairs and they are not at all insensitive to moral issues. Indeed writers like Niebuhr and Morgenthau *agonized* about moral issues. Their ideas were always tempered by a concern for humanity and by a genuine intellectual humility. Furthermore, realists have never claimed that the world will always be divided into sovereign states. They know that in much the same way as medieval Christendom gave way to the Westphalia system, so the present state-system may yet give way to something else; their claim is that it has not happened yet and will not happen merely because scholars or statesmen want it to happen.

If the realists have traditionally ignored 'planet earth' problems it is more because those issues have emerged fairly recently than because realism provides an inappropriate perspective for considering them. Actually, realism provides an illuminating perspective on environmental issues because it highlights their intractability. Of course, that is precisely why it is unpopular with those who favour a 'global politics' paradigm. In short, the argument of these last paragraphs is that there is more to realism than its critics sometimes claim. It may be premature to jettison a tradition of thinking which is probably flexible enough to accommodate many of the criticisms levelled against it.

Nevertheless, interdependence is now an established fact of life, though precisely how much of it there is and how important it is, is very difficult to determine. Kenneth Waltz, for example, has argued that levels of interdependence are not high, growing, or likely to promote peace.[38] However, the general feeling among scholars is that the interdependence theorists are on to something. They have drawn our attention to hitherto neglected features of the modern world, and they have provided an illuminating alternative and corrective to state-centric perspectives.

But they have not vanquished realism and, so far, they have not erected an intellectual edifice of comparable scope or sophistication. Loosely speaking, as we have seen, interdependence is a paradigm which focuses on the connections between actors of all kinds on the world stage. As such it is a very narrowly focused perspective which has virtually nothing to say about so many of the issues which troubled the realists. Students of interdependence literature will look in vain for discussions about international morality, law, reason, historical change, human nature, balance of power, and nationalism. What the interdependence theorists have produced is a limited but highly suggestive analysis of international transactions between a variety of actors who are increasingly aware that they share a common fate. Perhaps the main thrust behind the interdependence paradigm is the realization that, in the words of Zbigniew Brzezinski, we live 'between two ages', between the past age of the nation-state and some unknown future.[39] In this twilight zone, neither realism nor interdependence perspectives are alone sufficient. Both are necessary.

## Notes

1. Oran R. Young, 'The Actors in World Politics', in J. N. Rosenau, V. Davis, and M. A. East (eds.), *The Analysis of International Politics* (New York: Free Press, 1972), 127.
2. See, for example, J. R. Strayer, *On the Medieval Origins of the Modern State* (Princeton, NJ: Princeton University Press, 1970); and D. C. North and R. P. Thomas, *The Rise of the Western World—A New Economic History* (Cambridge: Cambridge University Press, 1973). An excellent brief account of the rise of the nation-state is to be found in R. Gilpin, *War and Change in World Politics* (Cambridge: Cambridge University Press, 1981), 116–23.
3. A clear and balanced overview of the realist tradition is to be found in M. J. Smith, *Realist Thought from Weber to Kissinger* (Baton Rouge, La., and London: Louisiana State University Press, 1986).
4. M. Oakeshott, *Rationalism in Politics* (London: Methuen, 1962), 127.
5. See R. Niebuhr, *Moral Man and Immoral Society* (New York and London: Charles Scribner's Sons, 1932); H. Butterfield quoted in K. W. Thompson, *Political Realism and the Crisis of World Politics* (Princeton, NJ: Princeton University Press, 1960), 53; and G. F. Kennan, *American Diplomacy 1900–1950* (Chicago: Chicago University Press, 1951), 78.
6. T. Hobbes, *Leviathan*, ed. M. Oakeshott (Oxford: Basil Blackwell, 1946), 64.
7. G. Harland, quoted in A. Herzog, *The War–Peace Establishment* (New York and London: Harper and Row, 1963), 88.
8. H. J. Morgenthau, *Politics among Nations*, 2nd edn. (New York: Alfred A. Knopf, 1956), 4.
9. J. H. Herz, *International Politics in the Atomic Age* (New York and London: Columbia University Press, 1962).
10. E. L. Morse, *Modernization and the Transformation of International Relations* (New York: Free Press, 1976), 85.
11. Ibid. 85.
12. C. P. Kindleberger, *American Business Abroad* (New Haven, Conn.: Yale University Press, 1969), 207.
13. T. A. Couloumbis and J. H. Wolfe, *Introduction to International Relations: Power and Justice*, 4th edn. (Englewood Cliffs, NJ: Prentice-Hall), 385.
14. R. A. Falk, *A Study of Future Worlds* (New York: Free Press, 1975), 2.
15. R. W. Mansbach, Y. H. Ferguson, and D. E. Lambert, *The Web of World Politics: Nonstate Actors in the Global System* (Englewood Cliffs, NJ: Prentice-Hall, 1976), 46–64.
16. Couloumbis and Wolfe, *Introduction to International Relations*, 361.

17. Quoted by Mansbach, *et al.*, *The Web of World Politics*, 28.
18. Quoted by Couloumbis and Wolfe, *Introduction to International Relations*, 358.
19. Falk, *A Study of Future Worlds*, 2.
20. Mansbach, *et al.*, *The Web of World Politics*, 66.
21. Mansbach, 'The Realists Ride Again: Counter-Revolution in International Relations', in J. N. Rosenau and H. Tromp (eds.), *Interdependence and Conflict in World Politics* (Aldershot: Aveburg Gower Publishing Co., 1989), 224.
22. J. W. Burton, *World Society* (Cambridge: Cambridge University Press, 1972), 35–45.
23. There are two editions of this book. The first edition was published in 1977. The second edition (1989) contains the authors' comments on some of the criticisms levelled at it by reviewers and commentators.
24. R. O. Keohane and J. S. Nye, *Power and Interdependence: World Politics in Transition*, 2nd edn. (Glenview, Boston, and London: Scott Foresman and Co., 1989), 25–6.
25. Ibid. 26–7.
26. Ibid. 27–9.
27. G. Goodwin, 'International Institutions and the Limits of Interdependence', in A. Shlaim (ed.), *Yearbook 1975* (London: Croom Helm, 1976), 26.
28. R. Rosecrance, 'International Interdependence', in G. L. Goodwin and A. Linklater (eds.), *New Dimensions of World Politics* (London: Croom Helm, 1975), 21.
29. Keohane and Nye, *Power and Interdependence* (1989), 11–19.
30. Ibid. 8–19.
31. Quoted by D. A. Baldwin, 'Interdependence and Power: A Conceptual Analysis', *International Organization*, 34/4 (1980), 501.
32. Keohane and Nye, *Power and Interdependence* (1989), 19.
33. S. D. Krasner, 'Structural Causes and Regime Consequences. Regimes as Intervening Variables', in S. D. Krasner (ed.), *International Regimes* (Ithaca, NY and London: Cornell University Press, 1983), 2.
34. Keohane and Nye, *Power and Interdependence* (1989), 24.
35. P. Willetts, 'Interdependence: New Wine in Old Bottles', in Rosenau and Tromp, 196.
36. R. Gilpin, 'The Richness of the Tradition of Political Realism', in Keohane (ed.), *Neorealism and its Critics* (New York: Columbia University Press, 1986), 318.
37. Keohane and Nye, *Power and Interdependence* (1989), 23–4.
38. K. Waltz, 'The Myth of National Interdependence', in R. Maghroori and B. Ramberg (eds.), *Globalism Versus Realism: International Relations' Third Debate* (Boulder, Colo.: Westview Press, 1982), 81–96.

39. Z. Brzezinski, *Between Two Ages: America's Role in the Technetronic Era* (Harmondsworth: Penguin Books, 1976). According to Brzezinski, 'While the formal rules of the game maintain the illusion that it is played only by those players called "states"—and, when war breaks out, the states become the only significant players,—short of war the game is truly played on a much more informal basis, with more mixed participation' (p. 5).

# THREE

# Culture, Society, and Order in World Politics

*Nicholas J. Rengger*

Culture is one of those terms that often prompts people (especially international relations scholars) to reach for their revolvers. It seems to represent everything that good, positivistically trained international relations specialists should hate. It is an inevitably loose concept that defies rigour and precision and is open to endless reinterpretation. Yet its significance for world politics cannot really be doubted. Depending how the phenomenon is viewed, the existence of radically different and divergent cultures on the planet can be seen as a curse, a blessing, a blight on the future, the best hope for future growth, or even (as we shall see) an irrelevance. In many respects it can be all of these.

More problematically still, the notion of culture is inextricably linked to one of the most important but disputed notions in international relations, the idea that there is an international society as well as an international system manifest in contemporary world politics. We shall explore this conception in some detail in a moment.

This chapter seeks to examine the theoretical dilemma created by the interrelationship between these two ideas and to assess its implications for what is held to be produced by international society—the notion of international order. Essentially, there are two different and almost opposite claims that provide the parameters for the dilemmas associated with culture and society in world politics. I shall term these first, the claim from cultural relativity and second, the claim for cultural synthesis or dominance. I shall outline each of them before discussing the problems associated with each and looking at possible solutions. Before I begin, however, let me turn to the notion of international society and suggest why it is so inextricably entwined with discussions of culture in world politics.

## I. How Should we Understand International Society?

For Martin Wight the idea of international society, found in past political thinkers as varied as Suarez, De Toqueville, De Visscher, and Burke, is best defined as 'the habitual intercourse of independent communities, beginning in the Christendom of Western Europe and gradually extending throughout the world'.[1] The nature of this society, Wight goes on to argue, is 'manifest in the diplomatic system; in the conscious maintenance of the balance of power to preserve the independence of the member communities; in the regular operations of international law . . . in economic, social and technical interdependence and the functional international institutions established . . . to regulate it. All these presuppose an international social consciousness, a world wide community sentiment.'[2] In Hedley Bull and Adam Watson's handsomely mounted and edited collection *The Expansion of International Society*, which can almost be read as an extended elaboration of Wight's argument, Bull identifies the First World War as the time by which 'international society', previously primarily self-consciously Euro-centric, had become a universal international society, and the period following the Second World War as that in which attempts were made 'to transform a universal society of states into one of peoples'.[3] Wight, however, implies that international society as he understood it accepted that states were not its exclusive members and suggests that it is only in the eighteenth century, with Wolff and Vattel, that there was seen to be a problem with the ascription of international rights to actors with, as it were, non-state personalities. Moreover, this transition was not, Wight believes, entirely eclipsed by the rise of the notion of state personality, expressed in more recent times by, amongst others, international lawyers like Westlake, Brierly, and Jessup.

In his book *The Anarchical Society*, Hedley Bull builds on Wight's argument, but departs from it in subtle but important ways. For Bull the idea of international society is conceived by the natural law tradition of the sixteenth to the eighteenth centuries, most prominently in the writings of Victoria, Suarez, Gentili, Grotius, and Pufendorf. This period of international society, according to Bull, has five principal characteristics: Christian values; the ambiguity highlighted above as to the membership of international society; the primacy of natural, as opposed to positive, international law; the assumption of universal society (*respublica Christiana*); and finally the lack of a set of institutions deriving from the co-operation of states. Bull's argument goes on to suggest, however, that the notion of the idea of international society develops through two further major stages, 'European International Society' and 'world international society'. Bull's conclusion, echoing Wight's assertion of the tension implicit in 'western values in international relations' in his most famous essay,[4] is that the element of international society is only one element in world politics but that 'The idea of international society has a basis in reality that is sometimes precarious but has at no stage disappeared'.[5] He concludes by attacking notions of 'international anarchy' (for understandings of this term see the introduction and Chapter 1) that ignore this persistence of the idea of international society as relying overly on an overstated domestic analogy that in its turn ignores the elements of uniqueness in the predicament of states and states-systems. This uniqueness, according to Bull, was recognized by certain theorists of international society in the eighteenth century and is implicit in the gradual abandonment of the idea of the law of nature in favour of 'the law of nations' and ultimately of the adoption of the term international law (by, as we noted in the introduction, Jeremy Bentham). This is coupled by Bull with a repetition of Wight's point that it was also in the eighteenth century that the key statement that states are the true and proper members of international society is made.

Bull is, moreover, insistent that the notion of society in world politics is intimately connected with the idea of order in world politics. *The Anarchical Society* is, of course, subtitled 'A Study of Order in World Politics'. By order Bull is clear that he means a pattern of regularity of social life such that it promotes certain goals and values. This will have three component parts; first, the fact that all societies seek to ensure that life will be in some measure secure against violence, secondly, that all societies will seek to ensure that all agreements, once made, will be kept, and thirdly, that all societies will seek to ensure relative stability of possession. These Bull refers to as the elementary and primary goals of societies. As far as world politics is concerned, then, Bull suggests a division of the notion of order into international order, which he describes as a pattern of activity conducive to the maintenance of the elementary and primary goals of the society of states, and world order, described as a pattern of activity conducive to the maintenance of the elementary and primary goals of human social life as such. The latter, he thinks, is also in important respects prior to the former. Thus, in terms of Bull's breakdown of the evolution of the notion of international society after 1945 as attempting a transformation from a society of states to a society of peoples, we can say that, in addition, it is engaged in attempting a transition from international order to world order.

Inevitably, the notion of society deployed here is dependent on seeing society and culture as locked in a parasitic embrace. The values and shared understandings that mark out international society must be culturally generated and sustained, which, of course, implies that international and/or world order is equally dependent on such cultural generation and maintenance. It is clear, then, that the way we see the role and character of culture in world politics will have important implications for our conceptions of international society and international or world order.

## II. Does Cultural Diversity Imply Conceptual, as well as Systemic, Anarchy?

The first problem that I shall look at, then, is the claim that the existence of many different cultures in the contemporary world has two stark implications for contemporary world politics. The first is the loss of agreement over the set of values which governs the international society. The second is the idea that all cultural claims have, prima facie, the same validity. If true, these two claims would imply a weakening, perhaps a collapse, of those elements of the international system that help it to constitute a society on the understanding sketched above. The second would also imply that it was an irrecoverable loss. Let me examine both these propositions in more detail as they might be said to affect world politics.

Let me consider the second of these claims first, as it is the stronger. It is central to the argument of many (though not all) of those critical theorists discussed briefly in the introduction referred to as radical interpretivists. It is the argument recently pursued, for example, by Richard Ashley and Rob Walker.[6] They suggest that, in fact, both world politics and the ways it is studied are each undergoing what amounts to a cultural crisis due both to the acknowledgement of the huge variety of contemporary cultural realities and to the collapse of the legitimacy of the hegemonic culture of the last 200 years, western culture. This crisis, which they date in its specifically modern form from the late eighteenth century, is congruent with the emergence of 'modernity'. This term, hotly disputed though it is, they take to mean the set of assumptions which became especially dominant at that time and immediately thereafter and which have very powerfully contributed to dominant understandings of western culture from that time onwards. The paradigmatic status of natural science and the types of knowledge and rationality associated with it are the primary 'set' of cultural values that are held to make up modernity from this perspective but, in international relations, it is also the period where characteristically modern notions of state, system, and society emerged. Thus the strategy employed by Ashley and Walker is to celebrate this event and to suggest that what it opens up, both intellectually and practically, is the space for marginalized voices, for different cultural projects, for dissenting understandings of the world and of its politics and polities. The implications of this reading for world politics, both its study and its practice, are profound.

The second, and rather weaker, response to the claim from cultural relativity is made, for example, by Adda Bozeman in her chapter in *The Expansion of International Society*. Bozeman argues that western culture is different from most other world cultures in the weight it puts on the principle of individuation. This principle, she argues, 'rooted in the linguistic and intellectual heritage of Greece and Rome, was to remain the guiding force in Western approaches to arts, science and letters as well as to religion, ethics, politics and law. The primary concern here . . . was . . . the individual human being . . . as the exclusive source of thought and the carrier of rights as well as obligations.'[7]

Bozeman's conclusion from this analysis is that the result of this principle and its effect on western culture has been, amongst other things, the characteristically western ways of thinking about world politics but that since these views are not shared by other cultures 'we do not have . . . a globally meaningful system because the world consists today, as it did before the nineteenth century, of a plurality of diverse political systems, each an outgrowth of culture specific concepts'.[8]

Her conclusion is, therefore, rather different from that of Ashley and Walker. Their cultural relativism bites deep into the heart of 'western culture' as much as it draws attention to the levels of cultural diversity in contemporary political life. For Bozeman, however, the 'cultural crisis' lies only in the fact that western culture no longer commands wide acceptance in the global system. This means, she thinks, that the global system will be less ordered, less organized, and more prone to conflict and to violence; that it will, in other words, increasingly cease to display those elements that Bull would describe as societal and this is because of the cultural diversity that characterizes the modern world.

Both these arguments, despite their differences, stress the levels of fragmentation in contemporary world politics. Ashley and Walker essentially see this as a cause for celebration, Bozeman for regret, but each thinks that it is perhaps the most crucial feature of the contemporary world. Thus, the dilemma that arises out of this is whether the undeniable fact that the western norms which largely created international norms and institutions and are now much less acceptable than ever before, means simply that international society will be very different (Bozeman) or that our ways of conceiving of and operating within society *per se* must be remade (Ashley and Walker). I shall return to each of these claims later on.

## III.  Are We Moving Towards a 'World Culture'?

Opposing these arguments of cultural relativity, however, are those views that suggest that we may be seeing the emergence of at least an embryonic global culture. Some institutionalist writers (for example, Ronald Dore, John Burton, and Richard Falk[9]) argue this case and it is also argued in rather different ways by critical interpretive theorists such as Linklater and Hoffman who adopt what they call a 'cosmopolitan' position on world politics.

Inevitably, therefore, there are differences in how various writers see this development. Some, for example the historian Theodore Von Laue, see the emerging global culture as the concluding part of a long process of 'westernization'.[10] For Von Laue, 'The world revolution of westernization has run its course. It has created an interdependent world supporting five and more billions of human lives . . . interdependence has been built on universalised western terms, on western accomplishments in institutions and command over nature. It forms an external and still superficial framework of human existence within which incompatible cultures . . . clash.'[11]

In fact, Von Laue's view is that what he calls 'the liberating discipline of globalism' can help us avoid the dangers to which such a situation is obviously prone and his concluding chapter urges all of us to a 'higher' loyalty. Essentially, therefore, he too appeals to what is usually termed 'cosmopolitanism' and in so doing adopts a similar strategy to writers such as Hoffman and Linklater.

Cosmopolitanism for critical theorists like Hoffman is based on an ethical position derived from the German philosopher Immanuel Kant, to the effect that 'a violation or wrong felt in one place should be felt in all others'.[12] Another theorist who makes similar claims, although his conclusions are somewhat different, is Charles Beitz. He suggests that cosmopolitan conceptions are 'concerned with the moral relations of members of a universal community in which state boundaries have a merely derivative significance'.[13]

Versions of the claim from cultural unity that stress this 'cosmopolitan' thesis obviously emphasize the ethical and normative aspects of world politics, although they would usually argue that social, economic, or technical changes are also in part responsible for the 'globalizing' they discuss. In the terms we used in the introduction, they will be either institutionalists or, more usually, critical theorists and they will tend to be on the interpretive end of the methodological spectrum. They are not united by any particular conclusions, however. Some, for example, would see human rights as the language of the emergent cosmopolitan culture (to some extent Beitz might qualify here)[14] others would argue for a less rights-based and more emancipatory theory.[15] None the less, the primary locus of the global culture for these writers is an ethical one.

Other writers, however, have suggested that the motor of the new global culture will be the need to solve problems that are inevitably insoluble by any one state acting alone, however powerful; for example, environmental problems or the problems of co-ordinating economic policies in an interdependent world economy. Keohane and Nye[16] adopt this course as do many other writers who stress interdependence and 'regimes'.[17] Here most writers would be institutionalists and would tend toward the positivistic end of our methodological axis. Some, however, veer towards integrating realist insights with the changing circum-stances of contemporary world politics (this is explicitly Keohane and Nye's endeavour[18]) while others are much closer to critical analyses (James Rosenau's latest book *Turbulence in World Politics*, for example).[19]

None of these authors suggests that the obvious differences that currently exist between cultures are not real or that they are unimportant. They attempt, however, to elaborate one or more of a number of strategies to suggest that they are being gradually overcome. For Hoffman and Linklater they are transcended by a cosmopolitan ethic, for Von Laue by both this and by the gathering pace of the world revolution of westernization; for Keohane, especially in his more recent work,[20] by the mechanisms available for co-operation in international institutions. However, all these views coalesce around the claim that the world must increasingly be seen as a whole, and that the lens for seeing this whole is, at least predominantly, a western one, however modified it may in the end turn out to be.

In important respects, therefore, this claim is that what we are observing in contemporary world politics is the triumph of western culture. This is, of course, essentially Von Laue's argument and it is also expressed in different ways by a number of other writers. Francis Fukayama, for example, in a now notorious article in the American journal *The National Interest* in 1990, suggested that with the decline of Communism as a viable challenger to western capitalist liberal democracy we had, to all intents and purposes, reached 'the end of history' (the title of the article) at least as far as discovering the institutional norms of the good life. Many of the responses to Fukayama's article as well as critiques of the work of the cosmopolitan theorists (from various perspectives) has expressed a considerable concern at what might appear overwhelming western arrogance.

However, the Globalizers have an answer to this. It has been perhaps best put by Ronald Dore who has suggested that this concern with western dominance is only problematic because of the west's colonial past and its current position at the top of the international heap. 'When that ceases to be the case', he argues, the problem will diminish rapidly, but

world culture will still be basically western culture. Many post-Confucian elements may be absorbed: geisha parties might replace cocktail parties at the UN and there may be more talk of benevolence and less of justice in the rhetoric. But the modes of international law and conference procedure, the shape of the novel and the structure and functioning of universities will still be of western origin.[21]

In this series of arguments, therefore, we see an emphasis on the unifying power of technology and modernization as agents of westernization rather than on the elements of crisis between or within cultures. The co-relative assumption is that this process, for all its problems and difficulties, is at least in principle a benevolent one even if it is also inevitable at least to some degree. Thus, it might lead to a very different type of world politics (as, for example, cosmopolitan theorists have been arguing at least since Kant); one that is, for the first time, truly global in scope, concern, and focus.

## IV. What are the Problems with these Arguments?

I said above that these two claims, the claims of cultural relativity and the claims of cultural unity, have set the parameters of the debate about culture, society, and world politics. Let me now look at some objections that have been raised to these arguments. Of course, at one level the most powerful set of criticisms of each claim comes from the other one. There are also, however, a large number of other objections. To examine these in anything like a comprehensive fashion is beyond the scope of this book. But it is important, I think, to look briefly at those objections directly relevant to world politics not related to either of the groups we have already examined.

The first set of objections, then, comes from a broadly realist perspective. This argument is essentially that culture, in the sense we have been using it here, is, strictly speaking, irrelevant to world politics. Of course, some realists are aware that culture is relevant in the sense that to understand, say, a particular state's military posture it is important to look at what is called its 'strategic culture',[22] but this is simply 'knowing your enemy'. What is irrelevant, they say, is to assume that cultural differences can result in differences to world politics at the systemic level. The clearest argument of this sort is that of Kenneth Waltz. As outlined in the introduction, his position is that the anarchic nature of the system constrains all states (from all cultures) to act in a functionally undifferentiated way. Thus, while either of the claims discussed above might be true in whole or in part they are incapable of affecting the nature of the international system and are therefore irrelevant at that level.

This argument seems to me to be entirely mistaken. To begin with, it assumes what it sets out to show, i.e., that culture does not affect world politics. It assumes, for example, that one can have a culturally independent way of seeing the world, that the categories developed by western social science are themselves suitable tools for such a culturally neutral view and that all institutions on the world stage are perceived in the same way at least in terms of their functions. None of these statements is unchallengeable. It is demonstrable, I think, that many states in the world are of a very different order from those on which the realist model of international relations is patterned[23] and it is also at least arguable that realism is predicated on a particular western understanding of the problems of politics.[24] For all its variety, for example, an Islamic understanding of world politics, even if broadly sympathetic to the idea of territorial states and the impedimenta of the western international system, would see things very differently (see Chapter 11 for a discussion of the dilemmas posed by Islam).

A second possible objection might arise from those who adopt a 'strong' positivist methodology. If we take three of the best general world politics textbooks written from an essentially positivistic standpoint we find that the word culture is mentioned only twice in Kegley and Wittkopf,[25] once in Holsti (and this a relatively curious usage),[26] and not at all in Russett and Starr.[27] Such a consistent neglect needs an explanation. In part, it might have something to do with the resistance to empirical theory of the term 'culture', noted at the outset of this chapter. On the other hand many positivist writers, Singer, for example, and Holsti in a recent book,[28] have stressed that it is important not to ignore normative questions and so this seems unlikely. A second reason might be found in a similar type of argument to that of the realists sketched above, i.e., that 'culture' is simply not a problem for world politics *as a subject of study*. Here the claim would not be that it is necessarily irrelevant to the facts of world politics (the realist case) but that it is something that must not be allowed to affect the way that we *study* world politics. The root of this claim would lie in the distinction that all positivists would draw between the world of 'facts' and that of 'values'. Culture, they would argue, defines the values that are held, celebrated, defended, attacked, and so on at a particular time and place. As such it is something to be investigated and not something through which to investigate. From this perspective, then, they would criticize all critical theorists and many institutionalists for failing to note this fundamental aspect of enquiry and confusing the facts of the world (which may include cultural facts) with the values we use to investigate them.

At one level, this criticism is a powerful one. It is perfectly fair to say that we can investigate phenomena without believing in the truth of the phenomena we investigate. A historian of political thought, for example, can investigate the reasons why a particular past thinker believed in witchcraft (say) without themselves believing in witchcraft. This takes us into important areas of contemporary and social theory and the problems of meaning and explanation. However, the emphasis that the argument from cultural relativity places on culture is a slightly different one. It claims either that the existence of different cultures means that truth claims cannot be validated outside the matrix of that particular culture (not that in order to recognize them we must believe them) or that, in any case, the notion of truth claims in this sense is itself at the centre of a cultural crisis. Either of these positions can be disputed, of course, but they are not susceptible to refutation by a simple disjunction between facts and values.

A third possible objection, directed this time at the second of our two claims, might be rather more subtle. This might suggest that, of course culture could be influential and might have been in the past, but that it is not so today due to precisely the developments that advocates of the second view stress: i.e., globalization and modernization. Proponents of this view might even be prepared to accept that culture is still relevant in certain regions of the world, at least for the time being, but only because such regions were not fully 'westernized'.

This view has much in common, of course, with the claim of embryonic cultural unity, save only that its adherents de-emphasize, rather than stress, the affect of this cultural unity as a systemic determinant. For them, growing cultural unity is a fact of contemporary world politics but it does not give rise to any problems. To this extent, they would object at least to the cosmopolitan side of the cultural unity argument.

Of course, these objections are not in themselves unanswerable. What they clearly indicate, however, is the range of views that exist in accounts of world politics as to the provenance or relevance of cultural questions. What I want to do now, however, is to suggest one particular way of approaching this question.

## V. Culture and Tradition: A New Approach to Culture and World Politics?

To begin with, I want to suggest that there is a way of conceiving of the role and influence of culture in world politics that avoids the problems outlined above and that enables us to bring the notion of international society into play once more in order to illuminate the importance that culture can play in contemporary world politics. To start with it seems sensible, I think, to accept that we are in a position at present in world politics where the general norms of western culture as they affect the international system are being challenged as they have not been before, at least since the late eighteenth century. It is also important, however, to accept the claim that many western norms have been adopted globally. In other words, my starting-point is to accept aspects of both the claim from cultural relativity and the claim from cultural dominance.

However, it seems to me that these 'global' assumptions, which Benjamin Barber has felicitously called the assumptions of 'McWorld', the world of the Macintosh computer and the McDonald hamburger,[29] of information technology and global capital markets, are not embryonic of a 'global culture', if by culture we mean (amongst other things) a shared set of normative understandings of the world leading to patterns of activity supportive of the primary goals of a society, whether this society is considered one of states or of peoples. The assumptions of McWorld have an entirely derivative, second order significance. Rather than being an overarching framework, superficial at present but embryonically the beginnings of global culture, they are a subculture, a set of assumptions shared only by those who have already accepted aspects of the westernized culture currently in place.

This brings me to a second point. Obviously I disagree with the realists that culture is irrelevant to world politics, but I would argue that there is a small nugget of truth in their dismissal of it. This is that 'unified cultures', in the sense seemingly presupposed by Bozeman, do not really exist. Here, radical interpretivists are correct to assume that western culture is fragmented, but many are wrong, I think, to assume that it (or any other culture) has ever been anything else. Cultures are inevitably fashioned by inter-penetration, continual change, and constant reinterpretation.

Here, therefore, I would suggest we introduce the notion of traditions of thought within cultures. Now, of course, it must be admitted that the notion of a tradition is every bit as disputed as that of culture itself. None the less, it can, I think, perform a useful function in the present context in that it helps to break down the rather unwieldy mass of whole 'cultures' into rather more manageable elements. It also enables us to emphasize the links between traditions of thought that may be important or relevant cross-culturally and so build in a sense on the fact that while 'cultures' may be incommensurable, traditions are always interpenetrative in their own time and place.

Let me briefly outline how I think we should use the term tradition in this context. Adam Roberts and Ben Kingsbury have very usefully defined four senses in which the term tradition has been used in international relations in connection with the notion that there is a 'Grotian tradition' of thought.[30] These are first, a proposition that there can be discerned a pattern of issues, and approaches to them with which the tradition concerned has been centrally and distinctively concerned. Secondly, simply a body of textual material around the work of a single author (such as Grotius). Thirdly, the view most associated with Quentin Skinner, that traditions can only be recovered by the exhaustive study of intellectual contexts. Fourthly, and lastly, they conclude there is the sense drawn from the writings of the philosopher Alisdair MacIntyre,[31] where a tradition is perceived as 'more than a coherent movement of thought. It is such a movement in the course of which those engaging in that movement become aware of it and of its direction and in self-aware fashion attempt to engage its debates and to carry its enquiries forward.'[32]

This last view is the one that Roberts and Kingsbury think scholars such as Martin Wight and Hedley Bull have basically followed, though they point out that there are considerable difficulties with it. What I suggest is that an approach that combines this with the contextual readings and historical recovery of Skinner would actually give us a clear, if complex, way of seeing the development of cultural interactions on international relations and thus to assess its impact. For example, Islamic Aristoteleanism in the twelfth and thirteenth centuries strongly influenced Christian thinking and helped a very strong (and still very powerful) tradition of Catholic thought to emerge—Thomism.[33] It would be incorrect to say that Islam and Catholicism today were commensurable world views, of course, but it is clear that there have been many interpenetrations and cross-fertilizations and that in order to understand how traditions of thought have influenced each other (whether from within the culture or from without) we have to see the way in which traditions of thought within a particular culture have evolved and that, of course, requires a historical (but not radical) interpretivism similar to that of Skinner.[34]

What I think that this implies is that in order to understand the essential relevance of culture for world politics in any given situation, time-period, or issue-area, the traditions of thought and action operative at that time, or in that place or over that issue-area should be understood and interpreted in their cultural context. It should be clear that this activity does not, therefore, accept the radical interprevist claim that such interpretation is not possible at all, although it is sympathetic to many other aspects of their projects. Equally, however, it would only accept with very heavy qualification most versions of the cosmopolitan view as it does take seriously the very real differences that have existed and continued to do so not only between cultures but also within them. On these grounds, then, we do not have to accept the global culture thesis in order to acknowledge the very powerful effect of the westernizing tendencies inherent in many aspects of world politics (especially the economic and technological aspects). Nor, however, need we argue that, as a result, there is a complete and unbridgeable incommensurability between the cultures that exist in world politics because such cultures are explicable and recoverable through examining the interpenetrations and inter-actions between the traditions that constitute them.

This brings us back to our starting-point, however. If there is a sense in which we can deploy notions of culture in world politics, what are its implications for understandings of international society and international order?

## VI. Does Cultural Diversity Necessarily Weaken International Society and International Order or can it Strengthen Them?

As we saw earlier, Hedley Bull is the scholar who has done most this century to investigate the nature of international society.[35] He has also focused on the chief problem for theorists who wish to assert (as he does) that international society is the crucial 'glue' that holds the international system together. That problem is primarily created by the alleged fragmentation of the western norms that created the society in the first place and, in any case, their questioning or rejection by many in contemporary world politics. Bull himself believed that this fragmentation had not yet fully occurred (although it was certainly threatened) and was relatively optimistic about the prospects for international society.[36]

However, there are clearly problems with such optimism. At one level (the level of 'McWorld') there are, as we have seen, forces making some global set of rules necessary, but these will not necessarily be the sort of rules that generate a society in the required sense. In order for this to be a realistic proposition the rules must include norms that provide support for the self-identification of the various groups that are held to make up international society since only this will actually provide support for a pattern of behaviour which will sustain the elementary or primary goals of social life. The simple fact of interdependence, or of globalization, is not enough for this. Equally, however, a simplistic nationalism or identification with a particular ethos is clearly not enough either. The international system has had plenty of that over the last one hundred years and it cannot be said to have been an unalloyed benefit.

Given that both these tendencies are present in contemporary world politics surely a sensible position is to recognize that the difference and diversity of cultures is both inevitable and welcome in at least one sense. This is that there does not seem to me to be any reason why the fact of diversity should logically require us to abandon beliefs about international relations (or, indeed, anything else) that we happen to hold to be true. An understanding of the importance and role of culture that adopts the approach I sketched above will be similar to the historian who is asking why a particular individual believed in witchcraft; we are not obliged to accept his reasons as good ones for us, though we accept that they may be (or have been) good ones for him. Thus we might well understand why certain groups in the contemporary world do not accept much western thinking about territoriality, for example, without necessarily refusing to accept it ourselves. Moreover we might also be able more clearly to suggest that there are traditions of thought in western culture which have been overlooked and which we might think are now more appropriate to the circumstances in which we find ourselves. As I remarked above, neither traditions of thought, nor the cultures in which they have their being, stand still; they are always changing and evolving.

Of course, it might well be true (indeed, I think it is) that the way in which these two Janus-like tendencies are manifesting themselves currently in world politics will be to strongly reinforce the trends that are weakening international society. My point, however, is that this is not a necessary condition merely a contingent one. We still have the capacity to interpret them differently and make them serve the cause of international society rather than be its gravedigger.

This understanding would seem to imply that the one activity that is perhaps most conducive to the elementary and primary goals of the society of states is tolerance of alternative readings of our circumstances. These are, after all, likely to be of use to us, at least so long as such alternative readings are equally tolerant of our own. This would in turn imply that international order bespeaks tolerance at the same time as it remains clear that certain forms of activity (clear aggression, whether externally or internally directed, for example) should be relegated from it. It also implies, I think, that Bull is incorrect to assume that world order ought to replace international order as the primary concern of world politics.[37] Politics is now global, it is true, but society is still largely international because it is still primarily in terms of national identities (note I do not say state identities) that groups express themselves and their identities, even if the radical interpretivists are right that they often do so in a contested and fragmented way.

What I hope is clear from all of this is that I do not think that the study of world politics can afford to ignore cultural issues at any level. Whatever hope we do have to claim that some cosmopolitan norms might exist (and I am sympathetic to that claim) they can only be given expression in practical terms through the many manifestations of the different cultural practices of the Earth. How we can give such expression without fuelling conflict and violence creates for us some of our greatest dilemmas of all. It also alerts us to the fact that only by so doing might we create sufficient 'patterns of activity' to prevent the tenuous and fragile international society we do possess from vanishing completely.

## Notes

1. Wight, *Power Politics* (Harmondsworth: Penguin, 1970), 96.
2. Ibid. 96–7.
3. Hedley Bull and A. Watson (eds.), *The Expansion of International Society* (Oxford: Clarendon Press, 1986), 125–6.
4. See Wight, 'Western Values in International Relations', in H. Butterfield and M. Wight (eds.), *Diplomatic Investigations* (London: George Allen & Unwin, 1966).
5. See Bull, *The Anarchical Society* (London: Macmillan, 1977), 42.
6. In their concluding essay to the Sept. 1990 special issue of *International Studies Quarterly*, 'Speaking the Language of Exile: Dissidence in International Studies'.

7. In Bull and Watson, *The Expansion of International Society*, 404.
8. Ibid.
9. See, for example: Dore's essay ibid.; John Burton, *World Society* (Cambridge: Cambridge University Press, 1968); Richard Falk, *The End of World Order* (New York: Holmes and Maier, 1983).
10. See Theodore Von Laue, *The World Revolution of Westernisation* (Oxford: Oxford University Press, 1987).
11. Ibid. 361.
12. See Mark Hoffman, 'States, Cosmopolitanism and Normative International Theory', *Paradigms*, 2/1 (1988), 67.
13. Charles Beitz, *Political Theory and International Relations* (Princeton, NJ: Princeton University Press, 1979), 182.
14. For the best general discussion of human rights and international relations, see R. J. Vincent, *Human Rights and International Relations* (Cambridge: Cambridge University Press, 1986).
15. This would certainly be the position of Hoffman and Linklater. See M. Hoffman, 'States, Cosmopolitanism and Normative International Theory', and A. Linklater, *Men and Citizens in International Relations*, 2nd edn. (London: Macmillan, 1990).
16. See R. Keohane and J. S. Nye, *Power and Interdependence: World Politics in Transition*, 2nd edn. (Boston: Little-Brown, 1987).
17. For example, the chapters by Oran Young and D. J. Puchala and R. F. Hopkins in Stephen Krasner (ed.), *International Regimes* (Princeton, NJ: Princeton University Press, 1982). For a fuller discussion, see John Garnett's chapter above.
18. See Keohane and Nye, *Power and Interdependence*, p. xi.
19. James N. Rosenau, *Turbulence in World Politics: A Theory of Change and Continuity* (Hemel Hempstead: Harvester, 1990).
20. See, for example, *After Hegemony* (Princeton, NJ: Princeton University Press, 1984). See also his concluding essay, co-authored with Robert Axelrod, in Kenneth Oye (ed.), *Co-operation under Anarchy* (Princeton, NJ: Princeton University Press, 1985).
21. Ronald Dore, 'Unity and Diversity in World Culture', in Bull and Watson, *The Expansion of International Society*.
22. This term was coined by the American scholar Jack Snyder, though pioneering work was also done by Ken Booth in his brilliant book *Strategy and Ethnocentrism* (London: Croom Helm, 1979). One realist writer who has made extensive use of this term is Colin Gray in his *Nuclear Strategy and National Style* (London: Hamilton Press, 1986).
23. See, for example, the argument of Robert Jackson in *Quasi-States* (Cambridge: Cambridge University Press, 1991).
24. This, of course, would be argued by many critical theorists.

25. C. Kegley and E. Wittkopf, *World Politics: Trend and Transformation*, 3rd edn. (London: Macmillan, 1989).

26. Kalevi J. Holsti, *International Politics: A Framework for Analysis* (Princeton, NJ: Prentice-Hall, 1988).

27. B. Russet and H. Starr, *World Politics: The Menu for Choice*, 2nd edn. (New York: Freeman, 1989).

28. Holsti, *Peace and War: Armed Conflicts and International Order 1648–1989* (Cambridge: Cambridge University Press, 1991).

29. In his plenary lecture to the annual conference of the Political Studies Association of Great Britain held at Lancaster, 15–17 Apr. 1991.

30. See Hedley Bull, Adam Roberts, and Benedict Kingsbury (eds.), *Hugo Grotius and International Relations* (Oxford: Clarendon Press, 1990), 51–64.

31. Especially his *After Virtue* (London: Duckworth, 1981); *Whose Justice? Which Rationality?* (London: Duckworth, 1988); and *Three Rival Versions of Moral Enquiry* (London: Duckworth, 1990).

32. Bull, Roberts, and Kingsbury *Hugo Grotius*, 54, citing MacIntyre's *Whose Justice? Which Rationality*.

33. After the writings of St Thomas Aquinas. Some international theorists have been strongly influenced by this. For example, writers like Victoria and Suarez were both late Thomistic writers in the 16th century and, in our own day, writers as different as Michael Donelan and Brian Midgely have been influenced by this tradition of thought. See Donelan (ed.), *The Reason of States* (London: George Allen & Unwin, 1978), and E. B. F. Midgely, *The Natural Law Tradition and the Theory of International Relations* (London: Elek, 1975).

34. It would not be the same. I have tried to elaborate both the differences and the similarities in: 'Serpents and Doves in Classical International Theory', *Millennium: Journal of International Studies*, 17/2; 'The Fearful Sphere of International Relations', *Review of International Studies* (October 1990); and *Tradition Transition in International Society* (forthcoming).

35. See Bull, *The Anarchical Society*, and id., *The Expansion of International Society*.

36. See the conclusion to *The Expansion of International Society*.

37. For a fuller discussion of the claim that international order must be seen as prior to world order see N. J. Rengger, 'No Longer a Tournament of Distinctive Knights: Systemic Transition and the Priority of International Order', in R. Brown and M. Bowker (eds.), *Theory and World Politics in the 1980s* (Cambridge: Cambridge University Press, forthcoming).

# PART II. INSTITUTIONS

# FOUR

# The Global Political Economy

*Rowland Maddock*

## I. What is The Global Political Economy?

Although politicians and statesmen have always understood the interdependence of politics and economics, the intellectual disciplines of political science and economics have long been separate. There are good pedagogic reasons for this, and both disciplines have benefited from this intellectual separation. It is at the same time unsatisfactory. Political economy is the intellectual discipline which investigates the rich interface between economics and politics. International political economy is the extension of that investigation to the international sphere. Although political economy often offers a more fruitful description of events and outcomes, there exist real methodological problems of academic inquiry.

The unit of investigation, or the actors, in each discipline are assumed to be motivated by different objectives. In economics, firms, consumers, wage earners, even governments are assumed to maximize an economic variable: profit, income, or welfare. In political science the same governments are assumed to seek other objectives: security, status, or political stability. Although it is possible at the state level to construct objective functions which include welfare as well as security, the analysis loses simplicity, one of the virtues of theory.

Moreover for the state, territoriality, that is borders which keep out those whose loyalty cannot be guaranteed, is a precondition of existence, and to a considerable degree the practice of international politics is designed to maintain exclusivity. For the firm, the prime economic agent, exclusivity is arbitrary and inefficient.

National boundaries have no economic rationale and decrease profits. Firms seek to expand beyond and even destroy boundaries, and therefore come into conflict with the essential function of the state. In respect to territory the motivation for economic and political behaviour differs. In other respects, however, firms and states need and depend on one another. Firms depend on states for protection and for establishing and maintaining the rules of the game. Governments, outside pure command economies, depend on firms to create wealth, to increase the tax base essential to the pursuit of security.

Formal economic theory derives by and large from the assumption of *ceteris paribus*, i.e., everything which is not essential for the investigation at hand is assumed to be constant, and can therefore be ignored. This usually means all non-economic motivation and behaviour. Politics is assumed to be an irrational departure from optimal behaviour and economic efficiency. Political scientists make no such assumption. So-called irrational behaviour is the very stuff of analysis and though some schools assume a hierarchy of assumptions political science has not developed the formal rigorous and mathematical body of theory which the *ceteris paribus* assumption makes possible in economics. Logically the two methodologies cannot be reconciled. Political economy proceeds therefore in an eclectic manner picking and choosing from both disciplines what appears useful. As such it lacks the intellectual elegance of formal economic analysis and the empirical richness of political science. Analysis is also complicated by competing ideological viewpoints: the liberal, the realist, and the Marxist being the ones most usually identified. More recently the epistemological basis of the positivist framework which informs most academic writing on international political economy has been attacked as inadequate.

In short, international political economy is not a tightly defined and exclusive discipline with a well-established methodology. It is more a set of issues which need investigating and which tend to be ignored by the more established disciplines, using whatever tools are to hand.

The present chapter is in that mould. Ignoring the methodological problems and eschewing a strongly ideological stance it identifies a small number of key interdisciplinary issues.

After investigating the creation in the 1940s of the liberal global order, which delimits the non-socialist international economic order, the chapter considers some Third World criticisms of the liberal economy, and the steps Third World governments have taken to negotiate a more equitable alternative. A dominant hegemonic power is argued to have been an essential prerequisite for international harmony and co-operation. An investigation of why this might be so is followed by a discussion of the likely consequences of the apparent decline of American hegemony. The chapter also considers the consequence of Soviet hegemonic decline on the international socialist economy. A brief conclusion looks at some outstanding global issues: managing the system of exchange rates, global debt, and economic regionalism.

Nations seek some optimal combination of economic welfare and national security, given material and non-material constraints. In the short term welfare and security may well be substitutes in that more of one means less of the other. For instance, higher defence spending reduces civilian consumption or investment, while more trade increases vulnerability to outside influences. In the long run, however, security and welfare are more likely to be positively correlated. Secure borders provide the stability which encourages investment and innovation and richer societies have larger surpluses which can be mobilized for security purposes. The optimal policy choice between security and welfare, the long term and short term is necessarily complex. Neither realist political nor economic models which specify a simple hierarchy of objectives provide wholly acceptable analyses of global political economy. They do, however, provide useful starting-points.

Economists show that, given quite plausible assumptions international trade and investment increase national and global welfare. Trade allows nations to specialize in the production of goods and services in which they are most efficient. Specialization maximizes the static gains from trade and the dynamic benefits of scale and competition. Other things being equal, welfare in individual countries is positively correlated with the overall efficiency and stability of the global system. Nations are therefore induced to respond positively to the principles, norms, rules, and decision-making procedures which maximize global benefits; that is to pursue policies of free trade.

Furthermore, international trade and investment create inter-dependencies and mutual vulnerabilities, which increase the cost and therefore reduce the incentive to serious conflict and war. In short, free trade increases welfare and decreases the likelihood of war. Casual empiricism gives a measure of support to these theoretical insights. Nevertheless, free trade has historically been the exception rather than the rule.

The benefits of trade, though real and substantial, are diffuse, difficult to identify and to quantify. The costs of trade on the other hand are immediate, easily identifiable, concentrated, and therefore highly politicized. Although trade benefits the community as a whole, particular regions, industries, and workers are adversely affected. Since the intensity of loss of employment is usually greater than the gain to living standards from cheap imports, the numbers of people affected lower, and the source of distress easily identified, the incentive to mobilize political action against imports is high and the transactions costs of so doing low. Nations seek to avoid political turbulence and instability and may therefore be prepared to forgo long-term, narrowly defined economic efficiency for the short-term more diffuse benefits of state building. Nations are in short simultaneously induced to co-operate and to defect from the liberal international order. The perceived balance of gain and loss varies between nations and periods.

## II. What were the Principles Underlying the Creation of the Post-War Global Economic Order?

In 1945 the victorious allies faced just such a dilemma. For some, in particular the USA, trade offered an opportunity to increase living standards at home, power and influence abroad. For the European nations free trade threatened ungovernable turbulence. Although all accepted with greater or lesser conviction the eventual superiority of market capitalism, and therefore the positive role of international trade, the pace at which they could contemplate reducing barriers which had been erected in peacetime depression and in war varied enormously.

In 1945 the USA accounted for 40 per cent of world industrial production and held 70 per cent of world gold reserves. The war had dragged the economy from depression to full and productive employment, poised to penetrate overseas markets. American leaders, recognizing their responsibilities to (and America's benefit

from) a liberal international economy rejected traditional isolationism with the, often reluctant, support of Congress. Moreover,
they argued that economic nationalism had been a major cause of
the Second World War. Free trade would increase welfare not only
in the USA but ultimately the whole world, and thereby provide a
positive stimulus to peace and security.

The Europeans had to be persuaded, if not intellectually, then
materially of the virtues of the American viewpoint. Detailed
compulsion and interference would probably prove counter-
productive and was in any case inconsistent with *laissez-faire*
principles. Nevertheless some degree of intervention was essential.
Unilateral reductions in trade barriers would undoubtedly de-
stabilize already vulnerable economies. If, however, the Europeans
could be induced to reduce tariffs and other restrictions jointly,
loss in one economic sector for any one country would probably
by compensated by benefit in another. If, moreover, they could be
induced not to seek unfair advantage by competitive devaluations,
the systemic stability thereby created would encourage traders
and investors. In short, nations which faced balance of payments
deficits if they reduced tariffs and which were prohibited from
devaluing the currency had to be materially compensated. Liberal
values and procedures had to be embodied in new institutions: the
International Monetary Fund (IMF), the General Agreement on
Tariffs and Trade (GATT), and the International Bank for Reconstruction and Development (IBRD).

The Soviet Union participated in the initial discussion on post-
war reconstruction, but following its ideological preferences soon
withdrew behind autarkic barriers, forcing its client East European
allies to follow. From the late 1940s, therefore, American
initiatives were motivated by Cold War containment. Liberal
principles would if necessary be sacrificed for pragmatic concerns
about alliance stability. Wealthy nations were believed to be less
susceptible to socialist pressure or enticement, but weak nations
forced to embrace economic liberalism without external support
might succumb to short-term instability. Despite their ideological
preferences for free trade, American political leaders not only
accepted European protection, but encouraged discrimination
against American exports. Marshall Aid to Europe was conditional
on the Europeans reducing trade and monetary barriers between
themselves and therefore at the expense of others.

Economic recovery was rapid, so much so that the liquidity-creating provisions of the IMF proved inadequate to meet international demand for the reserves which were by and large prerequisites for liberal policies. Gold was limited, and the only feasible alternative was the dollar. America's balance of trade surplus, which reflected its economic superiority in the world economy, had therefore to be transformed into a balance of payments deficit, the mechanism for increasing the dollar reserves of Western Europe and Japan. In the process the dollar became an instrument of American economic hegemony. The USA gave economic and military aid to Europe and Japan, bore a disproportionate share of the collective defence effort, and facilitated foreign investment by American multinational companies. In exchange Europe and Japan conceded leadership of the capitalist world to the USA. The so-called 'imperial burden' transformed a balance of trade surplus into a balance of payments deficit. In 1960, for instance, a balance of trade surplus of $4 billion was turned into a payments deficit of $3.8 billion, America's political and security interests were enhanced, global liquidity and therefore welfare increased, and the dollar established as the key currency.

The outcome was, by historical standards, exceptionally high and stable growth, at the core of which was the dynamic international liberal order. Between 1953 and 1973 world trade grew on average by 8 per cent per annum, compared with 4.7 per cent per annum between 1830 and 1860, 3.3 per cent per annum between 1873 and 1913, and 0.9 per cent per annum between 1913 and 1939. The Bretton Woods system not only increased welfare, it also established the liberal paradigm as the superior organizing principle for the international economy against which others had to be measured, and in official circles at least, found wanting. Although the fixed exchange-rate system eventually collapsed in 1971, the principles of openness and co-operation have remained supreme even when policies fail to measure up.

## III. How do Third World Countries View the Liberal Economic Order?

Liberal theory shows that in the long run all nations can benefit from international trade. Those which in practice fail to take advantage of the opportunities available do so because of domestic distortions and inhibitions. Not only is the international economic system not responsible for underdevelopment, it is a positive force for progress destroying the atavistic forces in developing nations which hold back modernization. Underdevelopment is therefore a condition of late insertion into the trading system, the appropriate policy response to which is openness and not protectionism.

Despite obligatory reference to their special problems, less-developed countries played no role in the creation of the post-war international economy. Nevertheless, as a group they grew faster on average during the Bretton Woods period than did the group of developed or the group of socialist nations.

The growth index alone, however, could not disguise what the Third World argued were fundamental imperfections in the global economy. Whereas the developed nations by and large sought efficiency and stability, the underdeveloped nations, though clearly not indifferent to these, were also concerned with matters of equity and justice, the distribution as well as the size of the global product. In 1964 in the wake of rapid de-colonization they managed to create a United Nations Conference on Trade and Development (UNCTAD) which actively pursued such Third World objectives as preferential access to the markets of the rich nations, though with little success.

Third World nations sought not growth so much as development. They were as a group largely dependent on exports of raw materials and primary products, the price of which were wholly determined by world markets beyond their control and which, their spokesmen claimed, tended to long-term secular decline. The intellectual attack on the theory and practice of liberal non-intervention took many guises. One of the most influential was that which described Third World relations with the global economy as one of dependency, especially articulated by a group of Latin American economists and sociologists. According to *dependencia* theorists underdevelopment was not a condition of lateness but a necessary feature of international capitalism, a structural process of exploitation. The global economy, they argued, is divided into two types of countries. The core countries are those which control the sources of capital and technology and which, in consequence, can achieve self-sustaining growth. In periphery countries expansion is conditioned by and dependent on growth elsewhere. They are integrated into the world economy, but on unequal terms.

In the colonial period, international companies, the agents of world capitalism, invested in the primary producing sectors of less-developed countries, rubber, tin, etc. Productive export sectors linked by capital to the international economy existed as enclaves in otherwise underdeveloped economies unable to take advantage of such external economies as were potentially available. After the Second World War the pattern of foreign investment changed. Multinational companies, seeking to integrate production world-wide, invested in industrial and manufacturing as well as the traditional primary producing sectors. For the recipient nation the benefits, often described as 'trickle down' were limited. Local markets are ill-developed, profits are repatriated to the host state, and the better-known, better-organized international companies attract local savings away from indigenous firms. The process of dependency cannot, however, be created without the active support of local élites which are integrated into a class alliance with the transnational bourgeoisie, adopting their life-styles and consumption patterns. Because of dependent development, poverty, with the exception of the small élite group, has been transformed from a matter of class to one of nationality.

Dependency theory has been criticized from various ideological and empirical standpoints. Irrespective of any intellectual short-comings, however, it was important in providing a rational counterpoint to the prevailing liberal orthodoxy, and as such a rallying focus for Third World political activity.

Increased turbulence in the international economy after 1971 fuelled expectations of change. The real trigger for a determined assault on liberal norms was the crisis in international capitalism brought on by the increase in oil prices in 1973–4. The devaluation of the dollar in 1971 appeared to compromise American economic leadership, and the oil crisis highlighted disagreement among the developed states as each sought to guarantee its own supplies of oil. Many, in both the developing and the developed worlds, believed that oil power was harbinger of more encompassing resource power. Although this eventually turned out to be a chimera the perception of global resource scarcity did for a period increase the bargaining-power of the Third World, and therefore provide the basis for a sustained challenge to liberal norms of non-intervention. Because of its superior voting power the Third World located its challenge to the existing order in the United Nations, which at the Sixth Special Session in 1973 passed a Declaration for Establishing a New International Economic Order. In summary this required:

(i) revising international resource transfers;
(ii) restructuring international markets for primary products;
(iii) reorganizing international financial flows.

Consistent with *dependencia* theory, Third World countries wanted more than a fairer share of the global product. They also demanded more control over their economic environment, possible only if unregulated markets were replaced by authoritative regimes willing and able to intervene in and manage international economic affairs. Some developed nations acknowledged the just cause of many Third World complaints, and, responsive to an increasing concern with global interdependence, were willing to concede on some issues. As a group, however, the developed nations would not compromise the essential principles which had brought them, for the most part, such astounding prosperity and stability. The South, supported in general by the socialist bloc, negotiated with the North at a series of meetings in Nairobi, Havana, Manila, and elsewhere over the New International Economic Order. By 1980 the negotiations were effectively at an end, without achieving any substantiative Third World objectives. The explanations for failure are many and complex, ranging from lack of real commitment to fundamental change by Third World negotiators to new-found solidarity amongst the developed nations. In a nutshell, however, the Third World lacked the power to force the developed countries to accede to its demands, and had little to offer to induce substantive concessions.

Apart from those few Newly Industrialized Countries which have successfully penetrated the international economy the relative position of the Third World remains essentially unchanged, and in some regions such as sub-Sahara Africa worse than before the negotiations for the NIEO began. Short of a systemic crisis real bargaining-power remains with the rich and powerful core nations. Despite disagreements amongst themselves, they are sufficiently united to ward off a fundamental challenge to their basic interests. The essential rules of the game are determined by the dominant players, and, as the negotiations to resolve the global debt crisis subsequently showed, these rules are interpreted by and for the benefit of the rich and the powerful.

The 1970s also showed that without power, global negotiations are not useful mechanisms for achieving basic Third World objectives. Bilateral or small-group bargaining between interested parties, on single issues, which do not compromise the essential interests of the developed nations offer a more likely avenue of success. Indeed, some liberal theorists argue that the concept of the Third World as a distinct and separate entity is no longer relevant.


## IV. Does International Economic Co-operation Require a Hegemonic Power?

One reason for Third World optimism in the mid-1970s was a widely held perception of declining American hegemony. Histori-cally, periods of openness, growth, and relative stability had coincided with the existence of a single dominating hegemonic power: Britain in the mid- to late nineteenth-century, the USA after 1945. The inter-war period, by contrast, when no nation either would or could exercise leadership, was characterized by depression and turbulence. There are two, not wholly consistent, reasons why hegemony might be necessary, though not sufficient, for openness. The dominant version draws its inspiration from the economic theory of public goods. Creating and sustaining open international orders is costly, if only in the sense of domestic autonomy forgone. Nations, especially if they are small, cannot be prevented from enjoying the benefits of openness, even if they make no corresponding contribution to its success. They are induced to 'free-ride'.

Capitalist systems, despite their overall efficiency, do periodically slide into depression and instability, during which nations are strongly induced to close themselves from economic perturbations emanating abroad. Protectionism by one country provokes retalia-tion. To prevent wholesale defection the hegemony must bear the cost of sustaining the liberal system. It alone has the resources to offer a market for distress goods, to supply a counter-cyclical flow of capital and adequate liquidity. It must also manage the system of exchange rates and co-ordinate international monetary policy. If the hegemony is successful all nations benefit, but because they free-ride the non-hegemonic nations benefit disproportionately.

Realist and neo-realist theorists dismiss the exclusive focus on economic welfare. Nations are also concerned with security, given which, relative benefit may be quite as important as, perhaps more important than, the absolute gains from trade which underlie the economic model. Liberal hegemonies lead by consent so that for the community of nations within the hegemonic ambit there are fundamental values for instance the very essence of the capitalist system itself, which demand co-operation. Within that co-operative framework, however, the hegemony and the smaller states disagree over the distribution of costs and benefits. To exercise effective political leadership and thereby achieve its fundamental security objectives in a non-coercive system, the hegemony is obliged, and is able, to bear a disproportionate share of the economic cost.

The dollar standard, established after 1945, reflected and was an instrument of American hegemony. It contained at its core, however, a fatal flaw. In 1945, and for years afterward the dollar was inviolable, more sought after than gold by other nations, because unlike metal, dollar reserves paid income, and the USA was legally obliged to exchange dollars for gold at a fixed price. So long as America's gold reserves comfortably exceeded its liabilities the dollar could be, and was, held with absolute confidence by other countries. The balance of payments surplus, which stemmed from America's geopolitical objectives, and which fuelled global expansion, logically and inevitably redressed the balance between reserves and liabilities. As America's gold reserves declined and its dollar liabilities increased, so the once unassailable confidence in the stability of the dollar began to evaporate. Currency speculation, fuelled after 1967 by the devaluation of sterling, gradually but with increasing potency weakened the dollar. The final decisive blow was the inflationary consequence of Vietnam War financing. After a series of spectacular speculations against the dollar which modest reform of the international monetary system failed to assuage, the USA in August 1971 unilaterally destroyed the fixed exchange rate system it had so carefully constructed and managed. President Nixon announced that the dollar would no longer be convertible to gold at a fixed price and imposed a temporary surcharge on imports. Despite subsequent negotiations to devalue the dollar and realign currency values the system of fixed exchange rates could not be rescued. The stable dollar standard was replaced by one of floating exchange rates where in theory the value of each currency was left to find its natural price in response to demand and supply. A powerful prop of American economic hegemony had been removed. Other economic indices such as ratios of world trade and production, and the political fall-out associated with the Vietnam War and the Watergate break-in confirmed the perception of declining hegemony.

## V. How did the Socialist Bloc Organize its Economic Relationships?

Hegemonic power leads to open international systems only if they are in the interest of the dominant state. For productive nations, the benefits of openness can be expected to exceed the costs. Where the hegemonic power is not economically efficient the anticipated benefit from free trade is small. Leadership is replaced by domination, and the system takes on the aspects of imperialism. Such was the case with the USSR which unlike the USA depended almost exclusively on military superiority.

Having distanced itself from the world capitalist economy, the Soviet Union set out to create an international socialist system with itself at the core. Autarky, though never efficient, was not prohibitively costly for the USSR given its large domestic market and rich resource base. It was, moreover, ideologically rational. For its East European allies which it forced into the same constricting economic mould autarky was most certainly not rational. Trade provides an essential spur to competition in small countries and the East Europeans had traditionally traded westwards, in particular with Germany. After the war they were forced into a radial pattern of bilateral trade with the USSR which, because of its own inefficiency, failed to provide the essential spur to systemic competition. Although late industrialization and high investment created high growth initially it was inefficiently achieved. Consumer living-standards failed to increase commensurately and fell below those prevailing in Western Europe by increasingly large margins. As the hegemonic leader, the Soviet Union had constantly to trade-off regime stability against alliance cohesion. To offset systemic and policy-induced inefficiencies, it allowed the East Europeans to depart from the strict command model so long as this was not politically destabilizing. It also allowed them to trade with the West though the low quality of their manufactured goods kept exports low. Its major act of hegemonic leadership was its subsidy of the East European economies. This took a variety of forms importing soft currency goods at higher than world prices, and accommodating bilateral trade surpluses. Its most effective subsidy was the sale of hard currency goods, in particular, oil, below world prices. In the decade or so after 1974, this subsidy has been estimated at $60 billion to $110 billion in exchange for which it gained the military benefit of a buffer zone on its western borders, and the ideological and political benefits of leadership of a group of important European nations.

Systemic inefficiency was aggravated in the 1970s by a series of poor and unlucky policy decisions. After 1974 western capital was plentiful and cheap and many East European countries borrowed heavily. The strategy was rational enough; with the borrowed capital the East Europeans planned to modernize their economies, export the finished products back to the West, and thereby pay off their debt. The strategy was overtaken by the crisis caused by the increase in oil prices. Exports failed to grow and interest rates increased. Debt mounted, and living standards stagnated and in some countries fell. The implicit social contract between the Communist élites and the people, fragile at best, began to disintegrate. Furthermore the Soviet Union, beset by poor economic performance, proved increasingly reluctant to bear the high cost of empire. In 1981, for instance, to the surprise of most observers, it refused to accept responsibility for Poland's external debt, ultimately a factor in the creation of Solidarity. Economic sclerosis, the onerous cost of the arms race, perestroika, and Gorbachev's repudiation of the Brezhnev doctrine all in their own and different ways played a part in undermining Soviet economic hegemony. The Soviet model was patently failing to meet the expectations of the people, and socialism it appeared was losing the systemic competition with capitalism. For the East Europeans the command model was also a symbol of Soviet rule, a further reason for its rejection. International organizations such as COMECON had failed to integrate the socialist economies, and in 1989 the various forces coalesced in a massive, universal repudiation of the Soviet model.

## VI. Why don't States Co-operate?

Despite some increase in protectionism and discrimination, closure of the international economy had been less than many had predicted. Potentially de-stabilizing changes such as floating exchange rates, debt, inflation, and recession, have not reduced international trade which has by and large outgrown world production. It may be that the models of state behaviour which show strong incentives to defect are mis-specified. International trade is not a pure public good. Nations can be excluded from some of the benefits, access to markets, or to capital, for instance, if they do not accept the rules of the game.

Much of the logic of defection derives from simple game theory, in particular that known as the Prisoner's Dilemma. The Prisoner's Dilemma shows logically how given certain pay-off structures, nations which seek the first best solution or to avoid the worst, in fact obtain a less than possible level of reward. This is best illustrated by means of a simple numerical example. Assume for simplicity a two-country model, where each has two policy options: to co-operate, e.g., reduce barriers to trade or to defect and increase protectionism. Free trade is more beneficial than protectionism, but is not costless. The optimal policy mix for any country is for its partner to pursue free-trade policies, but for it to have the option of putting tariffs and quotas on imports, to reduce political turbulence. If we designate co-operation as C and defection as D the preferred policy mix for each country is

$$DC > CC > DD > CD$$

Since the first-choice policy mix for one country is the last choice for the other, the extreme choices DC and CD become effectively unavailable. Despite the fact that a policy of mutual co-operation is superior to one of mutual defection, the logic of the game shows that mutual defection will be chosen by the two countries. We measure the relative benefits of co-operation and defection by

*Country A*

| | | Co-operation | | Defection | |
|---|---|---|---|---|---|
| | | *A* | *B* | *A* | *B* |
| *Country B* | Co-operation | 6 | 6 | 8 | 4 |
| | Defection | *A* | *B* | *A* | *B* |
| | | 4 | 8 | 5 | 5 |

Fig. 1. Mutual Co-operation and Mutual Defection

means of ordinal indices, whereby a higher number indicates more utility, and therefore a preferred outcome, than a lower number, In Fig. 1 the top-left-hand box shows that mutual co-operation is superior to the bottom-right-hand box, mutual defection. If we now go through the various policy options, first from country A's point of view, we obtain the following outcomes:

If B co-operates:

A co-operates     benefit 6
A defects         benefit 8

If B defects:

A co-operates     benefit 4
A defects         benefit 5

From B's perspective:

If A co-operates:

B co-operates     benefit 6
B defects         benefit 8

If A defects:

B co-operates     benefit 4
B defects         benefit 5

For each country, whatever the policy pursued by the other, it is in its interest to defect. Despite the superiority of the top-left-hand box, mutual co-operation, the two countries will logically end up in the bottom-right-hand box, mutual defection.

The surprising (to many) buoyancy of the global economy suggests that despite its internal consistency the Prisoner's

Dilemma may not in fact usefully describe the web of international economic relations. The game gives the logically most likely outcome in a one-off exchange, whereas international trade by its very nature is dense and iterative. The benefit to one player of defection in a one-off play is almost certainly less than that of co-operation over a long period unless the bargainers suffer from extended myopia. Nations are not unitary actors as the theory implies, nor can relative costs and benefits be so simply calculated and compared. Or perhaps American hegemony has not declined to the degree generally assumed. Many of the quantitative indices of decline were halted and even reversed during the 1980s. By virtue of its uniquely dominant role in global production, financial, knowledge, and security spheres its structural power remains unmatched. American values and norms are widely disseminated and the habit of co-operation is firmly entrenched in the leading trading nations.

Finally, policy preferences are unlikely to be exclusive functions of relative and absolute scale. They are also likely to reflect productivity levels. Efficient nations which can expect to benefit from an open economy will be induced to co-operate, especially if they could believe that their defection will provoke retaliation. Thus the small group of large traders: Japan, Germany, Britain, and France are powerfully induced to co-operate, despite or perhaps because of declining American hegemony, though the commitment to co-operation may erode in a serious crisis which, according to the original formulation, was the special virtue of hegemony.

Even in periods when trade was least restricted, protection and discrimination were not wholly absent. Despite the views of liberal economists, protectionism is not an aberration, a fall from grace, for nations are never exclusively concerned with economic efficiency and welfare. Typically, nations seek an optimal balance between political power and economic wealth. Changing circumstances alter both the preferred balance and the means by which it is achieved.

In new nation-states when economic and political power was centralized, mercantilism provided an efficient organizing principle. When economic activity was decentralized, and domestic and international politics stabilized, mercantilism ceased to be efficient. Restrictions on the free play of markets were removed and the state raised revenue for security and other purposes indirectly through taxation. Free trade was the extension of the market to the international sector. If it eventually ceases to provide the means by which the optimal balance between security and welfare is attained, it too will be modified.

Furthermore, because multinational corporations which have global horizons move capital and productive resources between nations easily and quickly, comparative advantage is no longer a static reflection of relatively fixed resources. It can be created and destroyed by purposeful behaviour by firms and by nations. Trade patterns are therefore fluid, and because they have access to cheap labour less-developed nations can perform many industrial processes efficiently and provide superior investment returns to multinational companies. Mature nations concerned at potential turbulence caused by loss of production, tax base, and employment, are induced to manipulate nominal comparative advantage and thus destroy the essential precondition for free trade. Nations also seek to retain industries they believe to be particularly vital to technological progress or to national security.

A large and increasing proportion of world trade is that between different plants of single multinational firms. Inter-firm trade depends on internal pricing and investment policies of the multinational firms and is therefore less influenced by conventional protective devices. In short the trend towards protectionism which some discern in the wake of declining hegemony many be less damaging to global welfare and security than has conventionally been thought.

## VII. What are the Major Economic Problems Facing the International Community?

Despite perturbations in the international economy the global system has remained surprisingly buoyant. Nevertheless, problems remain. Although the abandonment of fixed exchange rates in 1971 was due mainly to the pressure of events, intellectual opinion by then had shifted towards the virtues of freely fluctuating currencies. Fluctuating exchange rates, it was argued, had not been responsible for monetary instability in the inter-war period, which was, rather, due to domestic monetary mismanagement.

Countries resorted to devaluation only in a crisis when all else had failed. The exchange rate is a price and like any other should be left to find its natural level, in response to supply and demand. Politicians should not try and second-guess the markets. If exchange rates were allowed to float, they would eventually prove to be stabilizing. The balance of payments would automatically tend to equilibrium, and a floating exchange system would economize on international liquidity. In the event these sanguine predictions have not been borne out. They were, often implicitly, based on the assumption that exchange rates should and would reflect real economic conditions in the trading countries, i.e., purchasing power parity. In fact, purely speculative movements across the exchanges in response to interest-rate or exchange-rate differentials have swamped international trade. Improved communications, deregulation of domestic capital markets, and high savings, have all increased the transnational flow of speculative capital, to the degree that it now dominates trade in goods and services by a ratio of 50 : 1. Quite small changes in financial variables or even political rumour bring about disproportionately large swings in exchange rates.

Moreover, nations are induced deliberately to manipulate exchange rates for domestic policy purposes. Exchange rates have different consequences on real and financial variables. A devaluation, for instance, reduces the international price of domestic goods and therefore stimulates exports. It also increases the price of imports and thus inflation. As policy priorities shift between inflation and unemployment, so governments try to manipulate the exchange rate. They cannot control the exchange rate, however, for at least one other country and usually many more, plus private traders are involved. Policy-induced and private transactions have together created a volatile exchange-rate system. Between 1971 and 1990, the dollar, for example, depreciated by 28 per cent, appreciated by 69 per cent, and depreciated again by 39 per cent.

Despite the intellectual preference for free exchange rates, by the middle of the 1980s the major economic powers were forced to reassess the practical consequences of benign neglect. Although it may be possible to identify what exchange rates should not be, by, for instance, gross payments imbalance, it is more difficult to determine what they should be and to bring preferred alignments into being. The major trading nations which seek actively to manage exchange rates must contend not only with private dealers, but must also be prepared to forgo for domestic purposes a potent economic instrument. So far multilateral agreements have been limited to broad exchange targets agreed by the group of seven economically most powerful nations, initially in the Plaza Communiqué in 1985 and then the Louvre Accord in 1987. For the G-7 countries exchange rate stability is of prime importance. For others, more immediate problems demand their attention.

In many Third World countries, the single most critical problem is the level of external debt. In 1990 Third World external debt stood at approximately $1.3 billion, equivalent to 44 per cent of their GDP. Although other nations have higher debt ratios, the largest debtors are Brazil with a debt of $115 billion, Mexico $97 billion, and Argentina $57 billion. Far from being a short-term liquidity problem, as was initially believed, the debt and related problems of many Third World countries have worsened. The initial fear that over-exposure to Third World debt would de-stabilize the Western banking system has turned out to be unfounded. Commercial banks have made provisions against bad debt, though a banking crisis brought on by de-stabilizing factors elsewhere in the global economy might yet reactivate the problem of over-exposure. Bank profits and dividends have been reduced, but the major burdens have been borne by the Third World debtor nations. Despite attempts to increase new lending to the debtor nations via the Baker plan and the Brady plan, little has been achieved. Since 1982, the debtor countries have transferred over $150 billion net to their creditors, yet their total debt keeps growing. Rescue packages to maintain the short-term solvency of borrowers have been highly conditional reflecting IMF and liberal values so that the debtor nations take steps to resolve the basic internal imbalances. These have required increasing exports, reducing imports, and cutting back on government spending. The consequence has been lower growth and falling living-standards. During the 1980s living-standards in Latin America are estimated to have declined by 10 per cent, borne mainly by the poorer and weaker sections of the society. So far the political consequences have been limited, though in 1989 riots in Venezuela—generally regarded as being one of the more stable Latin American democracies—are widely believed to have been directly stimulated by the austerity programme imposed by the IMF. By judicious short-term measures, the creditor nations have managed to divide the large debtors and keep them from maximizing their bargaining-power through collective action.

In Africa, though the absolute levels of debt are lower, the adverse consequences have been much more severe, because of the structural weakness in the economic and political systems and other problems such as hunger and malnutrition.

Debt is not an exclusively Third World phenomenon, however. The world's largest single debtor is the USA, though unlike the Third World nations it also holds substantial foreign assets. In addition, being an indicator of declining hegemony, America's huge debt impacts directly on global economic outcomes. The debt is due, in part, to America's large budget deficit, which keeps interest rates high. It and the associated payments' deficit influences American relations with its major creditor nations, especially Japan. Together they inhibit the USA from exercising global leadership in some areas of international economic affairs. So long as economic return and political stability is high, the debt, though eventually costly to US citizens, is manageable. If either of these pre-conditions ceases to hold, the consequences for the USA and for the global economy are likely to be profoundly de-stabilizing.

Having rejected the command model, the newly transformed Commonwealth of Independent States (formerly USSR) and the East European states also seek to change the geographical pattern of foreign trade and investment, looking westwards also for aid and intellectual blueprints for privatization. They are, however, ill-prepared to enter the competitive global economy unprotected. Production and investment have been systematically distorted, the price system needs thoroughgoing reform, and labour markets are inefficient. Restrictions on efficiency and the market mechanism must be lifted before the East Europeans can enter the global economy and become fully participating members of the great international economic institutions. Short-run adjustment will inevitably create unemployment, increased prices, and lower living-standards. If the short-term transition costs and the social distress which will derive from them can be successfully negotiated, longer-term prospects are favourable.

European Community leaders are faced with the challenge of

simultaneously negotiating deeper and wider integration. The single European market and European monetary union signify a more organic integration of the core members of the European Community. More extensive if less intense economic co-operation with those members of the European Free Trade Association who either cannot or choose not to become full members of the Community, the newly liberated East European nations, and the CIS itself pose a quite different set of problems and opportunities. Although a more integrated Europe need not be discriminatory, the very dynamic of integration is necessarily exclusive to a greater or lesser degree. Economic integration in Europe reflects trends elsewhere in the global economy. On the 'Pacific rim'—an economic region located around Japanese economic and financial hegemony—and in the Americas, free-trade agreements between the USA on the one hand and Canada on the other, and closer economic links with the West Indies and Mexico and Latin America in general, signal increasing salience of regional economic blocks.

Historically, economic blocks, especially if dominated by a single hegemonic power, have been strongly mercantilist with destabilizing political consequences. This need not necessarily be the case, however. All three regions are located around dominant nations where international trade and investment are crucial to the wealth-creating process and can be expected to seek to maintain the liberal economic order. When mercantilism dominated international economic relations, foreign territory contributed directly towards security and welfare. This is no longer the case, and control over foreign territory may even be counter-productive. The emerging economic regions are sufficiently large and diverse that dynamic trade-creating benefits are likely to exceed the trade-diverting outcomes. They also offer a stable political framework which may encourage nations to pursue liberal expansionary and therefore trade-creating policies. In conventional analysis outcomes in the global economy can eventually be traced back to the distribution of power, which does, however, beg the question of what power is in this context. Power relates to the abilities and interests of states. Such a state-centric conception of international economic relations has recently been attacked as unrepresentative of the complex web of global economics interrelationships. States, or rather their governments, cannot exclusively determine what is on the international agenda and how the issues are resolved. Non-governmental actors such as multinational corporations, international scientific associations, and environmentalists not only force to centre-stage issues which governments have traditionally neglected, but induce a search for solutions not based exclusively on the distribution of power. Such, for instance, is the case with global environmentalism discussed elsewhere in this volume.

New actors, new issues promote new ways of understanding and explaining international economic affairs, such as what has come to be known as regime theory. Regimes have been defined as sets of implicit or explicit principles, norms, rules, and decision-making procedures around which actor expectations converge. It is the presence of principles and norms which are of particular interest in that they explain behaviour as other than dominated exclusively by calculation of narrow self-interest. They are conventionally understood as an intervening variable between structure and outcome. Regimes have been described for international trade, money, food, and environmental resources. Despite a wide though not universal acceptance of their significance, important theoretical and empirical issues have yet to be resolved: how are they formed? How do they change outcomes? Perhaps most intriguing of all is the relationship between the principles embodied in regimes and the interests of powerful nations.

## Notes

This chapter is based on the following sources:

BUNCE, V., The Empire Strikes Back: The Evolution of the Eastern Bloc from a Soviet Asset to a Soviet Liability', *International Organization*, 32/1 (1985).

BUZAN, B., 'Economic Structure and International Security: The Limits of the Liberal Case', *International Organization*, 38 (1984).

CALLEO, D., 'Inflation and American Power', *Foreign Affairs* (Spring 1981).

DOS SANTOS, T., 'The Structure of Dependence', *American Economic Review*, 60 (1970).

DRUKER, P., 'The Changed World Economy', *Foreign Affairs* (Spring 1986).

GEIGER, T., *The Future of the International System: The United States and the World Political Economy* (London: Unwin Hyman, 1988).

HAGGARD, S., & SIMMONS, B., 'Theories of International Regimes', *International Organization*, 41 (1987).

HERI, J., & RASCH, B., 'Hegemonic Decline and the Possibility of International Cooperation', *Cooperation and Conflict*, 21 (1986).

KINDLESBERGER, C., 'Dominance and Leadership in the International Economy', *International Studies Quarterly* (June 1981).

ROTHSTEIN, R., 'Epitaph for a Monument to a Failed Protest? A North–South Retrospective, *International Organization*, 42 (1988).

SCAMMEL, W., *The International Economy since 1945*, 2nd edn. (London: Macmillan, 1983).

SPERO, J. E. *The Politics of International Economic Relations*, 4th edn. (London: Unwin Hyman, 1990).

STRANGE, S. (ed.), *Paths to International Political Economy* (London: George Allen & Unwin, 1986).

# FIVE

# Technology and Modern Warfare

*Colin McInnes*

Throughout history technology has had a major impact upon the strategy and conduct of war. The twentieth century, however, is unusual in that technological change has been continuous and at a speed hitherto unknown. In addition, armed forces, strategists, and doctrines have become increasingly influenced by and dependent upon technology, and less upon the fighting man. This has led to a change in the nature of thinking about strategy. Whereas classical (i.e., pre-nuclear) strategists concentrated upon the principles of war and the correct organization of forces for battle, more contemporary strategists have concentrated upon the relationship between technology and war.[1] Therefore although there has always been a relationship between on the one hand the nature of war, its conduct, and the strategy and tactics used, and on the other the technology available (particularly weapons technology, but also support services such as transport and communications), in the twentieth century this relationship has become closer, and armed forces more sensitive to change in technology. This chapter examines the evolution of military technology since 1945, and some of the important features to have emerged from this. It begins with the 'revolutionary' impact of nuclear weapons and an examination of the nuclear arms race. It then considers the development of conventional weapons and their impact upon the nature and conduct of modern warfare.

## I. To What Extent was the Nuclear Arms Race a Case of the United States Leading and the Soviet Union Following?

On 6 August 1945 the US B 29 bomber *Enola Gay* dropped the first atomic bomb on the Japanese city of Hiroshima. The bomb was a comparatively simple device, effectively shooting one lump of the uranium isotope U 235 at another such lump to form a critical mass, which was simultaneously bombarded with neutrons, thus producing a sufficiently fast chain-reaction for an explosion. The second bomb, dropped a few days later over Nagasaki, was a more complicated design, imploding a quantity of the manufactured element plutonium to form a critical mass. Unlike the Hiroshima bomb which had never been tested, this latter design had been tested in the New Mexico desert on 16 July 1945 in the first nuclear explosion. Designing and producing these bombs had taken the United States five years of massive financial and scientific effort, costing over $2 billion and involving some of the best physicists of that generation. Although other Allied scientists, particularly the British but also French and Canadians, had assisted in the project, the lion's share of the research and development, and easily most of the cost had been borne by the United States.[2] This, coupled to the scientific complexity and sheer scale of the project led many to expect that the United States would retain its atomic monopoly for some years.

The two atomic bombs dropped at the end of the Second World War have commonly been seen as ushering in a new age of warfare, one in which the awesome destructive power of these new weapons rendered traditional ideas about war—and perhaps war itself—obsolete. Writing within a year of their use against Japan, the strategist Bernard Brodie famously pronounced 'Thus far the chief purpose of our military establishment has been to win wars. From now on its chief purpose must be to avert them. It can have almost no other useful purpose'.[3] Nuclear weapons shifted the balance of strategic thinking away from defence in the event of war, to deterring wars from occurring in the first place. But Brodie's comment was prophetic rather than an accurate analysis of the situation when he wrote. Until the 1950s the US atomic arsenal was surprisingly small, consisting for most of the late

1940s of only a few dozen bombs. Moreover these bombs were of limited destructive power. The bomb dropped on Hiroshima, for example, was the equivalent of 20,000 tons of TNT, considerably less explosive power than that used in the massed bomber raids over Germany and Japan. Although atomic bombs also produced lethal radiation, this effect was little understood at the time, and the bomb's utility was seen more in terms of its destructive power than its ability to kill through radiation. The fact that enormous damage could be accomplished by a single bomb was of course important, but the small number of bombs available and the difficulty in producing them at that time reduced somewhat the military potential of the US atomic arsenal. Nor were these weapons widely distributed, being deployed on strategic bombers alone. Development of naval and army nuclear weapons, and of shorter-range weapons for tactical or battlefield use had to wait, sometimes until the 1960s. Therefore the nuclear age may have begun in 1945, but the nuclear weapons available in the 1940s had somewhat less of a military capability than might be supposed.

An extended period of US atomic monopoly was not to be, and in 1949 the Soviet Union exploded its first atomic bomb, somewhat earlier than had been widely expected. This acted as a catalyst for the United States not merely to expand its small nuclear arsenal, but to develop more powerful thermonuclear weapons. Whereas atomic weapons worked by splitting atoms and releasing the power which held atoms together (fission), thermonuclear weapons forced atoms together so that the much stronger force which kept them apart was released (fusion). The result was a much more powerful bomb, capable of destroying large cities on its own. The fusion process required an element with a simple atomic structure, and initial interest focused on two isotopes of the hydrogen atom (deuterium and tritium) from which the hydrogen bomb gained its name.[4]

The first hydrogen bomb was tested by the United States in November 1952, followed in 1953 by a successful Soviet test. Britain, France, China, and India all followed suit in public, while in secret Israel and possibly South Africa also developed nuclear weapons. Over the years these weapons have grown smaller in both physical size and, perhaps surprisingly, explosive yield as accuracy was increased and as more discriminating targeting policies were developed (moving away from city-busting to targeting military forces). This culminated in the development of the neutron bomb by the United States in the 1970s. This bomb was designed to maximize radiation and minimize blast effects.[5] The bomb was to be used against invading armies, destroying the armies without demolishing large sectors of Europe's cities. European fears that this indicated a US preference to fight a nuclear war in Europe, however, prevented the United States from deploying such weapons.

The focus of the nuclear arms race, however, quickly shifted away from the weapons themselves towards launch platforms. Three main types of platforms are now used to deliver strategic (i.e., long-range) nuclear weapons: manned bombers; land-based intercontinental ballistic missiles (ICBMs); and submarine-launched ballistic missiles (SLBMs).[6] Initial post-war interest concentrated upon the further development of strategic bombers as used in the Second World War since they were the only proven delivery means. Because of limited range, the first US nuclear bombers (B 29s) had to use foreign bases. In 1948 the first intercontinental bomber was deployed, the B 36, with its replacement (the B 52) already being designed. But given the availability of bases in the UK and problems over the technology involved in intercontinental range, attention focused on development of a new medium-range jet bomber, the B 47. In addition to increased range, designers sought improvements in speed and altitude to enable bombers to penetrate defences. Jet technology in particular was seized upon as allowing bombers to fly higher and faster to avoid enemy interceptors, with both the British and Americans producing successful designs.

The shooting down of Gary Powers's U-2 spy plane over the Soviet Union in 1960 by a surface-to-air missile, however, demonstrated the growing vulnerability of high flying aircraft. Since these missiles are principally guided by radar, and since radars also provide early warning of attack, attention shifted to the problem of avoiding radar detection. By flying low bombers could use the radar 'shadows' of hills to avoid detection. Even if detected, electronic counter-measures (ECM) carried by the aircraft could jam or deceive radars. US and British bomber technology therefore shifted away from high, fast flight to low flight with sophisticated ECM. Although existing airframes were retained (particularly the US B 52 and British Vulcan bombers) these were fitted with new avionics and electronic warfare suites for the new attack profile.

Soviet bomber technology initially lagged behind that of the United States. The two main Soviet designs of the 1950s were the Tu 95 Bear and M 4 Bison. Although the Bison was a jet-engined bomber, it suffered from poor range and payload, and is not generally considered a successful design. In contrast the Bear, although large, ponderous, and powered by turbo-prop engines, has proved a useful workhorse and has been continuously modified as a weapons and sensor platform.[7]

Throughout the 1960s it was generally considered that Soviet interest in strategic bombers was slight compared to that of the United States. In the 1970s, however, the deployment of the sophisticated, medium-range supersonic Backfire bomber, followed in the 1980s by the strategic Blackjack, indicated a renewed Soviet interest in bomber technology. Both the Backfire and Blackjack were capable of fast flight and low flight, with low radar signatures and probably a reasonably sophisticated ECM suite. Both could launch missiles some way from the target if so desired, so avoiding the problem of having to penetrate enemy defences (though the Blackjack would probably be used primarily as a penetration bomber). The appearance of the Backfire gave added impetus to the development of a new US bomber, the B 1, which was specifically designed for low flight using sophisticated ECM. But the B 1 was cancelled by the Carter Administration in 1977 on cost grounds in favour of a further development of the B 52 as a platform for long-range cruise missiles. The Reagan Administration, however, reactivated the B 1 programme in 1981 as part of a two-bomber strategy. The B 52 would retain its role as a stand-off cruise missile platform, and the upgraded B 1B would be used as a penetrating bomber. The Reagan Administration also began development of a successor to the B 1B, the B 2, which would assume the penetrating role in the 1990s as the B 1B became vulnerable to Soviet air defence developments. The B 52s would then be retired and the B 1B would assume the stand-off cruise missile carrier role. The B 2 bomber exploits radical new 'stealth' design concepts aimed at minimizing its vulnerability to radar detection. The precision engineering and composite materials required for this has led to an extremely high price-tag of perhaps $750 million each, depending on the numbers bought. The high cost of the B 2 and the ending of the Cold War has raised doubts as to whether or not the bomber is needed, and its cancellation is possible.[8]

One reason perhaps why the Soviets deployed considerably fewer strategic bombers than the United States was because of the attention paid by Moscow to the development of ICBMs. This led to a number of 'scares' in the United States when Soviet ballistic missile developments appeared to give Moscow an edge in the nuclear arms race (particularly the launch of Sputnik in 1957, fears of a 'missile gap' in the late 1950s to early 1960s, and the 'window of vulnerability' in the late 1970s to early 1980s). In retrospect these fears seem to have been exaggerated, and the Soviet Union has consistently lagged behind the United States in ICBM technology.[9] At the end of the Second World War both the United States and the Soviet Union acquired ballistic-missile technology from the German V-2 project. However, it was only in 1954 that US scientists concluded that an intercontinental missile was possible, and in 1955 development of the Atlas ICBM was accelerated. Like most 1950s missiles, the Atlas used a liquid fuel propellant. This was difficult to handle, unreliable, and required considerable launch warning (making the missiles vulnerable to surprise attack). The United States therefore conducted research into the more reliable solid fuel technology. In 1955 it began development of the solid fuel Titan ICBM and in 1958 the more advanced Minuteman missile. By the 1960s most US ICBMs used solid fuel, requiring minimal warning before launch, and displaying considerable reliability in flight.[10] The 1960s also saw the United States develop and deploy missiles with multiple warheads. The first such design was the MRV (multiple re-entry vehicle) which spread a number of warheads across a target in a set pattern. This was followed by the MIRV (multiple independently-targetable re-entry vehicle) which enabled warheads from the same missile to be launched against different targets. A further planned development was to give warheads a manœuvre capability to avoid anti-ballistic missiles (ABMs), but this was scrapped in the 1970s due to its high cost and the poor quality of Soviet ABMs. The accuracy of US ICBMs also improved such that, despite a range of several thousand miles at several times the speed of sound, warheads might be expected to land within a thousand feet of their target. This enabled strategic planners to consider attacking hardened military targets (such as enemy ICBMs) as well as cities.

Despite their success in being the first to place an object in space with Sputnik, the Soviets continually lagged behind American developments in ICBM technology. After a series of tests on the V-2 in the late 1940s, the Soviets began development of the SS-3 ballistic missile in 1950, and in 1957 launched Sputnik on an SS-6 booster. Although Sputnik demonstrated that the Soviets were capable of producing ICBMs, the slow deployment rate of the SS-6 seemed to indicate at least an uncertainty over their grasp of missile technology.[11] Development of missile types continued though, and by the early 1970s the Soviets had overtaken the Americans in terms of numbers of missiles deployed—although the level of technology used was still well behind that of the US Minuteman force (particularly in the use of MIRVs and solid fuel propellants). In the mid-1970s, however, the Soviets deployed two new missiles, the SS-18 and SS-19, which were in most respects a match for the Minuteman force, and in some respects superior (particularly in the number of warheads carried). This created something of a scare in the United States, which was at the time developing a successor to the Minuteman, the M-X or Peacekeeper. The M-X was bedevilled throughout the late 1970s and 1980s, though, by the problem of devising a basing mode which was both secure from attack (given improvements in Soviet missile accuracy) and politically acceptable. After a whole series of different plans being accepted and then rejected, the Bush Administration now envisages the missile being launched from specially designed railway cars which would be moved around the country in times of crisis to avoid detection. This solution of mobility to enhance survivability has also been adopted by the Soviets with the rail-mobile SS-24 and land-mobile SS-25, while the United States is currently pursuing the development of a small, land-mobile missile to complement the Peacekeeper, dubbed 'Midgetman'.

The most survivable leg of the strategic triad though remains the submarine-launched ballistic missile (SLBM). Despite advances in anti-submarine warfare technology, strategic missile sub-marines remain almost undetectable, and are likely to continue to do so for the foreseeable future. The United States has led the development of this technology, with the Polaris programme its first operational design. The first nuclear-powered Polaris boat was commissioned in December 1959 and sailed on its first patrol in November 1960. The Polaris missile design continued to be improved upon in the 1960s with increases in range and the incorporation of MRV technology. Each Polaris boat carried 16 missiles which (with the A3 missile) could launch 3 MRVs over 2,500 miles. The second generation Poseidon SLBM, first deployed in 1971, offered MIRV technology with up to 14 warheads per missile, though with little improvement in range. Increased range was addressed with the Trident I/C4 missile, first deployed in 1978. Although of a similar size to Poseidon, the C4 could carry much the same payload up to a distance of 4,600 miles. This was important in vastly increasing the operating area available to submarines, and therefore increasing the amount of sea in which the boat could hide. The Trident I is to be replaced in the 1990s by the much larger Trident II/D5 missile with increased payload and accuracy sufficient for it to be used against hardened military targets.[12]

Although the Soviet Union conducted its first SLBM test in 1955 and deployed its first ballistic missile armed submarine in 1958, two years before the first Polaris boat went on patrol, both the missile and submarine suffered from severe operational limitations. The conventionally powered Golf submarine carried just three SLBMs, and its SS-N-4 missile had to be launched on the surface with a range of just 300 nautical miles. This meant that the submarine had to approach quite close to its target and then surface to fire, making it vulnerable to attack. It was only in 1967, with the nuclear-powered Yankee class submarine armed with 16 SS-N-6 missiles that the Soviets approached the technological level of Polaris. Even then, the SS-N-6 was significantly inferior to Polaris, being liquid fuelled with a range of 1,300 nautical miles, and carrying just two MRVs of limited accuracy. The missiles' range limitations meant that the Yankee submarines had to patrol close to the US coast, far from friendly bases, while the US Polaris boats could use bases in Scotland and were able to operate in comparatively friendly waters. Range improvements came for the Soviets with the single warhead SS-N-8, and its MIRVed successor the SS-N-18. The latter was first deployed in 1978 and was of a similar style to Poseidon, though offering a lesser capability in many areas. These missiles are carried by the more sophisticated Delta class nuclear submarines, as well as a handful of diesel-powered Golf III and Hotel III class boats. The increased range of the SS-N-8 and -18 allowed the Soviets to operate these submarines close to home waters in defended bastions, as opposed to the US practice of hiding in the vastness of the open ocean. The Soviets also tended to keep fewer boats on station than US practice, possibly because of poor reliability, but also perhaps to allow them to send a larger number to sea in a crisis than would be the case if a significant proportion of the fleet was kept permanently at sea.

The SS-N-18 was further improved upon with the SS-N-23, deployed in the late 1980s in new Delta IV class boats. But it was only with the SS-N-20, deployed in the massive Typhoon class submarines in the mid-1980s, that the Soviets successfully developed a solid fuel SLBM. Although the SS-N-20's range and payload are similar to that of the Trident I/C4, it is less accurate, and falls well short of the Trident II/D5's capabilities. The simultaneous production of the SS-N-23/Delta IV and SS-N-20/Typhoon systems has also led some to suggest that the Soviets are not fully confident with the solid fuel technology of the SS-N-20, and maintain the SS-N-23/Delta series as a hedge against failure.[13]

Defence against strategic attack can involve either the protection of targets (passive defence), or the attempt to destroy attacking forces (active defence). Although both Superpowers have at some time considered large-scale civil defence schemes, the difficulties involved are extreme and the cost excessive. The United States abandoned its schemes in the 1960s, and though the Soviet Union maintained at least the pretence of civil defence beyond this, its capabilities were poor at best. In contrast a number of fixed military installations of strategic value have been protected by both Superpowers, usually by concrete and steel bunkers. In particular, ICBMs have been placed in hardened silos to protect them against nuclear attacks. With improvements in missile accuracy however, even these hardened shelters might be vulnerable, and the trend is clearly towards mobility to avoid attack rather than protection from attack.

As far as active defence is concerned, there are two distinct threats to protect against. One is from bombers and cruise missiles which remain within the atmosphere and seek to avoid detection to aid penetration (air defence); the other is from ballistic missiles, which use high re-entry speeds to penetrate defences (ballistic missile defence, or BMD). The Soviets have paid considerably more attention to air defence than the United States, partly because the latter faces a minimal threat from Soviet bombers. There are, however, substantial doubts as to the efficiency of the Soviet air defence network. These doubts were highlighted when a young West German pilot penetrated Soviet airspace in a light civil aircraft and landed in Red Square in the mid-1980s. With the development of missile technology in the 1950s, the Superpowers began research into anti-ballistic missiles (ABMs) for ballistic missile defence. Both the Soviet Union and the United States deployed systems in the late 1960s to early 1970s, but technological problems as well as doubts over the strategic benefits of ABMs led to the ABM Treaty of 1972 severely limiting the deployment and testing of ballistic missile defences by the Superpowers. The US abandoned its ABM system in the mid-1970s, though the Soviets retained their rather rudimentary Galosh system to defend Moscow. Both Superpowers continued ABM research through the 1970s and into the 1980s, though at a fairly low key given the lack of interest and the limitations imposed by the ABM Treaty. The Soviets deployed an upgraded version of the Galosh system in the 1980s, but it was Ronald Reagan's 1983 announcement of the Strategic Defense Initiative (SDI, or 'Star Wars') that rekindled interest in BMD. Attention now shifted to more exotic technologies such as lasers, particle beam weapons, and the rail gun, which raised the prospect of a high technology shield to protect the United States from missile atttack. Like the ABM in the 1960s though, serious doubts were raised over the technological feasibility and strategic desirability of the weapons envisaged. Although both superpowers have continued to fund SDI research into the 1990s, many of the technologies remain on the horizon, with doubts over when a system might be deployed and how efficiently it might work.[14]

Aside from strategic nuclear weapons, literally thousands of shorter-range nuclear weapons have been deployed. The two major categories into which these can be divided are battlefield nuclear weapons and intermediate range nuclear forces (INF). From the 1950s on, both the United States and the Soviet Union developed and deployed INF missiles with increasing capabilities. The most capable on the Soviet and American sides were the SS-20 and Pershing 2 respectively. The SS-20, first deployed in 1977, was a mobile, MIRVed solid-fuel missile with an accuracy of c.2,000 feet. The Pershing 2 missile, deployed in West Germany in the mid-1980s, was similarly mobile and solid fuelled, but its single warhead had an accuracy of under 150 feet. The trend with INF missiles, as with strategic, was clearly towards mobility and accuracy. Although the 1987 INF Treaty banned the deployment of all land-based intermediate-range nuclear missiles by the Superpowers world-wide, this still left substantial numbers of nuclear-capable aircraft and submarine-launched missiles at the INF level. In addition, the several thousand battlefield nuclear weapons in Europe remained unaffected by the INF Treaty. These principally consist of artillery shells and short-range missiles. The military utility of these weapons is somewhat uncertain given that they would be used close to friendly troops, and with the disintegration of the Warsaw Pact pressure for the removal of these weapons has mounted (though difficulties in verification at the very least make a treaty unlikely in the short term). Even with an arms-control agreement, a world-wide ban is unlikely, and the proliferation of short-range nuclear weapons by new nuclear powers is probably the more likely scenario.

## II. What have been the Major Developments in Conventional Warfare since 1945?

Land forces have seen three major changes since the Second World War.[15] First, the increased weight and accuracy of firepower has led to fighting units being armoured and mobile for survival on the battlefield: survivability lies in mobility. Modern infantry ride into battle in armoured 'battle taxis', and may even fight from armoured vehicles; much of modern artillery is placed on mobile, armoured platforms so that to the lay eye they often look like tanks; and forward command posts and anti-aircraft guns are similarly encased in protective shells on wheels or tracks. As a result battle has become very mobile and fast-moving. Recent developments in sensor technology though have threatened to create a 'transparent battlefield', whereby large armoured formations and even individual vehicles can be spotted at distance and targeted with long-range, precision-guided munitions. If so, armoured mobility may no longer be the best means of survival on the modern battlefield.

The second major feature of land warfare has been the arms race between armoured vehicles (in particular tanks), and anti-armour weapons. The anti-tank guided munition (ATGM) first made an impact in the 1973 Middle East War. In the early days of the war Egyptian infantry achieved disproportionate success with these relatively cheap weapons against Israeli tanks. As a result the balance of modern warfare seemed to have been upset, with expensive armoured vehicles vulnerable to cheap infantry weapons, and the main offensive weapon of land warfare (the tank) incapable of overrunning defensive infantry positions. Re-evaluation after the 1973 war, however, showed that the initial estimates of ATGM success had been exaggerated. In particular the weapons had proved difficult to use, were inaccurate and had too small a warhead to penetrate some types of armour. Nevertheless, the potential of the ATGM was not lost on military planners, and a technological arms race followed between improvements in ATGMs and in protective armour. As a result ATGMs are no longer necessarily cheap, using sophisticated warheads and guidance systems, and may be so large that they have to be carried by an expensive platform such as a helicopter rather than simple 'leg infantry'.

Two types of armour have been developed to counter this threat: composite armour, such as the British Chobham armour, which uses a variety of materials of different density to disrupt the kinetic energy of an enemy projectile; and explosive reactive armour (ERA), boxes fitted outside the armoured shell which when hit explode outwards, disrupting the shaped-charge warhead of an ATGM. Composite armour is particularly useful against the heavy metal darts fired by tanks, while explosive reactive armour is purely designed to counter ATGMs. ERA was first used in combat by the Israelis in the Lebanon in 1982, and caused considerable consternation amongst NATO military commanders in the mid-1980s when fitted to Soviet main battle tanks, creating fears that its deployment rendered NATO's ATGMs obsolete.[16] What this demonstrates though is not so much the obsolescence of the ATGM—indeed ATGMs capable of overcoming ERA are already well under development—but rather the technological arms race of measure-counter-measure which has become a common pattern in modern weapons' development.

The third important feature of modern land warfare is the degree of air support required for land operations. Although this had begun to appear at the end of the Second World War, the importance and close integration of air operations to the land battle is now such that the two are more accurately seen as different dimensions of the same battle, rather than separate battles. In particular helicopters offer enormous flexibility both as transport and as highly mobile sources of firepower, the latter role also filled by many different aircraft types including specialist 'tank busters' such as the American A-10 aircraft. The Israeli use of helicopters in the anti-tank role in 1982, firing ATGMs from beyond the range of tank guns, provoked much discussion, and anti-tank helicopters now feature prominently in most advanced armies' arsenals. Similarly, the emphasis placed by coalition forces on gaining air superiority in the 1991 war against Iraq before they would consider a ground offensive indicates the importance placed on air support in modern land warfare. Questions, however, remain over the survivability of both specialist aircraft and especially helicopters in the forward battle area. Without air superiority these comparatively slow and unwieldy vehicles might be extremely vulnerable to enemy jet fighters, while troops on the ground might be armed with a profusion of lethal anti-aircraft guns and missiles.

Air power in general has displayed two major characteristics since 1945: flexibility and sensitivity to technological change. The flexibility of modern air power is much commented upon. Although most of the roles performed by modern aircraft are fairly traditional, many aircraft can now perform not one but a variety of roles, sometimes in the same mission, and with vastly enhanced capabilities than in the Second World War. The four major combat roles for air power are those of air superiority, close air support of ground operations, interdiction of lines of communication, and attack (bombing). In addition aircraft perform a number of support functions, principally reconnaissance, transport, radar early warning and battle control, electronic warfare, and air-to-air refuelling. But whereas there might be little change in the roles of modern air power, there have been vast changes in aircraft technology. Air power has been an extremely dynamic technological arena, and as a result the cost of aircraft has increased dramatically. A modern combat aircraft can cost anything from $10 million to close to $50 million, with most 1980s aircraft costing around $20 million each. This excludes the often very high costs of maintenance, weapons, and of training the pilots and ground crew. Modern combat aircraft use low flight and/or electronic countermeasures to aid survival, and from the 1950s on air-launched missiles have been used both for air-to-air combat (sometimes beyond visual range) and for ground attack.

The growing sophistication of air-launched weapons and electronic countermeasures in the late 1950s to 1960s led to the pilot being overburdened with jobs to do, and so a second crew member was often added to new designs of aircraft. This second crew member would navigate and operate the aircraft's offensive and defensive systems while the pilot concentrated on flying the aircraft. This required a high degree of co-ordination and teamwork, and so with advances in automation the trend has reverted to single-seat aircraft (for example, the US F/A-18). Whereas a 1950s-style fighter such as the US F-104 or Soviet MiG 21 had a single jet engine, a couple of short-range missiles, a fairly unsophisticated radar and a maximum loaded weight of c.30,000 lbs, the US F-15 fighter designed in the late 1960s boasted two jet engines, a wide variety of ordnance, an extremely sophisticated multimode pulse doppler radar, a host of other electronic aids, and a maximum loaded weight twice that of the F-104. The cost accordingly soared, which led the United States to look for a cheap, single-engine fighter to complement the sophisticated F-15. The resulting F-16, however, proved to have enormous potential, such that the United States failed to keep it a simple, cheap fighter. In particular, the F-16 became the test-bed for new fly-by-wire technology: to gain greater manoeuvrability the aircraft was made deliberately unstable in flight, and used a computer continuously to adjust the control surfaces to ensure that the aircraft did not crash. This increased agility is being further exploited by aircraft currently under design, including the European Fighter Aircraft, while the application of Stealth technology to the US F-117A has indicated another very expensive area of design to be pursued further in the 1990s—though the cancellation of the A-12 Stealth attack aircraft in 1991 due to its high cost indicated that there is a financial ceiling limiting the development of aircraft technology.

The complex technology, high cost, and long research and development (frequently over a decade) involved in modern fighter production has led to a growing call for the more extensive use of remotely piloted vehicles (RPVs) in place of manned aircraft for a variety of tasks. This has been resisted not merely because of entrenched service interests, but because of the RPVs inherent lack of flexibility. Although the 1980s saw the widespread development of the RPV as an important means of gaining battlefield intelligence, whether it has a future in any other role seems uncertain.

Navies have also seen a number of important changes since the Second World War, not the least being the introduction of nuclear weapons. Although nuclear weapons have been incorporated into naval arsenals, offering increased firepower for a variety of weapons (from the depth charge to the land attack missile), the process of incorporation has been surprisingly slow. Throughout the 1940s naval arsenals were relatively unaffected by nuclear technology, and it was only in the 1960s that the US Navy became the first navy to deploy a full spectrum of naval nuclear weapons. Even then, with the exception of the SLBM, these weapons did little in the way of creating new roles, rather they tended to offer increased firepower for existing roles.

Where nuclear weapons did have a dramatic impact, though, was in questioning the viability of navies in the nuclear age. Doubts came from two directions. First, there were those who doubted the survivability of modern warships against nuclear weapons. Nuclear warheads costing perhaps a few million dollars apiece placed $100 million-plus frigates and even billion-dollar supercarriers in a position of unprecedented vulnerability. The response was to force navies into ever-more sophisticated defences in the hope that they could shoot down a nuclear weapon before it exploded. The second area of doubt concerned the length of a nuclear war. A nuclear war might be over in days, weeks at the most. In contrast, western navies might take a fortnight to assemble and move a single convoy across the Atlantic, while more traditional tactics such as the blockade appeared to have an absurdly long-term impact. To justify their existence, navies were forced to emphasize their flexibility in meeting a variety of challenges world-wide, not merely the single and unlikely scenario of a nuclear war in Europe, as well as devising strategies to give them an important role in any Superpower conflict.[17]

A second important naval development has been the advent of the guided missile. These small, comparatively cheap weapons appeared to be revolutionary because of their combination of long range, high accuracy, and destructive power, though it took over two decades of the missile age before these weapons were sufficiently well developed to have a decisive impact on naval thinking. Partly, this was because of the length of time taken to develop mature missiles: even after their potential had been demonstrated when the Egyptians sank the Israeli destroyer Eilat in 1967 with a Soviet-supplied anti-ship missile, it was only in the 1970s that reliable and effective missiles became available. Although the Falklands Conflict of 1982 demonstrated the potential of missiles such as Exocet, it was also apparent that these weapons were far from perfect. They were vulnerable to countermeasures, they could be shot down, and they were dependent upon launch platforms which might prove vulnerable. Thus their true capabilities have perhaps failed to match the 'revolutionary' tag which they acquired in the 1960s to 1970s. Guided missiles are also less than revolutionary in that they are merely an alternative method of delivering ordnance from well-established platforms (ships, aircraft, or submarines), though with perhaps greater range and accuracy than other weapons. But guided missiles do have a number of important consequences for naval warfare. These missiles can be mounted on small boats which can then attack much larger craft with some hope of success. They have also led to the demise of the big gun in ship-to-ship combat (the big guns on the four American battleships reactivated in the 1980s were for coastal bombardment purposes, not ship-to-ship), and in some instances to the development of all-missile ships. Guided missiles have also improved aircraft capabilities in that they can stand off from their targets thus improving survivability, while precision guidance improves the chances of hitting relatively small targets at very long ranges. Finally, when coupled to long-range sensors, these missiles have greatly increased the combat radius of modern warships, while the comparatively small number of missiles deployed on board most ships has reduced the probable length of any naval engagement.

A third area of change concerns ship propulsion, particularly the development of gas-turbine- and nuclear-powered engines. These new technologies enable propulsion systems to be smaller (especially when fuel is considered), with greater power and endurance. When coupled to better hull design, modern ships are faster and can stay at sea longer than their Second World War equivalents. Improvements though have been incremental. Ships are still slow compared to other means of transport, taking days if not weeks to reach areas of crisis. In battle, and particularly in anti-submarine warfare, this has led to the increasing use of ship-based helicopters and land-based aircraft to react quickly over wide areas of sea. Further, despite their increased endurance, ships are still dependent upon other ships for supplies. Even 90,000-ton nuclear-powered Nimitz class aircraft-carriers, which can sail around the world without refuelling, require frequent resupplies of fuel for their aircraft. Perhaps the area where new propulsion technology has had greatest impact then is with submarines. Nuclear submarines can now stay underwater throughout a patrol rather than having to surface at regular intervals and thus betray their presence, while diesel-powered boats have achieved new levels of quietness, making them extremely difficult to find.

The final major advance in naval warfare has been in C3I (command, control, communications, and intelligence). Ships can now co-ordinate their actions over great areas of ocean, data links enable them to share information, building up a composite intelligence picture, while satellites and radars can offer accurate intelligence on surface ship and aircraft movements. When coupled to increased weapon range the result has been the development of the single theatre sea, whereby a single naval task force can cover, or control, the actions of friendly forces within an ocean (excepting perhaps the Atlantic and Pacific). Improved communications has also increased the potential for commanders far removed from a battle to exercise greater central control of military operations. This was attempted in the Falklands with not wholly satisfactory results, commanders in the South Atlantic often resenting orders from on high which might lack the necessary 'feel' for forces at the sharp end.

In addition to land, sea, and air warfare, from the 1960s on satellites have been used extensively for military purposes. Satellites are currently only used for support roles—communication, navigation, and intelligence—but with SDI they might also acquire a role as weapons platforms. The major advantage of satellites is their area of coverage, whether in enabling fast communications from one side of the globe to the other, or in offering intelligence on activities in areas where aircraft cannot fly. But satellites also suffer from two main disadvantages. First, they are extremely expensive and complex to construct, and there is an uncomfortably high failure rate when it comes to placing them in orbit. And secondly, they are very vulnerable to developments in anti-satellite weapons, being delicate and highly visible targets.

## III. What Impact has Technology had on Modern Conventional Weapons?

A number of features are apparent concerning the relationship between technology and modern conventional forces. The first is the speed of technological change. This is perhaps one of the dominant features of life in general in the late twentieth century: the speed with which developments such as pocket calculators, digital watches, microwave ovens, and compact discs pass from the innovative to the everyday is remarkable. The speed of change with military equipment, though, has been both faster and slower than that in other areas. It has been fast in that, in the competitive relationship of the Cold War, the fear of being left at a critical disadvantage through failure to chase technological innovation led to a qualitative arms race. This was fostered by the West's use of technology as a force multiplier, whereby the superior weapons technology of the West would help to offset its numerical inferiority to the Warsaw Pact. The pace of change was also maintained by the high level of military funding for advanced research and development, and the close, sometimes incestuous relationship between the military and defence industries (what President Eisenhower termed the military-industrial complex).

But change has also been surprisingly slow. The increased cost of major weapons platforms (ships, aircraft, etc.) has meant that these platforms are kept for as long as possible, using modernization packages to prevent them from becoming technologically obsolete. Thus aircraft may be retained for over twenty years, main battle tanks may see up to three decades of service, and warships may still be operating forty years after being commissioned. In addition many weapons systems tend to be progressively improved by new versions being made available rather than completely new systems being designed. Thus aircraft like the US F-4 Phantom or the Soviet MiG 21 may go through half a dozen or more major design updates on the original. Change has also been slow in that the major weapons systems of modern war—the tank, aircraft, and ship—remain unchanged from the Second World War. Military technology is stuck in a paradigm set by combat fifty years ago, one which has seen improvements in capabilities, and the development of some new weapons and platforms, but whose basic structure remains unchanged.[18] Finally, change has been slow because of the amount of time required to develop a modern weapons system—often a decade or more. This has become especially problematic given the fast change in some subsystems, particularly electronics and computers. Computer half-life, for example, may be as little as two to three years before another generation of technology becomes available and existing systems begin to obsolesce. Thus major weapons systems now begin their design cycle in the knowledge that the electronics and computers they will eventually use are not one but two or perhaps three generations ahead of existing technology, with capabilities and requirements that can only be guessed at. Statements concerning the rapid or revolutionary pace of technological change are common. But these statements are only partially correct. The leading edge of technology may be fast, particularly for electronic and computing subsystems, but for major weapons systems development cycles are long, and the period of time spent in service is often very considerable.

A second major feature is the improvement in range and accuracy of modern conventional weapons. This has had a number of important effects. With precision terminal guidance, accuracy is no longer a function of range. If a target can be 'seen', visually or electronically, then it can probably be hit, while collateral damage might be minimized (though some new weapons such as cluster bombs and fuel-air explosives still rely on devastating an area rather than hitting a particular enemy target). This increased accuracy was clearly demonstrated in the coalition air offensive which opened the 1991 Gulf War. Precision guidance allowed weapons to be targeted very accurately upon small targets, in the case of cruise missiles perhaps hundreds of miles from their launch point. Because of this high accuracy, coalition air forces were able to minimize the number of civilian casualties. The increased range of many modern weapons has also increased the depth of the battlefield, both in terms of the immediate contact battle and the interdiction of forces moving to the front line. This long range has also led to the requirement for sensors operating beyond the visual range, increasing the complexity of battle, and creating a synergistic relationship between intelligence, command, communications, and weapons.

The increased destructive power of modern weapons, when linked to improvements in range and accuracy, has greatly increased their lethality. This has forced the development of a whole range of defensive countermeasures, from improved armour to electronics, to anti-missile missiles. Thus a dialectic of measure and countermeasure has been established, fuelling the technological arms race and adding to the spiralling costs of weapons systems. But unless an adequate counter can be found to a new development then survivability will be low due to the lethality of modern weapons. This tends to suggest a highly unstable situation where a comparatively slight technological edge may lead to disproportionate military results.

In addition to being more lethal, weapons have also become more complex. This complexity is most obvious in the way weapons work, which has tended to increase the repair and maintenance requirements (though recent advances in self-diagnostic technology may reduce this). Doubts have been raised about the reliability of complex weaponry, though this would seem to be as much a question of the maturity of a given technology rather than its complexity: the reliability of modern television sets, for example, displays the potential robustness of a mature technology. But the increased complexity of war is apparent in more than the technology used in the construction of a weapon; rather it is manifest in the way in which weapons are used. This is the case from the operating procedures for the use of a weapon, often involving many complex stages and specialized training, to the synergism of modern armed forces. Land battle is a combined arms battle, combining not merely the combat arms of infantry, artillery, and armour, but the traditional support services (engineers, supply, etc.), air power, and the increasingly important C3I to knit the disparate elements together into an efficient whole. Similarly, surface naval power now tends to operate in groupings of ships, the ultimate expression being the US carrier battle group. Although a powerful platform capable of many tasks, an aircraft carrier cannot operate successfully on its own. Rather it is part of a synergistic grouping, including anti-aircraft/anti-missile ships, anti-submarine warfare ships, and a number of supply ships.

One reason for this complexity in the design and operation of weapons is the growth of electronic warfare. The widespread use of radar and radio, attempts to disrupt their use (electronic countermeasures), attempts to foil this disruption (electronic counter-countermeasures), and the use of computers to process information and assist in the command and control of forces has created a new dimension to modern warfare. Electronic warfare is not merely a support service, but an area of combat activity where opposing sides challenge for supremacy. Successful electronic warfare capabilities are essential to the survival of modern weapons platforms (as the destruction of HMS *Sheffield* and the *Atlantic Conveyer* in the South Atlantic demonstrated), and superiority in this area can prove decisive. Modern warfare has also become much more of a continuous affair, with little or no halt for night or bad weather (as the Gulf War of 1991 demonstrated). Modern aircraft are equipped with sensors allowing low-level flight at night, armoured vehicles and infantry are equipped with infra-red night vision aids, and there has even been talk of using drugs to enable troops to fight for perhaps seventy-two hours without rest. As well as being continuous, the pace of battle has increased. Forces move more quickly, threats emerge with dramatic suddenness, and events can move with an alarming rapidity. The time allowed for reaction to an inbound missile threat, for example, is a matter of seconds, allowing a bare minimum of reaction time and reinforcing the trend towards automation: when the increasing tempo of combat is coupled to the growing complexity and diversity of weapons and sensors, automation is fast becoming a necessity, not an option.

The increased pace of battle also has implications for the speed with which ammunition and fuel stockpiles are used up. The experience of the Arab–Israeli wars, to a lesser extent the Falklands War, and estimates for warfare in NATO's central front all indicated that the consumption of munitions in modern warfare is astounding.[19] When this is linked to the tendency to buy fewer modern weapons because of their high cost, it seems unlikely that a modern high technology war can be sustained for any length of time. This problem of sustainability is further compounded by the vastly increased capabilities of most modern weapons systems: though weapon cost has increased dramatically, so has effectiveness. In the 1943 US bombing raid against Schweinfurt in Germany, 291 B 17 bombers were launched. 60 of these bombers were shot down. Only 228 reached the target, and only about 10 per cent of the bombs then dropped hit their target. Estimates suggest that eight modern US F/A-18 aircraft could fly the same mission profile, dropping almost all of their bombs on the target.[20] These increased capabilities reduce sustainability by increasing the lethality of war. John Pay illustrates this phenomenon with the example of the US AH-64 Apache helicopter:

The US Army currently plans to buy 48,000 Hellfire anti-tank missiles, which would allow the 600 or so planned AH 64 helicopters 80 missiles each. This would permit each helicopter to fly five sorties carrying a full load of 16 missiles. Each helicopter could fly 5–10 sorties per day. Given that each attack helicopter might destroy 20 tanks before it was itself destroyed, simple mathematics suggests that after very few days of combat there will be very few helicopters, even fewer missiles and fewer Soviet tanks left on the battlefield.[21]

Finally, modern conventional weaponry is beginning to reach the stage where the capability of the human operator is a major limiting factor. The speed and complexity of combat is entering an area beyond human limitations. The idea of an automated battlefield where humans are operators of systems and removed from battle may still be some time away, but the trend is clearly towards increased automation and reduced human participation. An illustration of this is the US Navy Aegis system which is designed to destroy a salvo of dozens of missiles fired against a group of surface warships with anti-missile missiles. The speed and numbers of missiles which might be fired by both sides is such that the Aegis system is fully automated, tracking incoming targets, deciding which to attack and in what order, and firing its own missiles all automatically. It would simply be too complex a task for a human to do in the very short space of time available. Similarly, jet aircraft can now be designed to turn so sharply at such high speed that pilots cannot take the strain of the g-force imposed. Again, technology has moved beyond human capabilities.

## IV.  What Problems are Created by Technological Developments?

These trends in modern weapons technology pose a number of problems, the most readily quantifiable being that of increased cost. The cost of major weapons systems has increased dramatically, much more than inflation alone can account for. Even attempts at cheap alternatives tend to end up costing more, while genuinely cheap alternatives may lack the capabilities necessary to compete successfully in a high technology war. This is demonstrated by US aircraft procurement in the 1970s–1980s. With the F-15 air superiority fighter reaching new heights of expense, the US began developing the F-16 as a cheap fighter to complement the F-15. But as capabilities were added to ensure the survivability and effectiveness of the F-16, as well as to exploit the potential of the aircraft, so the cost began to increase. In contrast, the privately developed F-20 was a genuinely cheap alternative, but failed to secure any orders due to its limited capabilities. Even revolutionary cheap weapons such as the anti-tank guided munition become expensive as they are locked into the measures–counter-measures spiral. This increased cost means that fewer weapons can be afforded, creating the phenomenon of structural disarmament. During the Second World War, for example, the United States produced 139,000 combat aircraft, but in 1986 the US Navy, Marines, and Air Force together only ordered 399 aircraft. In 1990 the world's largest single combat aircraft programme was the US Advanced Tactical Fighter, but only 1,300 are to be produced for the US Air Force and Navy at an estimated cost of $140 billion (over $100 million each).[22]

Increased cost has led to attempts at different procurement methods to minimize cost. One such method is international collaboration, which aims to reduce costs by spreading the research and development (R. & D.) burden, and by enabling economies of scale through ordering more units. In practice, though, international collaboration does not seem to have significantly reduced costs; it has merely made the unaffordable affordable by spreading the R. & D. burden. An alternative method has been to buy off the shelf from an alternative producer (e.g., the purchase of US F-16 aircraft by European nations). In this way R.

& D. risks are avoided, and probably only a small proportion of the R. & D. costs are incurred as a compensation payment to the producer. The corollary of this is a loss of independence in weapons production and a potential loss of industrial benefits, particularly in terms of employment (though some agreements allow for assembly and even licensed production in the purchaser's own country). The reverse of this approach is to recoup costs by selling weapons to other countries. Export markets may, however, be limited by political considerations, competition is tough, and there is a danger that weapons might be developed with arms sales in mind rather than national defence requirements. A final method is to use competition to keep costs down, though financing the development of two or more prototype designs may prove costly,[23] while outside the United States competition may be limited by the fact that most states have monopoly suppliers of specialized defence goods. In Britain, for example, British Aerospace are monopoly suppliers of fast jets, VSEL of submarines, and Vickers of main battle tanks. Competition in these areas would therefore involve bids from foreign suppliers, which muddies the water by adding political calculations of dependency upon foreign suppliers, as well as the economic implications of substantial contracts being placed overseas (including possible closure of factories, or even companies going bankrupt).

Costs do not inevitably increase, however, and as technologies mature so cheaper means of production may be found. Optical fibre in the late 1970s cost £10 per metre, now the price is nearer 10p per metre. Similar cost reductions occurred with the transistor and the microprocessor. But it should be noted that this applies by and large to *components* and not *systems*: although the cost of individual components may fall, the cost of a new generation weapons system, with new capabilities, and exploiting new technological advances, is unlikely to fall. Using these weapons in war is also extremely expensive, as Operation Desert Storm demonstrated. The degree of financial assistance to coalition powers in the Gulf War from non-participants such as Germany and Japan was highly revealing: an economic and military Superpower such as the United States was unable to fight and win a war against a medium-sized state without the risk of incurring excessive opportunity costs. This cost is reflected in peacetime as well. Some weapons are rarely fired in exercises owing to the cost

(British tanks in Germany, for example, might fire their main tank gun on only one exercise a year). This, and the damage caused to land and the environment by large-scale exercises, has produced a growing reliance on simulators. Troops frequently train on and 'fire' their weapons on sophisticated computer simulators rather than on the real thing, a trend which is likely to increase rather than reduce. Good though many of these simulators are (and some are very good), they cannot reproduce the full reality of modern weaponry, the sensation of their use, and the environment in which they are used. There is, therefore, a danger that training might become unrealistic, degrading combat ability.

The cost of war is not merely financial, but physical in terms of the human loss of life and the destruction of property. It may also be political in the damage done to a government's reputation internally and externally. The Second World War broke the back of the British economy (though it regenerated the US economy), while the Iran–Iraq war shattered the economies of two of the richest states in the Middle East. The Soviet invasion of Afghanistan led to much international criticism as well as a growing internal disillusionment, while the Israeli invasion of Lebanon in 1982 led to similar international and domestic political repercussions. Force is not a cheap option, and the increasingly destructive nature of war, with nuclear weapons as the ultimate expression of this, has led to growing doubts as to whether it remains an effective or useful tool of foreign policy.

The second problem area is that of technological over-reliance, and particularly the implications of increased automation. This problem is approached from two angles. The first is to question the military utility of an increased reliance on technology. Will the technology work, and work efficiently in a hostile environment? How reliable will it be? Will increased weapons complexity make support and maintenance too difficult? Will the high-quality manpower necessary to operate and support such sophisticated systems be available? And will the synergism produced by modern technologies break down all too easily if, whilst in battle, one critical component of a system fails? The second angle is to question the implications of increased automation for the nature of war and the ability to control weapons and war. The shooting down of an Iranian civilian airliner in the Gulf by the US Aegis cruiser *Vincennes* highlighted the problem of an inability to control high threat situations when there is a proliferation of high technology systems. As humans are increasingly removed from the sharp end of war, so the ability to control crises and wars might be severely affected.

Finally, the development and deployment of new technologies has been a major factor in promoting and maintaining the arms race. The arms race is as much a qualitative as a quantitative phenomenon, covering both nuclear and conventional spheres. Both sides attempt not merely to match and improve technologies, but to develop counters to them, creating pressures for the continued development of the initial technology. The arms race has therefore been portrayed as an action–reaction phenomenon, whereby the development of a new technology or weapons system by one state leads to a reaction by its adversary, creating a self-sustaining process of competitive weapons development. But the arms race can also be seen as a dynamic originating within a state. The vested interests of defence industry and the armed services, coupled to the seemingly inevitable march of technological progress, can combine to create pressure for new weapons systems. Weapons development might therefore be more a product of bureaucratic politics and technological determinism than of reaction to an external threat (though such a threat might be important in creating the permissive atmosphere necessary for major expenditure on weapons). Whatever the reason for the arms race, the result tends to be at best no increase in security at a greater financial cost, and at worst a reduction in security through the fear and mistrust created, and through the risk of the development of a destabilizing new technology by one side.

## V. Conclusion

The quest for new weapons through the development of technology has been one of the defining features of post-war military competition. The result has been weapons systems which are more capable, more destructive, and more expensive than their predecessors. Although all of the major weapons platforms of the Second World War are still present in the military arsenals of today (particularly tanks, manned aircraft, surface ships, and submarines), their capabilities have evolved beyond recognition.

In particular, many of the subsystems carried by these platforms—both support systems and weapons systems—are entirely new, or considerably enhanced since the Second World War. These developments have produced weapons of longer range, greater accuracy, and greater lethality. The size of the battlefield has been greatly expanded, and the complexity of warfare hugely increased. Not just the weapons but their operation, and their incorporation into a sophisticated, synergistic network of sensors, computers, and munitions has produced a complexity never previously known in warfare. Moreover, the pace of war has increased dramatically. Missiles and aircraft travel supersonically over long distances, arriving at their target with little or no warning, main battle tanks can cross rough terrain at high speeds (perhaps over 40 m.p.h.), and even infantry are carried to battle in armoured vehicles. Rates of fire and numbers of aircraft sorties flown have similarly increased: in the Vietnam War the United States managed some 400 sorties a day, in the 1991 Gulf War the United States generated over 2,000 sorties a day, supported by several hundred sorties from its coalition partners. Nor does battle stop for night or bad weather. Modern armies possess night-vision capabilities both for expensive platforms and individual soldiers, and although bad weather might hinder operations it is unlikely to stop them. This pace and complexity of battle has placed huge strains on the men (and, increasingly, women) who fight wars. Indeed, in some areas technology has moved beyond human capacity to control its operation, leading towards increased automation.

Technological change has been unremitting, though perhaps not always as fast as might initially appear to be the case. With this constant change problems have arisen: modern weapons are more expensive from one generation to the next; there is a growing tendency to rely on technology to solve problems; and weapons' development can create an arms race, reducing stability and security. But perhaps most tellingly the character of modern warfare has led military thinkers to question whether a high intensity conflict could ever be worth the costs involved (regardless of whether nuclear weapons are used), and even if such a war did occur, whether it could be sustained for any length of time.

## Notes

1. Stephen Canby, 'The Quest for Technological Superiority: A Misunderstanding of War?', in *The Changing Strategic Landscape*, pt. III, Adelphi Paper 237 (London: IISS, 1989), 26.

2. Richard G. Hewlett and Oscar E. Anderson, Jr., *A History of the United States Atomic Energy Commission*, i, *The New World 1939–46* (University Park: Pennsylvania State University Press, 1962); Dietrich Schroeer, *Science, Technology and the Nuclear Arms Race* (New York: John Wiley and Sons, 1984), 24–36; Alice Kimball-Smith, 'The Manhattan Project', in Jack Dennis (ed.), *The Nuclear Almanac: Confronting the Atom in War and Peace* (Reading, Mass.: Addison-Wesley, 1984), 21–40; Margaret Gowing, *Britain and Atomic Energy, 1939–1945* (London: Macmillan, 1964).

3. Bernard Brodie, *The Absolute Weapon* (New York: Harcourt Brace, 1946), 76.

4. On the US decision to build the H-bomb, see: Warner Schilling, 'The H-Bomb Decision: How to Decide Without Really Choosing', *Political Science Quarterly*, 76 (March 1961), 24–46; David Alan Rosenberg, 'American Atomic Strategy and the Hydrogen Bomb Decision', *Journal of Contemporary American History*, 66 (June 1979), 62–87; Robert Gilpin, *American Scientists and Nuclear Weapons Policy* (Princeton, NJ: Princeton University Press, 1962), 64–111.

5. For an explanation of the physics of a nuclear explosion, see Kosta Tsipis, *Understanding Nuclear Weapons* (London: Wildwood House, 1983), 29–43.

6. The French also maintain a strategic triad, but both their bomber and land-based missile legs lack credibility, and are probably therefore more political than military. The British have now retired all of their strategic bombers and operate just four submarines, each armed with 16 Polaris missiles. These are to be replaced in the 1990s with four new boats, each carrying 16 Trident missiles. The Chinese have a very small number of land-based missiles with intercontinental range, but rather more medium-range missiles. They are also constructing a submarine-based force, but production appears to be extremely slow. Israel has no intercontinental capability, but has both aircraft and probably over 100 missiles capable of hitting targets in the Middle East. India has exploded a nuclear device, but has no weapons.

7. Paul Rogers, *Guide to Nuclear Weapons* (Oxford: Berg, 1988), 46–7.

8. Bill Sweetman, 'MAR: Well-balanced Plan or Costly Compromise', *Jane's Defence Weekly* (12 May 1990), 899.

9. See Lawrence Freedman, *US Intelligence and the Soviet Strategic Threat*, 2nd edn. (London: Macmillan, 1986).

10. Greville Rumble, *The Politics of Nuclear Defence* (Cambridge: Polity Press, 1985), 12.

11. Freedman, *US Intelligence and the Soviet Strategic Threat*, 75–7.

12. Rogers, *Guide to Nuclear Weapons*, 13–14.

13. Capt. J. E. Moore and Cdr. R. Compton-Hall, *Submarine Warfare Today and Tomorrow* (London: Michael Joseph, 1986), 239–40; Norman Friedman, *The US Maritime Strategy* (London: Jane's, 1988), 168; Rogers, *Guide to Nuclear Weapons*, 42–5.

14. Office of Technology Assessment, *Strategic Defences: Two Reports by the Office of Technology Assessment* (Princeton, NJ: Princeton University Press, 1986); Steven E. Miller and Stephen van Evera (eds.), *The Star Wars Controversy* (Princeton, NJ: Princeton University Press, 1986); Ashton B. Carter and David N. Schwartz (eds.),*Ballistic Missile Defense* (Washington, DC: Brookings Institute, 1984); William J. Broad, *Star Warriors* (London: Faber & Faber, 1986).

15. Attention here will concentrate on the most-developed armies—principally those in Europe and the Middle East. The pace of change has not been uniform, however, and some armies still display weapons and tactics little removed from the Second World War. This was particularly so with the Iranians in the Iran–Iraq war, whose manpower-oriented tactics sometimes appeared more akin to the First World War than to the modern battlefield.

16. 'Are Anti-Tank Weapons Obsolete?', *RUSI Newsbrief*, 9 (Oct. 1989), 79–80; Benjamin F. Schemmer, 'Army, Sec Def's Office at Logger-heads over Anti-Armour', *Armed Forces Journal International* (May 1989), 53–60.

17. G. Till, *et al.*, *Maritime Strategy and the Nuclear Age*, 2nd edn. (London: Macmillan, 1984); Friedman, *The US Maritime Strategy.*

18. This point is forcefully argued in Mary Kaldor, *The Baroque Arsenal* (London: André Deutsch, 1982).

19. In the Second World War, for example, guns fired on average 25 rounds a day; in the Falklands some British guns fired more than 400 rounds a day. John Pay, 'The Battlefield since 1945', in Colin McInnes and G. D. Sheffield (eds.), *Warfare in the Twentieth Century: Theory and Practice* (London: Unwin Hyman, 1988), 221.

20. John Lehman, 'Utility of Maritime Power: The Restoration of US Naval Strength', *RUSI Journal*, 128 (Sept. 1983), 15. See also Pay, 'The Battlefield since 1945', 223.

21. Pay, 'The Battlefield since 1945', 221.

22. Bill Sweetman, 'ATF: 21st Century Super Fighter', *Jane's Defence Weekly* (19 May 1990), 957; Pay, 'The Battlefield since 1945', 222.

23. The USAF is financing the competitive development of two different prototypes for the advanced tactical fighter, each of $691 m, but only one design will be used. See Sweetman, 'ATF: 21st Century Super Fighter'.

## SIX

# Diplomacy

*Adam Watson*

Many chapters of this book are concerned with issues of substance. Diplomacy is a means or process which helps states to realize their goals. The diplomatic dialogue between states enables each to know what the others want, and so to take its decisions in the light of that knowledge. It gives form to what would otherwise be a confused jumble of aims and fears, and ill-informed reactions. It thus acts as the lubrication of the system of states, without which international society would seize up. A knowledge of how diplomacy functions is essential to a clear understanding of international relations.

The term *diplomacy* in international relations has two conventional meanings today. The first is the actual conduct of negotiations, and the dialogue generally, that the states of our modern international society carry on with each other and with international bodies. It is usually associated in our minds with embassies and professional diplomats; but communication between rulers and governments stretches back at least as far as the earliest written records. The second meaning attaches to a statesman or country, as when we speak of Gorbachev's or Soviet diplomacy. This sense reminds us that it is the rulers and statesmen in charge of governments who conduct the diplomatic dialogue, and that professional diplomats are their agents. But it is a pity to extend this use of the word diplomacy to mean foreign policy, as is often done in journalism and in conversation, because that blunts the more precise meaning of negotiation and dialogue.

Diplomacy is a civilized and civilizing procedure. It is civilized because it involves communication and discussion, and because it attempts to reconcile interests and to lessen conflicts by compromise and adjustment, or by the horse-trading of give and take. Indeed, diplomacy is like trade, in that it normally benefits both sides, or in multilateral bargains all concerned. It is civilizing because it involves listening to others, understating their aims and fears, and so broadening one's vision of international relations beyond one's own immediate concerns. A maxim of professional diplomacy is that you should concentrate your efforts on mastering the other side's case, because it is assumed that you know your own. *Raison d'état* or reason of state, now an old-fashioned expression, involves adjusting your policy to take account of the policies of others; and beyond that *raison de système* involves the awareness that it pays every member state of an international system to abide by the rules and to make the system work. Diplomacy is by nature constructive, and develops a bias in favour of peaceful solutions of disputes. It sometimes achieves its aims by widening the scope of the negotiation to bring in other issues where it is easier for one side to make a concession than the other. But diplomacy, like any other useful invention, can be exploited for sinister purposes. Diplomatic exchanges can be deceitful (as for instance, Hitler's were) and mask aggressive plans or the intention to break a promise. The pun of Tudor times, that a diplomat is sent abroad to lie (i.e., to live) for his country, is funny because there is a grain of truth in it. Indeed diplomacy is a form of language, and all language can lie.

The practice of diplomacy has changed a great deal in the course of this century. That is not surprising. International politics, and indeed all politics, has been transformed, and diplomacy reflects that transformation. The states that conduct the dialogue, and especially the most powerful ones that set its tone, have changed; so have the subjects that they discuss with each other. The methods of diplomacy have been transformed above all by the speed and ease of modern communication. The rules and conventions of diplomacy are also changing with the times.

Before we examine these changes, we need to take a brief look at the history of diplomacy, in order to understand the present practice. Though the nature of diplomacy is determined to a large extent by the political environment in which it operates, its rules and practices are also inherited from the past, and based on what has previously been found to work.

## I. What can we Learn from the Historical Background?

Where communities bump up against one another, and especially where they have regular dealings, they feel the need to communicate with each other. The ruler or government of one community will send a messenger or *envoy* (from the French envoyer, to send) to talk to the ruler or government of the other. Australian aboriginal tribes sent women as envoys, perhaps because their immunity was more likely to be respected. In primitive societies most of these communications concern arrangements for trade; boundaries and limits; and the prospect of war—for instance, to seek an alliance against another community that threatens them both. We know of no group of communities or political entities closely involved with one another that do not have arrangements for communication.

Communications between more civilized communities conform to a regular pattern. Envoys have always been granted safe-conduct, or what we now call *diplomatic immunity*, because one government wants to hear what the other has to say or offer, and to send back a reply, even if the two governments are hostile. Some civilized governments have kept written records of these communications. The earliest that we still possess date back many thousands of years. From these records we can see that the aim of all diplomatic communication, from the earliest times to the present, is to induce or persuade another ruler or government to act as you wish. It is not to win an argument, as in a court of law before a judge, or before an arbitrator who can enforce his decision. The word diplomatic has therefore come to mean tactful, and able to persuade.

An amusing early example of diplomatic tact is contained in the exchange between the Egyptian Pharaohs and the Kings of the Hittites. One Hittite King received some gold bricks in payment from a Pharaoh, but when he cut them open they were filled with dross. He did not want to quarrel with the Pharaoh, so he sent the bricks back with a message that someone must be cheating his good friend, charging the full amount of gold to the Pharaoh's treasury but keeping most of it; and would the Pharaoh please send the agreed amount.

Envoys did not come and go only between independent states.

Subordinate rulers wanted to plead their cause with an overlord or suzerain ruler, and the overlord wanted to induce subordinate rulers to act as he wished. Sometimes the overlord used threats, open or implied; and sometimes the subordinate warned that unless the overlord acted in a certain way, the subordinate would not be able to meet his wishes. Much diplomatic communication in the past and today, however tactfully phrased, can be reduced to the basic formula 'or else'. At other times both overlord and subordinate resorted to promises. These promises often referred to military aid, as did communications between independent rulers or governments. Often also they referred to monetary payments, either tribute by the subordinate or a subsidy by the overlord. The money, like the troops, could move both ways; and sometimes the one was in effect an exchange for the other. Today subsidies are commoner than tribute, but the underlying pattern is much the same.

Two examples from ancient sources are worth reading as illustrations. Chapters 16 to 18 of the Second Book of Kings describe in detail the diplomatic exchanges between the King of Assyria, as overlord, and the Kingdoms of Israel and Judah as subordinates. There are threats and promises, money payments, and the efforts of every ruler, including the great King of Assyria, to induce the other party to conform to his wishes with the minimum expenditure of his own men and money. Similarly, Chapter 3 of Book I of Thucydides' history of the Peloponnesian War contains a good example among many of the efforts of envoys from Corinth, a junior ally, and from Athens, a near enemy, to persuade or threaten the Spartan assembly to act as they wished. Today all the member states of our international society are theoretically recognized as independent. But in practice this is often not the case. Many nominally independent states are in reality dependent on one of the two superpowers, a former colonial power, or some other state. The diplomatic dialogue then resembles that in the Book of Kings. The ancient Indian and Chinese records of the millennium before Christ are full of similar evidence.

When we come down to the rich and bellicose world of the Renaissance, about five hundred years ago, we find the rulers of the Italian states needing information about their neighbours and the rest of Europe more regularly and in greater detail than before, both for reasons of trade and for reasons of security and war. The Popes with their network of envoys, the Medici bankers who controlled Florence with their agents all over Europe and the Levant, and above all the merchant princes who governed Venice, received regular reports from their representatives. These representatives resided for long periods in the countries concerned, and also of course acted as channels of communication between their masters and the governments of the states where they lived. They were not proud noblemen or high prelates, but usually humble people who knew their business; and other governments respected them and their correspondence most of the time, because they wanted to communicate confidentially with important powers like the Pope and the Venetians. So developed that major invention of European diplomacy, the *resident embassy*.

The new and very useful system of permanent envoys gradually became amalgamated with the older practice of grand temporary embassies led by a nobleman or member of the royal family, which a King or prince would send to another, and which were in effect pieces of his court temporarily detached and sent to the court of the other ruler. Ambassadors and other envoys of Kings became resident noblemen who took part in court life, with professional secretaries to carry out the reporting and most of the negotiation. Embassies and other missions were not merely granted diplomatic immunity; international law regarded them as 'extra-territorial' or foreign soil, and within the compound the law of the ambassador's country, and not the law of the land prevailed. An ambassador's effectiveness depended on his being able to mix as a social equal with the makers of policy in the country to which he was accredited, and to entertain them in a way which was not only worthy of the monarch he represented, but would also make those who shaped foreign policy glad to be invited. The glittering side of embassy work still partly survives today, though much less in reality than in popular imagination. Envoys of foreign governments in London are still formally styled Ambassadors to the Court of St James.

The city states of ancient Greece and of Renaissance Italy were closely involved with one another, so that each was obliged to take account of what the others offered or threatened, in trade and in war. As the European international society developed, it became more integrated, both strategically and economically, and the member states became increasingly *interdependent*. Many rulers, valuing their sovereignty, resisted the integrating pressures of the system as much as they thought was prudent. Since states ceased to be the domains of monarchs who were related to one another, and became nation states, popular nationalism has increased the sense of difference between them. The gradual decolonization of the European empires overseas (since US independence in 1776) has also increased isolationism and the desire to avoid strategic entanglement, though there has been less resistance to international trade. The great Communist states, Russia and China, for a time tried autarky, or insulation from the non-Communist world. But the world has become continually more integrated, generally as a result of the development of technology, and also in particular in the field of international relations by the expansion of European international rules, institutions, and practices to bring the whole planet into a single system for the first time.[1]

## II. What is the Nature of Contemporary Diplomacy?

The officers in established foreign services have long since become professionalized, in the same way as officers in the armed services. Diplomats today have a professional knowledge of their country's interests abroad, and of the interests and policies of at least some other countries, or problems of international concern. Modern international relations are so complex, and the number of states in international society is now so large, that no professional diplomat can have expert knowledge of every aspect of his subject; and most diplomats therefore become specialists, as do lawyers and doctors. But every foreign service needs some generalists, who are able to see the problems of their country's foreign policy as a whole, though they may have to refer to experts on each particular aspect of it. Every professional diplomat also needs to master the art of negotiation, how to conduct the diplomatic dialogue, and the art of pertinent reporting on the country to which he may be sent.

Diplomatic missions in other countries are now colloquially referred to as embassies. They include embassies in the specific sense of an ambassador and his staff accredited to a foreign government; legations, which are junior embassies; high commissions exchanged between member states of the Commonwealth; and delegations to international bodies like the United Nations when headed by an ambassador. The number of embassies has *proliferated* enormously in the last forty years. Many capitals of large powers now house over a hundred embassies, and the largest ones like Washington over two hundred. For example, there are three British ambassadors in Brussels, accredited to the King of the Belgians, the European Community, and NATO, alongside two or three ambassadors each from several other countries.

Professional foreign services not only staff embassies and other missions abroad; they also staff foreign offices or *ministries of foreign affairs* in their own country. An effective ministry is staffed by professional officers who have gained experience in embassies abroad and expect further tours of service there. Today a ministry of foreign affairs is quite as important for the conduct of foreign policy as the network of embassies abroad, and perhaps more so. A ministry or foreign office must receive and collate the flow, nowadays immense, of information from embassies abroad and other sources. It must submit the distilled information, along with any questions requiring a government decision, to the Foreign Minister (in the UK usually called the Foreign Secretary, and in the US the Secretary of State). It must transmit the decisions of the government which come down from the Minister, often in general terms, to embassies abroad in the form of detailed instructions (usually by diplomatic wireless or by telephone); which the embassies then carry out and on which they report back. Thereupon the process begins again. An effective foreign ministry must also communicate incoming reports to, and coordinate outgoing instructions with, other government departments—especially the Prime Minister's or President's office, and the departments of the treasury or finance, defence, and trade.

A foreign ministry must also conduct a continuous dialogue with the foreign embassies accredited to the government, at many levels. It may seem cumbersome to have the two sets of dialogue running in parallel, often about the same subjects. But the practice is useful. Embassies convey the information, ask the questions, and carry on the negotiations, that their government wants, which is not the same as what the host government and its ministry want. Even where the subjects are the same, a valuable stereoscopic effect is obtained. In practice detailed negotiations are usually concentrated in one ministry and embassy to avoid duplication. The more responsive a ministry shows itself to an embassy, the more co-operation it can expect for its embassy from the other ministry. A good working relationship between the diplomats in a ministry and the embassies that visit it is fostered by the fact that they regard each other as colleagues, who have played each other's parts and will shortly do so again, and therefore want to facilitate each other's task within the limits of their country's interest. So also the embassies in a capital form a *diplomatic corps*, with similar professional functions and a similar need to safeguard their immunity and lines of communication. Within a diplomatic corps the embassies of governments that are allied or have similar outlooks find it useful to compare notes: they may act in concert or in parallel in making representations to the government, and compare the information on the country which they report back to their ministries. There is thus a vast network of bilateral dialogue between states, each strand of which is affected by the others even though the strands are separate.

Diplomacy is not merely bilateral. A rapidly growing field is *collective diplomacy*, or representation and negotiation in *international bodies*. As explained elsewhere, such bodies are of two main kinds. First, there are omnilateral organizations like the United Nations, whose function is to be universal rather than efficient, though it should be noted that some specialized bodies of the UN have partially managed to be both. Secondly, there are selectively multilateral alliances, leagues, and bodies of like-minded states. Some are alliances for strategic purposes, for instance, NATO; some are regional bodies with more general interests, like ASEAN and the Organization for African Unity; some have non-regional ties, like the Commonwealth; and some of the most important have specific economic purposes, like OPEC and the councils that regulate commodities such as sugar and coffee. These organizations are not legislatures or courts of justice, but *associations of states*. As Andrew Young, a former US ambassador to the UN put it: 'The United Nations was not designed to be, nor is it adequate to serve as, a law-making body for the world . . . It is a forum for diplomacy; and true diplomacy is the art of dialogue.' The same is true of the other collective machinery listed above, which are also forums for diplomacy.

Member states attach considerable importance to many of these collective organizations, including the headquarters of the UN in New York, alliances like NATO and the Warsaw pact, and specialized multilateral bodies like OPEC, where significant diplomatic work is done. They consequently assign some of the ablest members of their professional foreign services to represent them there permanently, and their ministers attend on a regular basis. Many collective organizations are still elastic and adaptable, and their innovative practice outruns their formal legitimacy. International organizations are apt to take on a life and character of their own. Some professional diplomats work not for an individual state but for international bodies, many of which have huge bureaucracies. The most conspicuous of the international diplomatic figures is the Secretary General of the UN, who is supported by a number of professional diplomats from various member states. This arrangement is sometimes criticized; but it helps the omnilateral organization to reflect the aims of its various members. *Raison de système*, which the UN symbolizes, involves the resolution of compromise of conflicting interests and principles.

The dialogue between states reaches increasingly beyond foreign ministries. The embassy of a major- or middle-ranking power deals with matters of primary concern to many other departments of government; and those departments often want to appoint their own experts, who can act on their behalf and report back to them. As a result, the more important embassies have in this century ceased to consist largely of professional diplomats—the ambassador and his counsellors and secretaries—and now house members of many government departments. A British embassy to another major state, or the British delegation to an international organization like the United Nations, is a microcosm of all Whitehall rather than just the Foreign Office.

The emphasis of the diplomatic dialogue is steadily shifting from high politics, which was its major concern, to *economic problems*. Trade has always been a subject of diplomacy since the earliest times. Now the increasing emphasis on economic issues tends to make the dialogue more difficult, and at times less effective. When statesmen were concerned with matters like boundaries and alliances, they could usually carry out what they undertook. Economics on the other hand is like quicksilver: it slips through the fingers of governments. The fact that governments can control economic activity very imperfectly (except by severely depressing it) makes them all the more anxious to discuss their economic policies with other governments, and co-ordinates action where this seems to be in their mutual interest (for instance over exchange rates for their currencies). The economic dialogue is so technical that it usually has to be conducted by financial and other experts, with a modicum of assistance from members of foreign services. It is possible to regard economic diplomacy as a profession in itself, which includes the world's leading bankers and others as well as government servants. Much economic diplomacy is carried on in specialized multilateral organizations, such as the World Bank and the International Monetary Fund, and informal associations like the Group of Seven.

The pressure on the diplomatic dialogue increases as the world becomes ever more interdependent, and the impact of strategic and economic decisions ever more rapid. It took Napoleon as long as Hannibal to cross the Alps, but modern weapons can reach any part of the globe in a few minutes. At the same time communications technology is shrinking the effective distance between capitals so fast that those who take decisions sense both the need to talk and the possibility of talking to each other directly. They meet, and they telephone each other, much more frequently than even a few decades ago. Some foreign ministers have become almost peripatetic. At a lower 'working' level, members of government departments are increasingly in direct touch. The diplomatic dialogue between governments passes *less through embassies* than before.

Governments can influence other governments not only by negotiation and through international bodies: they also try to *influence public opinion* in other countries. The techniques of disseminating genuine information and propaganda have greatly developed in recent years, and increasingly involve professional diplomats in embassies and at home. It is therefore perhaps legitimate to group these techniques, ranging from public state-ments by political leaders to embassy information officers and special broadcasts like Radio Free Europe, under the heading of 'public diplomacy'. Public diplomacy in this sense is not new. From the earliest times rulers and statesmen have wanted to make some policy statements to their neighbours in public, and some in private. The text of 2 Kings: 18 (mentioned above) records that the ministers of the King of Judah wanted a confidential negotiation, but the envoy of Assyria said, 'Has my master sent me to speak these words to your master and to you, and not to the men, sitting on the wall?' Where the people, the demos, is the ultimate sovereign rather than a ruler, it is a necessary function of diplomacy to persuade that sovereign. The Corinthian and Athenian envoys in the example from Thucydides were doing so, and their actions can be called public diplomacy. Here diplomacy takes on some characteristics of argument in a law court or a parliament.

## III. Is the Role of the Embassy Declining?

As the dialogue between governments has expanded and its pace has become faster, foreign ministries have grown in importance. Will the role of the resident embassy in the management of international affairs continue to diminish as foreign ministries and other government departments deal more directly with their counterparts, and other departments of sophisticated governments accumulate expertise about the other countries with which they deal? The part played by embassies will continue to change. But neither foreign ministries nor other government departments have found an effective substitute for regular confidential reporting by their resident representatives on developments of concern to them. Further evidence of the usefulness of embassies is the increasing importance which other government departments attach to representation in embassies. Reports by journalists keep the public informed, rapidly and at various levels of seriousness; but in practice they are too hastily compiled, too under-researched, and too slanted towards the new rather than the important, to be adequate alone.

A growing body of opinion within diplomatic services considers that the professional contribution which these services make is more needed the less other government departments are in direct contact with one another, and most indispensable in, for instance, the relations of the Western powers to the Soviet Union and China during the Cold War era. By contrast the dialogue between the member states of the European Community now flows through a great many channels in addition to embassies, including regular meetings of ministers and the interaction of departments with the collective Community institutions. The task of professional diplomats in the Community is to adapt themselves to new ways of facilitating the complex relations between member governments, and assuring that the interests of their country are adequately furthered in the process. The lubricating function of diplomacy remains, but the modalities change.

In addition to their practical functions, embassies also have an important *symbolic* value, like royal families and national flags. The symbolic value of the thousands of embassies in the world can be questioned, but it has increased with the proliferation of independent states. Small and new states that need to achieve recognition and to establish themselves as independent members of international society are especially anxious to appoint ambassadors to the United Kingdom and other international bodies, and in the major capitals of the world, as well as to receive ambassadors in their own newly sovereign capitals. More established states recognize the symbolic value of such embassies in their capitals. However, donors of aid and technical assistance prefer to conduct their diplomatic business through their own embassies in small and new states until the embassies of those states have learnt the necessary professional skills; and where the assessment and administration of aid programmes is involved the embassy of the donor power is likely to remain the effective instrument.

## IV. What Criticisms can be Levelled against Modern Diplomacy?

Some criticisms of present-day diplomacy are worth considering, and the debate about them is helping to change diplomatic practice. The most familiar concerns *secrecy*. Many people feel that secret diplomacy leads to intrigue and war, and that in this democratic century the public has a right to know what is being said in its name. President Wilson after the First World War called for 'open covenants, openly arrived at'. The diplomatic dialogue before the First World War was too secret for our standards today:

some whole agreements remained secret, like the Russian–German Reinsurance Treaty, and many others contained secret clauses. The media have a vested interest in the maximum of disclosure, and much of the public favours it. Governments, and especially professional diplomats, are less sure. If President Wilson's words are taken to mean that the general subjects of negotiation should be known, and that agreements when reached should be more fully public, most people in democracies would agree. But bargaining between governments, as between business corporations, needs a degree of discretion to succeed. The exploratory diplomacy that feels out the possibilities for a deal between states, or a resolution in the Security Council, has to take place in confidence if it is to realize its potential: especially when a broad package is under discussion, a number of options have to be examined on a 'what if' basis. In democracies, where every public offer will be criticized by the political opposition and the media, a bargain openly discussed will usually mean no bargain at all. Also, a government which discloses what other governments say to it in confidence will soon find itself excluded from the confidential diplomatic dialogue, to its own serious loss. It is a question of where to draw the line between secrecy and disclosure.

A criticism similar to the distrust of secret diplomacy is that the international relations of a democracy should not be left in the hands of professional diplomats. A diplomatic service, it is argued, is *unrepresentative*: it is a self-perpetuating body that does its own recruiting. It forms an unelected élite that evolves and keeps alive ideas about 'the national interest', as opposed to the wishes of the democracy, and persuades government ministers, who come and go, to accept these ideas and allow the diplomatic service to implement them. This criticism is parallel to the argument that professionals from the armed services, and especially the chiefs of staff, must not be allowed to determine defence policy. It is often coloured in Western countries by the belief that diplomatic services are drawn from an unrepresentative upper class and are ultra-conservative: a belief which today is quite out of date for the developed countries. The criticism itself, as opposed to the class gloss, needs to be taken seriously. The argument that the demos does not know what is wise or prudent in foreign affairs, that it is misinformed by propaganda and the media, and that elected governments are often ignorant and ideologically prejudiced, is an argument against democracy itself. Democracy certainly comes at a price: and that price is mitigated in the foreign field by having a body of professional experts who determine the long-term national interest in much greater detail than ministers have time or training for, and submit their conclusions as one factor for ministers to take into account. International relations should not be 'left in the hands of' civil servants: but in the Western democracies they are not.

On the other hand there is a case for ensuring that not only the statesmen who determine and increasingly conduct a democracy's diplomatic dialogue, but also the permanent envoys to some of the more important foreign capitals and international organizations, are political figures identified with the government of the day. The US practice of assigning ambassadorships to people who have contributed to election campaigns has obvious disadvantages; but there is a real gain both to the Administration and to the host government to have an American ambassdor who has easy access to the President and knows his mind. It can be argued that for the same reasons 'non-career' European ambassadors at posts like Washington, Tokyo, and the United Nations tend to be more effective politically than professional diplomats, provided they are supported by an adequate professional staff. But each case needs to be judged on its merits: as so often in diplomacy, there is no hard and fast rule.

## V. Conclusion

We can therefore see diplomacy as the process of managing international society, and the relations of member states with each other and with international bodies. Hans Morgenthau described the process as 'the translation of conflicting or inchoate interests into a common purpose of the conflicting parties'. Diplomacy is not limited to independent states, or to the activities of professionals. Even the network of bilateral dialogues has a collective quality. Diplomacy works in favour of mutual understanding, of compromise and peaceful co-operation, and against conflict, ideologies, and even principles and values. International society is changing rapidly, and the changes affect the modalities of diplomacy, though not its basic nature. Interdependence and ease of communication are speeding up the diplomatic dialogue and extending its subject-matter, and bringing statesmen into more frequent direct contact. The dialogue is increasingly taking place in multilateral bodies.

Omnilateral organizations, to which virtually every state belongs, may come to play an increasing role in international affairs, until ultimately their authority over their members puts them in the position of a super state or world government. But the world is still a long way from that vision, which some want and others fear. Until then, the United Nations and more specialized omnilateral organizations remain part of collective diplomacy, alongside the bilateral diplomacy of states talking to and negotiating with each other.

## Note

1. For a detailed description see Hedley Bull and A. Watson (eds.), *The Expansion of International Society* (Oxford: Clarendon Press, 1986).

# SEVEN

# International Organizations

*Marc Imber*

## I. Why Study International Organizations?

This chapter has three purposes. The first is to define international organizations, both in the narrow institutional sense and also in the broader context of their place in an international system dominated by the relations of states. The second purpose is to inquire further into the purpose of international organizations, to ask why are these institutions created? The third purpose of this chapter is to discuss why, despite much solid evidence of their utility, international organizations are none the less frequently marginalized, criticized for not fulfilling the more ambitious expectations that their creation raises.

For many years after 1945, international organization was regarded as a subsidiary branch of international relations. It was a field of inquiry subordinate to foreign policy and security studies. This attitude reflected the dominance of the realist perspective, in which the security dilemma of each sovereign state is interpreted in predominantly military terms. In this scheme international organizations may exist and perform useful functions in the fields of economic, social, and scientific co-operation, the so-called functional approach, but these endeavours are of only secondary importance in international relations. The work of international organizations is liable to suspension when relations between states degenerate to the point of armed force. This may be seen to have occurred in the case of the League of Nations which although still not dissolved until 1946, went, in 1940, into a hibernation from which it never awoke. This attitude to the role of international organizations was unfortunate but inevitable. It is, however, a perception that has changed dramatically in recent years.

A pluralist approach to international order recognizes the importance of the economic and technical fields of foreign policy, and furthermore recognizes the multilateral as well as the conventional bilateral basis of diplomacy. The growth of conference diplomacy has been one of the most notable changes in the style of diplomacy during this century. The rise of international organizations is in part the institutionalization of this trend. A standing conference, serviced by a permanent career civil-service, takes on many of the attributes of an international organization, and several of the most familiar organizations, such as the World Health Organization have their origins in this process. Others were created at a specific place and time, such as the United Nations at the July 1945 San Francisco Conference, but even in this case the origins of the UN may be traced through several years of inter-allied diplomacy after the Atlantic Charter of 1941.

## II. What are International Organizations?

International organizations are frequently discussed synonymously with international institutions. In the formal and legal sense the two terms can be used interchangeably. Archer suggests that international organizations are 'a formal continuous structure established by agreement between members (governmental and/or non-governmental) from two or more sovereign states with the aim of pursuing the common interest of the membership.'[1] A distinction that will be made later in this chapter is that international organizations *as organizations* represent the apex of a pyramid of multilateral diplomacy. At the base of this pyramid are the issues suitable for negotiation. Above this is the process of negotiation in which states agree norms or rules, and only in certain cases does this process of negotiation create the appropriate organization or institution. This distinction is the origin of the now famous quotation, used frequently in examination questions concerning the singular and plural forms of organization: 'International organization is a process: international organizations are the representative aspects of the phase of that process that has been reached at a given time.'[2] Claude uses the singular form to describe the pattern of multilateral negotiation, and the plural form to represent the creation of the organizations, and the powers invested in them.

The concept of *regime*, extraordinarily pervasive in the 1980s, refers to a more comprehensive idea. 'By creating and accepting procedures, rules or institutions for certain kinds of activity, governments regulate and control transnational and interstate relations. We refer to these governing arrangements as international regimes.'[3] The regime is therefore the 'governing arrangement' for a particular service or issue in the international system, it will include both formal and informal agreements, normative and legal elements, and will represent a degree of *organization*. Probably, but not necessarily, this will include a constitutionally independent international organization at its apex.

An example of this more comprehensive regimes approach would be the operation of the international monetary system between 1944 and 1971. In this period the International Monetary Fund (IMF), created in 1944, with the World Bank (originally known as the International Bank for Reconstruction and Development (IBRD)) both exercised substantial authority in regulating the financial stability of the western states. However, these two organizations operated as elements in an altogether more comprehensive regime. This included the commitment of the member states to fixed exchange rates, to a fixed gold price, and to dollar–gold convertibility. In practice the system also relied upon the willingness of the US to shoulder an unequal burden of economic adjustment, and upon the gradual erosion of sterling as a competitor to a dollar-based world economy. The abandonment of both fixed exchange rates and a fixed gold price, and the emergence of persistent, structural balance-of-payments surpluses on the part of Japan and West Germany, and US deficits, caused the regime to undergo a massive adjustment in the Smithsonian agreement of 1971. This created the system of floating (or, for some, sinking) exchange rates that has existed since then, and which the EC countries are now trying to regulate between themselves by the partial regime embodied in the Exchange Rate Mechanism (ERM). The IMF and IBRD remain in existence, but their functions and status in the regime have altered over time.

Another basic distinction in defining international organization is between governmental organizations (IGOs) and non-governmental organizations (INGOs). Formally, an IGO is a permanent institution created by three or more states to serve some mutual purpose. An INGO is one created by private citizens, or groups, drawn from three or more countries. INGOs may be studied in their own right, or as an adjunct to the mainstream study of IGOs. INGOs can certainly be greatly influential, especially in fields such as political campaigns, development awareness, disaster relief, and environmental issues. In this they rely heavily on their freedom to operate within a western-style, pluralist political system. Amnesty International, for example, is only able to operate, publicly, in a limited number of countries. The charitable status of some INGOs may be queried as in the peculiarly British cases of War on Want and Oxfam. For this reason conventional studies of international organization tend to downgrade the significance of INGOs. They are seen as vulnerable and dependent for their operations and success upon permissive political conditions. Ironically they are most frequently perceived by the general public to succeed exactly when they do successfully confront governmental power, and challenge orthodox opinions. The role of Greenpeace in the Save the Whale campaign and the dumping of toxic chemicals at sea is apposite. The reasons for this apparent paradox will be discussed later.

To press further the distinctiveness of international organization as a form or context of diplomatic activity we should note that, as Jacobson has written, 'IGOs are distinguished from the facilities of traditional diplomacy by their structure and permanence. IGOs have meetings of the member states at regular intervals, specified procedures for taking decisions and a permanent secretariat.'[4] As permanent institutions, they are characterized by at least three specific tiers of authority. First, international organizations possess some form of general conference or assembly in which all members may participate. Typically these are convened annually, although some, such as UNESCO may operate a two-year cycle. This general conference ensures that the principle of sovereignty is maintained. States choose to participate, and do so on the basis of equality. This respect for the principle of sovereign-equality is one reason why new, small, and weak states find international organizations congenial institutions. Most international organizations also have a second organ, a smaller, executive board, that is a group of states, elected by the general conference, which meets on a more frequent basis, typically quarterly. This executive group will be mandated by the conference to design programmes determined in outline by the larger conference. The policies and programmes determined by these two are then implemented by the third organ, the secretariat of the organization, sometimes referred to as the international civil-service, although no such unified body exists. These are career civil servants employed by and loyal to the organization. The Executive Head or Secretary General of the organization and his or her staff are pledged neither to seek nor receive the instructions or favour of any member state.

In the performance of their duties the Secretary General and the staff shall not seek or receive instructions from any Government or from any other authority external to the Organization. They shall refrain from any action which might reflect upon their position as international officials responsible only to the Organisation.

Each member of the United Nations undertakes to respect the exclusively international character of the responsibilities of the Secretary General and the staff and not to seek to influence them in the discharge of their responsibilities.[5]

Despite these reciprocal commitments towards the inviolability of the secretariat, all member states wish to see their citizens well represented within the secretariat. Overt interference and favouritism are not permitted, but members like to see the style and culture of the organization reflect familiar patterns. Within the larger UN agencies the requirement to recruit on grounds of professional excellence has to be balanced by the requirements of 'equitable geographical representation'.[6]

International organizations may also be classified by their pattern of membership. Some may comprise as few as three states, such as the Rhine Commission, others may be regional, such as the Organization of American States, or Arab League. Some may be potentially universal, such the United Nations itself, and the sixteen specialized agencies such as the World Health Organization (WHO) or International Labour Organization (ILO). These are only *potentially* universal, recognizing that a very small number of states may decline to join, or may indeed withdraw from these organizations. Switzerland has never joined the UN on the grounds that the Charter obligations, to provide military assistance on the bidding of the Security Council, are a violation of neutrality. The USA and the UK have both withdrawn from UNESCO since 1985, citing a variety of objections and disenchantments with the administration and financial conduct of the organization. Also, some states are subject to campaigns of exclusion, either on political grounds or because of representational disputes concerning rival claims to the seat. South Africa has largely withdrawn from the UN system on the former grounds. The communist government of China (1949–71), the two German states (1949–71), and, since 1979, the Cambodian government, have each in their time been unable to take up their UN seats.[7]

International organizations may be further classified by their voting systems. In almost all cases the members take decisions in the organization on the basis of sovereign equality, or one state, one vote. (Exceptions do exist, such as the IMF, in which voting rights are weighted to deposits contributed. Also in the Council of Ministers of the European Community where a complex weighting formula gives the four largest members ten votes, the smallest two votes, and intermediate values to the others.[8]) However, although the sovereign right to vote is egalitarian, the voting systems of international organizations vary widely. Some operate by simple majority, others by qualified majority, and some proceed only by consensus, that is without the objection of any party. (This last, is near to, but not the same as unanimity, which requires a formal vote of all in favour.) Sometimes several systems will be contained in one organization.

A complex example is the UN. In the universal membership General Assembly, resolutions are adopted by simple majority (except for the budget, which requires a two-thirds vote). In the fifteen-member Security Council, procedural resolutions need a qualified majority of at least nine of the fifteen (i.e. a 60 per cent majority). On substantive resolutions, in addition to the nine out of fifteen requirement, five of the fifteen, that is the permanent members, China, France, UK, USA, and USSR, can cast their veto, and so defeat a resolution on which the veto-holding state would otherwise be in a minority of one. A recent study of veto behaviour in the UN revealed that in the period 1946 to 1989 the USSR used its veto on 114 occasions, the USA on 67, the UK on 30, France on 18, and China just on 3.[9]

The voting system that members are willing to accept, especially any diminution of the principle of sovereign equality ('one member, one vote'), can sometimes reveal a great deal about the attitudes of the members to the organizations' true worth. Members will live with the possibility of defeat in an organization from which they derive, on balance, greater benefits than costs.

Where vital, or imagined, national interests are at stake, such as in the UN Security Council, and the EEC Council of Ministers, it is more likely to find a more restrictive voting system.

## III. Why do States Create International Organizations?

States create, use, and value international organizations for many different purposes. States may also misuse, and undervalue international organizations. However, once created, international organizations are only very rarely dissolved.

Harold Jacobson suggests that international organizations serve five purposes in international relations. They provide information for the benefit of their members. They create norms or standards of conduct. They can also create rules which are binding on the members. (This is almost always controversial. For instance, UN General Assembly resolutions are not binding, whereas Security Council resolutions *are* binding, but are often ignored; the European Communities' so-called regulations are directly binding on the twelve member states and are superior to domestic law in those countries.[10])

The fourth tier in Jacobson's scheme is that international organizations may be able to supervise the rules they set. This suggests the need for a quasi-juridical authority. However, supervision can take the more passive form of verification activities, such as the role of the International Atomic Energy Agency (IAEA). Under the terms of the Non-Proliferation Treaty (NPT) the IAEA has rights to monitor and inspect the nuclear reactor installations of the signatories. The inspections are designed to verify compliance with the treaty, under which the states pledge not to develop nuclear weapons as a by-product of civil power programmes. Finally, international organizations may provide programmes or services to the members and to the larger international community. Each of the specialized agencies is engaged in promoting economic development in the Third World membership. The WHO programme of immunization for the global eradication of smallpox is one famous case. The ILO and IAEA run major training programmes in their special fields. The UN's own organs such as the Children's Fund (Unicef) and the High Commission for Refugees (UNHCR) are engaged in humanitarian relief in places and on occasions when the state is literally unable, or unwilling, to discharge its duties to protect human life and welfare. The rescue and restoration of endangered monuments such as Abu Simbel, Machu Picchu, and Borobadur by Unesco, not only assists respectively, Egypt, Peru, and Indonesia but is an example of international action to preserve sites of world cultural heritage.

Jacobson's categories describe stages in the utility and acceptance of international organizations. Another way of describing their activity is to classify the fields of multilateral diplomacy in which they are appropriate, namely functional, regional, and security roles.

The multilateral foreign policy agenda increasingly challenges the centrality of bilateral relations, and international organizations are recognized as the places *where* multilateral diplomacy is conducted. The multilateral agenda has lengthened with the century, and international organizations which were originally created to manage what were then new technologies of mail and telegraphs, and to enforce new norms such as the suppression of piracy and slave traffic, now attempt the management of new technical and humanitarian problems. Examples of these would include: satellite communications, air-traffic control, copyright and patent protection, AIDS research, ozone depletion, basic needs for economic development such as water quality and the global eradication of smallpox, and also the conservation of Antarctica and of whale and fish stocks. These cases possess two distinctive characteristics. First, the issue concerned is intrinsically international, in that successful regulation cannot be achieved by one state acting alone. Secondly, the threat or use of military force is not a credible option to encourage compliance. When these two conditions coincide, the rationale for international organizations in their most ubiquitous *functional* role is found.

These economic, technical, and welfare functions are the realm of the specialized agencies and the UN's numerous organs. The specialized agencies, of which the International Telegraph Union of 1865 is the oldest, have therefore been a feature of international relations for over a century, and they pre-date the UN by eighty years. The functional approach at one level is an expression of the routine conduct of relations between states. The agencies provide the mechanism for states to engage in relationships of interdependence.[11]

The larger functional agencies were created by their members because some services useful to them are beyond the ability of the sovereign territorial state to provide. The state is an essentially seventeenth-century institution, and one which has been shown to be frequently less efficient, and sometime incapable of supplying its citizens with twentieth-century needs.[12]

The rationale for these agencies is essentially pragmatic and utilitarian. The rise of industrialization creates opportunities for the exploitation of new technologies which sometimes by their physical nature are beyond the capacity of a single state to supply, and which more often are capable of being operated with greater efficiency, or economies of scale, if shared between several states. This is the sort of practical purpose that lay behind the creation of the International Telegraph Union (ITU) in 1865, the Universal Postal Union (UPU) in 1874, and the World Meteorological Union (WMO) in 1873. These specialized agencies were created up to eighty years prior to the foundation of the United Nations with which they are now linked. New technologies have spawned new incentives for regulation, as in the cases of the International Civil Aviation Organization (ICAO) of 1948 and the International Atomic Energy Agency (IAEA) of 1957. Central to the functionalist's case for the creation of these organizations is the belief that these technical services are in some sense less political, or less controversial than many issues that cause deep divisions in international relations such as territorial disputes or ethnic antipathy. At its most modest the functional scheme suggests that states will be able to separate their functional and political interests and be willing to enter into elaborate schemes of international organization despite the other objective disputes they may have with each other.

The larger purpose of the functional agencies, dubbed the creation of a 'working peace system' by Mitrany, is a highly questionable construct so far as the universal agencies are concerned. Claude, particularly, suggests a quite contrary pro-position. Rather than states finding their conflicts moderated by their need to maintain common services, he suggests that states will only enter into functional co-operation, and the mutual vulnerability it implies, if they have a high degree of political trust in the other parties. In this viewpoint peace is the pre-condition not the product of functionalism. However, at the regional level, particularly in the example of the European Community, the process of renouncing force as an instrument of policy is seen as commonplace. The founding purpose of the original Coal and Steel Community (ECSC) was, in Robert Schuman's words, 'to make war not only unthinkable but materially impossible'. This view, ambitious or perhaps naïve in 1951, is now accepted as the *raison d'être* of the EC and its basis in Franco-German *rapprochement*.[13]

Regional organizations such as the Organization of American States (OAS), the Organization of African Unity (OAU), and the Arab League, offer their members an arena in which to debate matters of common concern, and for mediation of disputes and conflicts between members. The formulation of a common response to an external threat may dominate the proceedings of such organizations. The OAU has exhibited great cohesion on the question of South Africa, and the Arab League a similar unity concerning Israel. They are frequently less able to act as mediators in the more intractable intra-mural disputes between the members. The civil wars, attracting substantial cross-border interference from neighbours in the former Spanish Sahara, Sudan, Ethiopia, and Uganda have defied OAU solution. A greater degree of success has been noted in the cases of Chad (1985) and the Katangese insurgency in Zaire (1978). Perhaps significantly, it was the UN and a supporting group of western states including the US, West Germany, and the UK who as a contact group were able to achieve the successful negotiation of a tripartite pact between Angola, Cuba, and South Africa in December 1988. This provided for the termination of South African rule in Namibia and the withdrawal of Cuban forces from Angola. Boycott diplomacy (South Africa is *not* a member of the OAU), may compel a state to bargain, but by definition an ostracized state can only bargain with those states which will sit with it. The Arab League has been similarly unable to secure a necessary degree of cohesion to terminate the Lebanese civil war that raged from 1975 to 1990, and was bitterly divided on the question of Iraqi annexation of Kuwait in August 1990 and subsequent military operations against Iraq. The European Coal and Steel Community of 1951, the EEC, and Euratom of 1957, have evolved as the most thoroughly integrated regional organization in the modern international system. Twelve states of over 320 million persons have formed the largest free-trade area (by volume) in the world. Free movement of employment, capital, goods, and services is scheduled for 1992. The EC members have created habits and organs of co-operation across a range of economic, social, and political issues. By 1991 the Community had to face fundamental questions on monetary and political union, also the previously unmentionable question of defence collaboration in the post-Cold-War world. The process of integration had proceeded so far in some respects, that the logical, yet very divisive step of federation was openly canvassed. How far the UK was prepared to countenance the creation of a single European currency proved decisive in the events surrounding Margaret Thatcher's resignation as Prime Minister in December 1990. However, changing the Prime Minister did not change the question.

The most ambitious role proposed for international organization during this century has been in collective security. This was largely a preoccupation of the 1920 and 1930s, when international organization was associated with an idealist critique of the system of sovereign states, that is, with varieties of economic sanctions, collective military force, and world government. These approaches shared the belief that the 'international anarchy' of sovereign states could be regulated by law and organization, in a way analogous to the rule of law within each state.[14]

Collective security proposed that coercive power could be used as an instrument of international order by a majority of responsible, peace-loving states, acting in concert in a world organization. The incentive for any one state to use force would, in the first instance, be deterred, and failing deterrence, victims of aggression would be defended and their sovereignty restored by investing the right to use force in the collective responsibility and actions of the members. Since neither the League of Nations (1919–46) nor the United Nations since 1945 had their own autonomous military resources, in practice, collective security required the great powers of the day to act *in the name of* the organization. This explains the marginalization of collective security associated with the 1930s. In the cases of Japan's annexation of Manchuria in 1931, and Italy's aggression against Ethiopia (then Abyssinia) in 1935, France and Britain, the key powers, entrusted with the responsibility to initiate collective action, chose not to. National interests, and imperialist double-standards, inhibited the League's senior members from acting on the norms they had so solemnly agreed to at the creation of the organization in 1919.

Elements of collective security were resurrected in the UN charter in 1945, but were qualified by the previously cited veto powers of the five permanent members of the Security Council. In consequence the UN has only been able to make judgements on acts of aggression, and organize an economic or military response in those cases that meet the joint interests of China, France, the UK, USA, and USSR. The members of the UN confer upon the Security Council the primary responsibility for the maintenance of international peace and security (Article 24). Furthermore, the members agree to accept and carry out the decisions of the Security Council (Article 25). The Charter authorizes the Security Council to determine when an act of aggression, or a situation likely to lead to a breach of international peace and security had occurred (Article 39). Thereafter the Security Council may vote to apply economic sanctions, and may finally authorize collective military actions to uphold or to restore international order (Articles 41 and 42). The UN has no independent military resources. The Charter envisaged that forces committed under Article 42 would be volunteered by the members, and that the UN Military Staff Committee would appoint a commander (Articles 43 and 47). In practice the United Nations has never fully met these conditions. The Korean War, 1950–3, was fought under the auspices of the General Assembly, whilst the war for the restoration of Kuwait, initiated after 16 January 1991, under the terms of Resolution 678, was not under UN command. These cases, and the *ad hoc* development of an entirely separate concept of peacekeeping will be discussed shortly.

Prior to the actions taken against Iraq in 1991, the only previous occasion on which the Security Council had acted to authorize the use of force was in the first days of the Korean crisis in 1950. The Security Council was only able to act on the Korean question because the USSR was absent from the Security Council and therefore unable to use its veto. When the Soviets returned, and duly vetoed further Security Council action in Korea, the large western majority in the organization then utilized the General Assembly to continue to authorize actions in the UN's name for the duration of the Korean War. The Korean operation was fought under a UN flag, although the United States and South Korea provided approximately 90 per cent of the ground forces that were deployed. Bennett suggests: 'The Security Council resolutions gave legitimacy to [the] United States massive involvement in assisting the South Korean government and furnished the basis for the incorporation of contingents from other members into a United Nations army under United States command.'[15] From 1967 to 1980 the Security Council applied mandatory economic sanctions against Rhodesia (the former name for Zimbabwe), not on the grounds of aggression abroad, but in an attempt to reverse the unilateral declaration of independence made by the white minority government in defiance of British plans for independence under black majority rule. Sanctions in this case were undermined by the public refusal of South Africa and Portugal to apply the embargo. Similar attempts to apply mandatory sanctions to South Africa during the 1980s were obstructed by British and US objections.

The veto powers of the permanent members effectively prevented the UN from taking any role under Articles 41 and 42 for the duration of the Cold War. However, there did evolve within the UN a vital, although strictly limited, security role, namely peacekeeping. This innovation (for it was not anticipated) provides for the creation of lightly armed forces contributed by the member states and constituted as a UN force (the so-called blue-berets or blue-helmets, depending on the likely response to their presence!). Peacekeeping forces are deployed, with the consent of both parties, to supervise cease-fire agreements. They act as independent observers, to monitor compliance with withdrawal and cease-fire agreements. They act as a physical barrier separating the previously combatant and probably still hostile forces, and in some cases they can undertake humanitarian services amongst the divided civil population. Peacekeeping is seen at its most dramatic form in cease-fires between member states such as the UNDOF force on the Golan Heights, separating Israeli and Syrian forces since 1974, and the UNIIMOG operation separating Iranian and Iraqi forces since 1988. However, peacekeeping forces can also be deployed, with consent, into civil-war situations. UNFICYP has policed the Cyprus situation ever since 1964. In what is probably the most dangerous, and thankless, peacekeeping operation in the UN's history, 146 volunteer soldiers from a dozen nations have died since 1978 in the service of UNIFIL, separating Christian, Shiite, Palestinian, and Israeli forces in south Lebanon.[16]

During the period 1985 to 1990 the growing pace of American–Soviet *détente* led to a revival of the UN as an instrument in the resolution of several complex regional disputes. The Security Council members were able to agree complex formulas for negotiated settlements in which UN 'peacekeeping forces' played a third-party role to observe and verify the compliance of the parties with the agreements made. The withdrawal of Soviet forces from Afghanistan (UNGOMAP), the transition to independence in Namibia (UNTAG), Cuban troop evacuations from Angola (UNAVEM), and the supervision of a general election in Nicaragua (ONUCA) all benefited from this process. Peacekeeping has thus emerged as a distinctive contribution to maintenance of international peace and security, combining techniques of policing and verification acceptable to both parties.[17]

The Iraqi invasion of Kuwait on 2 August 1990 presented the Security Council with a very explicit case of aggression, followed days later by the formal announcement of the annexation of Kuwait by Iraq. The post-1989 solidarity of the Council was tested, and demonstrated, in a series of resolutions which attracted US–Soviet joint support, with dissent from Cuba and Yemen on some issues. The resolutions adopted condemned the invasion (Resolution 660 of 2 August), and applied mandatory economic sanctions, under Resolution 661 of 6 August. Further votes nullified the annexation (Resolution 662 of 9 August) and denounced the Iraqi seizure of foreign hostages and violations of diplomatic immunity (Resolution 664 of 18 August). Other resolutions, adopted over the next two months, concerned humanitarian aid and the enforcement of sanctions by naval blockade and air embargo. On 29 November the Security Council adopted Resolution 678, by 12 votes to 2 in favour, Cuba and Yemen opposed, and China abstaining. The resolution set a deadline of 15 January 1991 for Iraq to withdraw from Kuwait and rescind its annexation. Thereafter, the resolution authorized the member states to 'use all necessary means to uphold and implement Resolution 660 and all subsequent resolutions and to restore international peace and security in the area'. Sixteen hours after the expiry of the deadline US, British, Saudi, Kuwaiti,

French, and Italian air forces, deployed in the region since the August invasion, launched a massive aerial bombardment of Iraq's command and control centres, air-bases, and troop positions in both occupied Kuwait and Iraq. Critical opinions were expressed which suggested extending the time for sanctions to take effect. There was also criticism of the intensity of military attacks upon Iraq, considered operationally necessary to enforce the withdrawal from Kuwait. The 'Desert Storm' campaign, was launched entirely under the command and flags of the contributing states. The Security Council resolution 678 thus voted to legitimate the allies' actions, but it did not take responsibility for them, or take command of them, as a UN operation.

## IV.  What are the Limits of International Organization?

It is a commonplace observation that international organizations could do more to provide functional, regional, and security services for their members. International organizations represent 'islands' of organization and infrastructure in a 'sea' of relations between states. A similar gap between actual and potential responsibilities exists with respect to the provision of public goods and welfare services *within* states. It was fashionable in the 1980s to explain this gap in terms of an excess of expectations, or what conservatives called 'dependency culture'. Liberals instead blamed a failure of supply, or 'market failure', to explain the same phenomenon. However, a part of the explanation for this discrepancy can be found in politically neutral, and widely observed, problems in the provision of collective goods. This may be seen to apply internationally as well as domestically.

A characteristic of collective goods is that they are indivisible. My walking under a street light does not reduce the supply of street lighting available to others. A second characteristic is that collective goods can be consumed by people who do not pay for them. Street lights shine upon the poll-tax payer and the poll-tax dodger alike. This applies to similar goods provided on an international basis. A lighthouse guides both the drugs-smuggler and the merchant ship. In the days of fixed exchange rates, 1944–71, the IMF provided a degree of economic stability to members and non-members alike. Military alliances extend their security to countries that do not join them, and to members which do not contribute their full share of the burden. Great powers, or so-called hegemonic powers, will frequently tolerate smaller, 'free riders' because the great power will continue to provide that facility or service for reasons of its own national interest. It has been argued persuasively by writers on hegemony, notably Keohane, that many post-war functional regimes, such as the financial system built around the IMF, are based upon a hegemonic interest of the US which, incidently, provides a collective good, in this case currency stability, that is enjoyed by others as well as itself. Similar arguments were current in NATO throughout the 1970s and 1980s. The leading role of the UK in creating ITU and UPU may have similar great-power needs at its root.[18]

The school of thought associated with the decline of American hegemony widely and perhaps prematurely discussed since the mid-1970s, explained the disenchantment of the US with the UN system, during the 1980s, in terms of the loss of leadership. The US, increasingly outvoted and marginalized within the UN, partly withdrew from the multilateral system, and thus undermined it, in the way that the withdrawal of a minor member could not affect it. As the provider of 25 per cent of the assessed contributions (or membership subscriptions) to the UN and its sixteen specialized agencies, the US has a unique capacity for either constructive or destructive action. In addition to the withdrawal from the ILO 1977–80, and from UNESCO since 1985, already cited, through-out the 1980s the US applied severe financial penalties to the UN through the mechanism of reduced and late payments. The crisis peaked on 2 December 1987 when the UN Secretary General announced that the US owed $122 million for that year (previously paid, most helpfully, in quarterly instalments, but that year delayed until the twelfth month), arrears of $147 million from the preceding year, and a sum of $67 million deliberately withheld. The impact upon the UN may be judged when this cash shortfall of $320 million is compared to the annual budget of the UN of just $824 million (half of the biennial 1988–9 budget of $1,769 million). The Bush administration presented budgets to Congress during 1989–90 to restore the full funding of the UN and a five-year programme to clear accumulated arrearage. Congress approved these plans, and made the first full payment of UN dues for over five years, when it adopted HR 5021 in October 1990.[19]

In a rational-actor framework, individuals and states both frequently take selfish decisions whilst hoping that others will take the more onerous, expensive, or honourable course. Commuters drive to work alone, blaming others for traffic congestion. Some states continue to raise their levels of greenhouse-gas emissions whilst urging others to lower theirs. States may enlarge their nuclear weapons arsenals, in a time of lessening tensions, whilst querying other states' rights to practise nuclear proliferation. However, as equally rational actors, most other individuals and states also act selfishly, and so create, as a result of individually rational decisions, a situation in which *all* pay greater costs than would have been incurred had the more socially responsible option been chosen. Thus commuters sit in traffic jams rather than taking the train or sharing their cars; global warming proceeds as no one state is prepared to cut its emissions, and states expend great resources on arms races for no enhancement in their security. These very special conditions are known as a 'prisoner's dilemma'.[20] What is the contribution of international organizations in these situations? Individuals and states frequently suffer high penalties for their selfishness, and yet still persist in that selfish behaviour because they cannot make commitments which are binding, public, and simultaneous, three necessary conditions to prevent evasion, duplicity, and the 'you jump first' problem.

Families and social groups can enforce discipline on their members. States can enforce a degree of responsible behaviour within their frontiers through legislation, taxation, and by the provision of public utilities. Thus, both the free-rider problem can be controlled, and with it, the closely related impulse on the part of some citizens persistently to create 'prisoner's dilemmas' for themselves and others. When family and social order break down, the enforcement of responsible behaviour becomes harder. Yob culture and international relations share many common characteristics. However, states create, use, and largely abide by the rules of international organizations, because they represent the most explicit attempt on the part of sovereign, that is anarchic, or yob actors, to satisfy their own enlightened self-interest.

In an international organization membership is limited to those states which pay the required membership subscriptions. Each member can vote on proposals brought to the conference. In international organizations states make binding, simultaneous, and public commitments to each other, and so create in the international system the nearest approximation to legislation and taxation acceptable to a system of sovereigns. The form of such agreements may vary: a resolution adopted, a new programme or budget approved, a convention or treaty recommended for signature. The bargain upon which accommodation is reached may be to split the difference between the parties, that is to compromise; or they may agree on the lowest common denominator, that is to find a common, lowest standard; or they may identify a super-ordinate goal, that is a target that can only be attained by co-operation. An element of the Holy Grail attaches to the third. It is the stuff of the functional high-frontier. Negotiations on the law of the sea reflect the operation of all three modes. Competing claims to the North Sea continental shelf were resolved by the median-line principle, an example of splitting the difference. The numerous claims to extended territorial waters in the 1970s were resolved by allowing all coastal states a 12-mile territorial limit and a 200-mile Exclusive Economic Zone, an example of the lowest common denominator. (Some land-locked states might object that this was the highest common denominator.) The 1982 Treaty on the law of the sea recognized the ocean floor beyond the limits of territorial jurisdiction as a common heritage of mankind. The mineral wealth of this territory is to be exploited under a UN licensing and taxing system, and the profits channelled to development projects, an example of a super-ordinate goal. The first and second forms of agreement may appear the more mundane, political method. However, in numerous situations, such as the UK attitude to the EC budget in the 1980s, or attitudes to fixing ceilings on emission of $CO_2$ for the year 2000, real progress is measured by agreements struck in the manner of compromise and minimum standards.

International organizations may under-provide for the reasons associated with collective goods' theory and the prisoner's dilemma discussed above. Ironically they may also be neglected as victims of general prosperity. Private affluence and public squalor, often noted together as societies prosper, has its international equivalent. Prosperous states can sometimes neglect international organizations and may prefer to fund national solutions to what are really international problems. Some states may therefore reduce their support for international organizations, or withdraw from them, and leave the system for the poorer states to use on a declining financial base. This phenomenon, very evident in the attitude of the thirteen Geneva group nations to the UN in the 1980s, which has imposed a policy of 'zero budgetary growth' on the UN system, is exactly parallel to the neo-conservative critique of the domestic welfare system.[21]

Higher living standards permit an increasing proportion of the population to afford private solutions to what were, in their parents' time, public welfare problems. With higher disposable incomes, the choice of private schooling, a second car, and a private medical insurance scheme are preferable to public-sector schools, crowded buses, and NHS waiting lists. It is not a choice that is open to *all*, but this is why both public services *and* international organizations may suffer a decline in the quality and patronage of the services they provide as general prosperity rises. It is not accidental that the governments most actively promoting the last decade's vogue for privatization of public utilities have simultaneously been the most critical of UN pretensions to regulation at the universal level. This has been linked with some degree of validity to a subsidiary argument concerning the 'politicization' of the agencies, namely the subversion of their proper functional purpose by the extraneous 'political' issues. President Reagan and Prime Minister Thatcher both withdrew their countries from UNESCO, both declined to sign the Montego Bay Convention on the Law of the Sea, after a fourteen-year negotiation of a comprehensive 320 article treaty between 1968 and 1982. Both objected to the provisions for UN-licensed exploitation of the common-heritage sea-bed mining provisions. Both were also in the forefront of moves, during the 1980s, to impose the zero-budgetary growth throughout the UN and its agencies.

However, in international relations, unlike the US and UK, the poor are the massive majority, not a numerically marginal underclass, the inadequacies of infrastructure are more glaring, and the ability of sovereign states to service those needs most obviously inadequate. For these reasons the confrontation between the voting power of the poor majority of states and the financial power of the small minority of developed countries is acute, and has been a persistent feature of political discourse in international organizations, particularly within the UN, throughout the last decade.

The argument above suggests grounds to doubt the continuing appeal and relevance of international organizations. There are, however, some conditions in which national solutions cannot actually succeed. There is no national immunity to the threat of rising sea-levels, although the impact of this phenomenon will be uneven between states. Similarly the continued release of CFC and other ozone-damaging gases, if continued by even a small number of states, will produce consequences for all states, although again with uneven impacts, as susceptibility to skin cancers is highly variable within and between racial groups. Desertification continues to impact very adversely upon a comparatively small number of states, but the creation of large numbers of environmental refugees, and the possibility of new, or revived conflicts over water resources and marginal land will, by definition, create grave threats to the security of states with sustainable resources from neighbouring states with depleted resources. Therefore, even if climatic change, desertification, and loss of marginal lands are more likely to impact more adversely on Third World countries, developed countries cannot avoid costs to themselves if they fail to take appropriate actions, both unilaterally and collectively. In these situations the role of international organization is not only to provide the forum in which negotiation can occur. To move from norms to rules to the supervision of rules needs a comprehensive regime for verification (cheats will be detected), for sanctions (cheats will be penalized), and for redistribution (co-operative poorer parties will be rewarded). This last element is crucial to the cluster of prisoner's dilemmas surrounding the protection of the natural environment. The elimination of CFCs, the reduction in emissions of $CO_2$, and calls to create world heritage sites on other people's sovereign territory, such as the Brazilian rain-forest, logically require reimbursement for the poorest who forgo fast routes to economic growth already enjoyed by the historic polluters of the North.

## V. What Roles do INGOs Play?

INGOs are harder to define with precision than IGOs. At the margins of the INGO world are associations, campaigns, and movements which are more properly defined as transnational rather than international. That is to say that they are founded, headquartered, and run from one country, with subsidiary operations in several or many other countries. These essentially hierarchical organizations do not satisfy the criteria of participation and election, that is the degree of democratization characteristic of an organization, and are therefore not discussed here. The UN's own attempt to distinguish IGOs from INGOs was made in the Economic and Social Council Resolution 288 (X) of June 25 1968. This simply referred to 'any international organization which is not established by inter-governmental agreement'. The practice adopted here is to use the criteria established by the Union of International Associations, publishers of the biennial *Yearbook of International Organization*, an indispensable reference work for students of international organization.

The UIA criteria are exacting. Among the prominent exclusions are transnational, or so-called multinational corporations, religious orders, and criminal syndicates. To meet the criteria of the UIA, INGOs must have genuinely international aims with operations in at least three countries. Similarly, the membership must embrace at least three countries. INGOs must also possess a formal structure with a headquarters. The officers of the organizations should be elected and rotated. The financial resources of the organization must be drawn from at least three countries. This rule serves to exclude numerous 'front' organizations which are, in political reality, created to serve a foreign government interest. The organization must also be non-profit-making. This excludes business corporations, even those that make losses. The UIA also excludes educational institutions, social clubs, and any secret society, whether or not the members exchange funny handshakes.

Despite these exclusions over 4,000 organizations are classified as INGOs, and through these rules a very wide number of famous organizations are brought into the ambit of international organization studies, for example: the International Committee of the Red Cross, Amnesty International, Greenpeace, and the

International Planned Parenthood Federation. Some authors note that hybrid forms of international organization do exist, exactly on the question of their fusion of IGO and INGO elements. IGOs frequently admit INGOs as observers to their proceedings. The basis of the Ecosoc resolution referred to above was exactly to determine the rights of such observers. There are also organizations which seat both government and private representatives. The venerable International Labour Organization is in this category, with government, trade unions, and employers seated in the ratio 2 : 1 : 1 in all of the tiers of the organization. However, membership of the organization is a government decision which would seem firmly to establish the IGO-dominant basis of this particular hybrid.

INGOs frequently appear both more popular and more active than the functionally relevant IGO. In the field of disaster relief, famine relief, population control, the environmental consciousness-raising, for instance, Oxfam, the International Planned Parenthood Federation, and Greenpeace are better known to the general public than the appropriate UN organs: the UN Disaster Relief Organization (UNDRO), the UN Fund for Population Activities (UNFPA), and the UN Environmental Programme (UNEP). Partly this reflects different mandates, partly different house style. In the environmental case, for instance, Greenpeace exists to mobilize public opinion, to publicize gross incidents of pollution, species extinction, and corporate and governmental malpractice. UNEP, by contrast, exists as a research organization, and as a negotiating forum. It has played a crucial role in providing the forum in which the Vienna Convention and Montreal Protocols on ozone-depleting substances were negotiated. Its Inter-Governmental Panel on Climate Change (IPCC) is the most significant expert working group on global warming. However, UNEP delegates do not chain themselves to embassies, nor do its secretariat staff perform publicity stunts, nor do they employ rock-stars to promote Amazonian folk-lore. These are intrinsically more media-friendly activities than meetings of men in grey suits, which constitute the intergovernmental forum, and vote the funds for climatic research. The international system probably needs both sorts of activity.

Other INGOs, especially those in the field of disaster relief, have attracted a loyal and supportive public following. The sources of this are readily apparent. *Esprit de corps*, tight financial practices, a limited target of operations, and a staffing policy based upon volunteers and idealists, have advantages compared to some UN agency practices. Bureaucratization, overlapping competencies, a sectorial attitude to development and budgeting, and a recruitment and personnel policy constrained by considerations of 'equitable geographical representation', as well as poor standards, all contrast with INGOs and inhibit the IGO response.[22]

## VI.  Conclusion

International organizations are central, not peripheral to international relations. Whether individual readers approach the international system from a realist, pluralist, or structuralist perspective, international organizations are, at minimum, the place where an increasingly long and complex agenda of multilateral diplomacy is conducted. The issues discussed in the third part of this volume each present opportunities, and some necessities, for multilateral diplomacy.

The disappointments associated with the false promises of collective security did much to damage popular and academic assessment of the worth of international organization in the mid-century. Disputes continue today concerning the efficiency of the UN system, the overtly political role of many INGOs, and the limits to collective action, short of a federal union, to which the twelve members of the European Community can agree, on issues such as monetary union, foreign policy co-operation, and the vexed issue of a security co-operation. For the UN system the confrontations of the 1980s are easing. In particular, the financial crisis is near to resolution. The Committee of eighteen created by the Secretary General, which reported in August 1986, advocated seventy-one specific reforms of the UN's internal procedures. The most important of these, namely the adoption of budgetary reforms including the insistence upon consensus procedures in the crucial Committee for Programme and Co-ordination (CPC) converted the US administration to the resumption of full funding. The need for global negotiation on a range of environmental issues has raised the expectations of both governments and public in the early 1990s. The appropriateness of the UN as a forum to negotiate binding and simultaneous agreements on climate change, ozone protection, toxic-waste disposal, the conversation of biological diversity, and forestry resources, is not seriously questioned. What is open to question is the willingness of states to bargain seriously on the issues at stake. The 1985 Vienna Convention, and subsequent Montreal Protocol on the protection of the ozone layer, has demonstrated the capacity of the international system to act swiftly and convincingly on a multilateral issue of great importance. Most other issues on the agenda of environmental diplomacy will involve more complex compromises, and hence slower and less comprehensive agreements. At the close of the century the proper study of international organization is thus of renewed importance for the resolution of a new security dilemma, that of environmental security.

## Appendix: A Note on the UN System

In addition to the General Assembly, Security Council, and Secretariat, the other principal organs of the UN are the Economic and Social Council, the International Court of Justice, and the near-extinct Trusteeship Council. Additional activities are directed through a number of programmes tabled below.

### UN Organs Linked to the General Assembly
Membership is tied to the UN and the organs are funded partly from UN assessed contributions and partly from voluntary contributions.

> UNCTAD: Conference on Trade and Development, Geneva
> Unicef: Children's Fund, New York
> UNHCR: High Commission for Refugees, Geneva
> UNDP: Development Programme, New York
> UNEP: Environmental Programme, Nairobi
> WFP: World Food Programme, Rome
> UNFPA: Fund for Population Activities, New York

### Assessed Contributions
Membership subscriptions are calculated on a sliding scale ranging from 25 per cent for the USA to 0.01 per cent for the poorest smallest states. The assessed contributions fund all Security Council and General Assembly activities, the organs named above, all Secretariat costs, i.e., translation services for 159 states in six official languages (English, French, Spanish, Russian, Chinese, and Arabic), plus all salary costs of

professional staff. Peacekeeping activities are, however, charged to separate accounts.

## Bi-ennium budget
The UN 1990–1 budget was $1.9 billion.

## Peacekeeping
A total of eighteen UN peacekeeping operations have been mounted. They have ranged in size from thirty-eight observers currently serving in Kashmir to the 19,828 troops who served in the Congo, 1960–3. They range in duration from the operations of a year in West New Guinea in 1962–3 to the Truce Supervisory Organization that has operated continuously in Jerusalem since 1948. The leading contributors of military forces have been: Canada (twelve operations); Sweden (eleven); Denmark, Finland, and Ireland (nine); Norway and India (eight); Italy, Netherlands, and New Zealand (six).

## The Specialized Agencies in the UN System
These are independent organizations (IGOs) with their own membership and budgets. The Specialized Agencies are formally related to the UN by the annual report to EcoSoc.

| Agency, date of formation, and HQ | Membership |
| --- | --- |
| UPU: Universal Postal Union (1874) Berne | 168 |
| WHO: World Health Organization (1946) Geneva | 166 |
| ITU: International Telecommunications Union (1865) Geneva | 160 |
| FAO: Food and Agricultural Organization (1945) Rome | 158 |
| WMO: World Meteorological Organization (1873) Geneva | 158 |
| Unesco: United Nations Educational, Scientific, and Cultural Organization (1945) Paris | 158 |
| ICAO: International Civil Aviation Organization (1944) Montreal | 156 |
| ILO: International Labour Organization (1919) Geneva | 150 |
| IMF: International Monetary Fund (1944) Washington, DC | 149 |
| IBRD: International Bank for Reconstruction and Development (1945) | 148 |
| UNIDO: United Nations Industrial Development Organization (1967) Vienna | 136 |
| IDA: International Development Association (1960) Washington, DC | 133 |

| Agency, date of formation, and HQ | Membership |
|---|---|
| IMCO: International Maritime Consultative Organization (1948) London | 128 |
| IFC: International Finance Corporation (1956) Washington, DC | 127 |
| IAEA: International Atomic Energy Agency (1957) Vienna | 113 |
| GATT: General Agreement on Tariffs and Trade (1948) Geneva | 108 |

## Notes

1. C. Archer, *International Organizations* (London: Unwin-Hyman, 1983), 35. This concise, comprehensive, and affordable text contains a most comprehensive discussion of the definition and variety of international organization.
2. From Inis Claude, Jr., *Swords into Plowshares* (New York: Random House, 1964), 4.
3. See R. Keohane and J. Nye, *Power and Interdependence* (Boston: Little Brown, 1973), 5.
4. H. Jacobson, *Networks of Interdependence* (New York: Knopf, 1979), 8.
5. UN Charter, Art. 100. Very similar language is used in the equivalent Articles of other UN agencies. Despite their hybrid origins as government nominees, the European Commission are bound by a similar obligation and hence their popular description as guardians of the Treaty of Rome.
6. See, for example, UN Charter, Art. 101 (3), which states: 'Due regard shall be paid to the importance of recruiting staff on as wide a geographical basis as possible.'
7. See M. F. Imber, *The USA, ILO, UNESCO and IAEA: Politicization and Withdrawal in the Specialized Agencies* (London: Macmillan, 1989), for further discussion of politicization, and the cases of US withdrawal and boycott.
8. In full, the Council of Ministers scheme is: Germany, France, Italy, and UK (10 votes); Spain (8); Belgium, Greece, Netherlands, and Portugal (5); Denmark and Ireland (3); Luxemburg (2). Not only is the scheme weighted in the manner above, it is also a qualified system requiring 70% or 54 of the votes out of the 76 available. In certain circumstances the vote must be unanimous. See W. Nicoll and T. C. Salmon, *Understanding the European Communities* (London: Philip Allan, 1990), 56–7.
9. The 10 non-permanent members are elected on a regional formula for

two-year terms, 5 from the African-Asian group, 2 from Latin America, 1 from Eastern Europe, and 2 from the West Europe and Others (WEOG) group. The language of the relevant Article 27 refers to needing the affirmative votes of the 5. However, UN practice does not recognize either absence or abstention as a veto. This matter proved crucial to the debates on the outbreak of the Korean War when the Soviets believed their absence alone was enough to constitute a veto. The resolution to organize a military force for the defence of South Korea was only adopted in their absence. See A. Le Roy Bennett, *International Organization*, 3rd edn. (Englewood Cliffs, NJ: Prentice Hall, 1984), 152–3. For a comprehensive discussion of the use of the veto, 1946–89, see Sally Morphet, 'Resolutions and Vetos in the UN Security Council: Their Relevance and Significance', *Review of International Studies*, 16 (1990), 341–59.

10. Nicoll and Salmon, *Understanding the European Communities*, 77.
11. For a full discussion of the foundation and role of the functional organizations, see Douglas Williams, *The Specialized Agencies and the United Nations* (London: Hurst, 1987). For a fuller statement and critique of the functional theory, see Imber, *The USA, ILO, UNESCO and IAEA*.
12. Functionalism is most closely associated with the writings of David Mitrany in the 1930s. However, many of the specialized agencies have their origins in the late nineteenth century. Mitrany's contribution to understanding international organization lay in his suggestion that a system of such functional agencies could create a 'working peace system' of technological and economic interdependence that would moderate the conflicts of states on traditional issues such as territory. See his *The Functional Theory of Politics* (Oxford: Robertson, 1975). The coincidence of economic interdependence and the declining utility of military force to resolve the issues it affects is also discussed by Keohane and Nye, *Power and Interdependence*.
13. For discussion of these founding purposes of the European Community, see Nicoll and Salmon, *Understanding the European Communities*, Chap. 1.
14. The full flavour of the idealist approaches can be captured in a still widely available library volume, *The Intelligent Man's Way to Prevent War*, ed. Leonard Woolf (London: Gollancz, 1933). A fuller contemporary account of collective security may be found in all major textbooks of international organization, such as Archer, *International Organizations*; Bennett, *International Organization*; and Jacobson, *Networks of Interdependence*.
15. Bennett, *International Organizations*, 152.
16. For full discussion of peacekeeping in a number of Middle Eastern

cases, see J. Mackinlay, *The Peacekeepers* (London: Unwin-Hyman, 1989). This also compares the UN operations with the so-called multinational force sent by France, Italy, UK, and USA to Beirut in 1982. The latter, not a UN peacekeeping operation, met with a more problematic and violent reception.

17. The most comprehensive account of peacekeeping may be found in Alan James, *Peacekeeping* (London: Macmillan, 1990).

18. See R. Keohane, *After Hegemony* (Princeton, NJ: Princeton University Press, 1984).

19. See Imber, *The USA, ILO, UNESCO and IAEA*, 130–3 and *Keesings*, 34 (1988), 35868–9. Also *Washington Weekly Report*, UNA-USA, XVI-34 (19 Oct. 1990).

20. The name derives from a situation pioneered by game theorists in the 1950s. See K. Deutsch, *The Analysis of International Relations* (Englewood Cliffs, NJ: Prentice Hall, 1968), 120–2. Two prisoners of a corrupt regime are kept in solitary confinement. Each prisoner is separately made the following offer: make a false statement against the other, be released, and collect a reward. The other prisoner will then be convicted and hanged. 'What if I refuse to make such a statement?' asks the first prisoner. 'Well', says the warder, 'if the other prisoner makes a statement against you, he will be rewarded and freed and you will hang.' 'What if we both make statements?' asks the prisoner. 'You will both be given ten years' gaol for attempting to pervert the course of justice', comes the reply. 'What if neither of us makes such a statement?' asks the now desperate prisoner. 'Well, for want of evidence we will have to let you both go,' comes the reply. The 'game' (and a certain way to test a couple's affection for each other is to play this at parties) requires a decision between co-operation with or defection from the other player. The best outcome of defection is freedom and reward, the worst outcome of defection is ten years' imprisonment. The best outcome of co-operation is freedom, with no reward, the worst is death by hanging. Given the very real risk of the last, the rational actor will 'defect', both will therefore defect, and both play a heavy penalty for their failure to trust the other party.

In practice, the threat of death is only realistically applied in international relations when simulating first use of nuclear weapons. The more realistic opportunities to cheat or to co-operate repeatedly, as in, say, trade negotiations, create a form of indirect communication between the parties. Always playing the martyr or the saint can invite retaliation. See Robert Axelrod, *The Evolution of Cooperation* (Harmondsworth: Penguin, 1990).

21. The Geneva Group is an informal caucus of the western members in

the UN and each of the specialized agencies. The percentage contribution to the UN assessed contributions is noted below. Similar, but not identical apportionments are made to the agencies. Contributions are calculated by a complex and confidential formula which approximates to the share of world GNP. The group comprises: Australia (1.57%); Belgium (1.28%); Canada (3.08%); France (6.51%); W. Germany (8.54%); Italy (3.74%); Japan (10.32%); Netherlands (1.78%); Spain (1.93%); Sweden (1.32%); Switzerland (non member of UN); UK (4.67%); USA (25%). The Geneva Group therefore contribute 69.74% of assessed contributions. On the other hand the poorest 71 members of the UN contribute 0.01% and therefore have 71 votes out of 159 for less than 1% of the funds contributed. See Williams, *The Specialised Agencies and the United Nations.*

22. Maurice Bertrand, former director of the Joint Inspection Unit of the UN, was the author of a report in 1985 which revealed the extent of qualitative deficiencies in the personnel of the UN. See P. Taylor and A. J. R. Groom, *International Institutions at Work* (London: Pinter, 1988), 193–219.

# PART III. ISSUES

# EIGHT

# Nuclear Weapons and Arms Control

*Phil Williams*

## I. Do Nuclear Weapons Enhance or Undermine International Stability?

While many observers have regarded nuclear weapons as a danger, others have seen them as promoting a greater order and stability in interstate relations than has been evident at any time prior to the nuclear age. For some, the dominant reaction to the nuclear revolution has been fear and distaste; for others it has been a cautious optimism based partly on a belief that the weapons are too horrendous ever to be used and that the very possibility of their use imposes a degree of restraint upon governments that is unprecedented. These divergent attitudes are reflected in the current debate over European security in the post-Cold War era. Whereas opponents of nuclear deterrence regard the dismantling of the blocs and the removal of nuclear weapons from Europe as enhancing security, others see denuclearization as making Europe safe for a resurgence of ethnic and nationalist conflicts.[1]

To see prevailing attitudes towards nuclear weapons in terms of a simple dichotomy, however, would be a mistake. Views about the impact and utility of nuclear weapons are many and varied, and cover a wide range from those who believe that the weapons have no utility and should be abolished to those who believe that their very existence imposes a degree of prudence and stability that make them invaluable. In between are those who believe that they are crucial in deterring their use by others, but have no real purpose beyond this; those who believe they have real military utility and that serious plans should be made for their use; and those who believe that in so far as there are doctrines for operational use, then any use must be political and designed to convey messages to the adversary that would restore deterrence and bring hostilities to an end. For analytical convenience, however, the focus of this chapter will be on three groups: the abolitionists, the deterrers and arms controllers, and the targeteers.

## The Abolitionists

This group consists of those who believe the arms race is itself a potential cause of war and the crucial thing, therefore, is to eliminate the capacity for conducting hostilities. In this view nuclear weapons, as the most sophisticated and destructive form of armaments yet invented, are the single most important target for elimination. The implication is that by getting rid of the weapons it will be possible to reform international politics and move away from the situation described by Hobbes as a state of potential war. The abolitionists tend to be heir to liberal and radical ideas for the reform of world politics, and their proposals are often linked to an emphasis on international law and international organizations. For those who hold to this view weapons themselves, rather than other states, are regarded as the real enemy and the main target of their activities.

## The Deterrers and Arms Controllers

Members of this group believe that nuclear weapons have been positive in their effects, but that they are also dangerous. Consequently, it is necessary to ensure that the benefits are maintained while reducing or minimizing the dangers. This is a regulatory rather than a reformist approach to international politics, and one which has its intellectual roots in a Hobbesian view of the world. Members of this group traditionally see the problem in terms of managing a Superpower relationship in which both sides are not only heavily armed but locked in a series of highly dangerous security dilemmas. While stable deterrence advocates are generally pessimistic about the prospects for changing the character of international politics, they believe none the less that nuclear weapons have made it both necessary and possible to engage in prudent management of the international system. A criticism sometimes levelled at them is that although they are short-term pessimists about the prospects for fundamental change in international politics, they are long-term optimists about the prospects for successful management of the international system in the nuclear age.[2]

## The Targeteers

The third school of thought is that nuclear weapons, while obviously important, have not brought about the revolution in strategy that is sometimes claimed. War remains a continuation of politics by other means and the best way to prevent a nuclear war is to be prepared to fight and win it. Weapons may be more destructive than in the past, but the basic logic of warfare remains the same. Those who adhere to this position generally believe that nuclear weapons have military utility, that the prime target of nuclear weapons should be the adversary's military capabilities, that usable and controllable limited options are both necessary and feasible, and that deterrence can best be achieved through an evident capacity for nuclear war-fighting. In this view, nuclear weapons are different from earlier weapons in degree but not in kind and in order for them to have maximum peacetime impact, it is necessary to engage in rational policy planning for wartime use. Such planning has been seen as particularly important in order for the United States guarantee to Western Europe—so-called extended deterrence—to have any credibility in a situation in which the Soviet Union is capable of nuclear strikes on the American homeland.[3]

Many of those who hold to this third view—who have been appropriately characterized as 'strategic fundamentalists'—have tended to be less concerned with managing an anarchic and dangerous international system or handling a difficult relationship between two heavily armed Superpowers who have little understanding of each other, than with finding a way to inhibit an unscrupulous and inherently aggressive adversary.[4] The problem is seen not as how to alleviate the consequences of anarchy or reduce the tensions caused by the security dilemma but more simply in terms of preventing aggression by a malevolent state. Adhering to what Henry Kissinger once described as an 'inherent bad faith model' of the Soviet Union, many 'strategic fundamentalists' in the United States have traditionally believed that the Soviet Union could only be deterred from attacks not only on the American homeland but also, and almost equally important, on America's major allies, if the United States maintained strategic superiority. Not surprisingly, this group tended to regard disarmers as naïve and deterrence stability and arms control advocates as misguided. The problem in their view was the Soviet threat—nothing more and nothing less—a threat that stemmed from the inherent aggressiveness of a political system which extolled ideology, militarism, and totalitarian control.

It should be clear from this brief categorization that the three groups are divided about both the nature of the problem and the appropriate solution. They differ profoundly in terms of beliefs about whether nuclear weapons are positive or negative in their overall impact, the kind of plans that have to be made for their use, and the extent to which their use could be controlled as opposed to resulting in uncontrollable and potentially disastrous escalation. They also differ in their attitudes towards arms control. The abolitionists tend to be highly critical of anything which fails to achieve large-scale reductions in arms, while the military utility school generally resists restrictions on American weaponry and contends that force planning has to have priority over any effort to control or regulate armaments. The deterrence stability advocates in contrast tend to favour constraints on force structures and see arms control as a way of restraining force planners while still allowing governments to derive considerable utility from nuclear weapons.

Much of the debate over nuclear weapons can be seen in terms of the interplay among these groups and the positions they advocate. The respective impact of the groups, however, has fluctuated throughout the post-war period. In the 1950s it was the abolitionists who ostensibly set the terms of the debate; in the 1960s the arms controllers came to the fore—only to be challenged in the 1970s and early 1980s by the targeteers, before making something of a comeback in the later 1980s. Accordingly, the next section of this chapter looks briefly at the attempt to achieve nuclear disarmament as well as the subsequent emergence of deterrence and arms control theory. It also considers the purposes of arms control as defined by its proponents, the forms arms control can take, and the benefits that can be achieved through the implementation of arms control measures. The third section examines the arms control experience and suggests that there has been a significant departure from the theory both in terms of the purposes arms control was intended to serve and in the form that at least some arms control agreements have taken. The fourth section examines different views of the arms race and its consequences. The final section of the paper attempts to assess the future of arms control and gives particular attention to the impact of the end of the Cold War on the arms control agenda.

## II. How have Ideas about Arms Control Changed?

During the 1950s, the response to nuclear weapons took place at two distinct levels. At the public level there were insistent demands for general and complete disarmament (GCD) or, at the very least, the elimination of nuclear weapons. The idea was that all states, acting in concert, should divest themselves of their military capabilities, apart from those necessary to maintain domestic order. Such proposals, which were based on the conviction that weapons themselves cause war, were rooted in the pacifist tradition and in liberal and radical ideas about war and peace. Not surprisingly, therefore, the negotiations of the 1950s took place primarily in the United Nations framework, especially the Ten- and subsequently Eighteen-Nation Disarmament Committee.

The gap between the public advocacy and the policy level, however, was considerable. Although the negotiations were nominally multilateral, in practice it was the two Superpowers who dominated the agenda and took the initiative. Moreover, the Superpowers presented grandiose proposals which they knew would be unacceptable to each other. The Soviet Union accepted the need for nuclear disarmament but insisted that this must precede any efforts to verify that the agreed-upon measures were being implemented. The United States remained equally adamant that without adequate provision for verification no agreement was possible. Consequently, the negotiations were primarily exercises in propaganda and gamesmanship as Washington and Moscow introduced proposals which invariably included 'jokers', i.e., clauses which they knew would be rejected by the other side.

The adversary's rejection could then be held up as the reason for the breakdown of the negotiations.[5] In effect, these negotiations were little more than a continuation of the Superpower rivalry by other means. At the end of the 1950s and the beginning of the 1960s, however, there was an important transition in thinking about nuclear weapons and their role in the Superpower relationship.

The development of arms control theory was partly a response to the failure of the more ambitious schemes for disarmament, but it also reflected an acceptance of the virtues of nuclear deterrence. The philosophical underpinnings of this approach were enunciated in three separate studies: Hedley Bull's *Control of the Arms Race*, Donald Brennan's edited volume, *Arms Control, Disarmament and National Security*, and Thomas Schelling and Morton Halperin's *Strategy and Arms Control*.[6] Although there were differences over detail, the underlying philosophy of all three studies was very similar. The concern was with stabilizing the deterrence relationship between the Soviet Union and the United States. The basic theme was that arms control was more closely related to military strategy than it was to disarmament, and that it could best be understood as an attempt to regulate and stabilize the strategic relationship between the Superpowers. Indeed, arms control theory was based on an explicit acknowledgement that the military relationship with potential enemies involved strong elements of common interests. Although the Superpowers were adversaries and would remain so, this should not be allowed to obscure their mutual interest in avoiding a nuclear war, in minimizing the risks and the costs of the arms competition, and in curtailing the scope and violence of nuclear war should it occur in spite of all the efforts to prevent it. Accordingly arms control was defined by Schelling and Halperin as 'all forms of military cooperation between potential enemies in reducing the likelihood of war, its scope and violence . . . and the political and economic costs of being prepared for it'.[7] Bull's definition of arms control was very similar. In his view arms control was restraint, internationally exercised on the development, deployment, and use of armaments in order to promote national and international security.[8]

At this stage, strategy and arms control seemed to be natural accompaniments to one another, and the tensions between force

planning and arms control were neither fully appreciated nor fully
dealt with. The main concern in arms control thinking was
promoting stability and, initially, this did not seem inconsistent
with more traditional military thinking. Indeed, the focus on
stability grew, in part, out of Albert Wohlstetter's argument that
American deterrent forces also made tempting targets and that all
effort should be made, therefore, to make these forces invulnerable
and capable of retaliating after absorbing a surprise attack.[9]
Minimizing the vulnerability of United States strategic forces
made sense from a traditional military perspective and from the
perspective of stability. As a result there was no immediate
tension between arms control and nuclear force planning.

The concern with minimizing vulnerability, however, was not
simply a matter for the United States alone. This emerged very
clearly in the work of Schelling, and especially in his analysis of
the Sarajevo Crisis of July 1914. Schelling saw this crisis as a
situation in which the prevailing technology and the belief in the
advantage of striking first had placed a premium on speed—with
disastrous results. In effect, Schelling recognized the perverse
dynamics of the security dilemma, in which precautionary actions
are regarded by the adversary as preparatory for an attack.
Consequently they lead to counter-moves, which in turn generate
further precautionary measures. The result is a spiral of escalation
that is fuelled not by malevolence but by paranoia. Schelling and
other arms controllers were concerned that a similar process be
avoided in the nuclear age. Indeed, the definition of stability as
'assurance against being caught by surprise, the safety in waiting,
the absence of a premium on jumping the gun' reflected this
concern and the need to avoid what Schelling termed 'the
reciprocal fear of surprise attack'.[10]

This emphasis on reciprocal fear was one of the most important
factors which distinguished the arms controllers from the traditional strategists or the targeteers. By defining the problem as
inherent in the dynamics of US–Soviet relations, Schelling was
not only challenging the view that the Soviet Union was
exclusively responsible for the arms race, but was also recognizing
that Soviet behaviour could be driven by fear of the United States.
The 'strategic fundamentalists', in contrast, ascribed only aggressive motives to the Soviet Union, and were generally unwilling to
acknowledge that the United States might be seen in Moscow as a

threat. Not surprisingly, therefore, overt tension between the two groups began to emerge when the arms control advocates concluded that it was advantageous to minimize the vulnerability not only of one's own forces but also those of the adversary. The implication of this was that stability was best served if American strategic nuclear forces did not pose a threat to the strategic retaliatory forces of the Soviet Union. A stable balance of terror required that *neither* side have an advantage in going first and that *neither* be afraid that the other might perceive such an advantage.

The claim that it was not necessarily in the United States' interest for Soviet weapons to be vulnerable to a disarming first strike was rejected by those who approached strategic matters in more traditional terms. In their view, it was crucial that the United States retain a military advantage over the Soviet Union. Strategic superiority was deemed essential partly because of Soviet malevolence, but also because the United States had extended a nuclear guarantee to its allies in Western Europe and elsewhere. This guarantee would retain little credibility in a world where an American attack on the Soviet Union would be suicidal. Whereas arms control theorists gave priority to stability over extended deterrence, 'strategic fundamentalists' claimed that real stability would be achieved only through a continued American preponderance that would deter not only a nuclear attack upon the United States but nuclear and conventional attack on Western Europe. There is something of an irony here in that the West European allies have rarely been comfortable with the political assumptions of the targeteers even though it is this group which has been most sensitive to the requirements of extended deterrence. At the same time, the Europeans have been apprehensive that arms control arrangements might erode the credibility of nuclear deterrence of conventional attack in Europe. Their reasoning has been based on what Glenn Snyder termed the stability–instability paradox—actions that stabilize the nuclear deterrence relationship make lower levels of deterrence less credible.[11]

If the arms controllers have been concerned more about the central strategic relationship than alliance relations, they have also focused on ways to reduce the likelihood of accidental war, that is a war initiated in the belief that it had become unavoidable or had already been initiated by the adversary. For Schelling and Halperin, in particular, accidental war was pre-emptive war sparked by some unpredictable occurrence. Consequently, the stability that came from making strategic forces invulnerable would also make accidental war less likely. Measures to reduce the urgency of quick action could also be accompanied by steps to reduce the incidence of false alarm and to improve communications. Taken together such measures would minimize the prospects for surprise and reduce paranoia, thereby making pre-emption less necessary and accidental war far less probable.

Consequently, the arms control advocates were critical of those who opposed collaboration with the Soviet Union. Yet they were also critical of those who espoused schemes of disarmament (which they regarded as unrealistic) or who saw arms control as simply a way of saving money. Indeed, given that arms control was about promoting stability, and was concerned primarily with reducing incentives for initiating hostilities, its advocates acknowledged that it might actually cost more. Under certain circumstances, reductions in numbers could erode rather than enhance stability.[12] Conversely, a diversified force structure, which was inevitably rather costly, could help to maintain stability—and was worth developing in spite of the cost.

The concern with stability and with reducing the prospects of war through reciprocal insecurity, inadvertence, and accident provided the single most important theme in arms control thinking. It also meant that arms control advocates were less concerned with the form of arms control than with its consequences. Arms control could encompass any measures which enhanced stability or otherwise reduced the prospect of war. It included forms of restraint that could be exercised unilaterally and did not require formal agreement or even reciprocity by the adversary. The installation of permissive action links and other methods of ensuring that nuclear weapons could not be used without proper authorization was a form of unilateral arms control which the United States initiated in the 1960s. Although it was recognized that this did not require reciprocity to be beneficial, it was clearly in the American interest that the Soviet Union also improve its control procedures—and it appears that the United States provided some guidance on how best to do this.[13]

If reciprocity is not a prerequisite for certain forms of arms control, it may nevertheless be a desirable and important consequence of unilateral measures. In the early 1960s the idea of pursuing arms control through unilateral measures which encouraged reciprocal restraint by the adversary became a key theme in the writings of Charles Osgood. This notion, which was formally known as GRIT or graduated reciprocal reduction in tension, became a very popular idea.[14] Amitai Etzioni advocated the same kind of incremental policy and suggested that Soviet and American initiatives in halting nuclear testing prior to the Test Ban Treaty of 1963 showed the potential of such an approach.[15]

Although the GRIT idea was overtaken by more formal negotiations, the idea of unilateral initiatives emerged once again in the late 1980s and played a part in restoring momentum to the arms control process. Gorbachev's decision to make large uni-lateral cuts in Soviet troop levels, a decision that he announced at the United Nations in December 1988, was particularly important in this connection. In fact, there are some who argue that such unilateral initiatives are the most important model for the future: with the ending of the Cold War in Europe in November 1989, the best way to proceed with dismantling the military stand-off in Europe is through mutual unilateral reductions rather than through detailed set-piece negotiations which can easily become formalistic and bogged down in technicalities.[16] At the same time there are those who contend that without a formal agreement there is nothing to stop a state from reversing course and re-embarking on a military build-up. The arms control process of the future may in fact be something of a hybrid, with negotiation and unilateral actions taking place side by side. Although the govern-ments of NATO and the Warsaw Pact reached agreement on conventional force reductions in Europe in 1990, it seems very likely that negotiated reductions will be supplemented by unilateral arms reductions through the 1990s. While some observers believe that this is the best way to go others contend that the unilateral reductions will undermine the negotiations.

There has been general agreement between East and West, however, that the negotiations on conventional force reductions should also aim to create force structures that are defensive in nature and that minimize the fear of surprise attack. Arms control thinking that was developed at the nuclear level in the late 1950s and 1960s is being applied at the conventional level in the early 1990s. This can appropriately be described as structural arms control in that the main objective is to shape force structures in ways which enhance stability.

Whereas structural arms control constrains the size, shape, and possibly the deployment of each side's military forces, operational arms control—which is sometimes closely linked with confidence and security-building measures—imposes constraints on each side's military activities. By prohibiting or limiting particularly dangerous forms of military activity it helps to prevent clashes that could increase tension or cause incidents, thereby increasing the prospects of conflict between the nuclear powers. One of the first agreements of this kind was the 1972 Agreement on Avoiding Incidents at Sea. This measure effectively established rules for the road that both Soviet and American naval forces observed. The result was that the number of dangerous incidents and near collisions was significantly reduced.[17] In the last years of the 1980s as a major element in the Superpower dialogue there were increasing contacts between Soviet and American military leaders. These resulted in an agreement, signed in 1989, on avoiding dangerous military activities.

Although operational arms control stands in its own right, it overlaps with, and is sometimes seen as a contribution to confidence building measures or CBMs. These measures are designed to increase military transparency, enhance predictability, and minimize the prospects of surprise attack, thereby creating and enhancing confidence about the adversary's military activities. Advance notification of manœuvres, challenge inspection procedures, invitations to observers are some of the steps that have been taken in a process which began modestly with Basket One of the Helsinki Accords of 1975, was developed further in the Stockholm Agreement of 1986, and holds out considerable promise for Europe in the post-Cold-War era.

There is another kind of measure that fits the broad definitions of arms control offered by Schelling and Halperin and by Hedley Bull, and concerns communication between the governments of the United States and the Soviet Union. This form of arms control includes measures which maintain or improve communication channels between the rival powers, thereby enhancing the prospects for avoiding miscalculation or inadvertent escalation. The installation of the hot line in the aftermath of the Cuban Missile Crisis was designed to ensure that communication between the Superpowers in a crisis would be quick and easy. Although this was primarily a political rather than a military or strategic measure, it was a natural outgrowth of the concern with crisis stability, and in some respects the most important measure of arms control there has been. There have been several upgrades of the hot line to ensure a degree of redundancy. Moreover, in the early 1980s, prompted by both the rise in US–Soviet tensions and a number of false alarms in the United States' early warning system, there was considerable pressure from Senators Sam Nunn and John Warner for the creation of a nuclear-risk reduction centre. In the event, centres were established in Moscow and Washington in 1987, albeit on a very modest scale. Some critics argued that such centres were undesirable because they would add another layer of bureaucracy that could delay decisions in a crisis, while others claimed that they would be superfluous or irrelevant. Yet such measures extend the principle of the hot line in ways which facilitate serious communication, create a pattern of familiarity and understanding, and enhance what one analyst has termed 'procedural co-operation'.[18]

In other words, arms control can take different forms and contribute to the avoidance of war in a variety of ways. Although arms control theory was developed primarily in relation to the nuclear relationship between the Soviet Union and the United States it has been extended to embrace a variety of procedures and methods and to apply to the conventional as well as the nuclear level. The concern with stability also led very naturally into efforts to forestall the spread of nuclear weapons to other states. It was suggested that horizontal proliferation was potentially much more dangerous than continued vertical proliferation in the central strategic arms race. The argument was based partly on the grounds that Third World states would not be able to develop the control mechanisms and the invulnerable retaliatory forces that the Superpowers had developed, and partly on the fact that regional conflicts such as those in the Middle East and South Asia were in many respects more intractable and virulent than US–Soviet rivalry. The result of this concern was the Non-Proliferation Treaty, which was signed in 1968 and came into force in 1970. Although the Treaty has been signed by a large number of states, it has not succeeded in halting the spread of nuclear weapons. In addition to the major nuclear powers, it is clear that Israel, South

Africa, India, and Pakistan have a nuclear weapons capability. While the consensus opinion has been that proliferation is to be avoided where possible, Kenneth Waltz has argued that nuclear weapons compel those who have them and who have to deal with a nuclear armed adversary to behave with great prudence. Consequently, more may be better.[19] The great virtue of this argument is that it challenges the hypocrisy of governments which argue that it is necessary for them to have nuclear weapons but that others should not. The difficulty with it is that nuclear weapons do add new instabilities to regional conflicts and rivalries that are already very fraught. In the final analysis, the argument of arms control theorists that horizontal proliferation adds new challenges to stability is difficult to refute. In so far as arms control has been designed to avoid proliferation, however, it has had only partial success. What though of its impact on the central relationship between the United States and the Soviet Union during the Cold War era?

## III. What have been the Main Problems with Arms Control Negotiations?

Arms control theory had a certain elegance and persuasiveness, and it is not surprising that the Superpowers negotiated on strategic arms control almost continuously from the late 1960s. Their deliberations resulted in the SALT One Agreement of 1972, which included a Treaty limiting Anti-Ballistic Missile systems and an interim accord establishing ceilings on strategic offensive forces. In 1979, the United States and the Soviet Union signed a SALT Two Agreement which incorporated a more detailed set of ceilings and sub-ceilings on offensive forces. Although this agreement was tacitly observed by both the United States and the Soviet Union until the mid-1980s it was never ratified because of the deterioration in Superpower relations following the Soviet invasion of Afghanistan. From the early 1980s, though, the Superpowers negotiated deep cuts in strategic forces and finally achieved a START One accord in 1991 which will cut the forces in US and Soviet (now Russian) arsenals by around 25 to 30 per cent. With the disintegration of the Soviet Union following the START agreement, the future of further START talks, at least in the form they took up to 1991, was very much in doubt.

It is clear even from this brief overview of Superpower strategic arms control negotiations that they have encountered certain difficulties. Indeed, there were several factors which made it difficult to translate the theory into practice. The first and most important was that the theorists focused on the purposes of arms control largely in terms of stability. Yet in practice it was not always easy to translate abstract notions of stability into formal negotiated agreement.

This difficulty was accentuated by the fact that arms control theory was not fully sensitive to the politics of arms control, either at the domestic level or in terms of the negotiations with the adversary. At the domestic level, arms control was resisted by those who viewed it as an unwarranted restraint on necessary military preparations and activities, i.e., the military utility theorists or targeteers. The critics of arms control contended that it lulled the United States into a false sense of security, that the Soviet Union did not share the same conception of stability as the West and was using arms control to obtain unilateral advantage, that the Soviet Union cheated on agreements, and that Moscow was far more skilful at obtaining what it wanted in negotiation than was Washington. Some even went so far as to suggest that any agreement signed by the Soviet Union must, by its very nature, be inimical to United States security interests. Underlying these objections was reluctance to accept a rough equality between the United States and the Soviet Union as well as a fear that Moscow would move from equality to superiority.[20] Indeed, for those who believed in nuclear utility, arms control based on parity or acceptance of mutual vulnerability was anathema.

There were also dynamics in the negotiation process itself that had not been fully obvious in the theory. Although arms control theory emphasized the common interest in obtaining arms control agreements, the act of negotiating towards this common end was itself very competitive. Indeed, there were those who believed that arms control negotiations were simply a continuation of the arms race by other means, that the main purpose was to maximize one's own advantages while ensuring that no advantages were obtained by the adversary. The dynamics of negotiation were made even more difficult by the fact that there were also domestic constituencies which had to be satisfied by the outcome. Moreover, in order to obtain support from those groups who were unenthusiastic about arms control it was sometimes necessary to make concessions and to move in directions that were not constrained by agreement. In other words, rather than stop or slow down the arms race, arms control simply rechannelled it in different directions.

Another, not unrelated, difficulty is that arms control objectives are not restricted to controlling the arms race. Arms control is not immune from some of the problems which bedevilled the disarmament negotiations of the 1950s, and governments may enter and pursue negotiations for propaganda purposes rather than because they want an agreement. There may be powerful domestic political incentives for engaging in negotiations. It has become clear, for example, that American presidents are expected to pursue arms control with the Soviet Union as part of a two-track policy which combines policies of strength with dialogue.[21] Allied pressures too have made American presidents more sensitive to the value of negotiations. Yet this does not mean that agreement will result. Under some circumstances, it may be possible to satisfy domestic and allied demands for arms control simply through negotiating even if no agreement is reached. Conversely, agreements may prove politically controversial. The INF Agreement of 1987, for example, left the European allies worried about the future of American extended deterrence and made the German government unwilling to allow new nuclear deployments on German territory.

Yet another problem was that it became difficult to separate arms control from the state of the overall relationship between the Superpowers. Although arms control was something that was intended to reflect common interests even in a period of tension, inevitably it proved difficult to sustain when the broader political relationship between Moscow and Washington was in difficulties. This was increasingly obvious in the mid- and late 1970s when the arms control process became increasingly controversial. This took various forms. In the first place, there were those who argued that the Soviet Union needed arms control more than did the United States and that Soviet concessions therefore had to be forthcoming. Closely related were demands that arms control with the Soviets should not go ahead unless the Soviet Union exerted broad restraint in its foreign policy. Indeed, during the 1970s, it became clear that what was termed linkage between Soviet geopolitical behaviour and arms control was a fact of life in the American political system. Arms control agreements with the Soviet Union were not acceptable to the American body politic in periods of high tension and Soviet advances in the Third World. In these circumstances, arms control was extremely vulnerable to political attack as became evident with SALT Two.

If arms control did not prove politically resilient in the 1970s, it did undergo something of a resurgence in the mid-1980s as the Reagan Administration and the Soviet Union discussed the possibility of deep cuts in the Strategic Arms Reduction Talks (START). Yet some arms control theorists complained that their injunctions were being ignored, with the result that arms control had become disoriented. Schelling, in particular, argued that during the 1970s the emphasis on the character of weapons and on the concept of stability had been lost and replaced by an unwarranted 'emphasis on numbers, and specifically numbers within fixed categories, the categories having nothing to do with the weapon characteristics that most deserve attention'.[22] The Reagan Administration's focus on reductions in numbers was something that he saw as having little rationale. Yet neither the focus on fixed categories nor that on numbers was very surprising when it is remembered that arms control negotiations are less a matter of rational decision designed to achieve common goals than a process in which competitive and co-operative incentives are intermixed and which is significantly influenced by political and bureaucratic considerations.

Another problem which has emerged in arms control negotiations is that different arms control objectives may pull in different directions. One of the most interesting and complex issues in recent years has concerned the deployment of mobile ICBMs. On the one hand, land-based mobile missiles are difficult to verify, complicate efforts to achieve formal arms control agreements, and run counter to efforts to increase military transparency between the Superpowers. On the other hand, mobile missiles, by complicating the adversary's military planning and enhancing survivability contribute to second-strike stability—one of the major goals of arms control. In this particular instance the issue has been complicated by the question of what kind of mobile missile the United States should deploy. The arms control and deterrence stability advocates have generally preferred the small single-warhead ICBM, the Midgetman, while the targeteers in the late 1980s favoured the multi-warhead M-X Missile which had far greater hard-target kill capability. This goes back to the underlying philosophical differences between the two groups. The Midgetman proponents claimed that the small missile neither posed a threat to Soviet strategic forces nor offered a lucrative target and was therefore stabilizing. The M-X advocates contended that a missile with ten warheads was not only more cost-effective than a single-warhead missile but was also far more suited to the counter-force strategy that provided the most effective deterrent.

These difficulties help to explain why the strategic arms race has been so difficult to regulate. How much though does this matter? In order to answer this question it is necessary to examine more closely the internal dynamics of the arms race.

## IV.  Why do Arms Races Occur?

The term arms race is often used to describe virtually any new military development or deployment. Strictly speaking, however, it should be restricted to those measures which are part of the process whereby rival powers increase their military capabilities in response to or in anticipation of a real or perceived increase in the military provision of the adversary. Colin Gray has described an arms race as existing when 'two or more parties perceiving themselves to be in an adversary relationship . . . are increasing or improving their armaments at a rapid rate and structuring their respective military postures with a general attention to the past, current and anticipated military and political behavior of the other parties'.[23] Accepting this definition as a helpful starting-point, what drives the arms race?

The simplest model of the arms race is based on the idea that it is fuelled by a straightforward action–reaction phenomenon. In this view the connection between the increases and improvements made by each side are close and systematic. In other words, each takes action either to obtain a strategic advantage over the adversary or to offset a disadvantage. As Barry Buzan has pointed out, the image is one of two actors locked into a smooth, continuous, and self-reinforcing pattern of mutual military stimulation.[24] There are, however, several variants on this basic theme, revolving partly around the issue of whether the arms race is driven by defensive security concerns or by more ambitious and aggressive motives. Those who hold to the defensive view generally have a spiral model of the arms race and see it as driven by the security dilemma in which each state takes precautionary defensive measures only to have these construed by the adversary as threatening in nature. In this view, the arms race is a product of the underlying security dilemma that is an inescapable feature of international anarchy. The great powers are trapped in the security dilemma and each is reacting to the defensive measures of the adversary. Arms control is seen by deterrence stability and arms control theorists as a way of at least mitigating some of the aspects of the security dilemma.

In contrast, the nuclear weapons utility school sees the arms race dynamic in rather different terms. The argument here is that the arms race is fuelled by Soviet attempts to obtain strategic superiority and that the United States is doing little more than react to Soviet initiatives. There is, of course, a mirror image of this which sees the arms race as driven predominantly by the United States rather than the Soviet Union. According to this assessment, it is the United States which has generally been at the cutting edge of technology and which has used its technological superiority to determine the parameters of an arms race that has been predominantly qualitative in nature.

Whether one adheres to the spiral model of the arms race or sees it in terms of the drive to obtain or maintain superiority by Moscow or Washington, there is an interesting refinement of the reaction element in the model that has been elucidated by Johan Holst.[25] According to Holst, reactions can be of two types—imitative or offset. An imitative reaction is where one side attempts to emulate the adversary in either technology or force levels (e.g., the Soviet development and deployment of MIRVs); an offset reaction occurs when one attempts to take actions designed to detract from, or interdict, the adversary's capability (e.g., through defensive measures). This can be even more complicated when one considers not simply after the fact reactions, but anticipatory reactions based upon informed but not necessarily correct estimates of what the adversary's future military programmes will look like.

Nor is this the only refinement that can be made of the crude action–reaction model. Barry Buzan has suggested that there are several other dimensions which have to be considered. These include 'magnitude, in terms of what proportion the reaction bears to the triggering action; timing, in terms of the speed and sequence of interaction; and awareness, in terms of the extent to which the parties involved in the process are conscious of their impact on each other, and whether they govern their own behavior in the light of that consciousness.'[26] Although these refinements suggest that the action–reaction phenomenon is not as simple as it initially appears, even with the refinements the model is still based on implicit notions of government action as being the rational calculations of a single monolith rather than the outcome of a complex bargaining-process involving agencies and departments concerned with maximizing their domestic positions. Once this possibility is incorporated into the model, the adversary's actions can be understood less as a threat to national security than an opportunity to find new rationales (which can be cast in either imitative or offset terms) for programmes which enhance the organization's status and resources in internal bureaucratic and political battles. The implication is that one of the main engines for the arms race is domestic bureaucratic politics.

Other explanations of the arms race tend to emphasize domestic factors even more. Indeed, rather than seeing the arms race in action–reaction terms, they focus almost exclusively on domestic dynamics. These explanations of arms races include such influences as the vested interests of the 'military-industrial complex', the armaments manufacturers, or the vested interest of the services. In this view, the arms race is not so much a race, more an expression of basic domestic economic and political imperatives.

Another view of the arms race tends to see it neither in terms of action–reaction models nor in terms of domestic politics. Instead, the emphasis is on technology as the main engine driving the arms race. In this view, the rapid pace of modern technological development, in the civilian as well as the military sphere, contributes to a highly dynamic military environment. Technological push rather than political or strategic pull is seen as the most important factor leading to the development and deployment of new weapons systems.

Although technology is sometimes treated as the decisive factor, it can also be linked to other interpretations of arms race behaviour. Innovations in technology, for example, can be seen as contributing to the dynamics of the action–reaction phenomenon, especially when the arms race is predominantly qualitative. The technological dimension can also be linked to domestic factors, with the scientific, technological community providing much of the impetus for new weapons systems. In the final analysis, therefore, it is clear that no single explanation is sufficient: arms races do have an action–reaction quality, but are also influenced by domestic and technological factors.

Although there has been much discussion of the dynamics of arms racing there has been far less analysis of the consequences. Here again, of course, there are differences of approach and assessment. As suggested at the outset, those who advocate the abolition of nuclear weapons tend to be heirs to a tradition which sees weapons as the major cause of conflict. In this view arms races culminate in war. The Anglo-German naval race which preceded the First World War is often cited in support of this thesis. Yet Anglo-German naval rivalry far from being the decisive factor in the outbreak of war in July 1914 was peripheral to a crisis which had its roots in traditional great power rivalry in the Balkans. The implication is that the arms race was a function of more deep-seated rivalries rather than the cause of the 1914–18 war. But even if it is accepted that the arms race culminated in war, in this particular instance that does not mean that war is either a natural or an inevitable outcome of an arms race.

The nuclear arms race, for example, seems to have been most dangerous in its early stages when forces were at lower levels and concerns over the delicacy of the balance of terror were at their highest. Moreover, although the nuclear targeteers have resisted regulation, the United States and the Soviet Union have used arms control in an attempt to mitigate some of the more destabilizing consequences of the arms race. The Superpowers have realized, if only grudgingly, that unilateral attempts to obtain advantage are increasingly difficult in a world where there is considerable overkill. What does this mean though for the future of arms control?

# V. Does Arms Control have a Future?

The arms control agenda of the 1990s and into the next century will inevitably reflect broader changes that have taken place in international politics in the late 1980s. One of the most immediate items on the agenda, therefore, is to continue the process of regulation and reduction of strategic forces that has been an integral part of the attempt by the former Soviet Republics and the United States to move beyond the Cold War. Although the Russians and Americans seem to have entered a new phase in their relationship, the strategic underpinnings of this relationship will be influenced by nuclear deterrence for the foreseeable future. The role of arms control, therefore, is to ensure that the relationship remains both stable and relatively relaxed as all the states concerned feel that the strategic environment has become more predictable and less threatening.

A closely related item on the arms control agenda concerns Europe. In 1989 Europe moved beyond the Cold War as the dismantling of the Berlin Wall effectively removed the division between East and West. At the same time the democratization of Eastern Europe resulted in what was in effect the disintegration of the Warsaw Pact. Even so, the residue of the military confrontation in Europe remains. The CFE talks were an attempt greatly to reduce if not dismantle the military establishments that both blocs created in Europe. At the same time, there is a possibility that new dangers and instabilities will result from ethnic and nationalist tensions in Eastern Europe. In these circumstances, the development of mechanisms for crisis management is essential. Indeed, procedural mechanisms of co-operation are a necessary counterpart to structural arms control in Europe in the 1990s, and it seems very likely that they will be developed through the Conference on Security and Cooperation in Europe.

Although there may be some changes of emphasis in arms control in Europe, the main items on the arms control agenda are very traditional. There are also new problems, however, which will prove very difficult to deal with. Perhaps the most important of these is the spread of ballistic missile technology in the Third World. This problem has been growing for some time, reflecting both the ability of some Third World states to adapt missiles provided by the major powers and the growth of indigenous arms production in the Third World. It was highlighted most dramatically by the war of the cities in the closing stages of the Iran–Iraq War and during the 1991 Gulf War. Although a 'missile technology control regime' was established in 1987, neither the supply nor the demand sides of the ballistic missile problem have been adequately dealt with. The worst effects of missile proliferation, of course, would occur as this technology is allied with either chemical or nuclear weapons, thereby introducing new instabilities into regional conflicts. The long-term challenge, therefore, is to transform arms control into an effective means for dealing with problems that go well beyond the old Superpower relationship or the military balance in Europe. Arms control theory was designed to deal with a simple relationship between two powers; the task for the future is to manage relations in a more complex world where the technology of destruction has been widely diffused. The challenge is as urgent as it is inescapable.

## Notes

1. For this latter view, see John Mearsheimer, 'Why We will Soon Miss the Cold War', *Atlantic*, 266/2 (1990), 35–50.
2. This is a point that has been frequently made by Ken Booth.
3. For a powerful reiteration of this view, see Colin Gray, 'Nuclear Strategy: What is True, What is False, What is Arguable?', *Comparative Strategy*, 9/1 (1990).
4. For an incisive critique of this kind of approach, see Ken Booth's contributions to Ken Booth and John Baylis, *Britain, NATO and Nuclear Weapons* (London: Macmillan, 1989), especially 166–7. Although Booth applies it to all deterrence theorists his critique at this point is most relevant to the targeteers.
5. This is documented more fully in John Spanier and Joseph Nogee, *The Politics of Disarmament* (New York: Praeger, 1962).
6. Hedley Bull, *The Control of the Arms Race* (New York: Praeger, 1961); Donald Brennan (ed.), *Arms Control, Disarmament and National Security* (New York: Braziller, 1961), and Thomas Schelling and Morton Halperin, *Stategy and Arms Control* (New York: Twentieth Century Fund, 1961).
7. Thomas C. Schelling and Morton H. Halperin, *Strategy and Arms Control*, 2.
8. Bull, *The Control of the Arms Race*.

9. See A. Wohlstetter, 'The Delicate Balance of Terror', *Foreign Affairs*, 37/2 (1959).

10. Thomas Schelling, *Arms and Influence* (New Haven, Con.: Yale University Press, 1966), 235.

11. See Glenn Snyder, *Deterrence Defense* (Princeton, NJ: Princeton University Press, 1961).

12. Schelling and Halperin, *Strategy and Arms Control*, 57.

13. I am grateful to my colleague Dr Michael Brenner for this point.

14. See Charles Osgood, *An Alternative to War or Surrender* (Urbana: University of Illinois Press, 1963).

15. See Amitai Etzioni, *The Kennedy Experiment* (New York: Institute of War and Peace Studies, Columbia University, 1967).

16. Lawrence Freedman is a strong advocate of this view.

17. For a fuller analysis, see Sean Lynn-Jones, *Avoiding Confrontation at Sea: The 1972 US–Soviet Agreement on Naval Incidents*, Harvard Project on Avoiding Nuclear Wear, Occasional Paper Series, No. 2 (Boston: Kennedy School of Government, 1984).

18. See Christopher J. Lamb, *How to Think about Arms Control, Disarmament and Defense* (Englewood Cliffs, NJ: Prentice Hall, 1988), 41.

19. See Kenneth Waltz, *The Spread of Nuclear Weapons; More May Be Better*, Adelphi Paper, 171 (London: International Institute for Strategic Studies, 1981).

20. For a fuller analysis of the way in which this argument was developed during the 1970s, see Mike Bowker and Phil Williams, *Superpower Détente: A Reappraisal* (London: Sage for Royal Institute of International Affairs, 1988), especially chaps. 7 and 8.

21. This argument was developed in Bernard Firestone, *The Quest For Nuclear Stability* (London: Greenwood Press, 1982).

22. See Thomas C. Schelling, 'What Went Wrong with Arms Control?' in O. Osterud (ed.), *Studies of War and Peace* (Oslo: Norwegian University Press, 1986), 102.

23. Colin Gray quoted in Barry Buzan, *Strategic Studies* (London: Macmillan, 1987), 69.

24. Ibid. 8.

25. See Johan Holst, 'Missile Defense, the Soviet Union and the Arms Race', in John Holst and William Schneider (eds.), *Why ABM?* (New York: Pergamon, 1969), 161.

26. Buzan, *Strategic Studies*, 8.

# NINE

# International Terrorism: New Risks to World Order

*Paul Wilkinson*

Political and strategic concepts are notoriously difficult to define in a few sentences. Ask any two historians or social scientists to explain what they mean by 'war', 'insurgency', and 'revolution', for example, and you are likely to get two quite different answers. But this does not mean that these terms have no commonly accepted meanings. Scholars concerned with the study of major events in contemporary international politics could not get along without using such terminology.

'Terrorism' is one of the key concepts in the analysis of contemporary international politics.[1] It is true that it is often abused for propaganda purposes, but in this respect it is no different from 'democracy', 'imperialism', and 'national liberation'.

Among scholars of all disciplines who have studied political violence it is generally accepted that terrorism is a special form of political violence. It is *not* a philosophy or a political movement. Terrorism is a weapon or method which has been used throughout history by both states and sub-state organizations for a whole variety of political causes or purposes. This special form of political violence has five major characteristics:

- it is premeditated and aims to create a climate of extreme fear or terror;
- it is directed at a wider audience or target than the immediate victims of the violence;
- it inherently involves attacks on random and symbolic targets, including civilians;
- the acts of violence committed are seen by the society in

which they occur as extra-normal, in the literal sense that they breach the social norms, thus causing a sense of outrage; and

- terrorism is used to try to influence political behaviour in some way: for example to force opponents into conceding some or all of the perpetrators' demands, to provoke an over-reaction, to serve as a catalyst for a more general conflict, or to publicize a political cause.

As already noted, terror violence can be committed both by states and sub-state organizations. The activity becomes international terrorism when the citizens of more than one country are involved and internal terrorism when confined within the border of a single state. In practice, however, it is difficult to find any protracted and intensive terrorist campaign that remains purely internal as, almost invariably, the terrorists will look across their borders for political support, weapons, funds, and safe haven. Another key distinction is between pure terrorism used in isolation and terrorism used as an auxiliary weapon in a wider repertoire of violence. The terrorism experienced in Western Europe since the late 1960s has been used as the sole weapon of many groups. The 'mixed' form of terrorism is the general rule in all major areas of conflict throughout the world. For example, in Southern Africa and Latin America terrorism has been only one strand in conflicts involving rural guerrilla war, economic sabotage and disruption, and wider political struggle.[2]

This chapter does not aim to provide an in-depth analysis of counter-terrorist strategies for the liberal democracies. I have attempted this in my book *Terrorism and the Liberal State* (2nd edn. Basingstoke: Macmillan, 1986). The object of the present chapter is to assess the scale and significance of terrorism as a problem in the international system in the light of recent trends.

## I. What is the Historical Background of Terrorism?

Terrorism is not a recent invention.[3] It was used by the Sicarii and Zealots against the Roman occupation in Palestine. In the eleventh and twelfth centuries it was the chosen weapon of a radical Islamic sect, the Assassins, in their campaign to overthrow the existing Muslim authorities.[4] Revolutionaries, nihilists, and anarchists used the tactics of bombing and assassination in their unsuccessful efforts to destroy autocracy, for example in Russia and the Balkans. And in the 1940s and 1950s terrorism became the primary weapon of movements engaged in major anti-colonial struggles, for example by the Jews against the British Mandate in Palestine, by EOKA against British colonial rule in Cyprus, by FLOSY in Aden,[5] and by the FLN against the French in Algeria.[6]

These examples of anti-colonial struggles are historically significant because they are the only clear instances in modern history where sub-state organizations using terror as their major weapon were able to achieve their long-term political goals, i.e., the withdrawal of the colonial power and establishment of a form of government favoured by the insurgents. There is no other clear case where such results have been achieved. Moreover, it is foolish to deny that these strategic successes through the use of terrorism have inspired many other groups to emulate these methods, although often with little awareness that the conditions of such anti-colonial examples were uniquely propitious for the terrorist and most unlikely to be repeated. In each case the colonial authorities lacked any substantial support for maintaining their rule both in the colonial territory and among the population of the European colonial power. After the loss of life, destruction, and economic debilitation of the Second World War, neither the politicians nor the general public in Britain and France had any stomach for wars of attrition. They already saw their colonial commitments as liabilities, costly in lives and treasure, to be negotiated away as swiftly and honourably as possible. It should not be forgotten that for the most part the de-colonization process was completed without significant bloodshed, and terrorism played a key role in only a small number of cases. The real burgeoning of modern international terrorism did not occur until the end of the 1960s. International incidents of terrorism have increased tenfold since 1968 and now directly affect, to some degree, over half the countries in the international system.[7]

## II. What are the Underlying Causes and Implications of Modern Terrorism?

There is still considerable debate among specialists as to the reasons for the enormous growth of terrorism in the late 1960s and

1970s. The definitive history of twentieth-century terrorism is still to be written. Nevertheless it is clear that there are some key characteristics of the contemporary international system which are powerfully conducive to terrorist violence. The most important of these are the deep and bitter ethnic, religious, and ideological conflicts which remain unresolved and which fester in the international system, spawning many forms of violent conflict including terrorism, and periodically erupting into civil and international wars. By far the most significant of these is the Arab-Israeli conflict: in the wake of Israel's defeat of conventional military power of the Arab states in 1967 militant Palestinians decided that terrorism—hijacking, bombings, shooting attacks— was their only remaining weapon. This was the catalyst for a whole new wave of terrorist activity emanating from the Middle East or conducted within Middle Eastern countries.[8] Yet it must be borne in mind that other violent ethnic and religious conflicts around the world which have also given rise to a great deal of terrorism are also very far from being resolved. Separatist conflicts of this kind rage fiercely in many parts of the world, from Northern Ireland, Spain, and Corsica to the Central Asian republics of the former Soviet Union to the Punjab, Sri Lanka, and the Philippines.

De-colonization has not removed these problems: in many ways it has made them even more intractable. New and relatively fragile political systems with weak economies find themselves confronting fundamental challenges to their authority and legitimacy on the grounds that the new state is denying them the right of self-determination. Some new states in Asia and Africa have had more than a dozen movements ranged against them, often waging full-scale insurgencies, and frequently resorting to terrorism.[9]

Another underlying cause has been the global strategic balance which has prevailed throughout the period, from the early 1950s right through to the Gorbachev era. In the shadow of the nuclear balance of terror between the Superpowers methods of un-conventional and proxy war, such as terrorism, became more attractive as instruments of policy for states and sub-state organizations such as national liberation movements. Such methods are low-cost, relatively low-risk, and yet afford the possibilities of high yield in terms of weakening, penetrating, or even gaining control through covert means. Moreover, such methods carry far less cost and less risk of escalation than conventional war. State-sponsored international terrorism carries the added attraction for its perpetrators that it can be carried out secretly, and, if suspicions are voiced, plausibly denied.

This strategic factor has been of particular significance because it is linked to another central feature of the post-war international system; the influence of Marxist–Leninist regimes and their client Communist movements, many of which have used guerrilla war, terrorism, and other techniques of revolutionary warfare, on an extensive scale and which have acted as a major conduit for exporting theoretical and practical knowledge of these methods of warfare around the world. It would be foolish to underestimate the long-term influence of the major theoreticians, such as Mao Tse-tung, Vo Nguyen Giap, Fidel Castro, Che Guevara, and Carlos Marighela. The clear evidence of the world-wide decline in the support for Communist regimes and movements today should not blind us to the fact that they were enormously influential in the 1950s and 1960s, when they succeeded in disseminating their theories way beyond their own countries of origin. One sees this vividly illustrated in the shift of emphasis from rural guerrilla warfare to urban guerrilla activity and terrorism among the Latin American revolutionaries. The ideas of the Tupamaros certainly influenced the *Red Brigades*, and Marighela's *Minimanual of the Urban Guerrilla* was a strong influence on Ulrike Meinhof and others in the left-wing terrorist movements of Western Europe in the 1970s.[10]

The world-wide dissemination of new technology has also greatly facilitated the growth of terrorism. For example, the development of international civil aviation has created new vulnerabilities and lucrative targets for the terrorist to exploit.[11] TV satellites have brought about a media revolution: the terrorists can exploit this by gaining almost instantaneous world-wide publicity for an outrage, thus enabling them to magnify the element of fear and to disseminate awareness of their cause of demands on a scale that would have been unthinkable for the anarchist bomb-thrower or assassin of the nineteenth century.[12] Modern weapons technology has also proved a great boom to terrorists, providing them, for example, with modern plastic explosives such as Semtex and highly accurate lightweight portable firearms such as the Uzi sub-machine-gun.

Perhaps most important of all the factors encouraging the spread of terrorism has been the sheer success of this method in achieving short-term tactical objectives of great value to the terrorist. For although it is clear that terrorism rarely, if ever, wins strategic political goals it has an impressive record in gaining such things as massive world-wide publicity, extortion of large ransom payments, and the release of considerable numbers of imprisoned terrorists.

There are many reasons for the failure of certain states and the international community as a whole to take firm action against terrorists: they include weakness, double standards, and outright complicity. Terrorism, like piracy, will not be eradicated unless it is subjected to concerted and determined action by the entire international system. As this appears highly unlikely we must recognize that terrorism will remain a problem for the world community for some considerable time to come.

The problem of terrorism in the international system has serious implications at a number of different levels. It is an intolerable attack on the individual human rights of the innocent. It is true that wars are infinitely more destructive of human life, but the vast majority of fatalities through terrorism are caused by attacks on unarmed civilians who are going about their peaceful and lawful business. What more fundamental attack on human rights can there be than to deprive the innocent of the right to life? Does murder cease to be murder just because the killer believes human life is expendable in pursuit of some particular species of fanaticism?

When terrorism becomes severe and protracted it can also present a serious challenge to the well-being and security of local communities or even entire nation-states. For example, in the most severe cases, such as Colombia, Peru, Lebanon, Sri Lanka, and parts of India, terrorism has bred intensified inter-communal conflict and polarization. It has severely damaged the processes of law and orderly government and threatened the economy by damaging trade, destroying valuable resources, and scaring away investment. In the most severe cases terrorism can render whole areas of a country ungovernable, as in the cases of Lebanon and Sri Lanka, for example, and can provoke full-scale civil war.[13]

The implications for the international system as a whole can also be far more grave than is generally realized. State-sponsored terrorism, or even the mistaken belief that a state has sponsored terrorism against one's own state or citizen may provoke a retaliation which spirals into war. Full-scale military intervention and international war may result from a move to crush terrorist factions in a neighbouring state and/or to establish a secure zone within the territory hitherto utilized by terrorists. These motives, among others, lay behind the Israeli invasion of Lebanon in 1982. Sarajevo is the classic instance of an act of terrorism serving as the spark which sets off a giant international conflict.

In less dramatic circumstances terrorism can still present states with major national security problems. When the Iranian revolutionaries held the entire US diplomatic mission in Tehran as hostages, the White House, the National Security Council, and the Department of State became so embroiled in the effort to secure the hostages' release that the US administration's capacity to act on wider issues in the Middle East became almost paralysed.[14] And President Reagan was virtually compelled to alter his administration's policy on Lebanon and bring an end to the deployment of the peacekeeping Multi-National Force (MNF) following the massacre of 241 Marines in a truck bombing by *Hezbollah* terrorists. In this case the terrorists and their backers in Iran knew that they were using the psychological weapon of terror to reach over the head of President Reagan to the American public. They did so, and Mr Reagan's policy options on Lebanon were drastically narrowed.

## III. Can Terrorism ever be Morally Justified?

We live in an age when the idea of universal moral standards or principles is under severe attack. According to the sophistry of moral relativism and 'situational ethics' almost anything can be condoned. The oft-repeated cry 'One man's terrorist is another man's freedom fighter' is but one manifestation of the widespread confusion about the morality of terrorist forms of violence. Even in those clear cases where we may be persuaded that a terrorist group is motivated by a legitimate sense of injustice or grievance and can truly claim to 'speak' for a majority of its professed constituency, does this mean we must condone their use of terrorist means? Surely not, for this is to confuse means and ends.

Unless one is a pacifist, the use of force can certainly be justified under particular circumstances. But terrorism is a special form of violence involving deliberate attacks on innocent civilians. According to the doctrines of just war and just rebellion against tyranny a righteous cause can never justify the use of evil means.[15] But it is no longer fashionable to believe in good and evil. This writer has always taken the position that terrorism is an unmitigated evil. The undoubted fact that many state and non-state belligerents through history have flouted the most basic principles of the humanitarian law of conflict does not provide a moral argument for abandoning such standards completely and making terror permissible. On the contrary, the historical record of modern war and the heightened threat from weapons of mass destruction should spur the international community to greater efforts to impose recognition of the humanitarian law of conflict.

Yet the moral desirability of strengthening the protection of human rights in conflict provides no easy answer to the moral problems inherent in the use of terror. Suppose terror is used on a major scale against your own people, whether by state or non-state perpetrators, can this justify the use of terror as a means of resistance? Are there circumstances when the use of retaliatory terror can be condoned as the lesser evil? When whole groups or societies start a spiral of retaliation and counter-retaliation the danger is that anything becomes 'permissible' in the name of resistance.

On a more hopeful note, it is worth recalling that in Eastern Europe some of the most oppressive one-party regimes in modern history were overthrown without even initiating this spiral of terror and counter-terror: the liberation of these countries was achieved primarily by the moral and political pressure of internal resistance, by protests and mass demonstrations on the streets, and general economic collapse. What is astonishing is that, with the sad exception of the case of Romania, these revolutions from below were remarkably non-violent. It is also significant that there are no historical examples of a modern dictatorship or totalitarian regime having been overthrown by means of terrorism.

There is more general agreement, of course, that terrorism can never be a justified means of struggle within a liberal democracy. A truly democratic political system, by definition, offers numerous non-violent channels of political protest, lobbying, and electoral competition: it is patently a violation of democratic principle when fanatical minorities behave like petty tyrannies, resorting to the bomb and the gun to impose on their fellow citizens what they are unable to achieve through the ballot box.

In liberal democracies even the claim of terrorist groups to speak for the majority or the minority they claim to represent is generally spurious. It is only in democratic societies that terrorist groups have the option of forming political parties and fighting elections. Even when given the chance, few take it, and if they do their election results are generally derisory. However, in the few cases where the pro-terrorist parties manage to gain a more significant minority of votes (e.g., in Northern Ireland or the Basque region of Spain) this suggests a worrying degree of disaffection from the democratic political system and the relative success of terrorist propaganda. It does not establish the moral legitimacy of terrorist means.

## IV. Is International Terrorism Increasing or Decreasing?

As one would expect, the incidence of domestic terrorist crimes and the total casualties they cause vastly exceeds the figures for international terrorism: that is, incidents involving the citizens of more than one country. For example in Northern Ireland alone the number of deaths through domestic terrorist attacks in 1989 (sixty-two) was over four times the total deaths caused by international terrorism in the whole of Europe in that year. This pattern is repeated in Asia, Africa, and Latin America, where casualties and physical destruction caused by domestic attacks far outweigh those resulting from international incidents. However, few databases even attempt to keep tally of both domestic and international terrorist attacks world-wide.

Our data on international terrorist incidents for the 1980s is far more reliable and comprehensive. The total number climbed from over 500 a year in the early 1980s to 600 a year in 1984, rising to around 800 per year in the period 1985–8. The quite dramatic decline in the number of international incidents world-wide in 1989–90 shows a very encouraging underlying trend. It is particularly noteworthy that international attacks originating in the Middle East were reduced by almost 70 per cent in 1990 over the previous year's figures. However, there are three essential caveats. First, we must remember that internal or domestic terrorist incidents are not taken into account in these figures. Hence most of the savage violence afflicting countries such as Sri Lanka, Colombia, Peru, parts of India, and Lebanon does not appear in the international statistics. Secondly, there was a massive upsurge in the number of international incidents during the six weeks of the Gulf War against Iraq. This was hardly noticed by the western media at the time, partly because of their understandable preoccupation with the military conflict, but mainly owing to the fact that the majority of the attacks were non-lethal and rather low-level in character, mainly crude fire-bombings of buildings associated with the US and other coalition partners. Even so, the surprisingly high figures for the six weeks of Operation Desert Storm (166 terrorist incidents recorded world-wide including seventy-seven in Europe and fifty-five in the Near East and Asia) are a sharp reminder that trends in international terrorism can turn sharply upwards in times of crisis. Thirdly, despite the welcome reduction in the overall level of international terrorism in 1990, the statistics show a serious worsening of terrorism in regions of the Third World: a 25 per cent increase in international attacks in Latin America, and a doubling in the number of terrorist incidents and casualties in Asia. Hence, there are no grounds for assuming that levels of terrorism are set for a period of irreversible decline. Western ethnocentric attitudes often lead to the assumption that western experience within the industrial countries is a sound guide to trends in the rest of the world.

It is a foolish myth to present terror violence as an exclusively or primarily western problem. The tragic murder of Rajiv Gandhi was a reminder of the way in which violent fanaticism can threaten a Third World democracy. It is true that Indian democracy has survived previous major crises including the assassination of Rajiv's mother, Mrs Indira Gandhi; India is deeply imbued with the influence of democratic institutions and respect of the rule of law. There has been a remarkable expression of determination to close ranks and preserve the constitution. Nevertheless there is no doubt that the assassination of Rajiv Gandhi, probably by *Tamil Tiger* terrorists, removed at a stroke the major champion of secular democracy who had a real determination to defeat the forces of ethnic separation and fragmentation threatening Indian unity.

Moreover, statistics on the total numbers of examples and their regional distribution can be misleading. Incidents vary enormously in their lethality and overall impact. Sabotage bombing of airliners in flight has been rare compared with more conventional bombings, yet it accounts for a high proportion of the fatalities caused by international terrorism. For example, in 1988 the 270 deaths caused by the terrorist bombing of Pan Am 103 over Lockerbie accounted for over 40 per cent of the total deaths from international terrorism in that year. And in 1989 the terrorist bombings of the French UTA airliner over the Niger desert with the loss of 171 lives and the bombing of the Colombian Avianca airliner with the loss of 107 passengers and crew accounted for 70 per cent of the fatalities from international terrorism for the whole year. This underlines a worrying trend in international terrorism since 1982, and that is the pattern of increasingly indiscriminate and lethal attacks in which ordinary citizens are targeted. One manifestation of this trend is the mid-air sabotage bombings of airliners referred to above. Another is the use of the car bomb in public places with the object of creating maximum carnage. This development has not been confined to the Middle East. Paris experienced a horrifying example during a nine-day terrorist campaign in September 1986 which killed eight members of the public and wounded over 150. And in November 1987 the Provisional IRA exploded a bomb at a Remembrance Day service at Enniskillen which massacred ten people.

How does one explain this increase in indiscriminateness? In part it results from the terrorists' ever more desperate desire for publicity. With the media and the public satiated with reports of violence around the world, terrorist leaders have concluded that they must commit greater atrocities to capture the headlines. Another key factor is the growing attraction of soft targets to terrorists increasingly aware of the greater risks that face them if they seek to attack high-prestige targets which have been 'hardened' by improved physical protection, such as military and diplomatic installations. Some experienced observers have suggested that another major element may be a shift inside terrorist organizations away from the more pragmatic 'politically minded' terrorist leaders to fanatical hard men, obsessed with vengeance and violence.

A further important development which has stimulated considerable debate among specialists in the study of terrorism is the sharp drop in international incidents in 1989. Is this the beginning of a new and encouraging long-term trend, or is it simply a temporary lull in terrorist activity resulting from a special combination of factors? Are the terrorists simply regrouping with the aim of launching new and more destructive campaigns at the next opportunity?

It seems clear that three major developments combined to have a restraining effect on international terrorist activity in 1989. Firstly there were important shifts of policy and activity among the groups involved. In December 1988 Yasser Arafat renounced the use of terrorism, as part of the so-called Geneva declaration designed to create the conditions for formal diplomatic contact between the PLO and the US government. Although it is clear that many Palestinian militant groups did not agree with this line it is certainly true that there was a significant decline in the number of operations by groups under the PLO's umbrella.

Another factor affecting the level of terrorist group activity was severe internal dissension both within and between the various terrorist factions. It is reported that in 1989 over 120 members of one of the most notorious international terrorist groups, the *Abu Nidal* organization (ANO), died in an internal purge which virtually paralysed the group's activities. The ANO was also hampered by growing coolness on the part of one of its state sponsors, Libya, which was being strongly encouraged to distance itself from the ANO as part of the price for Gadaffi's badly needed improvement in relations with both the moderate Arab states and the European Community. The ANO also became embroiled in the growing inter-factional conflict and 'the war of the camps' in Lebanon, as did other Palestinian radical groups. This all diverted their energies and resources away from international terrorist operations further afield.

A further reason for the drop in international terrorist incidents was the shifts in policy on the part of several key state sponsors of terrorism. In 1987 and 1988 the Soviet-backed regime in Afghanistan conducted over 250 attacks in Pakistan, both in the North-West

Frontier Province and in cities such as Karachi, Islamabad, Lahore, and Peshawar. Casualties of these bombings were often extremely high. In 1987, seventy people were killed when the crowded market-place in Karachi was bombed, and fourteen died in the bombing at Peshawar in June 1988. In 1989 the Afghan government scaled down its backing for the WAD terrorist campaign, following the withdrawal of Soviet troops from Afghanistan. This had a considerable effect on the global total of international terrorist incidents: there was a sharp decline from over 120 such events in 1988 to around two dozen in 1989.

A third important trend which undoubtedly contributed to the decline of international terrorism in 1989 was the improvement in counter-terrorist measures by many governments and the increasing effectiveness of international co-operation between governments and security services. This has been particularly true in the European Community, where the *Trevi* network and bi-lateral police co-operation against terrorism has been gradually strengthened in preparation for the dismantling of internal frontier controls in 1992. For example, in 1989 improved European police co-operation led to the arrest of a number of members of terrorist groups including PIRA in West Germany and France, ETA in France, and *Red Brigades* in France, Spain, and Switzerland. This strengthening of international police and intelligence co-operation, combined with the greater organizational problems of operating abroad, has tended to discourage international terrorist attacks outside the borders of the terrorists' own country. It has been estimated that in 1989 almost 80 per cent of international incidents world-wide fell into the former category.

One other key trend of the 1980s needs to be highlighted. The problem of terrorism, especially domestic terrorism, has begun to afflict certain Third World states on a major scale. It is quite ridiculous to pretend that terrorism is primarily a problem for rich industrial countries. The scale of terrorist lethality and destructiveness in countries such as Lebanon, India, Sri Lanka, Colombia, and Peru totally overshadows the levels experienced by West European countries in the 1970s. Yet the Third World countries which have been the major victims of this type of violence in the 1980s lack the basic resources to deal with it.

# V. What are the Future Threats Posed by International Terrorism?

Terrorist groups make no secret of their threats: they generally lose no opportunity of putting out their propaganda messages, asserting the righteousness of their cause, the inevitability of their ultimate victory, and the dire consequences that face anyone who stands in their way. There are very few cases of terrorist groups voluntarily abandoning their activities and simply fading away. Some groups have gone under as the result of the death or capture of all their leading figures and cell structure. Others have been curtailed by the action of state sponsors or as a result of internecine strife. But when a terrorist group possesses unfulfilled political aims, leadership, weapons, manpower, and access to targets, it is a fair assumption that it will stay in business.

By far the most durable of these groups since the early 1970s have been those with a nationalist or separatist ideology, such as the radical Palestinian groups, the PIRA, and ETA. These groups have larger constituencies of potential recruits, supporters, and more political clout and resources than the extreme ideological groups. We can expect them to remain an important part of the terrorist scene. By contrast the ideological terrorists of the extreme left, such as the *Red Brigades, Action Directe*, and the *Combatant Communist Cells* have proved more vulnerable and ephemeral. They are a declining threat world-wide. Exceptions include the avowedly Maoist *New People's Army* in the Philippines and the Maoist *Shining Path (Sendero Luminoso)* movement in Peru. These both combine terrorism with rural guerrilla insurgency and have the ability to mount major threats to government.

## The Middle East

In the field of international terrorism the main threats in the future arise from the Middle East, the conflict-ridden region most closely linked with the development of international terrorism ever since the late 1960s. In 1990 a major new risk emerged in the shape of the reappearance of the Iraqi regime as a leading state sponsor of international terrorism. Saddam Hussein has a long record of sponsoring hard-line Palestinian groups and providing them with headquarters, training facilities, the back-up of the Iraqi diplomatic network, and weapons and funds. Baghdad provided these services for the *Abu Nidal* organization until 1983. This terrorist group has been responsible for over ninety attacks since 1974 in which 900 people have been killed or injured. From 1983 to 1987 the *Abu Nidal* group had its base in Syria, and from 1987 to 1989, in Libya.

Although Saddam was successful in attracting *Abu Nidal* and other Palestinian terrorist groups back to Iraq's sponsorships in 1990, and despite his repeated threats to unleash a campaign of 'Holy terror' against the coalition, one of the puzzles of the Gulf War is that Saddam's terrorism effort went off like a damp squib. It is true there were at least 166 terrorist incidents, mostly of a low level, during the six weeks of the war. There were incidents from the Philippines and Indonesia to Turkey, Greece, and Peru. But casualties were extremely low (nine killed and sixty-six injured) and spectacular terrorist atrocities were conspicuous by their absence. How can this be explained?

One important factor was the extremely effective preventive measures taken by the intelligence and police authorities of the coalition states. They had early warning of the possibility of Saddam-inspired terrorism, and by acting swiftly to detain and deport key suspects, including Iraqi agents working under diplomatic cover, they pre-empted many attacks which could have been quite serious: the Germans, the French, and the American authorities are convinced that heightened security nipped much terrorism in the bud. Another important factor was the enhanced intelligence co-operation between the coalition parties. In addition, the stunning effect of the allied air bombardment of Iraq destroyed, or at very least seriously disrupted, Iraqi command, control, and communications, making it far more difficult for Baghdad to co-ordinate international terrorism. It is also very likely that the terrorist groups enlisted by Saddam began to have second thoughts about making a major effort on his behalf, once they realized that Saddam was heading for a devastating defeat. Last but not least, there is general agreement among the security authorities in the coalition states that the Syrians and the Iranians, for their own strategic and political reasons, exerted considerable pressure on their terrorist clients and contacts to desist from anti-coalition terrorism in the greater interest of achieving the defeat of Saddam. It would be foolish to suppose that this policy was adopted for any reasons other than *raison d'état* and the desire to improve economic relations with the west. It does not mean that Tehran and Damascus have abandoned the weapon of terrorism. But it does show that even major state sponsors of terrorism can and do suspend these activities when they see tangible benefits in so doing.

Although Saddam has been expelled from Kuwait and suffered a massive military defeat the prospects of a recrudescence of Middle East terrorism remain as strong as ever. The Palestinian militants, their anger and frustration intensified by yet another military defeat, are showing every sign of their determination to resume a campaign of terrorist violence to achieve their goals. The apparent impasse in the US-promoted talks on the Arab–Israel conflict has again created a climate of increased disillusionment and bitterness over the failure of diplomatic efforts. The militant groups, particularly the Palestinian fundamentalists, such as *Hamas* and *Palestinian Islamic Jihad* (PIJ) are succeeding in mobilizing growing support, especially among Palestinian youth. Nor should we forget that some Palestinian rejectionist groups, such as *Abu Nidal* and the PFLP-GC, have structures of active terrorist cells already in place in a number of countries, prepared for further terrorist actions.

A further danger emanating from the Middle East is terrorism stemming from militant Islamic fundamentalist groups. Much of the impetus for these movements grew out of the Iranian Islamic Revolution which came to power in 1979–80. The *Hezbollah* movement in Lebanon and *Al-Dawa*, active in the Gulf states, are examples of Shiah movements aimed at establishing Iranian-style Islamic republics. But the Shiah constitute only 10 per cent of the population of the Muslim world. What is not sufficiently well understood is the existence of a strong fundamentalist tradition in many Sunni Muslim communities, for example in Egypt, Algeria, Tunisia, and even as far away as Pakistan and the Soviet Central Asian republics. Among the Palestinian Arabs in the Occupied Territories we have seen a weird alliance arise between Islamic fundamentalists like the *Hamas* group and the radical Palestinian groups such as the PFLP. Such alliances are potentially a powerful challenge to more traditional and moderate Arab political structures and they are capable of developing tactics of extreme violence.

## Ethnic Conflicts

Middle East conflicts are already closely linked with over 40 per cent of international terrorism. This proportion may well increase in the light of the trends described above. Yet it would be a grave mistake to see the Middle East as the sole source of emerging threats of terrorist violence. The collapse of Communist one-party regimes in Eastern Europe during 1989–90 has brought to the surface many long-suppressed ethnic conflicts and hatreds, many of which hark back to an earlier tradition of terror violence. One has only to refer to the history of Balkan nationalist movements in the nineteenth and early twentieth centuries to realize that most of them are steeped in their own traditions of political violence and terrorism: the Croatian *Ustashi*, the Serbian *Black Hand*, and the Macedonian *Internal Macedonian Revolutionary Organization* (IMRO) offer ample evidence. There are real dangers that some of the bitter ethnic conflicts that are now re-emerging in Eastern Europe will manifest themselves in full-scale campaigns of terror violence. Extremists may exploit the relative ease of operating in open and vulnerable new political systems. Is living with high levels of ethnic conflict and spasmodic terrorism going to be a price East Europeans have to pay for their new democratic way of life? We should also remember that the demographic distribution of these East European nationalities is geographically untidy, with every major ethnic group straddling one or more state frontiers. To complicate things still further, many of the ethnic minorities involved have *émigré* communities scattered in many western countries, and some of these could well be drawn into any fresh outbreak of inter-ethnic conflict. The whole international community has an interest in the peaceful resolution of these conflicts.

The same is even more true of the former Soviet Union where so many of the 197 officially recognized nationalities appear disaffected from the central government system and wish to attain independence or, at very least, a far greater degree of autonomy. In parts of the Soviet Union—for example, Azerbaijan, Armenia, Uzbekistan, and Tadjikistan—we have already seen Soviet troops deployed in an effort to suppress or head off violent ethnic clashes and confrontations with the authorities. The potential for ethnic terrorism in the former Soviet republics is even more evident than it is in the former Communist countries of Eastern Europe. And the Russian leaders are well aware that the Central Asian republics are not immune from the fundamentalist and radical movements based on the other side of their southern borders.

## VI. What are the Problems of Responding to International Terrorists?

### The Terrorist Threat to Civil Aviation

In *Conflict Study* 226, 'The Lessons of Lockerbie' (December 1989), the writer argued that, despite the Lockerbie tragedy and two more mid-air sabotage bombings in 1989 over Africa and Latin America, the world civil aviation system had failed to take the long-overdue measures to protect civil aviation against this major threat. It is depressing to report that another three years have gone by without any significant improvement in blocking the major loopholes. A number of terrorist groups and their state sponsors with track records of ruthlessness and lethal expertise are well aware of the vulnerabilities of civil aviation. It is a sad fact that very few countries have made any significant improvement in security measures against the sabotage bomber. Another Lockerbie could happen tomorrow and the carnage caused would, of course, be even greater if the terrorists succeeded in destroying an airliner above the residential areas of a major city.

Some countries, such as the USA and Britain, and certain major airlines, have introduced some welcome improvements in aviation security. For example, in Britain the new Aviation and Maritime Security Act gives the Secretary of State for Transport the power to suspended an airline's operations if they fall below required security standards, and has created an aviation security inspectorate with greater powers. These changes, together with improvements in airport security, were long overdue but none the less welcome.

However, the greatest weakness of aviation security is the failure to install in the world's airports explosive detection systems (EDS) capable of detecting plastic explosives. It is true that the US authorities, and, more recently the British, have conceded that 100 per cent screening of all baggage is their long-term objective. But how is this to be achieved? It is clearly impossible for the major aviation countries to adopt the extremely effective El Al security searches of luggage and intensive questioning of passengers by intelligence officers. This works well for Israel's specialized aviation needs, but it would soon bring world commercial aviation to a grinding halt if it became common practice. Rapid and totally reliable EDS is therefore an essential weapon in beating the aviation terrorist. Yet, although there are many excellent technologies capable of detecting plastic explosives, there has been no real international effort to make them available in airports, and the only country which has invested substantial R. & D. efforts to develop such equipment is the USA by means of the Federal Aviation Administration's programme to upgrade security. We also urgently need to install a foolproof positive baggage reconciliation system, using the IATA bar code, capable of being operated throughout the international aviation system. This would be an enormous asset in the battle against the terrorist suitcase bomber, and would easily pay for itself because it would save billions of dollars currently lost through misrouted luggage.

This is both a technological and a political challenge, because it is crucial to mobilize the political will and resources to make such improved security—including better management, staffing, and procedures—available to international aviation generally.[16] Enhancement of national systems is a vital first step, but governments, the industry, and passengers will need to join forces to internationalize an effective response. Urgent steps are needed to raise the necessary funds for this purpose, and to set up a system for monitoring, inspecting, and *enforcing* proper security standards world-wide, using aviation sanctions as necessary. It is clear that international and national problems of response to terrorism are interwoven. To be effective, action against terrorists must be synchronized at both levels. By tolerating the terrorists' capacity to provoke war the international community is playing with fire. And we have seen how, in severe cases, terrorists confront democracies internally with a ruthless challenge against the safety of their citizens, the security of the state, and the rule of law. Of course the nature of response required will vary according to the severity of the challenge, but it is vital to get it right, because strong national policies to deal with terrorism are the building-blocks of a more effective international response.

*Principles to Combat Terrorism*

In the current period, when Britain, Spain, Greece, and other democratic states face continuing campaigns of violence, it is important to reiterate the cardinal principles of an effective liberal-democratic response to terrorism. These are:

- no surrender to the terrorists, and an absolute determination to defeat terrorism within the framework of the rule of law and the democratic process;
- no deals and no concessions, even in the face of the most severe intimidation and blackmail;
- an intensified effort to bring terrorists to justice by prosecution and conviction before courts of law;
- firm measures to penalize state sponsors who give terrorists safe haven, weapons, explosives, cash, and moral and diplomatic support;
- a determination never to allow terrorist intimidation to block or derail political and diplomatic efforts to resolve the underlying conflicts in strife-torn regions, such as the Middle East: in many such areas terrorism has become a major threat to peace and stability, and its suppression therefore is in the common interests of international society.

It may be claimed that these principles are of a very general nature, and that most democratic states confronting terrorism have violated some or all of these guidelines in certain circumstances. It is also true that these general assumptions do not amount to anything like a detailed policy on counter-terrorism. Such policies obviously have to be developed and co-ordinated covering such aspects as intelligence, crisis management, emergency measures, and the development and deployment of specialist counter-terrorist units within the police and armed forces, with the technical resources to back them up.

It is true that some of the most serious failures in counter-terrorism occur at the operational and tactical levels; for example, weaknesses in co-ordination, intelligence failures, or serious gaps in training or logistic support. It is no good taking the trouble to get the general principles accepted if these are not adequately implemented.

Nevertheless, violations of the fundamental principles of the liberal-democratic response have far more serious long-term implications, causing much wider political damage. For example, policies of appeasement, doing 'deals' with terrorists, indiscriminate repression, abuses of the legal process, and similar breaches, damage not only the individuals immediately involved, but also the integrity and legitimacy of the entire system, and thus play into the hands of the terrorists. Hence, the liberal-democratic principles should never be viewed as being of purely cosmetic or rhetorical significance. They are the very *essence* of democracy, and any severe terrorist campaign puts them to one of their harshest possible tests.

## The Key Roles of Politics and Diplomacy

It is of course a dangerous illusion to believe that if only we could alight on the appropriate formula for a diplomatic settlement or political reform, the underlying grievances of terrorists would be met, and all the violence would melt away. The search for the perfect political solution to terrorism is as much of a will-o'-the-wisp as the pursuit of a military solution. The experience of democratic states in the twentieth century suggests that what is really needed to curb terrorism effectively is a concerted multipronged approach, carefully calibrated to the level required to deal with the scale of terrorism employed, and combining the most valuable elements of political, legal, police, military, and socioeconomic measures.

Nevertheless, it is the case that the potential role and value of political and diplomatic approaches in the overall context of efforts to defeat terrorists are generally seriously underestimated. Let us take the key example of the Arab–Israeli conflict. Let us suppose that by some miracle the Israeli government is persuaded to continue at the negotiating table with Palestinians and the leading Arab states, and succeeds in devising a major agreement reconciling the demands of Palestinians for self-determination with the demands of Israel for secure borders.

Of course we know that extremists on both sides would try to wreck the agreement because they would view it as a betrayal of their maximalist aims. Groups such as the *Abu Nidal* group on the one hand, the Jewish extremists, the modern *Sicarii*, on the other, would continue acts of terror in a desperate effort to block a settlement.[17] Nevertheless, who can deny that if a major diplomatic agreement could be achieved that satisfied at least mainstream opinion on both the Palestinian and Israeli sides it would have a considerable effect in reducing the amount of violence and would render the terrorist groups far more isolated, weaker, and less politically dangerous.

The same applies in the context of the most intractable and bitter internal conflicts. It was the great strength of Peter Brooke, the present Secretary of State for Northern Ireland, that he did recognize the crucial importance of achieving *political* progress in the Province. His patient diplomacy almost paid off in the summer of 1991, only to be blocked by Union differences over the Anglo–Irish conference being held while inter-Party talks were in progress. Mr Brooke's initiative gained the backing of all major parties at Westminster. If it develops it will help in several ways to improve the political climate and further to isolate and politically weaken the IRA. Meaningful political co-operation between the SDLP, the major party of the Catholic minority in Northern Ireland, and the Unionists, in the context of a power-sharing system would indeed be major progress towards healing the bitter divisions of the past. Furthermore, such an outcome would once again demonstrate the futility of the IRA's terrorist campaign. Mr Brooke rightly insisted that the Provisional Sinn Fein should not be able to take part in any key discussions about the political future in Northern Ireland unless it abandons terrorism.

As we noted earlier in the survey of recent trends, the Middle East is far and away the major source of conflicts which spawn terrorism, and the most serious and dangerous of these in the long run is undoubtedly the Arab–Israeli conflict.[18] A key success of US diplomacy in 1991–2 was persuading Israel and the Arab states to reopen serious diplomatic negotiations to find a way of resolving this festering problem. For the Israeli government the prospect of sitting on the powder-keg of 1.5 million Palestinian Arabs for years ahead is clearly incompatible with Israeli security. Other options must be explored as a matter of the greatest urgency.

The IRA is far and away the most dangerous terrorist movement in Europe. In the past twenty years more than 2,900 people have been killed through the conflict in Northern Ireland. The IRA is responsible for roughly 60 per cent of these deaths, two-thirds of them civilians.

The level of IRA activity outside Northern Ireland is higher than at any time since the mid-1970s. The only other European organization in the same league is the Basque extremist movement, ETA, which has killed more than 500 people in Spain over the same period, half of them civilians.

True, the security forces in Northern Ireland have had more success in thwarting attacks over the past two years. A better flow of intelligence and security has enabled them to prevent many explosions and the rate of arrests in the province has gone up dramatically. But on mainland Britain police are facing intensified IRA violence with an enormous handicap: they lack intelligence on IRA operations in Britain—the leaders and cells involved and their logistic support network—which is vital if they are to capture the cells and prevent further attacks.

Why has IRA terrorism proved so intractable? And what lessons could be learnt from the success of other European Community countries in tackling internal terrorism? One fundamental reason for the stubborn survival of the IRA is that it draws on the general support or sympathy of roughly 10 per cent of the population in the Province, providing a constant supply of terrorist recruits and collaborators. By terrorist standards, the IRA has a strong financial infrastructure, using racketeering, extortion, smuggling, and legitimate business to raise funds. Above all, it has three assets for mounting terrorist operations.

First, in the Republic, it enjoys logistic support and relative safety from Northern Irish and British justice. Secondly, from Colonel Gadaffi it has obtained Semtex and other weapons. Thirdly, twenty years of operations against the combined expertise of the Army and the RUC have made the IRA one of the most technically sophisticated terrorist groups in the world.

It is expert not only in bomb-making and operational planning, but in propaganda warfare, especially in its defamation campaign against the Northern Ireland judicial and penal systems. Its members have also proved themselves capable of adapting their mode of operations on mainland Britain and the Continent to make it far harder for the police to find them. They keep their distance from the Irish community, maintain secure links with the godfathers, and show great versatility in striking a wide range of soft military and civilian targets.

## VII.   What Lessons can be Learned from Other Countries?

By contrast, the threat from domestic terrorist groups in Continental Europe has declined sharply since the mid-1980s. The main internal threat in Italy, West Germany, mainland France, and Belgium comes from extreme-left, Red Army-style gangs, generally tiny in terms of hardcore membership. These groups have been far less lethal than the IRA. The *Red Brigades*, one of the more dangerous extreme-left groups, has killed about 150 people since its inception. Nevertheless, at the peak of its strength in the late 1970s, the group mounted a direct challenge to the Italian Republic, culminating in the kidnap and murder—on 9 May 1978—of Aldo Moro, a former prime minister.

In West Germany, the *Red Army Faction* has killed thirty-seven people since its formation. It is true that tiny residues of the Red Army-style groups are still at large and there has been a small number of assassinations and attempted killings. After the West German group's abortive attempt on Hans Neusel—the West German state secretary in charge of security at the Interior Ministry, in early August 1990—the terrorists issued a declaration of war against a greater German/West European Superpower.

These grandiose threats are oddly reminiscent of the 1985 claim by the *Red Army Faction*, France's *Action Directe* (AD), and Belgium's *Communist Combatant Cells* that they were forming a 'united guerrilla front' against NATO, an effort that soon fizzled out. The truth is that Red Army terrorism is a busted flush on the Continent: the AD has been inactive since its leaders were captured by the police; the *Red Army Faction* has lost its bolt-hole in East Germany, while the younger generation of German radicals views it as irrelevant to the concerns of the 1990s; and Italian police now see the Mafia as their main organized-crime problem.

A common factor in the Continent's success in suppressing Red Army terrorism is that all countries have developed strong national anti-terrorist co-ordination. After Moro's murder the

Italians appointed General Dalla Chiesa to co-ordinate anti-terrorist operations. He set up his own task-force to infiltrate the terrorist cells and helped devise the *Pentiti* law, which gave generous remission to captured terrorists who provided evidence leading to the arrest of their associates. This law led hundreds to collaborate and helped crack open the *Red Brigades'* cells and columns.

In West Germany, the BKA (the Federal Criminal Office) was the leading agency, with powers to co-ordinate anti-terrorism throughout the country. Horst Herold, head of the BKA until 1980, pioneered the use of sophisticated computerized anti-terrorist intelligence data, which he described as 'the material which gives us superiority over the terrorists'. West Germany's assets in computerized intelligence have greater practical value than ever following the introduction of machine-readable identity cards and passports, which make it far easier for police to trace suspects.

Given the severity of IRA terrorism, and the implications of dismantling the EC's internal borders in 1992, Dublin and London should study the advantages of the co-ordination and computerization of intelligence and Continental ID card and passport systems.

We could also learn from the experience of improved cross-border co-operation between France and Spain over ETA terrorism. Since 1987 there has been a radical improvement, particularly on intelligence-sharing and extradition, with more than 150 suspected Basque terrorists being expelled from France in 1987. The French and Spanish have also set up a joint police liaison office to strengthen co-operation further.

The British authorities need more substantial anti-terrorist co-operation with the Republic of Ireland. They hope the Republic will abide by its new commitment to extradite those wanted on terrorist charges. Dublin needs to improve its intelligence-gathering and policing to enable it to deal with the threat, perhaps through the creation of an EC fund to enhance anti-terrorist resources.

In our increasingly integrated Community we must learn that no member-state is an island, particularly in the modern world of terrorism and drug-trafficking. We need to create the understanding that one democracy's terrorist is another democracy's terrorist and devise a Europe-wide criminal justice system appropriate to a Europe without internal frontiers.

We can also learn some useful lessons from the American experience in fighting major crime. The Northern Ireland Office, the Home Office, and the security forces in Northern Ireland have shown considerable interest in the US American Racketeer-Influenced and Corrupt Organizations Act, which has been used very effectively against organized crime, especially the Mafia. It has long caused outrage and puzzlement that the godfathers of terrorism in Northern Ireland are able to walk the streets without fear of arrest. The US anti-Mafia-style law would help to put the godfathers behind bars. The purpose of the legislation is to enable the courts to convict individuals found guilty of being involved in or associated with a criminal organization through racketeering, extortion, and so on. In order to gather the necessary evidence to convict, surveillance (including telephone taps) would be needed over a long period. There would clearly need to be civil liberties' safeguards. However, there is no doubt that legislation modelled on the US example would be of enormous value in bringing the godfathers to book.

In addition to cracking down on the racketeering and corruption which helps to sustain the IRA's murder machine, the authorities should make use of the well-tried method of offering substantial financial rewards for members of the public who provide valuable information to the police leading to the apprehension and conviction of terrorists. In many cases members of the public are nervous of coming forward to help the police with their inquiries, and with good reason, for there may well be a substantial risk to them and members of their families. A generous reward scheme would help to give a greater incentive to take those risks. To work effectively such a scheme would need to be combined with an adequately resourced and professionally organized witness-protection scheme of the kind used so successfully in the USA.

## VIII. What Measures can be Taken against State-Sponsored Terrorism?

There is no doubt that the democratic revolution in Eastern Europe dealt a huge blow against state-sponsored terrorism.[19] All the one-party Communist regimes were deeply implicated in the sponsorship of terrorism throughout the 1970s, certainly with the full encouragement of the Soviet KGB. Information now leaking out from the files of the former security police has already confirmed that thousands of terrorists were trained and helped by Communist regimes, including Palestinian groups, and left-wing groups active in Western Europe. The East Germans helped the *Red Army Faction* by giving them safe haven, cover, and new identities. East German training camps like Finsterwalde, near Dresden, were particularly important for passing on techniques of terrorism and assassination. Czechoslovakia was an important source of Semtex and firearms for terrorists. Hungary served as a haven and base for 'Carlos', the notorious Latin American terrorist. Poland was for a long period used as a European base for the *Abu Nidal* group. There is a great deal more to come out about these involvements, and it is at least possible that the new democratic authorities, keen to clean the Augean stables, will bring some of the former officials responsible to trial. They should certainly be encouraged to do so.

However, despite the loss of this valuable network of state sponsors in East Europe international terrorists can still look to other states, such as Iraq, Iran, Syria, Libya, and Cuba for safe haven and sponsorship. Despite the fact that these states are flagrantly defying international law by organizing and participating in 'terrorist acts in another state' (the wording is taken from the *UN Declaration on Principles of International Law*), very little effective action has been taken by the world community to penalize them.[20]

State sponsorship greatly increases the danger of terrorism to the international community because it provides the client groups with far greater firepower than they would ever be likely to obtain in the normal arms market. An obvious example would be Libya's provision of vast quantities of Semtex and other weapons to the IRA, thus considerably tilting the balance in favour of the terrorists and against the security forces. It is also worth bearing in mind that state sponsors are strongly suspected of involvement in the mass murder of airline passengers at Lockerbie in 1988 and over the Niger Desert in 1989.

What can be done to stop state sponsorship? It is surely time for the powerful industrial nations to combine their economic and diplomatic power to impose harsh sanctions on the guilty states. Under certain circumstances the use of military measures may well be the most appropriate option. The evidence of the effect of the US bombing of Libya in 1986, however, is rather ambiguous. It certainly pushed Gaddafi off-balance for a while. But it did not apparently cause him to cease his covert support for terrorist groups, such as the IRA. On the other hand both Syria and Libya may be highly vulnerable to really tough and concerted economic sanctions, as both regimes have major weaknesses in their economies which make them highly dependent on external trade and financial links. It must be admitted, however, that the European Community has been extremely timid in taking economic action. This is yet another instance where the EC lacks clear evidence of collective will and coherent policy.

## 1992: Rising to the Challenge

It is widely recognized among security specialists that the proposed dismantling of the European Community's internal frontiers in 1992 carries a grave risk that terrorists and organized criminal gangs such as the Mafia will take full advantage of the Single European Market.[21]

The principle that the EC needs to strengthen its criminal justice system to compensate for the abolition of internal borders has already been conceded in the terms of the Schengen Agreement (1990) but the additional co-operation proposed between the Benelux countries, France, and Germany is extremely modest.

It is unrealistic to assume that terrorists, drug-traffickers, and other major criminals will restrict themselves to operating within certain national territories of the Single European Market. Surely, far more imaginative measures are needed to create a Euro-wide criminal justice system. It would be foolish simply to wait for the various national legal systems to 'evolve' into a more harmonized system. What is needed is a European Community criminal law statute providing for a European Community Criminal Court in which serious crime (such as terrorism, drug-trafficking, etc.) committed anywhere in the EC could be dealt with. The legal statute should provide for a court to investigate, try, and sentence in such cases. The Euro Court would have the enormous advantage of overriding all the tedious and often chauvinistic national arguments among EC states regarding the extradition of terrorists. Terrorists would know that they could not get safe haven simply by moving from one EC state to another. In addition the criminal law statute could provide a proper remit and legal basis for a Euro-style FBI of the kind proposed by Chancellor Kohl in 1989. This should greatly facilitate the fight against serious crime within the Community. Surely this concept of an EC criminal statute and court is worthy of serious study by the EC Ministers of Justice and Interior.[22] In a sense it would be a logical addition to the existing structures of the European Court of Justice and the Council of Europe's Human Rights Court. The absence of a European criminal court from our institution-building in Europe seems a somewhat glaring omission in the light of plans for 1992.

## IX. What Conclusions can we Draw?

Terrorism is not simply a problem for the richest and most powerful states. It is a challenge which has to be faced by the entire international community. Terrorism is, at the very least, a threat to individual human rights and the rule of law. But at its most severe levels it endangers the stability and well-being of whole communities and states and may, under certain circumstances, trigger internal and even international wars.

A key problem in responding to terrorism is to find the right balance of effective and proportionate measures which avoid the evils of both over-reaction and under-reaction. Democratic societies everywhere can take heart from the fact that a number of countries have succeeded in defeating major terrorist campaigns without losing their democratic process and rule of law. The successes of West Germany and Italy in virtually eradicating the threat from *Red Army* and *Red Brigade* terrorists offer two very encouraging examples.

Democracies are important in a more fundamental sense in the long-term battle against terrorism. While it is true that terrorists can exploit the freedoms of an open and democratic society to mount attacks, the very legitimacy of democracy in the eyes of its citizens provides a kind of inner moral strength which helps the system to withstand any attempt to subvert or overthrow it. In the final analysis the battle between democracy and terrorism is a test of moral strength and political will.

It is unrealistic to hope for an international system purged of all tyrannies and dictatorships, at least in the foreseeable future. All experience shows that as long as there continue to be tyrannies, terrorists will find sponsorship, support, succour, and safe haven. Yet this should not cause the democracies to sit on their hands and write off any effort to strengthen international co-operation to counter terrorism. Democratic states must work even more closely together for the suppression of terrorism. For it is in their common interests and in the interests of humanity to work together for the eradication of this scourge.

## Notes

The following abbreviations are used in this chapter

| | |
|---|---|
| EOKA | Ethniki Organosis Kypriakon Agoniston |
| ETA | Euskadi ta Askatasuna |
| FLN | Front de Libération Nationale |
| FLOSY | Front for the Liberation of Occupied South Yemen |
| PIRA | Provisional Irish Republican Army |
| PFLP-GC | Popular Front for the Liberation of Palestine—General Command |
| Trevi | Terrorism, Radicalism, Extremism and International Violence: set up as an intergovernmental forum under the European Political Co-operation (EPC) in 1976 |
| WAD | Afghan Ministry of State Security |

1. See Alex P. Schmid and A. Jongman (eds.), *Political Terrorism: A Research Guide to Concepts, Theories, Data Bases and Literature*, 2nd edn. (Amsterdam: North Holland Publishing Co., 1988).
2. For discussions of typology, see R. Shultz, 'Conceptualising Political Terrorism: A Typology', *Journal of International Affairs*, 32 (1978), 7–15; F. J. Hacker, *Crusaders, Criminals, Crazies* (London: Macmillan, 1974).
3. For general histories of terrorism, see A. Parry, *Terrorism from Robespierre to Arafat* (New York: Vanguard Press, 1976); W. Laqueur, *The Age of Terrorism* (London: Weidenfeld & Nicolson, 1978); W. Laqueur, *The Terrorism Reader: A Historical Anthology* (Philadelphia: Temple University Press, 1978); and Roland Gaucher, *The Terrorists: From Tsarist Russia to the OAS* (London: Secker & Warburg, 1968).
4. A detailed, authoritative account is given in B. Lewis, *The Assassins: A Radical Sect in Islam* (London: Weidenfeld & Nicolson, 1967).

5. A good historical survey of these conflicts is provided by C. Townshend, *Britain's Civil Wars: Counterinsurgency in the Twentieth Century* (London: Faber & Faber, 1986).

6. See Martha Crenshaw Hutchinson, *Revolutionary Terrorism: The FLN in Algeria, 1954–1962* (Stanford, Calif.: Stanford University Press, 1978); Yves Courrière, *La Guerre d'Algérie* (4 vols., Paris: Fayard).

7. Karen Gardela and Bruce Hoffman, *The RAND Chronology of International Terrorism for 1986* (Santa Monica, Calif.: RAND Corporation, 1990).

8. See, for example, John W. Amos, *The Palestinian Resistance* (New York: Pergamon Press, 1980); Helena Cobban, *The Palestinian Liberation Organization* (Cambridge: Cambridge University Press, 1984); Bard E. O'Neil, *Armed Struggle in Palestine* (Boulder, Colo.: Westview Press, 1978); Y. Harkabi, *The Arab's Position in their Conflict with Israel* (Jerusalem: Israel Universities Press, 1972); and John Laffin, *Fedayeen: The Arab–Israeli Dilemma* (New York: Free Press, 1973).

9. For a useful reference work on many of these movements, see Peter Janke, *Guerrilla and Terrorist Organisations: A World Directory* (Brighton: Harvester Press, 1983).

10. Carlos Marighela, 'Handbook of Urban Guerrilla Warfare', in *For the Liberation of Brazil* (Harmondsworth: Penguin Books, 1971).

11. See Peter Clyne, *An Anatomy of Skyjacking* (London: Abelard-Schuman, 1973); David Phillips, *Skyjack* (London: Harrap, 1973); Alona Evans, 'Aerial Hijacking', in M. Cherif Bassiouni (ed.), *International Terrorism and Political Crimes* (Springfield, Ill.: Charles C. Thomas, 1974); Kenneth C. Moore, *Airport, Aircraft and Airline Security* (Los Angeles: Security World Publishing, 1976); Alona E. Evans and John Murphy (eds.), *Legal Aspects of International Terrorism* (Lexington, Mass., Lexington Books, 1978) (see particularly section on aviation terrorism); and P. Wilkinson, *The Lessons of Lockerbie* (London: Research Institute for the Study of Conflict and Terrorism, 1989).

12. See R. Clutterbuck, *The Media and Political Violence* (London: Macmillan, 1981); A. Miller, *Terrorism: The Media and the Law* Dobbs Ferry, NY: Transaction Publishing, 1982); A. P. Schmid and Janny F. A. De Graff, *Violence as Communication: Insurgent Terrorism and the Western News Media* (Beverly Hills, Calif.: Sage, 1982); and B. M. Jenkins, *The Psychological Implications of Media-Covered Terrorism* (Santa Monica, Calif.: RAND Corporation, 1981).

13. On the effects of violence on Lebanon see David Gilmour, *Lebanon: The Fractured Country* (Oxford: Martin Robertson, 1983); John

Bulloch, *Death of a Country: Civil War in Lebanon* (London: Weidenfeld & Nicolson, 1977); and Itamar Rabinovich, *The War for Lebanon, 1970–1985* (Ithaca, NY: Cornell University Press, 1985). On Sri Lanka, see R. Kearney, 'Tension and Conflict in Sri-Lanka', *Current History* (March 1986), 109–12, and C. H. S. Jayewardene and H. Jayewardene, *Tea for Two: Ethnic Violence in Sri Lanka*(Ottawa, Ont.: Crimcare, 1984).

14. See Gary Sick, *All Fall Down: America's Tragic Encounter with Iran* (New York: Random House, 1985); Jimmy Carter, *Keeping Faith: Memoirs of a President* (New York: Bantam Books, 1982); and Warren Christopher, *et al.*, *American Hostages in Iran: The Conduct of a Crisis* (New Haven, Conn.: Yale University Press, 1985).

15. For a variety of views on this moral debate, see: Michael Walzer, *Just and Unjust Wars* (New York: Basic Books, 1973); David Rapoport and Yonah Alexander (eds.), *The Morality of Terrorism: Religions and Secular Justifications* (New York: Pergamon Press, 1982); Martin Warner and Roger Crisp (eds.), *Terrorism, Protest and Power* (Aldershot: Edward Elgar Publishing Company, 1990); and P. Wilkinson, 'Ethical Defences of Terrorism: Defending the Indefensible'; *Terrorism and Political Violence*, 1/1 (Jan. 1989), 7–20.

16. For a powerful and authoritative statement of the case for an enhanced US national aviation security system, see *Report of the President's Commission on Aviation Security and Terrorism* (Washington, DC: Government Printing Office, 1990).

17. The original Sicarii was a fanatical religious sect active in the Zealot struggle in Palestine (AD 66–73) against the Roman occupiers and those in the Jewish community prepared to co-operate peacefully with the Romans.

18. The Department of State's annual report on international terrorism in 1989 states: 'the Middle East continued to experience the largest number of incidents of international terrorism, incurring 1,993 attacks—37% of the total worldwide. The proportion of international terrorism connected with the Middle East increases to 45%, however, when Middle East spillover attacks into other regions are added.' *Patterns of Global Terrorism 1989* (Washington, DC: Office of the Coordinator for Counter-Terrorism, 1990), 1.

19. For a variety of approaches to the study of state sponsorship, see: Roberta Goren, *The Soviet Union and Terrorism* (London: George Allen & Unwin, 1984); Feliks Gross, *Violence in Politics: Terror and Political Assassination in Eastern Europe and Russia* (The Hague: Mouton, 1972); John F. Murphy, *State Support of International Terrorism* (Boulder, Colo.: Westview Press, 1989); G. M. Levitt, *Democracies Against Terror: The Western Response to State-Supported*

*Terrorism* (New Haven, Conn.: Yale Univ. Press, 1988); Michael Stohl and George Lopez, *State as Terrorist: Dynamics of Governmental Violence and Repression* (Westport, Conn.: Greenwood Press, 1984); and P. Wilkinson, 'State-sponsored International Terrorism: The Problems of Response', *The World Today* (July 1984), 292–8.

20. The language is taken from the UN Declaration on *Principles of International Law Concerning Friendly Relations and Cooperation Among States.*

21. For evidence of this concern in the UK, see House of Commons, Home Affairs Committee Memoranda of Evidence, Session 1989–90, *Practical Police Co-operation in the European Community* (London: HMSO, 1990).

22. The idea of an international court to try those accused of crimes of international terrorism is hardly new. It was first proposed during the League of Nations debate, following the 1934 assassinations of King Alexander of Yugoslavia and Louis Barthou, the French Foreign Minister. The idea was revived again in the 1970s when a draft convention on international crimes and a draft statute for an international criminal court were put forward by the International Law Association in 1972.

# TEN

# Third-Party Mediation and Conflict-Resolution in the Post-Cold War World

*Mark Hoffman*

The latter half of the 1980s saw a remarkable series of changes in the international system. In the initial euphoria regarding these events there was much talk of the 'end of history', a new age of peace, a new world order. As events continued to unfold, however, it became clear that, if anything, 'history' had returned with a vengeance.

For many, this situation was nothing new. The Cold War had not been a period of relative, though highly militarized, stability as it had been in Europe. The focus on US–Soviet relations and European security, defined largely in terms of containment, deterrence, and arms control, conditioned many to view the continuing violent conflicts elsewhere in the world as epiphenomena of the larger geopolitical struggle between East and West. Violent conflict in the 'periphery' was the price that was paid for 'peace' in the core.

This Cold War construct ignored the nature of many of these conflicts. The causes of conflict were not simply East–West competition (though they might be presented as such by the political leadership of fighting factions seeking external military aid) but often lay in ethnic tensions, economic inequalities, social injustices, and the tenuous legitimacy of political regimes. The reality of international conflict was not to be found in simple black-and-white dichotomies of East versus West but in a multiplicity of cross-cutting issues and a diverse range of actors with apparently irreconcilable differences over the protection and attainment of their material interests, the preservation of the historical and cultural values of a community, and the fulfilment of the need for some form of recognized identity.

The most intractable of these have been characterized as 'deep-rooted' or 'protracted social conflicts'.[1] The sources of such conflict are located in the denial of fundamental human needs for security, a distinctive identity, the recognition of that identity by others, and effective and legitimized participation in social, economic, and political systems. These needs are often expressed in and fulfilment sought via identity groups (e.g., religious, ethnic, racial). It is the suppression or lack of fulfilment of these needs, often manifest in structural economic, political, and social inequalities, which eventually leads to the outbreak of violent conflict. Such conflicts may entail an almost existential component as the conflicting parties perceive each other as posing a threat to their respective societies, institutions, culture, values, and identity.

The submergence of deep-rooted conflicts beneath the contours of Cold War confrontation had direct implications for the approaches taken toward conflict-management. During the Cold War, complex conflicts were handled through the traditional means of coercive diplomacy and crisis-management in the context of Superpower rivalry and competition. Containment, rather than resolution, was the objective. Yet the efficacy of these approaches needs to be seriously questioned. The flawed assumptions on which they are based, the inherent contradictions they entail, and their largely unsuccessful history in promoting sustainable solutions to violent conflicts are part of the legacy of the former Cold War system. More often than not, these methods served to exacerbate the conflicts while masking the underlying sources of conflict.

With the dramatic changes in the international system from the late 1980s onwards, the underlying sources of conflict in the international system have come more fully to the fore. The end of the Cold War has 'unfrozen' those aspects of international, regional, and intranational conflicts which had been contained within the dynamics of East–West relations. The most important consequence of these changes and the major dilemma to be faced in the post-Cold War international system is that the management of these conflicts has become increasingly more complex. As we move towards the twenty-first century, this complexity highlights not only the limitations of traditional means of dealing with and attempting to settle or resolve these conflicts but also creates pressures and opportunities for more innovative means of dealing with international conflict.

One of the most promising areas in the effort to develop innovative means of dealing with conflict in the post-Cold War international environment can be found in the practice and theory of third-party mediation and conflict-resolution. The initial development of third-party approaches to conflict-management and resolution began during the 1960s, continued to develop throughout the 1970s, and gained considerable momentum in the 1980s. The apparent success of such third-party efforts as the Camp David process, the increasingly evident stalemate in a number of international conflicts, and their resistance to settlement solely via traditional means has created an environment which is increasingly receptive to the possibilities offered by these approaches.[2]

The purpose of this chapter is to provide a brief description of these approaches. It will survey the contending frameworks found in the literature regarding third-party mediation and conflict-resolution and discuss some of the issues and debates that relate to these fields. Most importantly, it will argue that there is a complementarity and interconnectedness between what are seen in the literature as divergent, competing, and incompatible approaches to resolving conflicts.

## I. Has Third-Party Intervention been Employed in Conflict-Management?

Third-party intervention in international conflict has a long and well-established history. On the basis of empirical research and academic theorizing, a wide number of diverse and divergent aspects of third-party activities have been highlighted.[3] These can be differentiated according to the nature of the outcome being pursued (partial settlement versus integrative resolution), the processes used (arbitration, bargaining and negotiation, leveraged mediation, facilitative problem-solving workshops), the nature of the mediator (private individuals, scholar-practitioners, diplomats, regional organization, international organization, international non-governmental organization), the level or 'track'[4] at which they operate (official, unofficial), the nature of the conflict they are dealing with (dispute, conflict, protracted social conflict), and the level of conflict causation they are addressing (interests, values, or needs). These diverse elements are variously combined providing the basis for what are seen in the academic literature as distinct, often exclusionary, competing forms of third-party practices.

Thus, the range of possible third-party intervention covers a spectrum that runs from various forms of non-coercive facilitation and consultation through different types of mediation in which varying degrees of leverage are exerted to situations in which the decision-making authority is held by a third party via powers of arbitration. For the purposes of this chapter, these different types of third-party activities will be coalesced into several broad categories based on the identity, role, functions, techniques, and objectives of the third party.[5] These categories are arbitration, mediation, and facilitation, though only the last two will be addressed in any detail.

Arbitration is a form of binding, authoritative third-party intervention in which conflicting parties agree to hand the determination of a final settlement to outsiders. It is a formal, legal, or quasi-legal means of conflict-management which is provided for in many international agreements and treaties. Because it requires that all parties to a dispute or conflict agree to submit their respective claims to arbitration, it is of limited value in dealing with violent, protracted conflicts. Arbitration can work where the sources of the conflict are disputes over the interpretation or enactment of treaty provision, where the conflict has a strictly legal character. When these 'legal' disputes are the superficial manifestations of deeper, underlying conflicts or when the parties in conflict are not even willing to sit at the same table and engage in dialogue, then the focus turns to mediation and facilitation as the more viable and efficacious means of third-party intervention.

Within much of the literature real differences are perceived between third-party mediation and third-party facilitation. Mediation is construed as a device or means for *settling* disputes, often within the context of power politics and entailing a considerable degree of leverage on the part of the third party.[6] Conflict settlement is viewed as reaching an agreement on a particular aspect of a conflict rather than the conflict as a whole through a process of mediated bargaining and negotiation. It is a limited endeavour, focusing on the interests of the parties with the range of possible outcomes bounded by the parties participating and the contexts within which it takes place.

Third-party facilitation is often characterized as a means for *resolving* conflicts.[7] Conflict-resolution is the attainment of a non-hierarchical, non-coercive integrative solution that is derived from the parties themselves through a process of analytic problem-solving. It focuses on what it argues are the underlying non-material sources of the conflict and the establishment of acceptable relationships between adversaries.[8]

Within the literature, the dichotomy between these two approaches has been characterized in a number of different ways. Wehr refers to it as 'competitive/hierarchical versus collaborative/ network' approaches;[9] Jabri as bargaining versus facilitative approaches;[10] and Bercovitch as instrumental versus process approaches.[11] The dichotomy between the approaches is derivative of differing views on the identity, role, and objectives of the third parties and it is worth considering the differences between these approaches in more detail.

## II. What is the Nature of Third-Party Mediation?

Third-party mediation is a process in which parties to a dispute attempt to reach a mutually agreeable solution under the auspices of a third party. It developed as an alternative to arbitration and as an adjunct to more formalized negotiation processes in a number of different areas. Multi-disciplinary in nature, the theory and practice of mediation has drawn on research and practice in the fields of communications studies, industrial relations, business and management studies, political science, social-psychology, anthropology, and international relations. The work in these various fields has started to converge in recent years, producing an increasingly focused body of ideas. There are, however, important points of divergence linked to different disciplinary backgrounds and to the social contexts in which mediation takes place— interpersonal, intergroup, organization, intercommunal, or inter- national.[12]

The nature of third-party mediation is dependent on a number of factors: the sources of the conflict and the context in which it arose; the number and type of issues in a conflict; the history of trust or hostility between the parties; their predisposition to negotiate and compromise; and the nature and timing of the request or offer of mediation. Based on these factors, third-party mediators may serve a number of functions or act in a number of roles or capacities. Mediators may provide a conduit for communication between disputing parties, persuade parties to make concessions, provide a means for cutting losses while saving face, help the parties develop and explore alternative solutions, offer specific solutions, or provide the resources to make a settlement workable. Young[13] provides a fourfold characterization of the objectives of mediation: informational (offering information, increasing communication); tactical (offering services and resources); conceptual (offering ideas for settlement); and supervisory (monitoring agreements).

Within the literature and research dealing with third-party mediation in international conflicts, the structure of international politics is seen as imparting an important power political dimension to the nature, techniques, and outcomes of the mediation process. In consequence it has been dominated by the assumptions of what might be characterized as an outcome-oriented approach towards mediation. Bercovitch[14] has succinctly discussed the characteristic features of this approach. It is limited in its scope and characterized by its exclusiveness (not all parties to a conflict necessarily participate). Outcome-oriented mediation is focused on reducing the intensity of a conflict and facilitating concessions. The aim is to identify the range of an acceptable pay-off matrix or a zone of potential agreement for the conflicting parties. Using whatever leverage it has, the third party can then attempt to move the parties towards an outcome within that range. The mediator may offer incentives to increase receptiveness to particular outcomes, or 'frame' the conflict in ways that increase the possibility of agreement, or coerce the parties into concessions, hopefully without loss of face.

This approach sees the mediation process as an exercise in power and influence. It is directive and carried out within a defined structure of power relations in which the third party often becomes an 'outcome advocate' for a particular package.[15] The outcome that is often advocated is one that deals with a particular aspect of the conflict, usually seeking to alter those elements of the conflict situation which induce violent hostilities. However, the circumscribed focus of third-party mediation often leaves the general features of the conflict unaffected. In short, it focuses solely on the issues of immediate interest or importance to the parties in the mediation process—both disputants and mediators— and may not actually deal with the underlying, more fundamental issues at stake.

The centrality of the power political dimension is evident in much of the literature. Touval and Zartman,[16] for example, are clear that international mediation has to be defined, understood, and conducted in the context of power politics. Mediation must be power political or the mediator will have no leverage over the disputants. Not only that, but the mediators themselves, they argue, will only mediate if they have a set of interests in the conflict or in its settlement. The interests of mediators includes not only the abatement of conflict but also the protection or enhancement of their own political and economic interests. Mediators are not indifferent to the possible outcomes of negotiations. They may have 'defensive' interests (protecting threats to their interests) or 'expansive' interests (seeking to extend their influence). Thus, for Touval and Zartman, the motives and understanding of mediation are to be found in traditional power politics.

The affect of power politics on the mediation process is also evident in the question of determining when the conflict is 'ripe' for third-party intervention.[17] Pruitt and Rubin[18] and Touval and Zartman[19] have all argued that the ripe moment for mediation is linked to a situation of a 'mutually hurting stalemate' where the various parties to the conflict perceive that there is little to be gained from further escalation of the conflict. Pruitt and Rubin[20] and Touval and Zartman[21] go so far as to argue that it may be desirable for the mediator actually to produce a stalemate based on their view that 'stalemate is necessary to mediation, just as mediation is necessary to overcome stalemate'. The acceptance of mediation often signals such a state and the parties' desire for a negotiated end to their dispute. Once the hurting stalemate has been reached, mediation is sought or accepted because it provides a mechanism for reducing the costs of making concessions, particularly when the conflicting parties are accountable to a wider constituency.[22] Concessions can be characterized as being made to the mediator rather than the opposing party. Mediation may also be accepted because it is believed that the mediator may have some influence with the other parties (as in the case of US acceptance of Algerian mediation in the hostage crisis) or because it can reinforce compliance (for example, in Egyptian and Israeli acceptance of the Camp David Accords with US backing).

The important point that arises from this is that not only is it not necessary that a third-party mediator is impartial, it is undesirable and may be impossible. As Pruitt[23] argues, mediators with access to one or more of the parties and the capacity to influence them are more likely to be acceptable than those who are 'neutral'. Indeed, Touval, Zartman,[24] and others have argued that in the international context there is likely to be a significant relationship between the mediator and one or more of the disputants. The result is not mediation between two sides but a multi-cornered bargaining-process between the disputants and a mediator all pursuing their own interests.[25] The only requirement is that the mediator be acceptable to all the parties. What prevents lopsided or unequal solutions is the third parties' interest in having future dealings with all the parties in dispute. Therefore, third-party mediators, despite pursuing their own interests, will have more to gain by promoting evenhanded, equitable solutions.

The effectiveness of leveraged mediation will depend on the resources and capabilities of the third party and the strategies and tactics by which they are deployed. The tactics to be used in an outcome-oriented mediation approach will include: facilitation of communication; restructuring of issues; the formulation of proposals; and coalition building. The facilitation of communication is a central feature of third-party mediation, not only in providing a conduit for information between conflicting parties but also in altering their stated positions and inducing concessions. The mediator will be able to hold separate meetings with the disputing parties, allowing different ideas to be tested or aired. A disputant may be less concerned with the need to save face in the presence of a mediator. Mediators can take responsibility for concessions, eliminating the parties' concerns with looking weak, and creating expectations of further concessions. Indeed, it is argued that the mere presence of the mediator is likely to induce concessions.

The restructuring of the issues is the second central feature of outcome-oriented mediation. Here the mediator will use its leverage to create superordinate goals by stressing the existence of common interests above and outside the existing conflict. In addition, the mediator may expand the issue under discussion to create a set of multiple issues to be solved together (through off-setting compensation or log-rolling) rather than being settled sequentially.[26] This allows the mediator to foster trade-offs as the basis for a final agreement. Or the mediator may seek to introduce new issues or redefine issues so as to facilitate a solution. Or it may entail restructuring the agenda of issues so that easier issues are settled first providing momentum to the process and also fostering an element of trust.

The mediator may formulate, recommend, or seek to impose proposals for the settlement of the conflict. Indeed, some authors, such as Fisher and Ury,[27] advocate the advantages of 'single text negotiation' with the mediators providing the initial document on which subsequent discussions are based. These proposals need not be limited to the ideas of the disputing parties. In providing the initial framework for a solution the third party may create an environment conducive to flexibility on the part of the conflicting parties. It might also provide a basis on which the disputants would view their conflict from a different perspective. Such an approach assumes, however, that the mediator is able to uncover and clearly discern the interests and concerns of the disputing parties.

Finally, the third-party mediator will have to engage in a process of coalition building.[28] The coalition-building process works on two levels: at the level of agreements and at the level of the parties.[29] The former requires the creation of networks of linked agreements. This can be achieved by adding or subtracting parties to the negotiations, or linking agreement on one set of issues to agreement on another set of issues and, in doing so, altering the conflicting parties' perceptions of the range of alternative outcomes. The latter refers to the need to build coalitions of support for desired outcomes and against undesired outcomes among the conflicting parties themselves.

The major difficulty with this approach is that it often fails to address the underlying sources of conflict, particularly in protracted, violent conflicts. It relies in the end on a legalistic, sometimes coercive, framework in order to ensure that the parties comply with the concessions offered and promises made. Instead of producing outcomes with the prospect of long-term stability, it produces interim solutions which are subject to the stress and strains of the uneasy compromises on which it is based. Such agreements may provide the breathing space in which the parties regroup their resources to 'fight again another day' or may act as a litmus test of sincerity before moving on to more encompassing arrangements. More often than not, they become semi-permanent features of the wider conflict, providing a focal point for further hostility (often by excluded parties) and acting as impediments towards dealing with the deeper underlying sources of conflict.

## III. How does Third-Party Facilitation Differ from Third-Party Mediation?

In contrast to third-party mediation is third-party facilitation or consultation which seeks to promote the resolution of conflict. This approach argues that the third party should seek to promote integrative outcomes that are mutually acceptable to the parties. Third-party facilitation differs from third-party mediation because of the assumptions on which it is based, its objectives, the participants, the identity of the third party, and the nature of the outcomes.

The facilitation approach, also referred to as interactive problem-solving or third-party consultation, was developed by a group of scholar-practitioners interested in developing alternative techniques for conflict resolution. The approach developed as a reaction to the power political assumptions underpinning more traditional means of conflict management and drew on ideas in a wide range of literature: systems theory, functionalism, communications theory, organizational studies, social psychology, and socio-biology. Central to the approach is a focus on human rather than institutional behaviour and in particular on the idea of basic human needs. Most widely advocated by Burton as the theoretical and practical underpinnings of conflict resolution, these human needs are seen as inherent ontological and biological drives for human survival and development.[30] While there is no agreed list of what these needs are, most include the need for security, identity, and recognition. They are non-negotiable, cannot be compromised, and are suppressed only at a cost. It is the frustration, suppression, or denial of these basic human needs manifested in unequal, unjust, or illegitimate structural or institutional arrangements which is seen as the primary source of conflict.

The recognition of this leads naturally to an 'analytic problem-solving' approach to conflict which focuses on non-material, non-negotiable human needs rather than material, negotiable institutional interests. For Burton, this distinction between power political frameworks and a human-needs based framework is crucial. The former are seen as being pragmatic and expedient, offering considerable leeway to the third party based on the belief that with sufficient power the conflicting parties can be coerced into reaching an agreement. The latter is seen as delving beneath the hierarchy of positions, issues, interests, and values to the level of human needs and the basic relationship between the conflicting parties with the third party facilitating, rather than directing, constructive outcomes based on a restructuring of relationships and environment.

The process of third-party facilitation ideally operates in a co-operative, non-hierarchical, non-coercive fashion. Its essential feature is that it is an analytic process. It does not include direct bargaining or negotiation, nor does the third party advocate or impose specific solutions. Third-party facilitation is characterized by its inclusiveness (all parties to and all aspects of the conflict) and its diagnostic nature. Its scope and impact are intended to be extensive, affecting the entire system of interactions between conflicting parties. The central concern is the nature of the relationship between the conflicting parties and how to change the actual meaning, conditions, and circumstances of that relationship. Its inclusiveness allows it to focus on the structural, social, attitudinal, and interpersonal dimensions of the conflict relationship. It aims to perform a *transformative* function.

Its non-coercive, non-directive approach is aimed at increasing the capacity to determine goals and choose courses of action that help to avoid frustration and violence. Third-party facilitation has as its goal the improvement of the conflicting parties' own capabilities and resources to achieve a more creative decision-making process and resolution of the conflict. The process attempts to deal with the different concerns, values, interests, and goals of disputing parties precisely through fostering a dialogue about the parties' differing interpretations of the situation and in the process helps to redefine, refocus, and reframe their interests and values by fostering a recognition of their commonly held needs. The aim is to transform the situation from a conflict which divides the parties into a problem that they share and over which they need to co-operate if it is to be resolved. Compliance with agreements arrived at through problem-solving is enhanced because the solution arrived at has developed out of the consent of parties to the solution. A facilitated resolution promotes compliance because the solution is derived from the parties themselves. And, because the solution to the conflict is meant to derive from the conflicting parties themselves, third-party values and interests are excluded from the resolution process.

Third-party facilitation addresses not only the instrumental means and processes for achieving a resolution but also promotes a process of practical reasoning regarding the goals, interests, values, and needs at stake.[31] This reasoning process is fostered by the structure of the facilitation process itself.[32] In a confidential, neutral setting, representatives of the conflicting parties discuss their conflict under the guidance of a team of skilled facilitators. The workshop will normally move through three stages. The first entails an effort at coming to an accurate characterization and understanding of the conflict. This is done by having the representatives of each side present their view of the conflict with questions allowed to elicit information and to highlight the 'human dimension'. The second stage is aimed at redefining or reframing the conflict via the facilitators introducing analytic reformulations of information set out in the presentations and reference to other conflicts. Having identified the processes and institutionalized structures which have fostered the conflict, the third stage is the discussion of substantive issues and the identification of those processes and institutions that might foster and underpin creative responses.[33]

Central to the facilitative approach is getting the conflicting parties, who may fear the very act of communication with the other side, themselves to articulate and address their perceptions of the other parties and the nature and dynamics of the conflict, in an effort to remove the social-psychological blocks to creative decision-making. It puts participants in a situation where others do not necessarily share their interests and values or interpretation of a situation and through the process of communication and dialogue stimulates self-reflection on those positions. It has been characterized as an archaeological approach in which the third party helps the conflict parties dig down beneath their positions to their interests, from their interests to their values, and from their values to their needs, while connecting these to the institutional and structural contexts of their conflict.[34] Through promoting an awareness of common needs, it seeks to ensure that parties do not perceive only the possibility of winning or losing. At its core, third-party facilitation could be characterized as the promotion of consensual decision-making towards the resolution of conflict via a process of undistorted communication.

## IV. What are the Difficulties with a Human Needs Approach to Conflict Resolution?

Burton claims that conflict-resolution, because it is analytical, and based on the satisfaction of human needs, is non-ideological. But it is precisely with the idea of basic human needs that major questions have arisen with regards to this framework. These problems are fourfold: questions regarding its applicability at the level of international conflicts; the implications of the universality of needs; the cultural biases of needs; and questions surrounding the concept of needs itself.

The first set of questions raised regarding a needs-based approach to international conflict is whether it is applicable to conflicts at the international level involving large-scale structural and institutional entities such as states. This position has been most forcefully and cogently articulated by Bercovitch.[35] He argues that the human-needs-based approach is a special and ideal form of third-party intervention with limited applications in the international context. The possibilities of needs-based intervention are affected by the conjunction of a number of different conditions at the international level: its authoritarian climate; the distorted nature of communications; the inequality of parties; the lack of shared rationality; and the lack of an interdependent framework of attitudes and perceptions. The overlap between these various conditions undermines the possibility for a shared set of societal

norms which Bercovitch argues is a necessary condition for the
problem-solving approach to work. The consequence, Bercovitch
argues, is that the facilitative approach is not helpful in dealing
with international conflicts which involve diverse groups, most of
whom perceive a threat to their vital interests. In such conflicts
only more directive, instrumental, and leveraged forms of third-
party intervention offers the possibility of redefining or changing
status, prestige, and reduced forms of antagonisms.

The second set of problems arises from Burton's own arguments
regarding the genetic, ontological, and universal nature of needs.
Burton argues that human needs are universal and, therefore, held
in common.[36] Cultural and other values are shared to a large
degree in any society. Interests, however, separate members of
societies into groupings, frequently in opposition to each other.
The implications of this is that the fundamental goals of differing
ideologies are similar at the level of needs. It is at the level of
values and interests that differences occur. If this is the case, then
presumably once the commonality of needs are identified in the
resolution process, it will have to shift back towards the level of
differentiated satisfiers of those needs as embodied in societal
values and interests. If this is not the case, then implicit within
Burton's perspective is the homogeneity of values and interests
derived from commonly held needs.

The third set of problems starts to call into question the
universality of needs. This argues that the content of human
needs as identified by Burton and others is not non-ideological nor
acultural but is deeply imbued with Western conceptions of the
'self' and anterior notions of 'human development' by which to
measure the lack of fulfilment of need to the exclusion of other
cultural constructions of the 'person'. Indeed, as Avruch and
Black[37] have argued, Burton's position reduces culture to ir-
relevancy, marginalized to a non-role in the causes of conflict and
conflict-resolution.

The final set of questions surrounds the whole notion of needs
themselves. These questions have been raised in a wide range of
literature[38] but are cogently summarized by Mitchell.[39] They can
be coalesced into six categories. First, what does the list of human
needs contain and is there a hierarchy among them? Second, are
human needs universal and fundamental in all societies and
cultures? If there is a hierarchy of needs, is it the same across

different cultures? Third, even if needs are non-hierarchical, do they remain the same over time and space? Fourth, can needs be partially fulfilled? Fifth, are certain satisfiers linked to specific needs? Sixth, are these connections culturally determined? Mitchell argues that in order for there to be further development of a needs-based approach to conflict-theory and resolution the issues and contradictions raised by these questions need to be clarified and resolved.

More importantly, Mitchell notes that

one of the main effects of raising such issues . . . is that they begin to cast doubt on conflict researchers' stark distinction between conflict *settlement* (incomplete and temporary) and conflict *resolution* (durable, acceptable and permanent because it fulfils all previously frustrated needs completely). If some satisfiers fulfil particular needs completely and other needs partially, then conflict researchers are back in the business of providing better or worse solutions to conflict (depending on the partial fulfilment of some needs) rather than in the business of providing wholly satisfactory resolutions that *totally* fulfil all frustrated needs.[40]

The implication of Mitchell's comment is that rather than there being a dichotomy of levels and potential techniques of third-party intervention, there may be a spectrum of need-fulfilment. The implication is that we are dealing with the *degree* of needs-fulfilment, not whether there has been any or not. Even a settlement at the level of interests in the form of a cease-fire may partially fulfil the need for security. Mitchell concludes by arguing that human needs may provide the basis for a theory of conflict causes, while the focus on satisfiers and techniques for identifying them and gaining their acceptance may provide the basis for a theory of conflict solutions. This then points us in the direction of a connection between Burton's discrete levels of needs, values, and interests.

While all of these raise serious questions regarding the needs-based approach, it would be premature to dismiss it, particularly given its challenging and innovative nature. Instead, it may be more fruitful to build on Mitchell's concluding point and attempt to identify the place and role of needs-based third-party interventions in the context not only of a spectrum of third-party intervention, but viewing it as part of an interconnected process that includes more formalized negotiation processes.

## V. What is the Nature of the Third-Party Process?

Mitchell's argument raises important questions about the actual nature of the third-party process. Is it best characterized as a set of distinct and competing approaches as identified within the academic literature? Is it some kind of movement between them? Is it a combination of these distinct approaches? Or is it the case that at certain points in a conflict one approach may be more viable or efficacious than another? Do we need to engage in facilitative problem-solving at a pre-negotiation phase before we can move forward to a more traditionally developed settlement? Or is facilitative problem-solving more appropriate in the later stages of the process as a means of breaking the log-jam in negotiations resulting from basic mutual mistrust? Is there some kind of necessary and organic link or connection between these multiple levels or is it merely contingent?

In much of the literature, the above approaches are seen as largely independent of the others. Indeed, those theorists most closely wedded to a particular approach usually characterize it as standing in opposition to and in a superior relationship to others. But while this separation may make sense at the level of theory, providing useful pedagogical distinctions and the basis on which to develop 'ideal theory' necessary to the advancement of the theoretical and praxiological debates, it limits our ability to understand the third-party process as it develops 'on the ground'. Each of these characterizations may be an accurate account of one particularized form of third-party initiative, but they fail to capture the nature of the third-party process as a whole. What is needed is a 'thick' account of the whole of the third-party process which accurately captures and explains the dynamic connections between different third-party initiatives.

The need for such an account becomes obvious when we look at third-party practice in relation to any particular international conflict. What we find are consecutive, concurrent, parallel, or overlapping intiatives carried out by a variety of third parties. If we view these individual efforts as part of a larger, ongoing, and cumulative process, the result is a whole series of initiatives, each of which may embody one particular approach but which, taken as a whole, are difficult to characterize in anything other than an interconnected framework. Moreover, we find that there is a great deal of flexibility in the modalities of third-party intervention, not only between different individual efforts but also within particular efforts. In the course of the third-party process, viewed as a whole, there is a dynamic movement between different approaches which are seen as being discreet in theory. It therefore becomes important to distinguish between individual third-party *initiatives* and the larger third-party *process*.[41]

Third-party intervention, therefore, must be seen as an iterative process over an extended period of time involving a multiplicity of third-party actors operating at different levels addressing different elements of the conflict.[42] In any given conflict it is the case that a full explanation of the long and complex process leading to a solution needs to incorporate the multiple levels at which third-party activity takes place and the nature of the interconnections between them. And in relation to the latter, we need to develop a fuller understanding of the dynamics behind this process. In the effort to comprehend this dynamic, we need to address four basic questions: (1) what kind of third-party initiatives were being carried out?; (2) by whom were they being carried out?; (3) at what stage in the conflict were they carried out?; and (4) with what kind of outcome?[43] Addressing these questions may allow us to discern what are the appropriate intervention techniques to be carried out by what kinds of third parties at what stage in a conflict.

An initial step in answering these questions can be found in the 'contingency model of third-party intervention'.[44] In this model, the type of third-party activity is contingent on the stage of escalation and de-escalation the conflict is in. The argument is that, depending on the mix of objective and subjective causes of a conflict, different forms of intervention will be most effective when carried out at appropriate points in the conflict. What is required is an accurate identification of the particular stage in the conflict to serve as a triggering mechanism for the implementation of particular third-party strategies. Thus at the most destructive stage of conflict it may be necessary first to engage in 'mediation with muscle' linked to more traditional forms of peacekeeping in order to exert some control over the violence. If the conflict is left at this stage, however, it may induce long-term instabilities. In the short-term it may provide enough stability for movement towards more facilitative forms of mediation and analytic, consultative problem-solving, producing some form of a settlement, and possibly leading towards eventual reconciliation and resolution. These are more likely to be fruitful in the context of military de-escalation. The process may be further fostered by a focus on functional issues which cut across the conflict, such as water, communications, transportation, and agriculture promoting intercommunal contacts. This in turn may trigger a process of confidence-building measures, which may over a period of time provide the basis for renewed trust.

The interesting feature of the contingency approach is the connection that is made between third-party activities, particularly of an unofficial kind, and the more official and institutionalized element of conflict management, such as cease-fires and peace-keeping. Third-party facilitation or consultative problem-solving is seen as being carried out in a complementary and supplementary[45] fashion to more traditional forms of third-party activities. Importantly, it may provide a mechanism by which the results of the facilitative process can be transferred back into the more formalized negotiation process, as well as a means of moving away from the formalized negotiation process when it has reached a state of deadlock or stalemate.

A further implication of the contingency approach is that there may be some logical sequence for the application of different kinds of third-party interventions over the course of the third-party process. More than likely, however, we are likely to discover that there is no precise 'recipe' for managing conflict beyond some broad, generalized guidelines. The contextualities and contingencies of each individual conflict will come into play. This, in turn, will point to the need to develop an adaptive and co-ordinating component in the third-party process as a whole in which there is an element of feedback both within individual third-party efforts and between efforts as part of the larger overall process. During the course of the third-party process, the third parties will need to be responsive to situational factors which may create opportunities for pushing towards more integrative solutions, as well as being aware of the nature of constraints which may limit their endeavour to a more modest settlement in the short-term. This feedback and learning process means that the modalities of third-party initiatives need to be open to change at any given point in the process. Third-party intervention needs to be viewed as an experiential process which leads to modifications both in the approaches and techniques adopted as well as in the nature and contents of the agreements which are reached.

## VI. Conclusion

This movement towards viewing third-party initiatives as part of an overall process and within the context of a framework of contingency is a relatively recent development within the study of mediation and conflict-resolution. It has important implications for theory, research, and practice, particularly with reference to the deep-rooted, protracted social conflicts which pose the greatest dilemmas and greatest dangers in the post-Cold War World—conflicts such as Cyprus, Northern Ireland, Yugoslavia, the Middle East, Lebanon, Cambodia, South Africa, the Sudan, Ethiopia, and El Salvador to name but a few of the most obvious examples.

At the level of theory, the adoption of the interconnected framework and contingency approach resonates with developments in social and political theory and international theory which seek to move beyond the kinds of dichotomies that are evident in the literature on mediation and conflict resolution. This false dichotomy is readily evident when we recognize that the different approaches have their roots in, reinvoke, and reaffirm the dichotomy between human agency (which lies at the heart of needs-based approaches) and structure (which lies behind the interests-based approach). Moreover, this focus on the agency-structure relationships would lead logically to a concern with developing a deeper understanding of the civil society-state nexus in the process of conflict resolution.[46]

At the level of research it implies that we should not limit our investigation of third-party processes to single initiatives, but instead should examine it as a complex process over an extended period of time, involving a range and diversity of mediators. Such an approach might provide us with richer characterizations of the third-party process, demonstrating that the ideal types of theoretical frameworks do not provide literal representations of third-party initiatives, while highlighting the longitudinal nature of the third-party process and the conditions under which certain modes of third-party activity may be most appropriate, viable, and efficacious. It would also lead us to reassess the criteria of success and failure with which we judge third-party initiatives.

At the level of practice, it would shift us away from an adherence to and over-reliance on particular forms of conflict management—be they coercive diplomacy, leveraged mediation, or facilitative problem-solving. Different third-party techniques would no longer be seen as competing or contradictory. With a richer understanding of how different third-party initiatives may contribute to an overall solution, we will be able to approach violent, deep-rooted, and protracted conflicts with an ability to deploy a complex and varied range of complementary third-party initiatives in support of sustainable, integrative solutions.

## Notes

This article was written while in residence as a Fellow at the United States Institute of Peace. The views expressed are those of the author and do not necessarily represent the views of the Institute.

1. J. W. Burton, *Resolving Deep-Rooted Conflict: A Handbook* (Lanham, Md.: University Press of America, 1987), and E. E. Azar, *The Management of Protracted Social Conflicts* (Dartmouth: Dartmouth Publishing, 1990).

2. An additional impetus towards third-party mediation and conflict-resolution at the international level has been the degree to which forms of alternative dispute resolution (ADR) have become institutionalized in domestic settings, particularly, though not only, in the US. Indeed, many of the techniques, skills, and processes which are found in international facilitation were first developed in the domestic context to deal with marital, labour, and racial conflicts. Nevertheless, there are two important caveats which need to be mentioned. The first is whether ADR does not presume something like a highly developed legal system as is found in the US. The second, related concern, is what kinds of problems might be encountered or what adjustments need to be made in the transference of these techniques from the domestic to the international.

3. A number of studies have examined the nature and extent of third-party interventions in international conflicts and their degree of success. See M. W. Zacher, *International Conflicts and Collective Security: 1946–1977* (New York: Praeger, 1979); M. Haas, E. B. Butterworth, and J. S. Nye, *Conflict Management by International Organizations* (Morristown, NJ: GLP, 1972); R. L. Butterworth,

*Managing Interstate Conflicts: 1945–1976* (Pittsburgh, Pa.: University of Pittsburgh Press, 1976); J. Bercovitch, *Social Conflict and Third Parties: Strategies of Conflict Resolution* (Boulder, Colo.: Westview Press, 1984); R. Vayrynen, 'Third Parties in the Resolution of Regional Conflicts', *Bulletin of Peace Proposals*, 18/3 (1987), 293–308; H. Maill, *Peaceful Settlement of Post-1945 Conflicts: A Comparative Study* (Oxford: Oxford Research Group, 1990); and J. Bercovitch, J. T. Anagnoson, and D. L. Wille, 'Some Conceptual Issues and Empirical Trends in the Study of Successful Mediation in International Relations', *Journal of Peace Research* 28/1 (1991), 7–17. Most of these focus on incidents of official third-party mediation. The incidence of unofficial, second-track, and facilitative interventions is under-represented, though this is probably due to the confidential nature of such exercises.

4. John MacDonald, who along with J. Montville and others developed the notion of 'second-track diplomacy', has now identified nine tracks at which official and unofficial diplomacy work. Cf. J. W. MacDonald and D. B. Bendahmane, *Conflict Resolution: Track Two Diplomacy* (Washington, DC: FSI, 1987), and J. W. Macdonald and L. Diamond, *Multitrack Diplomacy: A System Guide and Analysis* (Grinnell, Ia.: Iowa Peace Institute, 1991).

5. These have been identified as the set of features on which third parties can be differentiated in R. J. Fisher, 'The Third Party Consultant: A Method for the Study and Resolution of Conflict', *Journal of Conflict Resolution*, 16/1 (1972), 67–94; J. Z. Rubin, *Dynamics of Third Party Intervention: Kissinger in the Middle East* (New York: Praeger, 1980); C. R. Mitchell, *Peacemaking and the Consultant's Role* (London: Gower, 1981); and H. C. Kelman and S. P. Cohen, 'Resolution of International Conflict: An Interactional Approach', in S. Worchel and W. G. Austin (eds.), *The Social Psychology of Intergroup Relations*, 2nd edn. (Chicago: Nelson-Hall, 1986), 323–42.

6. As an example of this view, see the 'Introduction' and 'Conclusions' in S. Touval and I. W. Zartman (eds.), *International Mediation in Theory and Practice* (Washington, DC: Westview Press for the SAIS, 1985).

7. See J. W. Burton, 'The Resolution of Conflict', *International Studies Quarterly* 16/1 (1972), 5–29, and Fisher, 'The Third Party Consultant'.

8. Mitchell has identified seven elements of conflict-termination which characterize a genuine resolution of a conflict: 1. *completeness*: the issues in conflict disappear or cease to have salience; 2. *acceptability*: the outcome is acceptable to all parties to a dispute, not just to one or to their élites; 3. *self-supporting*: there is no necessity for third-party sanctions to maintain the agreement; 4. *satisfactory*: all parties

perceive the outcome as 'just' according to their value systems; 5. *uncompromising*: in that no goals had to be sacrificed in the form of 'half-a-loaf' solutions; 6. *innovative*: the solution establishes new and positive relationships between the parties; 7. *un-coerced*: the adversaries freely arrive at the solution without imposition by outside authoritative agency. Mitchell also notes that based on these criteria, resolution of a conflict is often difficult to achieve. See C. R. Mitchell, 'Necessitous Man and Conflict Resolution: More Basic Questions about Basic Human Needs', in J. W. Burton (ed.), *Conflict: Human Needs Theory* (New York: St Martin's Press, 1990), 150–1.

9.  P. Wehr, 'Conflict Resolution Studies: What Do We Know?', paper presented at the Dispute Resolution Forum, quoted in D. J. D. Sandole, 'Paradigms, Movements and Shifts: Indicators of a Social Invention', in K. Webb and C. R. Mitchell (eds.), *New Approaches to International Mediation* (New York: Greenwood Press, 1988), 219–29.

10. V. Jabri, 'The Western Contact Group as Intermediary in the Conflict over Namibia', in Webb and Mitchell (eds.), *New Approaches to International Mediation*, 102–30, and V. Jabri, *Mediating Conflict: Decision-Making and Western Intervention in Namibia* (Manchester: Manchester University Press, 1990).

11. Bercovitch, *Social Conflict and Third Parties*.

12. For useful, extended surveys of mediation across a range of these areas of study, see: K. Kressel and D. G. Pruitt, 'Themes in the Mediation of Social Conflict', *Journal of Social Issues*, 41/2 (1985), 179–99; 'A Research Perspective on the Mediation of Social Conflict', in Kressel and Pruitt (eds.), *Mediation Research* (San Francisco: Jossey Bass, 1989); D. M. Kolb, *The Mediators* (Cambridge, Mass.: MIT Press, 1983); Kolb and J. Z. Rubin, 'Mediation through a Disciplinary Prism', *Research on Negotiations in Organizations, iii, Handbook on Negotiation Research* (New York: JAI Press, 1991), 231–57; and J. Bercovitch (ed.), 'Special Issue on Third Party Mediation', *Journal of Peace Research*, 28/1 (1991).

13. O. Young, *The Intermediaries: Third Parties in International Crises* (Princeton, NJ; Princeton University Press, 1976).

14. Bercovitch, *Social Conflict and Third Parties*, Chaps. 5 and 6.

15. Ibid. 129.

16. S. Touval and I. W. Zartman, 'Introduction: Mediation in Theory', in Touval and Zartman, *International Mediation in Theory and Practice*.

17. The concept of 'ripeness' is developed in T. W. Zartman, *Ripe for Resolution: Conflict and Intervention in Africa* (Oxford: Oxford University Press, 1985).

18. D. G. Pruitt and J. Z. Rubin, *Social Conflict: Escalation, Stalemate and Settlement* (New York: Random House, 1986).

19. Touval and Zartman, *International Mediation in Theory and Practice.*

20. Pruitt and Rubin, *Social Conflict.*

21. Touval and Zartman, *International Mediation in Theory and Practice.*

22. Recent case-study work has raised serious doubts about the validity of the hurting stalemate argument. See S. J. Stedman, *Peacemaking in Civil War: International Mediation in Zimbabwe, 1974–1980* (Boulder, Colo.: Lynne Reinner, 1991). Stedman, however, makes clear that this does not invalidate the usefulness of Zartman's concept of 'ripeness'. It does require that it be refined.

23. Pruitt, *Negotiation Behaviour* (New York: Academic Press, 1981).

24. S. Touval (ed.), *The Peace Brokers: Mediators in the Arab–Israeli Conflict 1948–1979* (Princeton, NJ: Princeton University Press, 1982).

25. Ibid.

26. Pruitt and Rubin, *Social Conflict.*

27. R. Fisher and W. L. Ury, *Getting to YES* (Boston:Houghton Mifflin, 1981).

28. The process of coaction building is discussed in D. Lax and J. Sebenius, *The Manager as Negotiator: Bargaining for Cooperation and Competitive Gain* (New York: Free Press, 1986).

29. Vivienne Jabri has also noted that this may occur at the level of the third party itself, creating its own unique set of decision-making problems. See Jabri, *Mediating Conflict.*

30. Burton is widely recognized as one of the founding figures in the facilitative or problem-solving approach to conflict-resolution. His publications over a span of five decades are extensive. While sometimes repetitive, the evolution of Burton's thought can readily be identified in his major publications. The functionalist influence can be seen in J. W. Burton, 'Restrictive and Constructive Intervention', Ph.D. thesis (University of London, 1941), and id., *Peace Theory: Pre-Conditions of Disarmament* (New York: Knopf, 1962). The impact of systems theory can be seen in id., *International Relations: A General Theory* (Cambridge: Cambridge University Press, 1965), and id., *Systems, States, Diplomacy and Rules* (Cambridge: Cambridge University Press, 1968). The effect of social-psychology, pluralism, interdependence and third-party practice can be found in id., *Conflict and Communication* (New York: Free Press, 1969), and id., *World Society* (Cambridge: Cambridge University Press, 1972). The turn towards basic human needs theory occurs with id., *Deviance Terrorism and War* (Oxford: Martin Robertson, 1979), and is used in the context of the Second Cold War in id., *Dear Survivors* (London: Pinter, 1982). The domestic sources of international conflict and the idea of deep-rooted conflict is developed in id., *Global Conflict* (Brighton: Wheatsheaf, 1984), and id., *Resolving Deep-Rooted Conflicts: A Handbook* (Lanham, Md.: University Press of America,

1987). These various components are all pulled together and connected with the idea of 'provention' in his latest work, *Conflict: Resolution and Provention* (New York: Macmillan, 1990). A set of essays offering a useful discussion and critique of Burton's ideas can be found in M. Banks (ed.), *Conflict in World Society* (Brighton: Wheatsheaf, 1984).

31. The role of practical reason and conflict theory is discussed in T. Nardin, 'Theory and Practice in Conflict Research', in T. R. Gurr (ed.), *Handbook of Political Conflict: Theory and Research* (New York: Free Press, 1980), 461–89, and, drawing on the work of Habermas, in J. S. Dryzek and S. Hunter, 'Environmental Mediation for International Problems', *International Studies Quarterly*, 31/1 (1987), 87–102.

32. The structure, form, and processes of the problem-solving workshop have been described and discussed by a number of scholar-practitioners. See Burton, *Conflict and Communication*; L. Doob and R. B. Stevens, 'The Fermeda Workshop: A Different Approach to Border Conflicts in Eastern Africa', *Journal of Psychology*, 73/2 (1969), 249–66; R. J. Fisher, 'The Third Party Consultant: A Method for the Study and Resolution of Conflict', *Journal of Conflict Resolution*, 16/1 (1972), 67–94; A. V. S. de Reuck, 'Controlled Communication: Rationale and Dynamics', *Human Context*, 6/1 (1974), 64–80; H. C. Kelman and S. P. Cohen, 'Reduction of International Conflict: An Interactional Approach', in W. G. Austin and S. Worchel (eds.), *The Social Psychology of Intergroup Relations* (Moneterey, Calif.: Brooks-Cole, 1979); C. R. Mitchell, *Peacemaking and the Consultant's Role* (Farnborough: Gower, 1981); M. Light, 'Problem-Solving Workshops', in M. Banks (ed.), *Conflict in World Society* (Brighton: Wheatsheaf, 1984); Burton, *Resolving Deep-Rooted Conflict: A Handbook* (Lanham, Md.: University Press of America, 1987); and J. Rothman, *Thinking and Acting for Peace* (Newbury Park, Calif.: Sage, 1992).

33. Fisher notes that there are a number of impediments to the continued development of facilitative conflict-resolution processes. First, the number of skilled practitioners is small and it is only relatively recently that centres for teaching and training these skills at the international level have become established. Second, is the limited institutional structures and support for those working in the area. Third is the problem of funding such exercises. See R. J. Fisher, *The Potential of Third Party Consultation as a Method of International Conflict Resolution* (Ottowa, Occasional Paper, Canadian Institute for International Peace and Security, 1991). Related to these problems is the question of the professionalization of the field. The issues here relate not only to the process of mentoring between generations in the field, but extends to a more difficult question given the state of

development of the field: is it time to professionalize? Is it desirable? If so, what standards should be used? The view on one side is that it is desirable and necessary in legitimizing the status of the field. The concern on the other side is that professionalization will lead to everything that those first working in the field sought to escape.

34. J. Laue, 'Conflict Resolution and Peace Research', NCPCR Conference, Charlotte, NC, 1991.

35. Bercovitch, 'Special Issue on Third Party Mediation', Chap. 6.

36. It is worth noting that many other advocates of needs theory are not as adamant as Burton on these questions. See the contributions in Burton, (ed.), *Conflict: Human Needs Theory* (New York: St Martin's Press, 1990).

37. K. Avruch and P. W. Black, 'Ideas of Human Nature in Contemporary Conflict Resolution Theory', *Negotiation Journal*, 6/3 (1990), 221–8. A parallel set of critiques could be raised from the perspective of feminist political theory though much of the literature on gender and conflict resolution is sympathetic to the broad outlines of Burton's position. See, for example, I. Sandole-Staroste, 'Overlapping Radivalisms: Convergence between Feminist and Human Needs Theories in Conflict Resolution', paper presented at the Conference on Gender and Conflict, George Mason University, 18–19 Jan. 1991.

38. For a discussion, see R. A. Coate and J. A. Rosati (eds.), *The Power of Human Needs in World Society* (Boulder, Colo.: Lynne Reinner, 1988), and Burton, *Conflict*.

39. C. R. Mitchell, 'Necessitous Man and Conflict Resolution: More Basic Questions about Basic Human Needs Theory', in Burton *Conflict*, 149–76. According to my count, Mitchell tables over 25 overlapping questions regarding Burton's and others' accounts of human needs.

40. Mitchell, 'Necessitous Man', 172.

41. See id., 'Person or Process', paper prepared for the Annual Conference of the International Society of Political Science, Helsinki, July 1991.

42. This argument is more fully developed in M. Hoffman, *The Interconnected Third Party Process in International Conflict: A Comparative Analysis* (Washington, DC: USIP, forthcoming).

43. A similar set of questions, though missing the focus on outcomes, is developed in L. Kriesberg, 'Formal and Quasi-Mediators in International Disputes: An Exploratory Analysis', *Journal of Peace Research*, 28/1 (1991), 21.

44. R. J. Fisher and L. Keashley, 'The Potential Complementarity of Mediation and Consultation within a Contingency Model of Third Party Intervention', *Journal of Peace Research*, 28/1 (1991), 29–42. It is also touched on in other pieces in the same Special Issue.

45. For the argument that facilitative problem-solving is best seen as a

form of supplemental diplomacy at the stage of pre-negotiation in protracted conflicts, see J. Rothman, 'Supplementing Tradition: A Theoretical and Practical Typology for International Conflict Management', *Negotiation Journal*, 5/3 (1989), 265–77. For discussion of the pre-negotiation stage in conflict-resolution, see J. Gross Stein, *Getting to the Table: The Processes of International Prenegotiation* (Baltimore, Md.: Johns Hopkins University Press, 1989), and Rothman (ed.), 'Special Issue on Prenegotiation Theory and Practice', *Jerusalem Journal of International Relations*, 13/1 (1991).

46. See Hoffman, 'Modes of Mediation', paper presented at the joint BISA/ ISA Conference, London, Mar. 1989.

# ELEVEN

# Environmental Issues in World Politics

*Ian H. Rowlands*

The move from the 1980s to the 1990s has been a time of great change in international relations. Unprecedented developments have brought a new set of issues to our field of study. Because of this transformation, the environment has arisen to take a position near the top of the new global agenda. And though it is unclear how today's revolutionary momentum will affect future arrangements of international society, it is apparent that the environment, being an intricate part of humankind's existence, will remain a key factor in global society. Accordingly, it will also continue to be a vital consideration in the study of international relations.

The outbreak of recent conferences, meetings, and declarations on international environmental concerns might lead one to believe that the arrival of these issues on the international relations agenda is a relatively recent phenomenon. This notion would be incorrect. Though it is true that they now occupy a more prominent and visible position in international affairs, it must be remembered that environmental issues have played a role in international society since the beginning of our modern state system.

The purpose of this chapter is to provide an overview of the major environmental issues that have been, and will continue to be, the dominant concerns in international relations. The discussion is divided into six sections in order to examine the most important debates and issues within this area. The sections are presented in chronological order, reflecting the sequence in which environmental problems first became a concern in international society. This method of presentation also illuminates the evolutionary nature of this issue; since all of the elements have remained a concern in international relations, the more general question of the environment in world politics has been growing and gaining momentum. The result is that it now occupies a prominent position in international affairs. Similarly, this evolutionary description presents an interesting parallel with the more general study of international relations. I will attempt to show that, with time, the dominant interpretations of international relations have become increasingly unable to deal with the new environmental issues in world politics. Indeed, more recent developments have effectively challenged the traditional interpretations, concepts, and frameworks that we use to study the discipline. I will conclude by arguing that a variety of approaches and methodologies must be employed if we are to gain a fuller understanding of the way in which environmental issues affect world politics.

## I. What are the Traditional Approaches to the Possession of Natural Resources?

The oldest aspect of environmental issues in world politics involves the possession of natural resources. For as long as the modern state-system has existed, countries have been concerned with their relative position in the hierarchical international system. Realist international relations theory teaches us that a state will attempt to increase its level of power—seeing this as the key to its security. One constituent element of a state's aggregate power is the quantity of natural resources that it possesses. The exploitation of natural resources allows a state to meet the basic needs of its peoples, to build up its economic and industrial base, and to prepare for war (all of which contribute to a state's power and security). It may be that the competitive drive for resources continues to motivate the rulers of states even today and thus can help to explain some of the events in world politics.

As an analytical device, this consideration can be usefully divided into two parts: 'non-living' resources and 'living' resources. The drive for non-living resources—for example, fresh water, non-fuel minerals or fuels—can often help to explain a state's particular actions. As a simple example, Paraguay successfully annexed Bolivia's Gran Chaco wilderness area during the Chaco

War of 1932–5. Paraguay undertook military action because it thought (incorrectly) that this area contained oil deposits.[1]

The desire for strategic natural resources might also motivate a decision-maker to pursue 'living resources'—for example, agricultural crops, forests, grasslands, or fish. Arthur Westing has recognized that: 'As human populations and human aspirations have grown in a global land area that has long been fully divided among the nations of the world, one of the time-honoured approaches to alleviating the problem of land shortage has been a resort to wars of conquest.[2] A state will often attempt to increase its land area so that its citizens can grow more food, harvest more trees, or graze more animals. For example, in July of 1969, El Salvador invaded Honduras in what has become known as the 'Football War'. It is generally believed that the large population gradient that existed between the two countries increased the motivation for the attack. The densely populated El Salvador was trying to prevent the sparsely populated Honduras from expelling its illegal Salvadorian immigrants. Obviously, this goal was directly related to Salvadorian concerns about the human pressures upon its resource base.[3]

Finally, it should be mentioned that these two categories are not mutually exclusive. There are international events that can be partially explained by recognizing a state's desire for both non-living and living resources. For example, though the Falklands/ Malvinas War of 1982 was motivated by a number of factors, the natural-resource issue was an important consideration. An Argentinean victory would have strengthened that state's claims to the mineral wealth of Antarctica and it would also have given Argentina control of the important fishing waters that surround the islands.[4]

This approach remains helpful today as we attempt to understand developments in world politics. The report of the World Commission on Environment and Development (commonly known as the Brundtland Report) recognized that: 'Such conflicts are likely to increase as these resources become scarcer and competition for them increases.'[5] With continued consumption of the Earth's non-living resources, the finite stock of these non-renewables is gradually being depleted. As increased scarcity is recognized, states place a higher value upon their possession and therefore pursue them more vigorously. The drive for both water and oil in the Middle East is a relevant, present-day example. Similarly, as the number of people in the world continues to rise, the demand for living resources will increase. Today, a key contributing factor to events in Africa is a shortage of food.

The natural resources issue fits comfortably into a zero-sum interpretation of world politics: an actor employs resources and privately accrues all of the benefits arising from their use. For the most part, any division of these commodities will mean that the derived benefits will also be divided. Though the increasing irrelevance of military force and the hardening of international borders challenge this assertion, it remains the case that a state has a variety of military, economic, diplomatic, and other tools with which it pursues natural resources. Accordingly, this traditional approach helps us to understand some events in contemporary international politics.

## II. Is the Environment an International Collective Good?

The modern state-system is based upon the twin principles of territoriality and sovereignty. A state has legitimate jurisdiction over a certain area within defined boundaries. The other members of the international system recognize and accept the absolute authority of the state within these geographical confines. Although this classical principle is functional for the land regions of the Earth, it starts to unravel when it is applied to other areas of the biosphere. There are a number of areas that must, if efficiency is to be realized, be managed by more than one sovereign state. These areas—for example, waterways and airsheds, areas often referred to as 'commons'—are properly studied under the category of international environmental issues. Furthermore, they have frequently been investigated by means of an important theoretical construct in the social sciences: collective goods.

Collective goods have been defined by two characteristics: they are joint in supply and they are non-exclusive. Joint in supply means that given a level of production of the good, consumption by one actor does not thereby lessen the quantity of the good potentially available for other actors. Non-exclusive indicates that if one actor is able to consume the good, then the good is available for all actors. Therefore, collective goods are goods that, once provided, are accessible to all. In the international system, examples of collective goods include: defence, human health standards, mail service, transportation regulations, and trading practices. Furthermore, there are a number of environmental issues which can be regarded as collective goods. I will return to these later, below.[6]

The recognition that certain commodities in international society could be modelled as collective goods had an important impact upon the state-system. It became increasingly accepted that co-operative action between states could help to realize mutual benefits. This challenged the realist understanding that unilateral action was the only determinant of security and prosperity in the international system. In the language of game theory, this development can be summarized quite simply: there was a recognition that, along with the traditional zero-sum games, certain international interactions could safely be regarded as positive-sum games.

More specifically, collective goods first came to the fore in the nineteenth century with regard to the question of shared bodies of water. At this time it was recognized that a single state could not unilaterally manage them since the actions of other, bordering states necessarily affected the resource in question. It therefore became clear that some sort of co-operation was necessary in order to avoid sub-optimal results.

The collective goods issues has not been restricted to small shared bodies of water—with time, common management was undertaken on, for example, the high seas, Antarctica, and outer space. Today's global problems of ozone layer depletion and climatic change (which I will return to in section VI) also fit into this category.

Though this proposition challenged traditional understandings of international relations, it did not necessarily displace them. For there are indeed instances when states have not engaged in international co-operation in order to try to realize a collective good. Within the international system, political realities dictate that competition does still exist among states. A government is expected not only to further the interest of its own people (and hence try to obtain absolute benefits), but it is also not expected to afford other states a disproportionate share of any benefit mutually achieved in an international dealing. If states are to pursue co-operative arrangements on collective goods issues, their leaders will expect not only to achieve an absolute gain, but also to avoid a relative loss. Thus, it may be that a state will forgo a collective good (and the benefit associated with it) or will unilaterally try to obtain the collective good (and therefore, though incurring a larger absolute cost, may also eventually realize a larger relative benefit). Furthermore, we must remember that the attainment of the collective good is dependent upon the action of other states. Therefore, even if a state commits itself to a co-operative effort, there is no guarantee that benefits will be forthcoming. Thus, either a mistrust in other members, or a conscious decision to 'free ride' (that is, not pay the cost, but perhaps receive the benefit nevertheless; and therefore realize a higher net gain) may be another impetus for a state to spurn co-operative efforts.

Nevertheless, an incentive for co-operation, not previously present, seemed to have arisen. Given that it is not automatic that states will co-operate on issues of international collective goods, there has been much interest among academics who study international relations on the question of what mechanisms affect the likelihood of co-operation. Much of this work can be found in the debates around regime theory, game theory, and international institutions and organizations.[7] Together these writings form a rich body of literature.

Dilemmas of collective action present interesting questions for international relations scholars. Not only will there be incentives for states to co-operate in order to obtain collective goods, there will also be logical reasons for states to avoid co-operation. Therefore, we can start to see that a flexible approach to the study of international relations is needed. If we are to further our understanding of world politics, we must be ready to incorporate a number of different theoretical concepts.

## III. Why has Trans-Boundary Material-Flow Become an Important Issue in International Relations?

As the quantity of industrial activity in the world increased, pollution became a major concern for states. An appreciation arose that local activity, though bringing about higher standards of material living, was also degrading the local environment. There was seen to be a direct correlation between decisions and actions taken by a local government and the quality of the environment locally. For example, attempts to clean up London (both its air[8] and its water (the Thames)[9] in the nineteenth century) were directed primarily by local authorities. Thus, though pollution control has been a concern of governments for a number of years, it has been accepted historically that it should be attempted at local or, at most, national levels. Only in the past quarter-century has 'pollution' become a major international issue. Nevertheless, there exist interesting empirical and theoretical connections between its domestic and international forms.

In the 1960s, a general increase in environmental awareness was accompanied by the emergence of a vigorous environmentalist movement. Though there are a number of factors that promoted its growth—the crash of the *Torrey Canyon*,[10] the publication of Rachel Carson's *Silent Spring*,[11] the student uprisings, and the general debate over global resource depletion[12] are but four examples—it is important to note that most of these stimuli can be related to domestic considerations (e.g., pressure groups, crises, legislation). These domestic forces propelled the environment issue to the forefront of a number of states' national agendas. It was from these national roots that it grew upward to reach the international agenda.

During the 1960s, three factors helped to realize this transition: an increase in domestic awareness, an increase in the absolute amount of pollution being discharged world-wide, and an increase in scientific knowledge. At this time it became clear that actions taken by one state within its own boundaries could have a direct impact upon another state. For example, toxic materials dumped in one state could be transported (by water or air) into another state. In this recipient state, the substances could affect its inhabitants' welfare by, for example, contaminating drinking water, lessening agricultural output, or reducing forestry yields.

Though this issue did not become a major consideration until the 1960s, the 'paradigm case' of trans-boundary pollution dates from much earlier. In the 1920s and early 1930s, a Canadian company in Trail, British Columbia, just ten miles north of the Canadian–American border, was smelting lead and zinc. Some of the fumes that it released were carried down the Columbia River valley and across into the United States, where they caused damage to the land and to other interests. An International Joint Commission was convened, found the Canadian company liable for this harm, and assessed damages of US $350,000 in 1935.[13]

Since that time, the question has become a larger issue in interstate relations.[14] For instance,

[i]n the early 1970s, German pastures in the Upper Rhine Valley and consequently cattle and milk in the area were severely contaminated by emissions resulting from a waste site where a French chemical plant deposited hazardous by-products of its pesticide production.[15]

It was clear that damage to German interests was inflicted by the French action. More recently, the 1986 Chernobyl incident is a vivid example of trans-boundary material flows. Furthermore, today one of the most important issues in interstate negotiations among the European countries and between Canada and the United States is acid precipitation. This case of trans-boundary pollution consists of the passage of sulphuric and nitric acids into another state. These acids damage forests, 'kill' lakes, and thereby affect the prosperity of the state.

The issue can also be expanded in order to include deforestation and desertification. At this point, the appropriateness of labelling these issues as 'international' might be challenged. But it is being acknowledged that these processes have important international ramifications. For example, logging activities in one state can cause an erosion of topsoil and an increased rate of flooding in another state (as Nepal has, in recent years, done to Bangladesh). In a similar way, land mismanagement in one state can cause a desert to encroach into another state (as has happened among the states of the Sahel). 'The recent destruction of much of Africa's dryland agricultural production was more severe than if an invading army had pursued a scorched-earth policy.'[16] It is being acknowledged that deforestation and desertification may have important international causes.

Trans-boundary material-flow will remain important in international relations for two reasons. First, it does not appear that the world is fast approaching any sort of post-industrial society, since industrial emissions have continued to climb over recent years. Thus there is unlikely to be a decrease in the amount of trans-boundary material-flow. Second, scientific knowledge has progressed in recent years. This evolution has meant that the recipient state has been able to identify and assess the impact of an attack with greater precision. If we assume that any new-found costs of material transfers will continue to outweigh any new-found benefits, then we can safely assert that the recipient state will place a greater value upon a successful resolution of the issue and thereby give it a higher position on its agenda of international affairs. Furthermore, with more reliable information, the state will be able to identify the source of transfers with greater confidence. The recipient state will then be more willing to take action against a known source rather than an uncertain originator. This has meant that states like the United States and the United Kingdom have no longer been able to hide behind blankets of scientific uncertainty with respect to the acid precipitation issue.

Conceptually, trans-boundary material-flow is interesting to the student of international relations for two major reasons. First, this issue has increased the challenge to our traditional interpretation of international relations by clearly revealing the true 'interdependence' of the global environment: trans-boundary material-flow tangibly demonstrates that one state's domestic actions can affect another state.

Second, it further illustrates the permeability of the realist's billiard ball by demonstrating that international issues can have their origins in domestic concerns. I would contend that this is a significant revelation and one that is playing a role in the resurgence of environmental interest, world-wide, today.

## IV. What is the Legacy of the Stockholm Environment Conference?

In June 1972, the United Nations Conference on the Human Environment took place in Stockholm, Sweden. This meeting remains the single most important reference in any discussion of international environmental issues. Representatives from 113 governments, nineteen intergovernmental agencies, and 400 other intergovernmental and non-governmental organizations (NGOs)[17] met for twelve days in order to examine environmental questions of an international nature. The conference is viewed as a landmark event for a number of different reasons. On an abstract level, it helped to advance the view that the human world and the natural Earth could not necessarily be divorced from one another.[18] From the date of the conference, policy-makers further accepted the proposition that at least some environmental problems needed to be addressed at the international level. More concretely, the conference also provided the 'Stockholm Declarations'—a set of twenty-six statements, which have served as a foundation for much of the subsequent international environmental law.[19] Finally, the conference was to provide the foundation for three themes that have played important roles in the debates since 1972.

First, non-governmental environmental organizations participated extensively at the international level for the first time. Though a variety of environmental groups had been operating at the national level for well over a century (for example, various conservation groups), the enormous concentrated activity of the NGOs at the Stockholm conference heralded the appearance of a new actor upon the international scene. Since 1972, NGOs have played a major role in environmental issues in international society in a variety of ways. First, they have created channels of communication that have later been used by states' representatives in order to conduct intergovernmental negotiations. Second, they have informed national and international public opinion in order to pressure governments to take national and international action on the environment. This has also, it can be argued, helped to create new international norms and thereby stimulated 'bottom-up' pressure from the grass roots. And third, they have contributed to the scientific debate and therefore helped to achieve common scientific understandings on the technical aspects of environmental problems.[20] In these, and other, ways, NGOs continue to play a role today.

Maintaining the theme of this chapter, it should be acknowledged that the rise of NGOs constitutes another effective challenge to the traditional understanding of international relations. In order to examine constructively today's global environmental issues, transnational actors in general, and environmental pressure groups in particular, must be studied both at the domestic and international levels.

A second important legacy of the Stockholm conference is the creation of another non-state actor: the United Nations Environment Programme (UNEP). Conceived during the conference and created by a UN General Assembly resolution in 1973, UNEP first took tangible form in 1974. It operates within the UN system, reporting to the Economic and Social Council (ECOSOC), which in turn is responsible to the General Assembly. UNEP's primary role is to provide co-ordinating and catalysing action on international environmental issues. It is not a specialized agency of the UN and its declarations do not have 'binding' status in international law. Nevertheless, it has been the focal point of attention for international environmental issues. The organization is based in Nairobi and it has an annual budget of approximately US $45 million.

UNEP's effectiveness has been the subject of much debate.[21] On the positive side, commentators recognize that the organization has been able, generally, to serve capably as a co-ordinating and leadership body. More specifically, many argue that UNEP's two greatest achievements have been its 'regional seas programme'[22] and its work on the stratospheric ozone depletion issue. However, its small budget (which has often been paid in arrears) and its limited influence have restricted the organization's role and performance. Nevertheless, UNEP is a functioning international organization that presently exists to address transnational environmental issues. Therefore, regardless of the verdict over its past performance, UNEP will be a key organization that will address the growing concerns about the international environment. Its continuing relevance is thus suggested.

Finally, the conference brought the development issue on to the international environmental agenda. Proceedings at the conference ensured that general North–South questions would necessarily be linked to the broader international environmental debate in any future discussions.

Environmental concerns are not viewed similarly by all states. It belabours the obvious to say that each state approaches the debate within its own national perspective. Nevertheless, in order to make some sense of this issue in international society, it is worth while to focus attention upon a basic distinction of perspective: that between the industrialized states (the 'North') and the non-industrialized states (the 'South'). Before we examine the question empirically, two observations must be made in order to place the issue in its proper context.

First, we must recognize that the North and the South place

different priorities upon the environment issue. Though the potential effects that environmental change can have upon international social systems are immense, a number of those changes still remain hypothetical, since they will occur, if at all, in the future. Contrast that with the fact that for a great number of individuals in the South, other issues have a more tangible presence and in fact threaten day-to-day existence. Thus, though a concern for the environment may be seen as being of primary importance for a large portion of society in the North, it is often seen as being subservient to the more immediate questions of survival in the South.

Second, industrialization in the North has resulted in two important consequences: a higher standard of living for these states and an increasingly fragile environment, world-wide. The North is now asking the South to join it in a global effort to stabilize the atmosphere. But the South has not significantly contributed to the deterioration of the global environment and therefore does not feel a responsibility to bear the burden of helping to solve this problem. There is a prevalent belief in the South that this burden may well jeopardize its prospects for a higher level of development. Therefore Northern pronouncements on the issue—e.g., calling for 'sustainable development'[23]—are often viewed with scepticism: citizens of the Southern states do not want to see this term used to justify the entrenchment of a neo-colonial eco-dependent relationship in the international system. Thus, the actors' perception on this issue is vital in order to gain a true understanding of the wider question.

Today, the Southern states are calling for unprecedented amounts of technical and financial resources to be transferred, free of charge, from the North to the South. Though these demands have been made (without measurable success) for a number of years, their link to the environment issue has given them a greater degree of urgency. The demands today are markedly different from the calls for a New International Economic Order in the early 1970s because the Southern states, with their potential to pollute the global environment, now hold a significant 'bargaining chip' in the negotiations. The Northern countries have realized that they must take note of these calls.[24] Therefore, we should not overlook the North–South axis, because the environmental issue has propelled these concerns to a higher level upon the international agenda.

Thus, the Stockholm Conference is remembered for a variety of reasons. The three which I have focused upon have each had a significant impact upon the practice and study of international relations since 1972.

## V. What is Ecological Security?

'Security' remains an important concept in the international system. Governments strive to ensure that their states are secure—secure in the sense that they are able to preserve their way of life, their ideals, their beliefs, and their territorial integrity from perceived threats by, and actual actions of, adverse foreign actors or events. It has traditionally been believed that military strength was necessary in order for a state to achieve a secure existence. Therefore, states have historically built up national military forces and/or entered into military alliances.

But, with the lessening of Superpower tensions and the 'end of the Cold War', an acceptance is emerging that security requires a broader interpretation than is usually allowed for in a traditional understanding of international relations. State security can no longer be interpreted solely as military security, because the challenges to a state's way of life, its ideals, or its beliefs need not be posed solely by armed forces. Therefore, state security can only be assessed by accounting for a large number of factors. In order to place the concept of ecological security in its wider context, let us first identify two other non-military threats to security.

Perhaps the economic threats are the ones that are most visible today within the international system. With greater world trade in a liberal global economic order, the security components of international economic relations are highlighted. Specialization can subject a nation to possible economic coercion, since the withholding of key materials and/or products can adversely affect the interests of the recipient state. And with the weakening of a country's economy, its values can also start to come under challenge. The importance of energy resources was brought to light by the Arab states in the early 1970s, when the normal way of life for Western, industrialized states was threatened. Further-more, the recent expansion of international financial markets has meant that interdependence in this area has increased. The 'knock-on' effects of the Crash of 1987 effectively demonstrated that a state's security can be threatened by more than solely military power.

Though less tangible than the economic considerations, social and cultural 'attacks' must today also be included in this category. With increased world-wide communication, a state's cultural, linguistic, and religious values may come under threat from sources outside its boundaries. These considerations run further than solely the 'Coca-Cola-i-zation' of the Third World or the, until recently, Voice-of-America-i-zation of the Communist bloc. Indeed, the volatile political situation in the Middle East demon-strates how religion has become an important trans-boundary force—Islamic fundamentalism threatens the security of a number of non-Islamic countries in that area. As a second example, Canada has recognized that a bombardment of American media could drown out a Canadian culture perceived as unique. There-fore, 'Canadian content rules' (in the media and elsewhere) have been employed as a defence against this threat. In this way, the country has attempted to protect its values.

It has also recently been recognized that environmental change can threaten the security of the state. A meeting of scientists and policy-makers from forty-six countries in Toronto in June 1988 acknowledged that 'continued alteration of the global atmosphere threatens global security'.[25] The participants also declared that the 'ultimate consequences could be second only to a global nuclear war'.[26] Changes in the natural world can threaten security in the social world in a number of different ways. Recalling the earlier sections of this chapter, we can see how some of the topics already discussed can be viewed as security threats. For example, trans-boundary material flows can affect state security by creating food shortages, reducing industrial output, or lowering the quality of life. This may give rise to environmental refugees (individuals who have been compelled to leave their homes because of environmental degradation), who in turn further weaken the state's security.

Additionally, the mismanagement of a commons may affect state security in a number of ways. For example, one country may be abusing the common region in such a way that it incites environmental degradation in another country. Alternatively, one country may not be shouldering its share of the burden in the co-operative arrangement (for example, it may not be party to an agreement or it may not be fulfilling its proclaimed obligations). Therefore, other states, either by citing tangible evidence or by acting out of sheer frustration, may conclude that the harm that they have incurred (either as a result of environmental degradation or as a result of shouldering too much of the responsibility) has been caused by the inaction of the offending state. They may then feel compelled to take sanctioning actions (military, economic, or diplomatic) against that state and thereby challenge its security.

Before we leave this discussion of a wider interpretation of security, one final observation needs to be made: though the integrity of the state system is not being threatened, these developments will undoubtedly promote the concept of 'common security'—a theme which has, in the past, seemed incompatible with realist international relations thought.[27] For, despite the fact that environmental changes are not equally distributed (some argue that the 'winners and losers' issue may continue to play a role in the global warming debate), it is clear that no state can insulate itself from some physical changes. Therefore, these variations in the natural Earth's equilibrium will definitely cause shifts in the political world's equilibrium. We cannot accurately predict the form that these changes will take, but we can hypothesize that, unless managed properly, they will be quite destabilizing. In this way, state and international security could be challenged.

## VI. What are the Challenges of Global Atmospheric Change?

In the introduction to this chapter, I presented the thesis that environmental issues in the international system have progressively accumulated. In other words, an increasing number of 'green' concerns have appeared on the global agenda, while the already present issues have become more established. This evolutionary explanation makes it clear that international environmental matters will continue to occupy a prominent position in the minds of decision-makers in the future.

This last substantive section examines an issue which effectively crowns (at least temporarily) the dual empirical and theoretical progressions that I have outlined. Global atmospheric change (as epitomized by the twin challenges of ozone layer depletion and global warming) will not only cause other environmental issues to remain relevant, but it will also continue to present challenges to the way in which we study world politics. Let us look, briefly, at the two major issues.

## Ozone Layer Depletion

The Earth is surrounded by a thin band of ozone that serves to absorb most of the incoming ultraviolet radiation. The natural equilibrium of the gases in this layer has been disrupted recently by a number of human-made substances that have been destroying the ozone. If these chemicals (the major one being chlorofluorocarbons (CFCs)) continue to be emitted and the globe experiences a depletion of its protective ozone layer, then more ultraviolet radiation will be able to penetrate the troposphere and hit the Earth's surface. Such an increase in ultraviolet flux would: increase the incidence of skin cancer and cataracts and decrease the effectiveness of the immune system of humans; decrease the productivity of animal-rearing (and perhaps even threaten the food chain); reduce crop yields; and weaken manufacturing materials.

## Global Warming

The Earth's atmosphere is constituted so that it allows most sunlight to stream in uninterrupted. After striking the Earth's surface, this solar energy is reflected as longer-wavelength infrared radiation. Some of this radiation is subsequently trapped in the atmosphere by clouds and 'greenhouse gases' (which include carbon dioxide, methane, nitrous oxide, and CFCs). Without this greenhouse effect, the surface of the Earth would be about 33°C cooler than it presently is, and thus the phenomenon is necessary for life, as we know it, on the planet. But since the Industrial Revolution, humankind has pumped more gases into the atmosphere and has, in effect, 'thickened' the greenhouse blanket that surrounds the Earth, therefore trapping more heat near the surface. As a result, it has been estimated that average global temperature may rise by between 1.5° and 4.5°C within forty years—a phenomenon generally known as 'global warming'. Such a development would cause sea-levels to rise and cause the climatic zones of the world to shift. These two major developments would also generate a number of other significant physical changes. Taken together, they would have immense global consequences.

Global atmospheric change will magnify the importance of all of those environmental issues that this chapter has identified. As I noted in section II, these two issues can be regarded as 'global commons' and therefore raise all of the considerations that were brought out in that section—yet on a world-wide scale. These physical changes will also reduce the availability of certain natural resources (section I) and will also cause trans-boundary material flows to increase (section III)—thus intensifying the significance of these two issues. (Further connections will be brought out later in this section.) Thus, from a purely empirical standpoint, it is clear that the challenge of global atmospheric change will sustain a wide range of international environmental issues.

If the challenges are to be managed effectively and justly, some sort of international co-operation will be necessary. Though there have been some co-operative efforts to date, comprehensive arrangements have yet to be realized.[28] Thus, to conclude this section, I would like to present a number of factors for co-operation on these issues of global atmospheric change. The purpose of this undertaking is twofold. First, it suggests what will be the trends and likely developments in the general issue of international environmental matters. And second, it substantiates the assertion that a wholly realist interpretation of world politics will not be able to make sense of these future developments. Instead, I will argue that we must accept a variety of theories and methodologies if we are to make some sense of the dynamic and complex world around us.

First of all, since states will continue to be the dominant actors in the international political system in the foreseeable future, any co-operative arrangement will have to be negotiated primarily among states. But before any country enters into a collective arrangement, their leaders will undertake some sort of cost–benefit analysis in order to help evaluate the proposed agreement.

The basic theoretical proposition being put forward here is that governments will not engage in co-operative arrangements if the agreements force them to make large economic sacrifices. Obviously, this statement specifies an approach to international politics that is characteristic of a 'rationalistic realist' who claims that there are always objectively defined choices in the international system. Though there are problems with this proposition, it is clear that this game-theory analysis can give us insight into the probable limitations upon future co-operation.

This view, however, must be tempered with some sort of 'reflective' admission.[29] In other words, though we should acknowledge that some sort of economic analysis will come into play (especially given the monumental economic costs that will have to be considered while addressing the issue of global atmospheric change), we must also recognize that the analysis will be transformed by changes in the prevailing norms and preferences in society. These factors (which determine the rationalist's costing) are affected by political leadership, by changes in fashion, and by learning from experience—therefore they (and thus the entire costing process) should not be considered to be static. Furthermore, an acceptance that preferences might change, and that these changes are important determinants of co-operation, would also direct the analysis to the key domestic processes that affect, and are affected by, changing calculations of costs and benefits. This examination would point to important considerations that are often missed by wholly rationalist and realist approaches. In this way, an acceptance that both the rationalist and reflective methods can make a contribution will give us a more complete insight.

Second, as I argued in section IV, the question of development will continue to be intricately linked to environmental issues. Any agreement will have to deal with the demands of the South for justice on this issue. More generally, this will change the focus of the bulk of international negotiations from the traditional (at least recently) East–West axis to the North–South axis.

Third, since these are collective goods issues, states will want some sort of assurance that all actors are addressing the problem and that some are not simply 'free-riding'. This suggests that effective co-operation will require states to publish production and emission figures for a wide variety of substances and industrial processes. Monitoring and verification will therefore become important, because no state will want to be making sacrifices while others 'cheat'. What may seem to be a straight-forward consideration is hampered by the important matter of data sovereignty. As Keohane has pointed out, information can be regarded as 'a significant variable in world politics'.[30] Indeed, data can be manipulated, to become powerful instruments of coercion. Thus, many governments, especially the weak and the suspicious, may think that environmental data will be used for other ends—goals which do not bring about world-wide collective benefits, but instead entrench a renewed imperialist, dependent relationship. Therefore it would seem that a degree of trust is a precondition for satisfactory expectation, which in turn, is a precondition for co-operation. This is a challenge to our traditional understanding of sovereignty, and that notion will necessarily have to be re-considered.[31]

Fourth, the presence of a scientific consensus is another key precondition. International co-operation will remain elusive as long as there is disagreement about the issue being discussed. Consensus will need to include an agreement upon the nature and identification of the problem under investigation; an agreement upon the data-collection process; and an agreement upon the method of data interpretation. (Another interesting aspect in this question involves the fact that there will be a demand for agreements to be concluded before scientific certainty has been established.) In order to build a scientific consensus, better theory and more data will be required. However, this requirement once again raises the consideration about data sovereignty. For the reasons outlined above, some governments may be reluctant to participate fully in the efforts to achieve scientific harmony, and therefore the fulfilment of this precondition may be hindered. Thus, scientific disagreement may well continue to be used as a reason for inaction. This might happen either because the dissenting player honestly does not accept the majority argument, or because the player has other reasons for avoiding a co-operative arrangement, but realizes that ostensible disagreement with the science and its findings is the most palatable rationale to cite in support of the political case.

There are a number of other important factors, though not necessarily preconditions, which will affect the international co-operative process. Briefly, these include political entrepreneurs, transnational actors, and crises. First of these is the actions of political entrepreneurs. 'Political entrepreneurs' are those actors that accept the task of facilitating international co-operation in return for private benefits. These benefits may include intangibles, such as an increase in international prestige or the returns derived from acting for simple altruistic reasons. Or the advantages may come in the form of tangibles, such as benefits in matters outside of the issue-area of the potential regime—in either international or domestic arenas. The second of these is the actions of transnational actors (in ways in which I outlined in section IV). The third of these is the influence of crises. By unifying perception on the subject, by increasing the cost of non-cooperation, or by lengthening the shadow of the future, a crisis will illuminate the importance of the issue and thus make players more eager to reach agreement.

It seems evident that as international environmental issues emerge, they will continue to challenge traditional conceptions of international relations. It should be clear that no single approach will be able adequately to interpret and explain the environmental events that will unfold in the international system. Instead, the student of international relations will have to be adaptable, using a host of tools with which he or she will analyse world politics. The world is constantly changing, and only a broad outlook will be able to make sense of the important developments of the next few years.

## VII. Summary

This chapter has examined the ways in which environmental issues have played a role in international relations. By examining six major issues, I have argued that they have come to be major items on today's international agenda through an evolutionary process. Similarly, I have also argued that international environmental issues are challenging the traditional theories by which we explain world politics. While presenting the analysis within this two-track approach, I have tried to make three points evident. First, international environmental issues occupy a predominant position among the concerns of decision-makers today. Second, this position is not precarious but is, in fact, firmly entrenched. It follows that international environmental issues will continue to be major concerns in the future. Finally, these issues present challenges that are unprecedented in the practice and study of international relations. Thus, it is clear that, in coming years, environmental issues will continue to present some of the most interesting concerns for the study and practice of international affairs.

## Notes

The research for this article was supported by grants from the Commonwealth Scholarship Commission in the United Kingdom and from the Canadian Institute for International Peace and Security. The author is grateful to these organizations for their generous support. The author would also like to thank Michael Banks for his comments upon an earlier draft of this chapter.

1. Arthur H. Westing, 'Environmental Factors in Strategic Policy and Action: An Overview', in id. (ed.), *Global Resources and International Conflict* (Oxford: Oxford University Press, 1986), 12.
2. Ibid. 7.
3. Ibid. 8.
4. Ibid. 16.
5. The World Commission on Environment and Development, *Our Common Future* (Oxford: Oxford University Press, 1987), 290.
6. Many environmental issues might, in fact, be more accurately represented by modelling them as 'free' goods. Free goods display the same characteristics as collective goods when they are available in large supply. However, they begin to display a private nature once scarcity is introduced, i.e., they are no longer joint in supply. Nevertheless, there is an important relationship between the analysis of collective goods and the environmental 'commons' problem. This relationship is tenuous, often controversial, and somewhat indirect. See Russell Hardin, *Collective Action* (Baltimore: Johns Hopkins University Press, 1982), and Robert Jervis, 'Realism, Game Theory and Cooperation', *World Politics*, 40 (1988), 317–49 for a fuller discussion.
7. See Further Reading Section.
8. Peter Brimblecombe, *The Big Smoke: A History of Air Pollution in London Since Medieval Times* (London: Methuen, 1987).
9. Bill Luckin, *Pollution and Control: A Social History of the Thames in the Nineteenth Century* (Bristol: Adam Hilger, 1986).

10. The supertanker *Torrey Canyon* crashed off the coast of England in 1967, causing a disastrous oil spill.
11. Rachel Carson, *Silent Spring* (Harmondsworth: Penguin, 1965).
12. The focus of this debate centred around the 'limits' versus 'technology' controversy. See the reading list at the end of the book for further sources on global modelling and the more general neo-Malthusian discussion which took place at this time.
13. Lynton Caldwell, *International Environmental Policy: Emergence and Dimensions* (Durham, NC: Duke University Press, 1984).
14. The issue of trans-boundary material-flow is a constant source of tension in international law. The principle of territorial sovereignty (a state's right to use its territory in whatever manner it sees fit) can clash with the principle of territorial integrity (a state's right to be free of any foreign violation of its territory). To attempt to find a balance between the two, the principle of 'good neighbourliness' ('that no state is entitled to use its territory or permit it to be used in a way that would infringe upon the rights of another state' (Jutta Brunee, *Acid Rain and Ozone Layer Depletion: International Law and Regulation* (New York: Transnational Publishers, 1988), 87)) is often used as a bench-mark. Also of relevance, Principle 21 of the 1972 Stockholm Declarations stated that 'States have, in accordance with the Charter of the United Nations and the principle of international law, the sovereign right to exploit their own resources pursuant to their own environmental policies, and the responsibility to ensure that activities within their jurisdiction or control do not cause damage to the environment or other States or of areas beyond the limits of national jurisdiction.' See 'United Nations Conference on the Human Environment: Final Documents', (1972) XI 1416–69, at 1420.
15. Brunee, *Acid Rain*, 92.
16. The World Commission on Environment and Development, *Our Common Future*, 7.
17. John McCormick, *The Global Environmental Movement* (London: Belhaven Press, 1989), 97.
18. The question of the interrelationship between the 'natural Earth' and the 'social world' is both relevant and interesting. See, for example, the work by James Lovelock, whose 'Gaia' theory has often been at the centre of the discussion: *Gaia: A New Look at Life on Earth* (Oxford: Oxford University Press, 1979), and *The Ages of Gaia: A Biography of our Living Earth* (Oxford: Oxford University Press, 1988).
19. See 'United Nations Conference on the Human Environment: Final Documents', 1420.
20. Some of the most sophisticated technical research is now being undertaken by NGOs. (This is a point that is often overlooked.)

21. See, for example, Robin Clarke and Lloyd Timberlake, *Stockholm Plus Ten: Promises, Promises?* (London: Earthscan for the IIED, 1982), and McCormick, *The Global Environmental Movement*, Chap. 6.

22. For an examination of one aspect of the regional seas programme (the Mediterranean Action Plan) that is also theoretically enlightening, see Peter M. Haas, *Saving the Mediterranean: The Politics of International Environmental Cooperation* (New York: Columbia University Press, 1990).

23. See The World Commission on Environment and Development, *Our Common Future*, and David Pearce, *et al.*, *Blueprint for a Green Economy* (London: Earthscan, 1990).

24. In June 1990, in London, the Parties to the Montreal Protocol on Substances that Deplete the Ozone Layer agreed to create a fund, valued at US $240 million for the initial three years, to assist the South to develop substitutes for CFCs. This agreement was unprecedented and could provide a model for other issues.

25. Conference statement of 'The Changing Atmosphere: Implications for Global Security' (Toronto, June 1988), 2.

26. Ibid. 1.

27. See the work on the League of Nations and, more recently, the Report of the Palme Commission: The Independent Commission on Disarmament and Security Issues, *Common Security: A Programme for Disarmament* (London: Pan Books, 1982).

28. Some co-operative arrangements have been reached on the ozone layer depletion issue (the Vienna Convention of 1985, the Montreal Protocol of 1987, and the 1990 amendments to the Protocol). In October 1990, however, no agreement had been reached on the issue of global climatic change. See the reading list at the end of this book.

29. For an interesting introduction to this rationalistic/reflective debate, see Robert O. Keohane, 'International Institutions: Two Approaches', *International Studies Quarterly*, 32/4 (1988), 379–96.

30. Id., *After Hegemony: Cooperation and Discord in the World Political Economy* (Princeton, NJ: Princeton University Press, 1984), 245.

31. The work that is being undertaken in arms control (verification and confidence-building measures) presents an interesting analogy.

# TWELVE

# Islam and World Politics

*James Piscatori*

The current revival of Islam arrived on the international political scene with an unmistakable force in the 1970s and has ever since continued to be an imposing presence. The Shah of Iran was toppled in an Islamic revolution that began in late 1978; American diplomats were taken hostage and held in that revolution's name for 444 days from late 1979 to January 1981; the Grand Mosque in Mecca, the religious focus of all Muslims, itself came under siege in November 1979 from fundamentalist critics of the Saudi regime; President Sadat of Egypt was murdered in October 1981 by a group which had proclaimed war against the impieties of Egyptian society; Shiah activists in Lebanon came to refer to themselves as 'the party of God' or as 'Islamic Jihad' from the early 1980s, and elements among them engaged in hostage-taking and suicide bombing, and throughout the 1980s and into the 1990s, violent confrontations between Muslim groups and the government, or between Muslim and non-Muslim groups, occurred in societies as diverse as Indonesia, Nigeria, India, and Trinidad. The publication of Salman Rushdie's novel, *The Satanic Verses*, in 1988, and Muslim reactions to the death sentence passed on him by Ayatollah Khomeini brought Muslim politics to the streets of even Western Europe and North America.

Such examples of Islamic activism have often been cited as signs of a new age of political integration among Muslims, but whether or not this is a salutary development has caused much dispute. Muslims may be expected to hold the view that greater political co-operation, even unity, of the believers is itself a wholly advantageous occurrence. Yet pronounced differences of ideology and policy among Muslim states and movements have led to little tangible integration beyond the rhetorical level, and profound disagreements exist as to what steps should be taken to improve the situation. By way of contrast, there has been agreement in the West, but of a disapproving kind: Muslim activism has widely been perceived as inherently 'militant' or 'fanatical', and, perhaps drawing on an entrenched mythology of natural civilizational confrontation, Western policy-makers have frequently feared that the contagion of 'Islamic revolution' would spread to the detriment of their interests. In the attempt to reach some conclusion as to whether the international system, or at least the Western political order, faces a radical pan-Islamic challenge, however, an examination of the various dimensions of Islam's impact on international relations must be undertaken.

## I. What are the Causes of the Islamic Resurgence?

It must first be noted that there has been an unhistorical tendency to conceive of the revival of Islam in the late twentieth century as a unique phenomenon. The reality, rather, is that a number of revivals have occurred in past centuries—in the eighth, tenth, early seventeenth, mid-eighteenth, and late nineteenth centuries, for instance—and it is probable that there is a cyclical pattern to revivalism or fundamentalism. At the outset of such a cycle, Muslims have come to accommodate themselves to prevailing social and political customs. But then, when an era of social and economic disequilibrium sets in, widespread discontent leads to the typical conclusion that Muslims have brought dishonour and punishment on themselves by deviating from orthodoxy. In response to this, reformist leaders and movements challenge the status quo in the name of purified Islam, but, after a period of upheaval, they finally return to an accommodation with the mores of the society in which they live.

The current revival is similarly the result of such a process of disillusionment and reform. Some observers credit this, however, to a kind of Muslim power and triumphalism as a result of the oil boom of the mid-1970s that gave impetus to internationally active patrons such as Saudi Arabia, Libya, and Iran. There is, of course, some validity to the argument that the 'international successes of Islam'[1]—institution-building and conferences—have helped to accent revivalist sentiment and organization within individual countries. But the availability of the means (oil) does not in itself account for the pursuit of the ends (revival). For this we must turn to deeper causes.

First, the defeat of Egypt, Syria, and Jordan in the 1967 war with Israel shattered the morale not only of the Arabs, but also most Muslims who had lost the holy city of Jerusalem. Sacred to Muslims not only because it, rather than Mecca, was the first direction of Muslim prayer, Jerusalem is also widely believed to be the place to which the Prophet Muhammad was transported on his famous 'night journey' and from which—on the spot where the Dome of the Rock now stands on Temple Mount—he temporarily ascended to heaven. The loss of Jerusalem was therefore not just a set-back or defeat; it was *al-nakba*, 'the disaster'—the culmination of a long series of humiliations which stretched back in modern times to the first militarily unsuccessful encounters of the Ottoman Muslims with the Europeans. These defeats had given rise to a sense of inferiority, which initially was based on an appreciation of technological inadequacy. But now, in the mid-twentieth century, the loss of sacred territory led many Muslims to conclude one of two things: either that Islam was an inferior religion, or, more plausibly, that they were inadequate believers who had not lived up to the ideals of Islam and thus deserved their fate.

Some Muslims, rejecting a public role for religion altogether, turned to secularism. But most Muslims experienced a religiously defined reaction to the defeat: they needed to be better Muslims, and their governments more Islamic, if God was to spare them further calamity, or if they were ever to have a chance of recapturing Jerusalem. Many Arab Muslims in particular had come to see a certain hollowness in Nasserism, the ideology of Gamal Abdul Nasser (1918–70), the Egyptian leader who had led the Arabs into the catastrophic losses of 1967. Once esteemed as virtually 'the voice of the Arabs' and his Arab nationalist, socialist, and secular ideology considered the panacea for the Arabs' problems, both man and programme were now spurned for ideas that were more familiar and coherent.

Second, the process of development has been a contributing factor. It has stimulated the revival in two main ways: first, it has often strained the social and political fabric, thereby leading people to turn to traditional symbols and values as a way of comforting and orienting themselves; and second, it has provided the means of speedy communication and easy dissemination of both domestic and international information.

The most important dimension of developmental stress has been the unsettling and unrelieved exodus of people from the country-side to the cities. In a pattern common throughout the Third World, the majority of rural migrants quickly become the urban poor, victims of their own hope, swallowed by the very process which they believed would liberate them. A powerful new sense of not belonging seems to lead naturally to the turn to religion. In some societies, such as Iran, where well-established religious institu-tions provide a degree of financial assistance, helping at least to cushion the move from the countryside, migrants inevitably come into close contact with the religious officials and develop ties of loyalty to them. In Lebanon, the Shiah who migrated from the south or the Beqaa valley to Beirut became more aware of sectarian identification, even before the politically charged turmoil of the late 1970s had set in. In the city and suburbs, as outsiders needing the patronage of families to which they did not belong, they felt that they had incurred dishonour and lowered the status that they had had in the countryside. In such an alien environment, the political point of reference was no longer family, as it has been in the village, but sect.[2] In other societies, such as Nigeria, where extreme economic imbalance and a climate of religious tension prevail, the migrants become natural recruits of millenarian movements, as in fact occurred in 1980–5.

If poverty and deprivation affect the attitudes of the rural migrants, relatively greater wealth and improved social position affect the attitudes of the urban middle classes in the midst of the developmental process. It is precisely because the middle classes are better off that they are dissatisfied; their appetite has been whetted and they want more. This is particularly true of the lower middle class. According to the standard profile of Egyptian Islamic militants of the late 1970s, over 70 per cent were from modest, not poor, backgrounds and were first-generation city-dwellers.[3] Most members of the middle classes will express their religious feeling through the state-controlled religious establishment and oppose a radical challenge to it. Yet some will turn to more radical alternatives as they sense that the religious establishment is indistinguishable from a regime, like that of Anwar Sadat (1918–81) in Egypt, whose policies appear to open doors to foreign political and business élites.

The other way in which the process of development has stimulated a sense of renewal is by advancing the dissemination of information throughout the developing world. Despite the overall adverse condition of many people, there have been substantial improvements in literacy in the general population; moreover, radios have become a common possession. As a result, people are now more in touch with what is going on in the rest of the world, and are especially able to know how dissatisfaction and protest against injustices can be framed by reference to Islam. The fast and efficient distribution within Iran of Ayatollah Khomeini's sermons, delivered in exile and recorded on cassettes—'revolution-by-cassette'—and those of other important religious figures, such as the Egyptian 'Abd al-Hamid Kishk, throughout the Middle East has also helped people to focus their discontent and build their identity around one set of ideas, even though the exponent of those ideas is far removed. Modern technology has thus dramatically projected the voice of Muslim opinion-makers and enhanced Islam's ability to function as a communications network.

The third general reason for the present revival, in addition to the intellectual and spiritual malaise since the 1967 war and the effects of the development process, is that Muslim societies have been caught up in the universal crisis of modernity. Like virtually everyone else, most Muslims are feeling ill at ease with a world that places less and less emphasis on the traditional loyalties of family and faith and seems to find religious institutions increasingly irrelevant. In the past century, there has been a discernible shift towards loosening the individual's dependence on the extended family, weakening parental authority, liberating women, and questioning the authority of the clergy. Though not causally related, there has also been an alarming increase in divorce, alcohol and drug addiction, nervous disorders, and crime. At the least, such facets of modernism have generated a time of 'secular discontents'[4] when many are seeking in religion the answer to basic questions of identity.

Muslims, and others, in a sense are looking for what Daniel Bell called 'new rites of incorporation',[5] which link today's deracinated individual to a community and history. To turn to religion is thus natural because it provides moral links and common world-views to its followers. In this one respect, born-again Christians and veiled-again Muslims are perhaps responding to the same broad phenomenon. But Islam supplies a particularly potent rite of incorporation because of its fervent devotion to the *umma* (community of believers), its view of the early Prophetic and caliphal community as constituting a golden age, and its graphic emphasis on the transcendence of trial and time in the afterlife.

Finally, the fourth general reason for the revival is that the conditions of political development in Muslim societies have tended to heighten the importance of Islam as a political ideology. Because most of these societies are poor in participatory institutions and dominated by unelected rulers, it is natural for those in power to look for a way of legitimizing themselves. Several monarchies have been especially adept at using Islamic symbols for this purpose: the Moroccan king makes much of his traditional title, Commander of the Faithful; the Saudi king finds a naturally sympathetic response when he speaks of his role as protector of Mecca and Medina, the two holiest cities of Islam; and the Jordanian king is careful to emphasize his descent from the Prophet. The leaders of republics have also found it expedient to put Islam to their service. Sadat, for example, found it useful—although it was extremely controversial—to have a religious-legal opinion (*fatwā*) from the Muslim establishment supporting his peace treaty with Israel. Similarly, Saddam Hussein, the Iraqi leader not previously noted for his deference to Muslim sentiment, appealed for support against the forces arrayed against him in the wake of his invasion of Kuwait in August 1990 by a calculated invocation of the resonant concept, jihād.

In these and many other examples, governments have felt able to use Islam because, as an ideology, it is vague in content yet highly charged, and its vocabulary is thoroughly familiar to everyone. Yet, for the very same reasons, Islam can be used to express opposition. This use has been increasing as well, partly as a result of the overthrow of the Shah and the advent of the Iranian revolution in 1978–9. But the use of Islam to express opposition has also been growing because in many countries in which regular outlets for political expression do not exist, Islam has been found to be an effective and relatively secure platform from which to make a political stand. Governments have been hesitant to suppress groups speaking in the name of Islam because of the need to appear orthodox themselves—in order either to forestall domestic opposition or to attract aid from Muslim 'patrons' such as Saudi Arabia. As a result, many Muslim groups have been relatively free to criticize their governments, albeit in a circumspect way. The Muslim Brotherhood in Jordan has been a case in point, as it was in the Sudan for most of the period of the Nimeiri regime (1969–85).

In regimes so repressive that they brook no dissent and regard Muslim criticism of any sort as a threat to their survival, the 'Islamic alternative' almost invariably has become more radical. It has become a kind of party, whose aim is to replace the regime, rather than a pressure group. Such conditions notably obtained in Iran where politics became increasingly polarized as all were caught up in a double revolution of expectations: peasants expecting the good life in the dazzling cities; professionals and intellectuals expecting greater influence, status, and political participation. Unable to defuse this explosive situation and unwilling to share power, the Shah's regime ceded moral and political ground to the opposition, the mullahs of 'Islamic revolution', who constituted an informal counter-élite.

## II. Is Islam the Enemy of the West?

So successful were these revolutionaries and so uncompromising their rhetoric, it is often assumed that the Iranian revolution has stripped away all illusion that Islam and the Western political order can coexist. This view builds on the hoary argument that Islam is pre-eminently concerned with the creation of a universal Muslim community and is intolerant of those who are not Muslims. The Qur'ān and traditions of the Prophet (hadīths) do indeed have many references to the need and desirability of fighting the unbelievers, often to the bitter end. This is one dimension of the idea of jihād, which is particularly emphasized in the case of polytheists. For example, the Qur'ān urges the believers to fight them 'wherever you find them' until they repent or are eliminated (9: 5), and a hadīth records the Prophet as saying, 'I am ordered to fight [the polytheists] until they say "there is no God but Allah".'[6] 'People of the book', other monotheists such as

Jews or Christians, are also to be fought until they pay a special tax and are 'subdued' or 'humbled' (9: 29). Generally, the *hadīths* tell us that 'whoever fights to make Allah's Word superior fights in God's cause', and that even a single journey for this purpose is 'better than the world and all that is in it'.[7]

It is this expansionist zeal which accounts for the medieval, 'Abbasid (750–1258) elaboration of a bifurcated and conflict-torn world—*dār al-islām* (the Islamic realm of peace) versus *dār al-harb* (the non-Islamic realm of war). Moreover, within the realm of Islam, non-Muslims who pay the tax in exchange for protection are to suffer certain disadvantages and are not to be treated equally with the Muslim citizens. For example, they are not allowed to display their religious symbols openly or to carry arms—the former condition, though obviously not the latter, applied to non-Muslim Western military forces stationed in Saudi Arabia as the result of the Persian Gulf crisis of 1990–1. This discrimination is entirely consistent with the Muslim view of Islam as the last and most perfect of revelations.

But it would be incorrect to conclude from this that a built-in political antipathy exists between the Muslim and Western worlds. One reason why such a conclusion is doubtful is that Islamic political theory is not as simple and clear-cut as just outlined. Rather, the Qur'ān and *hadīths* also elaborate a view that is distinctly at odds with the one which focuses on the jihād as an instrument of Islamic militancy and expansionism. This alternative view is of a tolerant, non-violent Islam that accommodates itself to the reality of political pluralism and non-Muslim centres of power. According to this, Qur'ānic, line of reasoning, there is to be no compulsion when it comes to religion (2: 256), for what matters is the quality, not the extent, of the faith. It is important for Muslims to commit their wealth and very lives (61: 11) to 'strive' ceaselessly against falsehood,[8] but actual combat constitutes the lesser form of 'striving' (jihād, literally) and is to be avoided if at all possible. Indeed, the Prophet is reported as saying that whereas 'war is deception',[9] the greater jihād is working for the good and against evil. Rather than relying primarily on the sword, the Muslim is to use his heart, tongue, and hands for the good of his own soul (29: 6) and to build the just society.

Fighting, to be sure, is enjoined in the cause of righteousness, but primarily for self-defence: 'Fight in the cause of God those who fight you, but do not be aggressive, for God does not love aggressors' (2: 190). There is, however, an obligation to fight in order to protect the non-Muslim subjects of an Islamic state, whose rights generally should be upheld and who should not be overtaxed.[10] Muslims are encouraged to end the fighting if the enemy has the momentary advantage[11] or withdraws from active hostilities (4: 90). They may even conclude a treaty with the enemy, which takes precedence over any obligation to their fellow Muslims. 'If they [Muslims] ask for help in the matter of religion, it is your duty to help them, except against a people with whom you have a treaty' (8: 72). And, as the Prophet did, they are to tolerate foreign delegations.[12]

Another basic problem with assuming the inherent antagonism of Muslims and Westerners is that it contradicts a long history of accommodation between them. Polemicists on both sides may prefer to invoke dark memories of the Crusades, but the historical record suggests a more variegated pattern of war and alliance, competition and co-operation. While they may not have conceded that Western states were equal to them, Muslim states regularly entered into territorial agreements and concluded peace with them, even, as an Ottoman treaty with Russia in 1739 states, 'perpetual, constant, and inviolate peace'.[13] From the sixteenth century, Muslim practice brought to a virtual close the earlier debates among Muslim jurists as to the length of a peace treaty, or truce, between Muslims and non-Muslims. Building on the example of the Hudaybiyya treaty which the Prophet himself had concluded with the then-polytheistic Meccans in 628, jurists of at least two law schools had argued that such agreements could last no more than ten years. But the treaty of 1535 between Suleiman the Magnificent, the Ottoman Sultan, and Francis I of France endorsed the idea of 'valid and sure peace' between them for their lifetimes,[14] and from this point historical experience redefined the theoretical approach.

A final difficulty with the presumption of automatic antipathy between Islam and the West is that it overstates the degree of coherence of each. Individuals—let alone governments—rarely think in civilizational terms and it is hard to conceive of Islam as speaking with one voice, or of the West as moving with one purpose. This is in part because of the shifting doctrinal or ideological bases of society to which reference has been made above. It is also because of intersecting loyalties and the multiple pulls on one's identity. Family, gender, ethnicity, race, class, education, nation, and combinations of these factors may be as, if not more, important than religion in motivating conduct. The reality is too complex to sustain the simple notion of inter-civilizational conflict between two monolithic blocs.

## III. Are Islam and Nationalism Compatible?

A more subtle proposition has been advanced which holds that Islam and the Western-inspired international political and legal order are incompatible because Islam is committed to a virulent universalism, whereas the international order is based on political and territorial pluralism. Adda Bozeman, for instance, has argued that Islam is inimical to the 'core idea of the state', and this has been specifically true of the Middle East, where 'communities of believers, or freely floating sects unconfined by spatial bounds', have been the norm.[15] But here too such conventional wisdom must be questioned.

It is undeniably true that Islamic political theory places substantial emphasis on the idea of world-wide community. There is no distinction among the believers except in piety, and the fraternity of the faith will inexorably extend, by various means, to the point where all peoples accept the indivisible unity of Allah and the final prophecy of Muhammad—the *sine qua non* of the Islamic creed. This imperative to advance the Islamic community (*umma*) accounts for the sharp hostility directed against those who profess to be Muslims but are not deemed to be sincere or loyal. According to the Qur'ān, the believers must fully conform, unlike the Bedouin of the desert, who only outwardly submitted (48: 16). Such bonds of loyalty as tribe and race as they affirmed must be displaced by common 'submission' (*islām*, literally) to the one God, and, as an influential modern writer, Abu'l-'Ala Mawdudi, said, the Islamic community can only be 'universal and all-embracing, its sphere of activity . . . coextensive with the whole of human life.'[16]

Yet one can also point to indicators of an Islam that recognizes, implicitly and explicitly, ideological, political, and territorial divisions. One reading of the Qur'ān, for instance, seems to sanction such divisions. It says that God divided men into nations and tribes for a purpose—to come to 'know each other' (49: 13)—and that the divisions of language and colour 'are signs for those who know' (30: 22). Moreover, in one injunction to obey God and His Prophet, it adds, in the plural, 'and those in authority among you' (4: 59). At another point, it says knowingly, 'If God had so willed, He would have made them one community' (42: 8). The texts of the various schools of law also accept territorial divisions as an inescapable fact to which the law must bend.

These recognitions that the reality of territorial divisions qualifies the ideal of Islamic universality set the stage for the medieval thinkers who accepted that there is pluralism within the Islamic realm as well as between it and the non-Islamic realm. They did this by casting a critical eye on the supposed unity of the Muslim community around the caliphate and finding it fictitious. For example, al-Mawardi (991–1058), the great theoretician of the caliphate, had made it seem that only one Caliph could rule and that he was the prime political authority. But Abu Hamid al-Ghazzali (1058–1111) argued that the Caliph has less power than is believed and that al-Mawardi had not explained how the Caliph owes his very position to the real centres of power.[17] Ibn Taymiyya (1263–1328) went further in stressing that, because of Islam's essential religious unity, it need not have only one political regime,[18] and Ibn Khaldun (1333–1406) endorsed the idea by arguing that the factual rise and decline of political units is entirely natural and, by implication, in accord with Islam. Group feeling and religious devotion are neither intrinsically nor practically incompatible. In fact, they reinforce each other and help the political units to grow bigger. Ultimately, however, these various 'states' are destined to come and go according to the whim of history, the laws of social logic, and the will of Allah.[19] Although the caliphate provided the façade of unity, then, large cracks were discoverable and were made to seem normal.

Parallel to this intellectual adaptation is the flexibility that Muslim statesmen have displayed over the centuries. As has already been noted, Muslim rulers found no difficulty in maintaining regular diplomatic intercourse with non-Muslim states. But they also came to accept the reality of separate centres of power within the Islamic community itself. This record runs counter to the argument of Elie Kedourie who says that the idea of 'the lively multiplicity of political authorities' is not endemic to a civilization in which 'loyalty to Islam . . . ought to constitute the sole political bond'.[20]

An early example of the contrary experience is the dispute between 'Ali (c.600–61), the Prophet's son-in-law and the fourth Caliph, and Mu'awiyya (c.602–80), the governor of Syria and later the first Umayyad Caliph, over the legitimate succession to the caliphate. The text of the arbitration between them is remarkable for the way it makes the men equal: 'Ali, the Caliph, is described as representing 'the people of Kufa [in Iraq] and their followers of the believers and Muslims', and Mu'awiyya, the rebel, is described as representing 'al-Sham [Syria] and their followers of the believers and Muslims'.[21]

Subsequent Islamic history confirms this tendency of the Muslim sovereign to concede that other, nominally subject, rulers had as much, if not more, power. This was the case at the 'Abbasid court when first the Barmaks and then the Buwayhids, with the connivance of the army, took charge. Later, the Sunni Ottomans were unable to force the submission of the Persian Shiah, but, in 1590, the two rivals concluded a treaty whereby the Persians agreed to stop the cursing of the first three Caliphs, whom the Shiah did not accept, and to cede large amounts of territory to the Ottomans. It was a religious and territorial compromise which Shah 'Abbas (1571–1629) felt that he had to make if he was to prevent the Uzbeks from moving in on his empire from the east. The two Muslim powers came to a *modus vivendi* in 1639, ambitiously designed to last 'till the day of resurrection';[22] and it did last, remarkably, for more than eighty years. Significantly, the treaty laid down a frontier between the two states of the *umma* which remained the undisputed border for two hundred years.

In the twentieth century, Muslim–Western relations and inter-Muslim relations came indisputably to be measured by the yardstick of territorial and national sovereignty. From the end of the eighteenth century, European colonialism had implanted itself, in turn fostering the growth of indigenous nationalisms. Local élites accepted that to rid themselves of imperial control, while simultaneously protecting their own prestige and power against rival claimants to post-colonial leadership, they had to play the international game. Playing this game meant first of all securing recognition from the great powers, and then enhancing the sense of their national individuality in the greater society of nation-states.

This commitment to national pluralism is demonstrated by the value that Muslim élites attached to the League of Nations, whose Covenant sanctified the territorial and political independence of every member. Persia and Iraq had good cause to be worried about this principle because they were involved in an ancient territorial dispute—a dispute that was to resurface in the 1980s as one of the causes of the bitter, eight-year-long Iran–Iraq war. In the 1930s, even though the Iraqi government had not been happy about the League's intervention on behalf of the Assyrian minority in Iraq in 1932, it appealed to the League's Council to take up the problem of control over the Shatt al-'Arab, the strategic waterway formed by the confluence of the Tigris and Euphrates rivers. There were pressing regional security reasons why the two countries came to an agreement in 1937, but the use of the League's machinery made the significant political point that both governments wanted to establish—that the dispute was international as were disputes between Muslim and Western states or between Western states themselves.

In inter-Muslim relations, the norm roughly from the 1930s to today has been to acknowledge the spiritual and cultural unity of faith while insisting on preserving the reality of territorial divisions. In 1936 Saudi Arabia and Iraq, for example, referred almost in the same breath to 'the ties of the Islamic faith and of racial unity which units them' and to the desire 'of safeguarding the integrity of their territories'.[23] Moreover, every multilateral agreement up to the present makes clear that the form of association contracted must not be seen as a derogation or qualification of the individual sovereignties of the contracting parties. The Arab League Pact (1945), although 'desirous of strengthening the close relations and numerous ties which link the Arab states', is committed to preserving the independence and sovereignty of its members and requires that 'each member state shall respect the systems of government established in the other member states and regard them as exclusive concerns of those states'.[24] The Charter of the Organization of the Islamic Conference (1972), which has members from across the broad Muslim world, spells out in unambiguous terms that the or-ganization is based on the principles of 'respect of the sovereignty, independence and territorial integrity of each member State' and of 'abstention from the threat or use of force against the territorial integrity, national unity or political independence of any member State'.[25]

When the weight of such historical experience is added to the intellectual evolution suggested earlier, it is no wonder that the overwhelming modern intellectual consensus among Muslims is that Islam and nationalism can coexist, even as it is thought that Islamic unity is ultimately desirable. The pervasive influence of modern, nationalized educational systems has also worked to confirm the trend. The great Indian philosopher and poet Muhammad Iqbal (1875–1938) may be seen as exemplifying this consensus: beginning with the assumption that Islam demands one integrated community, he ended with the view that unity first required the independence of every Muslim territory and the creation of a kind of Muslim League of Nations.[26]

There is no doubt, of course, that many Muslims reject the institution of the nation-state as alien and destructive of pan-Islamic union. Ayatollah Khomeini (1902–89) was the most notable recent exponent of this line of thought, and various other thinkers and groups, both Sunnis and Shiah, echo it. Principle 11 of revolutionary Iran's constitution commits the government to promoting Islamic unity. Yet for all his millenarianism Khomeini implicitly joined the consensus and accepted the territorial state: 'The Iranian nation must grow in power and resolution until it has vouchsafed Islam to the entire world'.[27] Even during the darkest days of the Iran–Iraq war, he could say, 'we have never violated the rights of the people of Iraq . . . We are brothers of the Iraqi nation and regard its soil as sacred'.[28] In effect, nationalism and the nation-state have become a powerful presence on the modern Muslim landscape.

## IV. What is the Role of Islam in Foreign Policy-Making?

Bernard Lewis, a prominent scholar of Islam, says that 'foreign policy is a European concept' and is 'alien and new in the world of Islam'.[29] Others, most often in the media, have talked of certain Muslim states, such as Iran, Pakistan, or Saudi Arabia, as so ideologically committed that they pursue an 'Islamic foreign policy'. Neither assumption of Islam's relevance, however, seems warranted by the facts, and the case of Saudi Arabia is particularly instructive.

In the wartime and post-Second World War period, there were two main issues which dominated Saudi foreign policy—Arab unity and Palestine. Regarding the former, there is no evidence that King 'Abd al-'Aziz (often known as Ibn Sa'ud, c.1880–1953) acted for any reason other than being, as the *Palestine Post* described him, 'a supporter of political realism'.[30] Although he encouraged individual movements like that of the Syrian nationalists, he was distinctly cool to any plans that aimed to reassemble the newly independent peoples into a larger unity. In particular, he opposed the Greater Syria Plan, which King 'Abdullah of Trans-Jordan advanced, and the Fertile Crescent Plan, which Nuri al-Said, the Iraqi Prime Minister, proposed. He naturally saw these as Hashimite, and perhaps British-backed, designs on his independence. Rather than being convinced that there was an ethnic and religious imperative for Arabs to unite, 'Abd al-'Aziz believed political decline would flow from such a projected union and especially feared financial loss from a customs union that would control the pilgrimage to Mecca and Medina in his kingdom.

But political and Islamic considerations affected the response to the second issue, Palestine. It is impossible to separate the motivations. 'Abd al-'Aziz could not ignore the risk to his position at home and abroad if he failed to be more vocal about the matter which so exercised Arab and Islamic sentiment. But he is also known to have shared with some Muslims a hostile view of the Jews, based in part on a misinterpretation of Islamic history, and to have thus believed that because the resurrection of all Muslims will take place in Palestine, that land must remain in the hands of Arab Muslims. To take it upon himself to pressure the West into resisting the Zionist demands was thus, in his view, the politically wise and only religiously proper thing to do.

Apart from the Palestine question, however, there is little evidence that Islamic values played a central role in the formulation of the foreign policy of the first Saudi king, or even in aiding its implementation. But the Islamic dimension became more pronounced under his successors, not necessarily because they were more devout but because different considerations presented themselves. The death of 'Abd al-'Aziz in 1953 roughly coincided with one of the most significant events in the modern Arab world—the launching of the Egyptian revolution. The accession of King Sa'ud at this time was unfortunate, for it brought an incompetent to the throne precisely at the time that the charismatic Nasser was making Egypt the premier Arab state.

The real catalyst for trouble between the two countries was the Yemeni civil war, which broke out in September 1962 and put the very survival of the neighbouring Saudi regime in question. After a period of hesitation and self-absorption, culminating in the deposition of Sa'ud, the new king, Faisal (c.1904–75), felt able to launch an initiative in 1965 that called for an alliance of all Muslims. Although he argued that there could be no conflict between Islamic and Arab co-operation, there is no doubt that he saw an Islamic *entente* as the counterweight to the leftist states in the Arab cold war. But little success was in fact to be culled from the policy since, although the more conservative states like Iran, Jordan, Pakistan, and Malaysia supported the Saudi initiative, the more radical states like Algeria, Syria, Iraq, and Indonesia vigorously opposed it.

The balance of forces dramatically shifted, however, with Nasser's and Egypt's defeat in the 1967 war. The Saudi *bête noire* now found himself in need of Saudi financial aid. When an attempt to burn down the al-Aqsa mosque in Jerusalem took place in 1969, the Saudis indisputably led Arab and Muslim opinion, blaming the outrage on the Israeli occupiers and organizing a summit of Muslim leaders.

It was this meeting that gave rise to the Organization of the Islamic Conference (OIC), which took formal shape in 1972 and was headquartered in the Saudi city of Jedda, 'pending the liberation of Jerusalem' (according to the charter). It provided a permanent institution through which the Saudis could express their views and emphasize their special role in the Muslim world, thereby in the process strengthening their position among the Arabs. Even, in 1989, at the time of inflamed Muslim sentiment in the wake of the publication of Salman Rushdie's allegedly blasphemous book, *The Satanic Verses*, the Saudis were able to influence the OIC away from endorsement of Ayatollah Khomeini's death-sentence against the author.

With regard to the Palestinian issue, Faisal had been financially cool towards the various Palestinian organizations and specifically the Palestine Liberation Organization (PLO) prior to the 1967 war because they were in league with the radical Arab states and had threatened the Saudi monarchy itself. But his attitude changed after the war, partly because of the more favourable regional configuration that has been noted and the need to be legitimized by appearing to be in the Arab political mainstream; but also because of his deeply felt religious belief that Jerusalem must be liberated from occupation. Saudi financial support of the PLO, while limited so as not to encourage the development of an uncontrollable organization, was thus constant from the late 1960s until 1990 when Iraq invaded Kuwait. Popular Palestinian support for the invasion and the alliance of Yasser 'Arafat (b. 1929), the PLO leader, with Saddam Hussein (b. 1937) were too much for the Saudis to bear, and the financial pipeline was cut.

The advent of the Iranian revolution brought other troubles. The Iranians have been unremittingly hostile to a royal family that they consider morally bankrupt and composed of Islamic impostors. Their avowed intention to export the revolution across the Gulf and eight years of war between Iran and Iraq (1980–8) convinced the Saudi regime that a deft calibration of foreign policy was required: strengthening the military through massive arms purchases, without appearing to be too closely allied to the United States; financial support of Iraq, without directly confronting Iran; competition with Iran for the mantle of Islamic leadership, by substantial aid to Muslim states and groups throughout the world, without encouraging the more radical Islamic current or abandoning the kingdom's leading role in Arab politics. The last was to be accomplished via the OIC and such other Saudi-backed institutions as the Muslim World League and the World Council of Mosques. Although the alliance with Iraq, which circumstances had impelled, proved self-defeating with the onset of the Kuwaiti crisis, the policy of containing the Islamic revolution in Iran was not a failure.

As this brief overview suggests, Islam plays a certain, though by no means pre-ordained, role in Saudi foreign policy. It has sometimes been important in the *formulation* of policy, as the support for the Palestinian cause demonstrates. But this has never occurred at the expense of the pragmatically determined *raison d'état*; the two have seemed to overlap and confirm each other.

More striking, however, has been the role that 'Islam' plays in the *implementation* of policy. Policy with an assertively Islamic label is typically legitimized and hence the chances of its effectiveness are improved, as the anti-Nasser and anti-Khomeini policies indicate. While important in this instrumental way, Islamic values are not, however, the sole determinant of the foreign policy of a Muslim country, and, as oil policy suggests, they are often not relevant at all. The presumption that Saudi Arabia, Iran, or any Muslim state follows an instinctively 'Islamic foreign policy' needs, therefore, to be placed in context.

## V. Does Islam Qualify the Idea of National Sovereignty?

It would be perfectly correct to conclude, on the basis of the preceding, that political Islam is naturally an international phenomenon. It is compatible with a nationally based public order and is bound up with the foreign policies of the Muslim states of that system. But as international politics has become more complex and is now more accurately described by the concept of 'world politics', so too Islam is more than simply 'international'. This is most readily borne out by the many Islamic movements, such as the Muslim Brotherhood (Ikhwan al-Muslimun) or the more radical Islamic Jihad, which operate in several countries simultaneously and which exhibit some degree of linkage between them. These are non-state actors, operating in the state environment and exercising an impact on the state system.

The several dimensions of Islamic transnationalism are illustrated by the controversy that ensued from the publication of the *The Satanic Verses* in 1988, the furore that immediately enveloped it as a result of the near-universal Muslim belief that it had blasphemed the Prophet Muhammad, and Ayatollah Khomeini's death-sentence against the author, Salman Rushdie. Britain and Iran broke off diplomatic relations over the affair and both the European Community and the OIC put it near the top of their agendas in 1989. But, in addition to these conventional foreign-policy concerns, a more complicated politics was at work.

The 'export' of the Iranian revolution has been a catch-phrase of the past ten years, and a body of scholarly and policy prescriptive work has substantiated the transnational linkages—the transfers of ideas, money, and men—that have developed between Iran and Islamic groups throughout the world.[31] Less research has been done on Saudi Arabia or Pakistan,[32] but these countries too have been involved in support of Muslim groups and movements beyond their national borders. Britain has not escaped becoming an arena in which such activities occur. In advancing their vision of a normatively preferable Islam, British Muslim groups inevitably espouse a political agenda, and those with close ties to groups or states outside Britain inevitably reflect, in part, the political views of their external supporters.

The Rushdie affair has brought this competition into the foreground, and one of its distinctive features has been the replication of the Saudi-Iranian rivalry on British soil. The Union of Muslim Organizations and the Islamic Cultural Centre in London were instrumental in the early stages in bringing Muslim objections to the attention of the government and public. Though these fall under Saudi patronage, the South Asian Jamaat-i-Islami played an important role as well. For example, it was influential in mobilizing the Islamic Foundation in Leicester to the cause. With the Ayatollah's edict (*fatwā*) against Rushdie in February 1989, however, the situation changed rapidly. Now the Saudis and their supporters in Britain, such as Sheikh Mughram al-Ghamdi, director of the Islamic Cultural Centre, seemed on the defensive. Iranian-inspired groups like The Muslim Institute have been vociferous, since the failure of the Saudis to endorse the *fatwā*, in their criticism of the Saudi position. *The Muslim Manifesto* issued by this Institute is typical: 'The Satanic Verses affair has exposed the insincerity of most Muslim governments, including the Saudi regime, towards issues that are vital for the defence of Islam and the honour of the Prophet of Islam, upon whom be peace.'[33]

The vast majority of British Muslims have not been as directly concerned with the Saudi-Iranian rivalry. Only a generation removed from their peasant origins in the subcontinent, they have been sensitive to appeals framed in terms of defence of honour and tradition—hence the particularly emotional response to *The Satanic Verses* and the openness to Khomeini's *fatwā* in Britain. However, there have also been internal rivalries at work. Muslims of South Asian origin in Britain—approximately 600,000 of the total of one million Muslims—are mainly Barelwis, who follow holy men (*pīrs*) and are mystical in orientation but are not entirely averse to political activity. Their primary competitors are the Deobandis, whose tendency is towards scripturalism in spiritual matters and apoliticism in worldly matters. They have been especially adept at disseminating their message of inner reform, owing largely to the Tablighi Jama'at, a singularly devoted missionary movement with branches in many countries.

Partly because of the lack of full assimilation into British economic, social, and political life, and the linguistic pluralism and ethnic rivalries (for example, among Mirpuris, Pathans, Bangladeshis, and Gujaratis), there is both a built-in competitiveness in British Muslim communities that is reflected in identifiably sectarian mosques and schools, and a susceptibility to outside influences. These latter include *pīrs*, Barelwi or Deobandi '*ulamā*' (religious officials), the Tablighi Jama'at, and Jamaat-i-Islami from the Indian subcontinent. To a considerable extent, the politics of British Muslims thus reflect the Pakistani or Indian politics of Islam.[34] Conversely, it can be said that what happens in Britain, particularly the reactions of Muslim groups and their degree of support for the *fatwā*, has an impact on the politics of Iran.

Indeed, the affair serves to remind us that 'states are intrinsically Janus-faced, standing at the intersection of transnational and domestic processes'.[35] As Kalim Siddiqui, the director of the Muslim Institute, has emphasized, Muslims in Britain, in order to survive, must both 'generate [their] own power . . . and plug into the global grid of the power of Islam.'[36] What may have sometimes appeared as pre-eminently a foreign-policy matter, a contest of political will between Britain and Iran, has involved in reality an intricate interplay of factors—at home and abroad—which has complicated the search for a solution to the diplomatic impasse.

## VI. Is Islam a Radically Destabilizing Factor in World Politics?

If the preceding discussion demonstrates anything, it is that the Islamic role in world politics is not what is normally expected. The revival of Islam has often been accompanied by militancy. But it most often has not, generally manifesting, rather, a kind of social and political activism that aims to improve the material as well as spiritual life of Muslims. The social dislocation that inevitably accompanies the process of modernization and the search for new anchors of identity in an uncertain world do not portend a rejection of development, *per se*, but of Westernization. The ability of Muslims to live within national frontiers in the modern world and, at the same time, the presence of Islamic concerns in both domestic politics and foreign policy further suggest that the vast majority of Muslims are seeking—for the foreseeable future—to create *Muslim* states, not to supplant the nation-state system itself.

Pan-Islamic aspirations have not disappeared, of course, and the ability of Muslim transnational organizations, ideologies, and communications to permeate national borders testifies that a greater degree of Muslim community is now apparent. This is a form of concretization of the *umma*, the community of believers, but, as the simultaneous acceptance of territorial and political pluralism and the manifold differences of foreign policy among Muslims indicate, pan-Islamic *political* integration remains limited. The Organization of the Islamic Conference, for example, has been riven by several disputes. The Algerians have generally given higher priority to the Non-Aligned Movement whereas the Libyans have tended to do just the reverse, stressing the Islamic movement's priority. With regard to an 'Islamic' issue such as the Muslim separatist movement in the Philippines, Libya has agitated for a strong commitment of support from OIC members, but Malaysia fears antagonizing a fellow member of the Association of South-east Asian Nations. Moreover, enmity between Muslim states cannot but penetrate into OIC deliberations, as the split between Iraq and Iran, and that between Saudi Arabia and Iran, demonstrated in the 1980s. The division that the Iraqi invasion of Kuwait created in the Arab League has patently been duplicated in the OIC and Muslim world.

When a former member of the British Cabinet in the 1970s says that 'Islam is a more powerful and enduring force in world affairs than the concept of Arabism',[37] he is most probably right. In an era of revivalist Islam, Muslim values and ideas at least seem more inspiring, relative to secular ideologies, than they did in the recent past. But it would be incorrect to deduce from this that Islam is by itself defining. As this chapter has suggested, it is, rather, one factor among several, and even as Muslims seek to displace or overthrow the status quo of their individual and collective lives, the 'Islamic challenge' to world order has not been as great as has been feared.

## Notes

1. Raphael Israeli, 'The New Wave of Islam', International Journal, 34 (Summer 1979), 370.

2. Fuad I. Khuri, 'Sectarian Loyalty among Rural Migrants in Two Lebanese Suburbs: A Stage between Family and National Allegiance', in Richard Antoun and Ilya Harik (eds.), Rural Politics and Social Change in the Middle East (Bloomington and London; Indiana University Press, 1972), 204–10.

3. Saad Eddin Ibrahim, 'Anatomy of Egypt's Militant Islamic Groups: Methodological Note and Preliminary Findings', International Journal of Middle Eastern Studies, 12 (December 1980), 438–9.

4. James Finn, 'Secular Discontents', Worldview, 24 (Mar. 1981), 5–8.

5. Daniel Bell, The Cultural Contradictions of Capitalism, 2nd edn. (London: Heinemann, 1979), 170.

6. Mukhtasar Sunān Abi Da'ud, ed. Ahmad Muhammad Shakir and Muhammad Hamid al-Faqi, iii (Beirut: Dar al-Ma'rifa, 1980), Kitāb al-Jihād, hadīth 2525, p. 424.

7. Sahīh al-Bukhārī, ed. Muhammad Tawfiq 'Uwayda, v. (Cairo: Lajna Ihya Kutab al-Sunna. 1390 AH, 1971), Kitāb al-Jihād, hadīth 2518, p. 50; hadīth 2505, p. 42.

8. Based on a hadīth related by Abu Da'ud: see compilation of Wali al-Din al-Tabrizi, Mishkāt al-Masābīh, ed. Abdul Hameed Siddiqui, i (New Delhi: Kitob Bhavan, 1980), Kitāb al-Imān, hadīth 59, p. 38.

9. Sahīh al-Bukhārī, hadīth 2710, p. 159.

10. Ibid., hadīth, 2729, pp. 174–5.

11. See Majid Khadduri's translation of Muhammad al-Shaybani's Siyar, The Islamic Law of Nations (Baltimore: Johns Hopkins Press, 1966), 154–5.

12. This, according to a hadīth: Sahīh al-Bukhārī, hadīth 2730, p. 172.

13. Text of treaty in J. C. Hurewitz (ed.), The Middle East and North Africa in World Politics: A Documentary Record, 2nd edn., i (New Haven, Conn.: Yale University Press, 1975), 27.

14. Ibid. 2.

15. Adda B. Bozeman, 'Iran: US Foreign Policy and the Tradition of Persian Statecraft', Orbis, 23 (Summer 1979), 389; and Bozeman, 'Decline of the West? Spengler Reconsidered', Virginia Quarterly Review, 59 (Spring 1983), 192–3.

16. Abul'l-'Ala Mawdudi, *Political Theory of Islam*, ed. Khurshid Ahmad (Lahore: Islamic Publications Ltd., 1960), 26.

17. See Leonard Binder, 'Al-Ghazzali's Theory of Islamic Government', *Muslim World*, 45 (July 1955), 229–41.

18. A. K. S. Lambton, 'Islamic Political Thought', in Joseph Schacht and C. E. Bosworth (eds.), *The Legacy of Islam*, 2nd edn. (Oxford: Clarendon Press, 1974), 415.

19. See Franz Rosenthal's translation of Ibn Khaldun's *Muqaddimah*, abridged and ed. H. J. Dawood (London: Routledge & Kegan Paul, 1967), Chap. 3.

20. See Elie Kedourie (ed.), *Nationalism in Asia and Africa* (London; Weidenfeld & Nicolson, 1970), 29, and Kedourie, 'Islam and Nationalism: A Recipe for Tension', *Times Higher Education Supplement* (14 Nov. 1980).

21. Quoted in Majid Khadduri, *War and Peace in the Law of Islam* (Baltimore: Johns Hopkins Press, 1955), 235.

22. Hurewitz, *The Middle East*, 27.

23. Preamble of the treaty, in the League of Nations, *Treaty Series*, 174 (1937), 132.

24. Preamble, Arts. 2 and 8 of the Pact, the text of which can be found in H. Hassouna, *The League of Arab States and Regional Disputes* (Dobbs Ferry, NY: Oceana Publications, 1975), 403–4, 406.

25. Art. 2(B) and Preamble [in order] of the Charter, the text of which can be found in Nizar Obaid Madani, 'The Islamic Content of the Foreign Policy of Saudi Arabia; King Faisal's Call for Islamic Solidarity, 1965–1975', Ph.D. thesis (American University, 1977), App. B, 200, 198 [in order].

26. See, for example, *Speeches and Statements of Iqbal* (Lahore: al-Manar Academy, 1948).

27. Quotation in R. K. Ramazani, 'Khumayni's Islam in Iran's Foreign Policy', in Adeed Dawisha (ed.), *Islam in Foreign Policy* (Cambridge: Cambridge University Press, 1983), 18.

28. From Khomeini's speech to Bangladesh Muslim leaders, as reported by Tehran Home Service, 8 Sept. 1982, in BBC, *Summary of World Broadcasts*, ME/7127/A/7 (10 Sept. 1982).

29. Bernard Lewis, *The Middle East and the West* (New York: Harper and Row, 1964), 115.

30. *Palestine Post* (17 Oct. 1935).

31. See, for example, R. K. Ramazani, *Revolutionary Iran: Challenge and Response in the Middle East* (Baltimore; Johns Hopkins University Press, 1986).

32. See, for example, Reinhard Schulze, *Islamischer Internationalismus im 20. Jahrhundert: Untersuchungen zur Geschichte der islamischen Weltliga* (Leiden: E. J. Brill, 1990).

33. *The Muslim Manifesto: A Strategy for Survival* (London: Muslim Institute, 15 June 1990), 21.

34. See Tariq Modood, 'British Asian Muslims and the Rushdie Affair', *Political Quarterly*, 61/2 (Apr.–June 1990), 143–60.

35. Peter B. Evans, Dietrich Rueschemeyer, and Theda Skocpol (eds.), *Bringing the State Back In* (Cambridge: Cambridge University Press, 1985), 350.

36. Kalim Siddiqui's speech, 'Generating Power Without Politics', conference on 'The Future of Muslims in Britain', London, 14 July 1990, p. 7.

37. Denis Healey, *The Time of My Life* (London: Michael Joseph, 1989), 216.

## THIRTEEN

# The United States: Superpower in Decline?

*Peter Savigear*

Winston Churchill called the Soviet Union 'an enigma' and more besides. Much the same could be said of the international role and foreign policies of the USA. Despite the great openness of the society and the impatient probing of the journalists, it is not easy to explain the place of the United States nor to be precise about the content and formation of policies. What is the role of the United States at a time when there appears to be great change in international relations?

## I. What are the Continuities and Inconsistencies in US Foreign Policy?

The old arguments that American policies and interests amounted to no more than marketing strategies and the support of the dollar now find less credence. Few states have applied sanctions to all manner of governments and commodities as steadfastly as the USA. China was banned to American business for years after the Communist party successfully took over the government of Peking. They have been applied to specific items, from electronic goods to arms, against the Russians, the Republic of South Africa, the Turks, and the Iranians. At the same time economic difficulties have come between the United States and some of its closest allies, notably those in the European Community. Difficulties over steel, all manner of agricultural produce, and other commodities have and continue to exist between these partners, yet they have never affected the fundamental closeness of the alliance nor the basic political identity of interest. Economics has always been the secondary element in American foreign policy, to be sacrificed for other ends. The Marxist critique was finally dealt a cruel blow when so many Communist economies turned to Western, free-market ideas for inspiration which might bring improvement in their performance. But what has been the nature of the policies of the USA and where have they left the greatest of Superpowers in the last decade of the twentieth century if dollar imperialism and economic performance are not the goal?

The very notion of a Superpower has come under attack. The old Soviet Union openly acknowledged a variety of political and economic problems which affect its behaviour. The collapse of the union in 1991 finally destroyed the claims to be a Superpower at all. The United States has also suffered a crisis of confidence after the years of Vietnam and apparently weak policies that followed that war. The growth in the number of states and their combined military and economic potential have reduced the former lead of the USA. There is therefore some doubt whether the United States is still as powerful as it once was. The brief period of joint domination with the Soviet Union appears to have ended. Their ideologies do not have the same pull and the world is no longer neatly divided into two camps, with the neutral and non-aligned states attempting to claw out some independent position. It could be argued that the USA has been obliged to alter its position and view of its role in international relations since the reduced place of the two Superpowers became evident. In many respects the presidency of Ronald Reagan is seen as an attempt to stem this slipping away of Superpower position for both Russia and the United States. The much heralded 'new Cold War' or second Cold War of the early years of the decade of the 1980s was partly an attempt to return to the clear-cut days of a divided world.[1] With the collapse of Soviet power and the leading role of the United States in the 1991 Gulf War the United States appeared to have reasserted herself, not only as the leading Superpower, but the only Superpower.

However, one of the aspects of the American enigma is the lack of clarity about foreign policy and how this is made. From the outside there is little firm ground on which to base assumptions. Presidents who have responsibility for foreign and defence matters in the union of American states change every four years—Ronald Reagan was the first to be re-elected since Eisenhower—and with the head of state come entirely new administrations and advisers. It is not easy to see continuity through such a system. Moreover, there are strange paradoxes, the most important of which is that the Democratic administrations, outwardly the more liberal and

international, have more often drawn the United States into
foreign entanglements, for whatever good or inappropriate reasons,
and the Republicans, the party of the states, of 'little America' and
isolationism, have brought agreements and settlements, through
the achievements of Eisenhower to those of Richard Nixon and
Ronald Reagan, despite the surface aggression and tough talking.
The operation in the Gulf in 1991 was carefully undertaken as an
international, United Nations operation by President George
Bush. In addition there are those who argue that in the last report
there are few major differences in policy between Republicans and
Democrats, and recent years have tended to endorse that assess-
ment, despite the initial impact of such different characters as
Jimmy Carter and Ronald Reagan.

Then there are other difficulties in understanding the process of
policy formation in Washington. No clear division of responsibilities
provides the kind of continuity that the British Foreign Office or
the Quai d'Orsay offer. Washington contains a range of offices and
bodies that have an input in the formation and discussion of
policy. The role of Congress and its committees, open to public
scrutiny for much of their work, further complicates the picture of
influences that go to the making of American policy. In particular
since the creation of important industrial centres linked to
generations of defence contracts, the impact of the many Congressional lobbies on the outcome of policy has become diffuse. There
is no single, overwhelmingly important agency or lobby or
individual lying at the heart of Washington's decision-making.
The inner cabinet that devised the operations at the time of the
Cuban missile crisis in October 1962 has proved the exception,
not the rule. Only the influence of Dr Henry Kissinger, during the
presidency of Richard Nixon, brought a single-mindedness to the
policy formulation in the United States. None of this has made
the location of American interests and position in international
affairs easy to discern from outside. The question can be posed,
does the United States have a foreign policy, or does the
government merely react to events on an *ad hoc* basis?

In some areas there remain distinct consistent policies. The
contemporary version of the Monroe doctrine pertained; the
United States would tolerate no alien power in the Caribbean and
central American region. This commitment brought invasions
and direct action throughout the decades since 1945. At times,

however, a compromise had to be accepted as was the case with Cuba. At other moments the implementation of policy met domestic and external resistance, as was the experience of President Reagan in his attempts to support the Contra movement in its conflict with the Marxist government in Nicaragua. Even under his successor, Congress has been reluctant to grant aid for other than humanitarian purposes—the sum of $49.8 million voted in April 1989 was for 'non-lethal' purposes only. The agonised 'love–hate' relationship between the USA and Latin America has also continued. The former keen to see change and accept the benefit of good relations, the latter critical of the inevitable weight of US economic and military influence, but eager for aid and support.

However, disillusionment characterized other elements of the United States and Americans' view of the world. The pain of seeing hostages held in an American embassy in Tehran was shown on the nation's television screens, each day carefully noted. The USA was obliged to accept the presence of the Marxist Sandinistas in Nicaragua throughout the 1980s, unable to remove the regime so hostile to the USA. American governments became very critical of the extravagance and the hostility of members of the United Nations. Support for UN bodies was withdrawn. Stability in international relations was thus not sought through that organization, a vast shift in American policy from the optimistic outlook for the United Nations in 1944 and 1945. However, the international opposition to the Iraqi invasion of Kuwait in August 1990 and subsequent fighting brought US policy closer to that of the UN majority.

In the fast-changing world of the 1990s, the nature of US policy is therefore an all-important matter to define. This chapter argues two things: there is a coherent basis for US policy and its international role, and the USA retains its special and central position.


## II. Has American Power Declined?

The changes that have occurred in the international political system since the end of the Second World War have left the USA in as prominent a position as the government of that State found itself to be in when that war ended. No state is as influential. No other government has the same global responsibilities and impact as does the government in Washington. As the century draws to a close, the USA has no rival in the claim to be the single dominant power in international relations.

The nature of this eminence is disputed. Some argue that the position of the USA, like that of the USSR, has diminished in importance. The precise role of the American and Russian Superpower has certainly changed since 1945. But there has been no sustained and successful challenge to the place of the USA in world politics. The Soviet Union between 1945 and 1991 built up a comparable military capacity, but did not managed the economic dynamism of the North Americans, the thrusting force of its dollars and marketing policies, nor the truly world-wide presence that the USA has been able to command so consistently for almost half a century.[2]

To many observers the role of the USA as the major world power has come as a surprise. Much of the debate about United States policy and influence has concentrated upon the limitations and failure that have beset governments in Washington, apparently suggesting a reduced role and a declining influence. There have indeed been numerous signs of a changing and even declining role for the USA. The problem is how to assess these factors; are they indicative of a real drop in the place of the United States in international relations, a mark of a Superpower in decline?

It is clear that the function of the two major states in world political relations from 1945 to 1991, the USA and the USSR, gradually altered in important respects over the years. In the immediate period after 1945 their control over events was remarkable. It seemed that no government could ignore the presence of the two giants, nor make policies that did not in large measure comply with the requirements of one or other of the Superpowers. A period of joint dominion was created under a dual umbrella, part military and part ideological. Vigorous debate continues about the relative importance of these elements—was the bipolar system, as it has been termed, more a product of clashing ideologies and views about the economic and social structures, capitalism versus Communism, or was it rather a result of competing powers, expressed in military language, in megatons and divisions? Whatever the answer to these questions, the dollar, the appeal to democracy and Western values, and the almost ubiquitous GI were the visible expressions of the American half of this balance of power between two Superpowers. Moreover, their influence affected war and peace in all continents. Until some time in the mid-1970s the USA and the USSR could pressure governments by their arms, supplies, financial weight, ideological pre-eminence, and demand compliance. No war could continue for long without their aid nor resist their voices. Superpower diplomacy seemed to shape international relations to an increasing extent, and the USA spread its influence in the Middle East, Asia, and Africa. The effects were felt in the capitals of other substantial states like the United Kingdom and France. The word of the government in Washington could end the Suez operation in October 1956 when a joint British, French, and Israeli force invaded Egypt. The war between Israel and Arab neighbours was ended by Soviet and American pressure in 1973. The fate of the world seemed to hang on the decisions taken in Washington and Moscow in October 1962 during the Cuban missile crisis. But all this joint dominion came to an end before the decade of the eighties.[3]

There was a considerable loss of authority by both Superpowers. Their decision no longer determined the outcome of wars and conflicts. Their influence could not end the war between Iran and Iraq nor achieve a political solution in the Lebanon or in the many conflicts in the African continent. Events in Eastern Europe in 1989 and 1990 totally escaped the joint control of the USA and USSR. Therefore the ending of the Superpower bipolar system brought not only the eclipse of Soviet power but also, in some ways, a decline in the role of the USA. Despite the formidable military capacity and the presence of American troops and diplomats in all corners of the globe, the government of the USA could not ensure that policies and events were to the liking and interests of the Americans. This was rudely emphasized in December 1989 when the government of President Bush decided to use its troops to overthrow the corrupt ruler of Panama, President Noriega, in support of the move towards more democratic rule. The operation was beset with difficulties and proved slower than anticipated to bring to a conclusion. The Panamanian leader found refuge in the Papal Embassy, defying the American plans. Thus, even in this North American 'backyard', easy and swift actions eluded the USA. The episode seemed symbolic of declining US status.

But this view required qualification and even revision with the appearance of a more determined US policy in 1990/1. When Iraq invaded Kuwait in August 1990 and ignored or rejected United Nations Security Council demands for withdrawal, and spurned independent attempts to prevent conflict, the USA organized an alliance of regional and other governments prepared to commit troops. In January 1991 these were used in a rapid campaign after a period of air attack. All military operations were dominated by the forces of the USA. In many respects it proved more straight-forward for the government of the USA to achieve these results, apparently so successfully, *because* the location was far from home. The logistics of the operation demanded international co-operation and there were several reasons for avoiding long-term political involvement—two conditions that did not apply in the Western Hemisphere. Not least of the reasons for avoiding embroilment were the lessons of US policy in South-East Asia almost thirty years earlier. The Gulf operation and diplomacy was possible *after* the Vietnamese experience.

The critical moment had come much earlier. When the last American troops left Vietnam in 1975, the humiliation of this Superpower was seen to have been complete. The experience of a war in which the USA was not only defeated for the first time and obliged to withdraw its forces and allow South Vietnam to be absorbed by the Communist North, but also which divided the American people as no previous war had done, was a turning-point in the foreign policy of the United States. That war was tremendously expensive in material and lives and emotional disruption. It lasted from 1961 until 1975. At its height there were more than 500,000 Americans in South Vietnam, and every act was photographed and reported in such an open and public manner that the world's attention and finally its disapproval fell upon the USA. They were no longer saviours as they had been in the First and Second World Wars, nor champions of democracy, but ineffective and cruel and themselves the victims of war, unable to control events and policies.

The effect of participation in the war in Vietnam was felt in the United States throughout the next decade. The very process by which foreign policy was made was drastically changed for the first time since the creation of the Union. What had been essentially a presidential matter, decisions taken on the basis of advice from bodies close to the president like the National Security Council and the Central Intelligence Agency, the Defense Intelligence Agency, and the Pentagon, now became subject to tighter control by Congress. The heart of the change came with the War Powers Act in 1973. Presidents were henceforth denied commitment of troops on foreign soil without express Congressional consent. In the following years, during the presidencies of Gerald Ford and Jimmy Carter, Congress nosed around all aspects of the foreign relations of the USA. Military and other forms of aid were examined and even refused. After the invasion of the island of Cyprus by the Turkish army in 1974, American military assistance was restricted to that crucial to NATO. Severe limits were placed upon aid to governments in all continents, and these continued through the two terms of President Reagan's administration when his desire to assist the opposition Contra movement in its struggle against the regime of the Sandinistas in Nicaragua was frequently thwarted by Congressional scrutiny. More and more corners of the presidential prerogative in foreign policy and military matters were investigated and dusted out by committees of Congress, none more murky and difficult than the so-called 'Irangate' episode, suggesting a secret deal between officials of the US administration and the Iranian regime involving arms which was never submitted for Congressional approval. In February 1989 Congress refused to endorse the nomination by the newly elected President George Bush of his defence secretary. Senator J. Tower was rejected and the President was obliged to find a replacement. The Vietnam war thus transformed the way in which the government of the USA could act in international affairs.

But there were further dimensions to the changes in the involvement by the United States in international relations. During the 1970s the global system of defence constructed in the years of the early Cold War collapsed. The outcome of the fighting in South-East Asia destroyed the SEATO as an effective defensive alliance. The revolution in Iran which brought to an end the rule of the Shah, one of the staunchest allies of the USA, also ended the already weakened Central Treaty Organization. Only in Europe was the leadership of the USA acknowledged and NATO apparently secure, although the changes that occurred in the regimes in Eastern Europe, the open policies of the Soviet leader Mr

Gorbachev, and the rapid move towards arms control agreements affecting the European fronts, have raised many questions about the future of that structure. By 1990 the USA no longer found themselves at the centre of a network of alliances and client states that formed one part of a bipolar international system.[4]

The impression of decline was enhanced by what seemed to be a weak presidency under Jimmy Carter. Not only was there further humiliation as the American embassy in Tehran was occupied by Iranian revolutionaries and rescue attempts failed, but it seemed that Soviet influence was extending while that of the United States declined. This was particularly the case on the African continent where Soviet advisers and Soviet directed Cuban troops assisted Marxist regimes and movements from Ethiopia to Angola. The USSR was able to deploy new and much improved missile systems, particularly on the European front—the SS 20 systems—whereas it was with difficulty and much opposition that both the governments of Presidents Carter and Reagan belatedly moved to the installation of more modern systems for NATO. The argument that the USA has declined in its international position stemmed from these important and substantial changes that followed involvement in the Vietnam war. By 1980 the previously dominant position of the USA had slipped away despite the efforts of President Carter to rebuild American military forces through the development and production of new weapons systems, cruise missiles and enhanced radiation weapons, and new generations of aircraft and tanks. President Reagan built on this policy and extended it during the following decade, but the pre-eminence had apparently disappeared. The United States could not bring stability to growing conflicts across the Middle East, from Beirut to the Arabian Gulf. Even the presence of American troops in the former and naval forces in the latter achieved no political resolution. Criticism of the USA was fiercely voiced in the United Nations General Assembly and the once 'mighty dollar' appeared feeble in the face of a series of price rises particularly in oil from 1973 through to 1981. By the 1980s, the USA faced a growth in military forces in all continents. Huge armies existed in several Asian states. Brazil became an important arms producer for newly ind'istrialized states that had no wish to become tied to either the USA or the Soviet Union.

The extent of the changed role of the USA was so pronounced

that talk of a return to isolation grew, a symptom of the transformation that followed the Vietnamese experience. The pressures were real—the cost of support for unstable and often unreliable regimes, the need to keep troops in so many parts of the world so long after the end of the Second World War, the strange evolution of Soviet–American relations which brought military negotiations and treaties, Strategic Arms Limitation Agreements, satisfactory political discussions like those in Helsinki in 1975, all of which had been suggested in the closing of the Cold War period. The events of 1989 and 1990 appeared to confirm this trend. The pressures for a less forward policy and less involvement are great. But that is to miss the point. The international order since 1945 has been based on a duality of power not merely an ideological clash.[5] The USA unlike the Soviet Union cannot fade away as a world power, allowing the farmers of the Dakotas and Wyoming to work in peace with no thought for the wider world.

The crucial question that remains for observers of the policies and role of the USA is how true is the sense of diminishing importance? Has the place of the USA declined or merely changed, adjusting to an altering international perspective?

The realities that came after Vietnam cannot be denied, but there was also a rapid realignment of United States thinking and action in international relations. This was not simply a matter of the firm stand on defence, the increased expenditure on arms, the rhetoric of Cold War diplomacy, that many saw in President Reagan. The realignment came earlier and was many faceted. The extent and success of this adjustment have enabled the USA to stand as powerful and distinct among the world's states in 1990 as in 1945.

First and perhaps most important of all factors surrounding the foreign policy of the USA has been the relationship with the other Superpower, the USSR. The slow and tentative steps that followed the 1962 Cuban missile crisis have not faltered. One achievement of the administration of President Nixon and his Secretary of State, Dr Henry Kissinger, was to keep open relations with the Soviet Union, indeed to improve those relations and initiate a series of agreements which later administrations could develop. International stability came from the American sustained desire to negotiate small but significant agreements with the Russians. These came steadily—arms agreements, the 1971–2 Four Power agreement on Berlin, talks on force reductions in Europe and on confidence-building measures. The series of bilateral talks between President Reagan and the Russian leaders, and the first summit between President Bush and Mr Gorbachev at Malta in December 1989, may not always have produced spectacular political initiatives. They indicated good will and opened the way to further arms control agreements, notably that of 1987 reducing the medium-range nuclear weapons from Europe. Not only has the USA accepted that the Cold War has faded, but it has joined in creating a new relationship, firstly with the Soviet Union, and more recently with the former Soviet Republics. At the height of the Cold War, in 1949 and the early 1950s, there were in effect no diplomatic and practical negotiations between the two powers, beyond the Berlin air traffic control centre. The USA has a continuing role in the period beyond the Cold War through negotiation with the former Soviet Republics.[6]

A second area in which the eminence of the United States has been diminished, some would say destroyed, is the moral force of its voice. There was little question that the Americans represented a force fighting for right, democracy, and freedom during the Second World War. This argument could be and was sustained during the Cold War years. But the action in Vietnam, linked to an increasingly sharp critique of American capitalism and marketing, deprived the United States of that moral voice. It was indeed strongly attacked from within by those opposed to the war and those urging greater respect for civil rights. Yet the need to base policy on a sound moral footing did not die despite Vietnam. It was the achievement of President Carter especially to re-emphasize that need. America's policies in the world had to be related to sound moral principles. This emerged as a stress on human rights. The political constraints that Congress had already imposed allowed President Carter to stress the moral dimension of his administration's foreign policy, notably in Africa and Latin America but also in Europe. The Soviet invasion of Afghanistan reinforced the argument that the USA had not abandoned a morally firm policy whereas the Soviet Union was intent on pursuing policies based solely upon power. This stress on the difference between a constitutional regime and a political system where issues of right and wrong were debated by political parties in an open and free way allowed the United States to point to a difference between the Western and the Soviet systems. Arms negotiations were one thing, but rights were another. The conferences that followed the European Conference on Security and Co-operation (CSCE) stressed the need to deal with violations of human rights. The Soviet Union came under severe Western criticism at the Madrid Conference which opened in 1980 on precisely these grounds. The changes that have occurred in Eastern Europe in 1989 and 1990 have seemingly confirmed this position. The leading role of the United States in the multinational coalition against Iraq in 1991 reinforced this trend. Thus the USA has been able to restore some of the vanished moral respectability.

Other policies have sharpened this edge. President Bush has pursued a forceful policy against large-scale drug operations in Central and Latin America, with operations in Panama and Colombia, the latter in close co-operation with the Colombian government. He has urged Congress to approve foreign aid budgets specifically aimed to help governments in the fight against drug dealers and producers. The 1990 budget includes $7.9 billion for this purpose, of which $291 million is earmarked for Peru, Bolivia, and Colombia. By such policies the United States has sought to restore a moral basis for foreign policy.

However, the accepted basis for the Superpower position has been the capacity to intervene and to possess the range of means of intervention in a substantial part of the globe. In this sense the USA now stands alone among states. Although most of the military operations undertaken by the United States since the withdrawal from Vietnam have been minor (with the exception of the 1991 Gulf War)—a landing on the island of Grenada to oust Cuban Communists, an air attack on targets in Libya, the Panamanian operation—and not universally regarded as even technically adept, there has been considerable strategic and tactical reappraisal of the military role of the USA. The result has been adjustment to the different demands of late-twentieth-century defence and security.

The policies of President Carter began the change. His administration initiated exploration of new types of weapons, a policy pushed to further lengths by President Reagan's funding of a Strategic Defence Initiative. This expensive research programme into a series of interrelated developments in the field of laser and communications technology intended to provide a complete missile protective shield has lost part of its political dynamism with the arms agreements and the planned phasing out of some missile systems. Congress cut the funding for this programme in 1989 as it did for the MX missile and the B 2 'Stealth' bomber, but development in the area of advanced weapons has retained a pre-eminent place for the United States. There is no real evidence of a military decline. But in the rethinking of security policy the years from 1975 to 1990 have seen the introduction of more flexible and more manœuvrable forces. Once again it was the Carter administration that took the initiative. The move towards a 600-ship navy, the basis for a more flexible policy, was laid then and received big increases in financing under the Republican administration of President Reagan. The shift away from large static bases for American forces was accelerated with the creation of a Rapid Deployment Force, as much a symbol of the new emphasis on flexibility as a fundamental innovation in military doctrine.

Of greater significance in this realignment of strategic planning was the move away from dependence on a few key allies, the so-called Nixon doctrine. It was this policy that had led to big military and other investment in states like Iran and Saudi Arabia. The Iranian revolution had demonstrated the fragility of this policy and the possible weakness in some of Washington's assessments about political stability. By the turn of the decade and with the strong stance of the Reagan administration, the USA had adopted a more cautious and selective policy, using a few carefully prepared bases, often islands, which could be kept on a short-term contract, supporting the growing naval forces. Thus islands like Diego Garcia and the former British base on Gan in the Indian Ocean acquired American contracts as supply points, less politically dangerous than the huge involvement in a state like Iran.

The predicted military decline of the USA has not occurred. Clearly the staggering dominance of 1945 had disappeared, but that went when the Soviet Union became a nuclear power in 1949 and began an effective space programme in the 1950s. The United States is still the most significant military power in the world. When the French prepared and executed an invasion of the rebellious province of Shaba in 1977, in Zaire, they required the assistance of American aircraft. In 1990, France, a state that has jealously guarded its military independence and maintained a large defence industry and export trade in order to minimize any dependence on other states, is debating whether to buy American fighter aircraft for the next generation of military aircraft and abandon its domestic product. The British invasion of the Falkland Islands in 1982 required the signals assistance of the USA to carry out operations in greater security, and the operation 'Desert Storm' against Iraq in 1991 was predominantly a successful US military and logistic action. The USA remains a military Superpower, the standard by which all other states judge their military capabilities.

In another sphere too there had been predictions of serious decline in the position of the United States. The American economy had been the motor for world economic recovery after 1945. Some states had benefited directly, through schemes such as Marshall Aid or through special arrangements as was the case with Japan. All states had been affected by the power of the dollar and the demand of the American market. Cold War and war itself had stimulated the economy, during the Korean War, during the arms race that pumped money into defence spending, during the Vietnam war. But a number of indications hinted at major recession, the collapse of the dollar, the decline of the American economy as the principal economic element in the international economy. Rivals began to appear. Japan challenged the American producers in several areas, notably in vehicles and electronics. By 1990 the Japanese were major investors in the American economy and gripped whole sectors of the market. The European Community also emerged as a rival to the United States with a fast-producing agricultural sector that excluded American products, and with several major companies that could compete effectively in quality and price with the Americans. The European Community possessed a larger internal market than that of the United States, and events in the 1980s encouraged the expansion of that market. New members, Spain and Portugal, joined the Community and approaches from East European states make the economic success of the Community yet more secure. But the United States has an economy that has withstood before such competition and such stresses.

Low points in the American stock market and undoubted pressures on the economy have occurred, but the remarkable feature of the last two decades has been the resilience of the American economy. The arguments among economists rage, but a number of elements have clearly contributed to this unanticipated survival. The strength of a home market and the business acumen and experience have provided a continued growth. The existing market has been increased by the free-trade agreement finally signed with the government of the Canadian federation. The American economy still dominates those of other states on the continent. But the progress of the dollar has perhaps been as remarkable since the end of the war in Vietnam and the boom that war encouraged. The dollar remains the single most important currency in the world economic system. Despite the price increases in oil and other primary commodities during the 1970s, those commodities were largely handled in dollars and rapid price increases resulted in large holdings of dollars. The subsequent drop in prices did not significantly affect the dollar and lower primary products benefited developed economies including that of the USA. Therefore against many predictions and significant indications, the economy of the United States held its powerful position, underpinning the international role of the USA.

## III. How has the American Approach to International Order Changed?

With these economic and military resources intact, the role of the United States remains exceptional. Fewer formal ties, greater flexibility and the ability to stand aside from some conflicts, all helped to maintain the role as 'the world's policeman' that has been attributed to the USA. What is now recognized is that the Americans cannot be responsible for order and stability in and among more than 150 independent states. The role is now seen as more cautious, intervening only where certain boundaries are crossed. There has thus been no lack of American commitment to Israel and the security of its sovereignty. Aid to Israel is still the largest item in the aid budget of the USA, $3,000 million in the last budget, out of a total $15,000 million. Such policies as this commitment to the integrity of the state of Israel, or the determination to take action where apparently disruptive policies have been pursued by governments like that of Libya, suggest that the heart of American foreign policy remains the search for a stable world order. Although this can no longer be achieved by the joint action of the two Superpowers, working on states that respond directly to their ideologies of Communism and capitalism, this is not indicative of the decline in the importance of the USA. The American/Soviet condominion has ended, as André Fontaine pointed out in an article in the French daily newspaper *Le Monde* in the early 1980s,[7] but the United States has not diminished the commitment to stability which was assumed so firmly in 1945. It is changes in the overall international system that require this search to be carried out differently and not a reduction in the role played by the USA in the search for stability.

Many of the policies pursued by successive governments in Washington have been coloured by this fundamental approach. The action against states which have protected terrorist groups or even assisted their actions, was particularly clear. But the condemnation of any Iranian support for terrorist groups has not prevented the consistent search by the American administrations of Presidents Reagan and Bush to draw Iran back into the international order, encouraging more stable policies from Tehran.[8] In Africa too a cautious and positive policy has been adopted by the United States. The USA has been definite in the application of some economic sanctions to the Republic of South Africa. No threat of possible intervention in the internal affairs of the indebted and weak states of sub-Saharan Africa has been suggested, but the USA remains the largest provider of aid and assistance, both from the public and private sectors, and an advocate of organized programmes for the reduction of debt. This last policy was explicitly urged by President Reagan when he attended the Cancun meeting of developed and less developed and primary producer states in 1981. Similar policies have characterized this phase of American policy in Asia. The emphasis since the end of the war in Vietnam has been on co-operation and the search for stability— support for the regime of Mrs Aquino in the Philippines, no severe economic reaction to Japanese business expansion, and assistance for its growing military industry (in April 1989, the two governments agreed to develop a Japanese-built fighter-aircraft, with the American share limited to 40 per cent), and even some sympathetic reaction to Vietnamese requirements for economic aid. It is clear that earlier policies of intervention and support for corrupt or insecure regimes that drew the USA into the politics of South-east Asia and the Middle East, did not bring the stability that was the fundamental principle behind American policies. Co-operation and shared institutions for future co-operation have replaced those old and often flawed policies. In Asia, therefore, the USA has tried to draw more states into collaborative economic programmes. In 1989, the People's Republic of China, Hong Kong, and Taiwan were invited to join the Asia-Pacific Economic Co-operation Conference with the active support of the USA (at the Australian meeting of the existing twelve members). No government in these regions can afford to ignore the position of the United States and in this respect there has been little change in the international order. No other government has such a broad impact.

## IV. Have American Foreign Policy Objectives Changed?

This co-operative policy towards the states of the Pacific basin might be seen as a reflection of a significant change in United States foreign policy. The many changes in military thinking, in the way in which policies were formed and scrutinized, the reluctance to become too deeply involved, suggested a shift in priorities. No longer was Europe the centre of American interests as it had been since 1941, when all other conflicts could be understood only in terms of the great clash of might and principle across the Iron Curtain. It seemed that Europe had to take its place among a range of American concerns with the Pacific regions, if not the Far East in general, the major interest. This had followed the opening of relations with the People's Republic of China and the experience of war in Asia.

There were other reasons why this might be so. The economic interest of the USA was increasingly located in the Far East. New markets of all kinds were opening. Japan was an economic rival and leading trade partner. States which had once looked to Europe now looked to the USA for their economic development—Indonesia, Australia and New Zealand, even Hong Kong and Singapore. Moreover the region was beset with many unsettling threats and conflicts, some ideological, others racial and even rooted deep in the history of local rivalries. Little was secure in Cambodia, Thailand, Indonesia, or the Philippines; even in New Guinea there were guerrilla movements. The newly industrialized states of the area were heavily armed and not easily controlled from outside by diplomacy or force. The world really did not seem so Euro-centric from Reagan's Californian ranch as it had for the previous 'East coast' presidents.

Yet the shift was neither complete nor even certain. This was rather part of the more flexible and truly global policy adopted by the USA, different from the narrowly viewed perspective of a conflict between Russia and America. Here was a measured, careful adjustment in the foreign policies of the United States.

The United States has exercised some degree of caution as events in Europe have taken on the pace of almost revolutionary change. Close communication with the USSR, and subsequently the former Soviet Republics, and a determination to move towards a series of arms-reduction agreements between the two parts of Europe, have been the formal characteristics of American policy, but without any wavering in the commitment to NATO. The reaction of President Bush to the suggestion that the Soviet Union might move to a closer and more integrated relationship with the economic system of the free market world, is characteristic: 'I think it's premature.' The United States has been cautious therefore in reaction to German unification, eager to avoid a drift towards a less stable Europe. Ironically, it is the former Marxist journalist and keen critic of the Americans, Regis Debray, who writes of the changing times in Europe that 'Our Europe can and must enlist alongside the United States in the complex cultural space called "the West", of which they and we are a part, on the basis of equality, but that no continent in particular symbolises or directs.'[9] The changing world may thus see Europe and the United States coming closer together, not pulled apart by the necessity for troop and armament reductions.

In the changing world of the late twentieth century, therefore, the USA continues to offer a conservative and stabilizing policy. For this to have any substance the governments in Washington have also continued to build on the exceptional strengths of the Union: economic resilience, technical innovation, and marketing expertise—the knowledge required to provide an efficient and thoroughly equipped military force. The governments of the United States have learned through this century that the cautious and stable international order which they favour and which is in the American interest, can only be urged upon the world if other governments are obliged to take notice of the USA. Thus, in the fiscal year 1990 the defence authorization budget is still a vast $305.4 billion, twenty times the foreign aid allocation. There is little evidence that the United States has seriously declined in its international position. The nation remains the strongest—indeed has emerged as unchallengeable in that role. Although other economies have special strengths and rates of growth superior to those of the USA, it is the all-round capacity of the United States that enables this dominance to be sustained.

What is also clear is that as the Superpower role, in the sense of joint control and management of international relations, has declined, the place of the United States has acquired an even greater significance. The range and power of so many new states, the declining importance of ideology, and the ending of Cold War bipolarity, and especially the collapse of Soviet power, have reduced the need for the Superpowers. Moreover, they have lost their former role, acting together. But in place of the co-dominion in international affairs, has come a new form of pre-eminence for the United States.

## Notes

1. Several works have appeared which stress this theme, notably that of F. Halliday, *The New Cold War* (London: Macmillan, 1980).
2. See Chap. 14.
3. The question is thus posed whether the result is not greater international disorder. See Michael Cox, 'From the Truman Doctrine to the Second Superpower Détente: The Rise and Fall of the Cold War', *Journal of Peace Research*, 27/1 (1990), 25–41.
4. An important aspect of US policy towards the government of Iraq after the latter's invasion of Kuwait in Aug. 1990 was the creation of what seemed to be an alliance system. Bilateral links, with Saudi Arabia and with European states like UK and France, were welded into a United Nations Alliance on the basis of Security Council resolutions. The traditional grounds for intervention, a defensive alliance in the region, were actually missing and had to be created in this way. In this sense the actions of the USA in mustering a huge force of more than 400,000 troops and thousands of aircraft, and the invasion of Kuwait and Iraq in January 1991, were of a special nature and did not rest on formal alliances.
5. See the discussion by P. Williams, 'US–Soviet relations: Beyond the Cold War?' *International Affairs*, 65/2 (Spring 1989), 273–88.

6. Jean Kirkpatrick, 'Beyond the Cold War' *Foreign Affairs*, 69/1 (1990), 1–32. The writer points out that the government of the United States finds itself closer to the position of the Soviet Union than to that of a close ally like Federal Germany (p. 11).

7. André Fontaine, *Le Monde*, (6 May 1982).

8. It was precisely this policy that was pursued by George Bush during the tension and conflict following Iraqi occupation of Kuwait between Aug. 1990 and Mar. 1991. This event and the suspicion between the governments of Iran and Iraq enabled Washington to pursue this aim, just as the opposition between the government of Syria and that of Iraq enabled US/Syrian relations to be restored and Syrian participation in the multinational force established against Iraq to be negotiated by President Bush's Secretary of State, Mr Baker, despite recent Syrian involvement with some terrorist groups.

9. Regis Debray, *Tous azimuts* (Paris: Odile Jacob Foundation, 1989), 123.

# FOURTEEN

# The Collapse of the Soviet Union: The Implications for World Politics

*Eric Herring*

During the three days 19–21 August 1991, hardliners tried to take control of the Soviet Union in a coup which removed Soviet President Mikhail Gorbachev briefly from power. They failed mainly because the armed security forces of the military, the Ministry of the Interior, and the KGB (Committee for State Security) generally refused to use force against mass popular demonstrations in the cities led by Boris Yeltsin, directly elected President of the Russian Federation. Once the people were no longer afraid of armed repression such as that which occurred in China in Tiananmen Square on 3 and 4 June 1989, they used the opportunity to overthrow the Soviet system. The Gorbachev revolution from above brought about the end of the Cold War to reform Communism, whereas the Yeltsin revolution from below brought about the end of the Soviet Union in order to save the radical trend towards democratization and independence for the fifteen republics which made up the Union of Soviet Socialist Republics (USSR). Now some of the republics have seceded entirely, while most are joining a free confederation, called for the moment the Commonwealth of Independent States (CIS).

To what extent was the Soviet Union powerful in world politics from 1945 on, and what are the implications of the transformation of the USSR into the CIS? These questions will be answered by looking in turn at whether or not the Soviet Union was a proper Superpower; at the limitations of Soviet military, economic, and ideological power; at Soviet achievements (or lack of them) in Europe and the Pacific (the two key regions of the world by virtue of their economic power outside US and Soviet territory) and in the Third World; and in conclusion at current trends and likely developments in the post-Soviet states from pessimistic and optimistic perspectives.

## I. Was the Soviet Union a Proper Superpower?

For many observers, the Soviet Union ceased to be a Superpower in the late 1980s. For others, it never was one, or at least not a fully fledged one. Paul Dibb called the Soviet Union an 'incomplete' Superpower, and Zbigniew Brzezinski described the Soviet Union as a 'one-dimensional superpower', the one dimension being military power.[1] The term 'Superpower' was coined by William T. R. Fox in 1944.[2] According to Fox, there were to be three—the United States, the Soviet Union, and Britain. His approach, based on the nineteenth-century idea of 'world powers', was to distinguish states which were powerful, especially militarily, in Asia as well as Europe from regional powers whose interests and power were restricted to one area of the world. Although 'Superpower' is a pre-nuclear concept, Gerald Segal sums up the conventional wisdom by saying that 'For a brief few decades since 1945, there emerged two so-called Superpowers who had the nuclear weapons capable of destroying all of civilization in a nuclear holocaust, alongside the awesome ability to deploy military forces around the globe.'[3] On this definition, the Soviet Union did not commence its 'brief few decades' as a Superpower until the late 1960s at the earliest when it had built up its military capabilities.

A basic problem with referring to a state as a Superpower is that the term may exaggerate its power: it makes it sound as though a Superpower can easily impose its preferences on other members of the international system. It implies that Superpowers are actually super-powerful, in spite of the fact that there are many occasions when they are not. Indeed, when one reads the work of regional specialists as opposed to those who look at the world through the lens of US–Soviet competition, the limits of Soviet influence are striking. The exaggeration of the extent to which the Soviet Union was a Superpower is linked to a more general problem with the concept of power, namely, that it is used to refer both to characteristics—such as large armed forces—as well as to influence.

The characteristics of a country are easily quantifiable in terms of steel output, numbers of tanks, and so on: there is some value in this kind of analysis, but it is not enough on its own. These characteristics are usually referred to as potential power or capabilities.

Even the term capabilities involves an exaggeration of the positive, as so-called capabilities may prove to be *liabilities* and nearly always involve direct or opportunity costs.[4] For example, the Soviet Union was large geographically. This provided the strategic asset of territory into which it could retreat, but also saddled it with the problem of controlling subject nations. Similarly, although a large population can be valuable as a labour force and as an army, the Chinese have realized that a large population can be difficult to feed and have therefore tried to limit their population growth. The Soviet Union had vast armed forces, but providing for these drained capital away from productive investment, provoked counter-arming by fearful neighbours, and made those neighbours suspicious of Soviet motives. Thus apparent capabilities may make it more *or less* likely that a state will be powerful.

The most important and yet the most slippery approach to the concept of power is its use with reference to causation—making someone do what they would not otherwise have done.[5] Power is only meaningful relative to the power of others and to the objectives pursued—in what sense is a state powerful if it cannot exercise influence? Thus *a state is a Superpower only if it can achieve its objectives in the most important regions of the world as often as a regional great power.* The two most important regions of the world are—and will probably continue to be— Europe and the Pacific rather than Latin America or Africa. This is a strict definition of Superpower in that its requirements are very difficult to fulfil. Indeed, only the United States has ever really been this kind of superpower. The Soviet Union was a central actor in Eastern Europe but did not normally bring about important outcomes which it desired elsewhere in the world.

## II. What has been the Role of Military Power?

There is a widespread fallacy that military power is the ultimate or most basic form of power. The idea behind this is that if the leaders of a state do not get their way on an issue, they can use force as a last resort. Experience has shown that in many cases military force is not a viable option. Acquiring military capability can also be the most rapid way of exacerbating the hostility of other states, and the military power of the coup against Gorbachev was neutralized by 'people power'.[6] A central element of the Gorbachev and Yeltsin revolutions has been an accelerating trend away from an emphasis on the value of military capabilities for foreign policy purposes, although conventional forces are still likely to be important for internal security.

## The Nuclear Weapon: The Great Leveller

In the nuclear arena, the United States and the CIS are still well ahead of any other country in raw numbers and are thus regarded as nuclear Superpowers. Their deployment figures in 1989 were 14,530 and 12,403 intercontinental strategic warheads respectively. In comparison, China had 320 nuclear weapons (other than tactical weapons) on delivery vehicles capable of hitting the Soviet Union, twenty of which could also hit the United States. In the same year Britain had 192 strategic warheads and France 336. China, Britain, and France all have programmes in place to increase these numbers substantially.[7] For example, Britain is deploying four new submarines, each of which will carry sixteen Trident missiles armed with probably eight warheads, which adds up to a total of 512 warheads.

The United States and the Soviet Union went far beyond a capability for Mutual Assured Destruction (MAD), that is, the ability to inflict unacceptable damage after absorbing a surprise first strike. With MAD, the choice is not simply 'suicide or surrender' in a nuclear conflict, as both sides may still choose to use their forces in a limited way, but the potential for escalation to all-out mutual destruction is there. Until recently, the leaders of both countries have been unhappy with the idea within MAD that their security in the end must rely on the restraint of the other side (because both sides are vulnerable to retaliation) and have either sought nuclear superiority or have pursued strategic arms competition out of fear that the other side will gain a military or political advantage.[8]

In the end, neither side has been able to have any confidence in its ability to fight and win a nuclear war, so that what we have now is MAD at very high force levels. Furthermore, the political leverage which nuclear weapons have provided over the smaller nuclear and non-nuclear states has been very limited.[9] There has been some recognition of this, although ambivalence and hedging remain on both sides. The Strategic Arms Reduction Talks (START) treaty signed in August 1991 was designed to bring about a reduction of roughly one-third of the current United States and Soviet strategic warheads down to roughly 9,000 warheads each. Although after this cut the two sides will still have as many warheads as they did in the mid-1970s, it does indicate acceptance for the moment that neither side can gain superiority. The Soviet Union saw nuclear weapons as the great leveller which helped to equalize the status of the Soviet Union and United States.[10]

Since the defeat of the coup, the signs have been very encouraging. The Ukraine and Kazakhstan have both declared their intention to be nuclear-free, and none of the other post-Soviet states has shown an interest in possession of nuclear weapons. Yeltsin is proposing to the West that rather than go through a process of moving all nuclear weapons to the Russian Federation, which might take twenty years and 20 to 25 billion roubles to implement, they should simply cut their post-START forces by 50 per cent.[11] There is a good chance that Russia will cut these forces unilaterally, cease nuclear-weapon testing altogether, and scrap most or all of its short-range nuclear weapons.[12] Certainly, there is no sign that the new leaders attach any prestige value to nuclear weapons.

The CIS does still have the capability to inflict immense nuclear devastation world-wide, so that instability must be a cause for concern. This is one of the primary reasons that Western decision-makers have been more concerned that there be a viable central government than about supporting republics which are seeking to break away, even if they are trying to establish democracies. However, the CIS is much more likely to implode than to explode: there may be bloody conflict, but if it occurs it will be with conventional forces and take place within or between the republics. The nature of the current instability does not provide any incentive to start a nuclear war, partly because of the reciprocal devastation it would probably bring about, but mainly because it would not serve the political purposes of any of the political factions.

*Reductions in Conventional Forces*

Gorbachev showed through unilateral military reductions, withdrawal from Afghanistan and withdrawal from Eastern Europe, concessions in the Conventional Forces in Europe (CFE) talks, and mutual military cuts with China on their border that he had little faith in conventional military capability as an instrument of foreign policy. Instead, his primary concern was the economic dimension of power. Soviet spokesman Gennadi Gerasimov teased US journalists when he referred to the Soviet Union as being 'number two' in the world. When asked to confirm his statement, Gerasimov said 'You heard me correctly: after all we must be fair to Japan.' The reformers in the Soviet Union believed that it need not prepare for global war for the foreseeable future. Soviet economic weakness provided the motive for *perestroika* (restructuring) and the perception of the absence of any serious external military threat provided the opportunity.

## III. A Leaner, Meaner Threat or Common Security?

The changes in Soviet policies cannot simply be explained by a desire for a breathing space (*peredyshka*) so that the West would face at some later date a 'leaner, meaner threat'. The thinking which underpinned the Soviet policies changed. The background to the 'new political thinking' was economic failure at home and the prospect of a renewed high-technology arms race symbolized by the US Strategic Defence Initiative (SDI) in which the Soviet Union expected to be at a disadvantage. Gorbachev realized that the Soviet Union was going to have to reorganize its economy in order to safeguard its economic and military base. Soviet tolerance of radical change was linked to the new thinking concepts of 'reasonable sufficiency' and 'common security'. Reasonable sufficiency means that there was no need symbolically to match the West in all categories of weapons. Common security is founded on the notion that a state cannot be secure if its potential adversaries feel insecure because an arms race and hostility will result.[13]

New thinking assumed that Western hostility was conditional on Soviet actions and was not simply a product of inevitable capitalist hostility to socialism. In particular, NATO was not seen as an offensive military threat. This provided the Soviet Union with an incentive to restrain its behaviour in order to maintain good relations.[14] Another assumption was that in conventional military strategy the defence is superior to the offence and politically less provocative. The Soviets tried to develop a military posture in which their forces would be 'structurally incapable of offensive operations'. According to new thinking, the withdrawal from Eastern Europe was a way of getting rid of an enormous economic liability, and was not the reluctant loss of an asset. Soviet trade subsidies alone to Eastern Europe for the period 1960 to 1980 have been estimated at $87,000 million.[15] As no war was expected with NATO, there was no need to hold on to the region as a buffer zone.

As a result of the new thinking, the Soviet Union allowed changes which had previously been unthinkable, such as the liberation of Eastern Europe, the reunification of Germany as a capitalist democracy, the ending of the Communist Party's monopoly of power, the establishment of a Presidential system of government, and declarations of sovereignty by all of the Soviet republics. The Soviet leadership did not want these events to occur (and even described them as 'unacceptable' when it looked as though they might), but its willingness to tolerate them was a vitally important sign of its intentions. The governments of Poland, Czechoslovakia, and Hungary said that they were not worried about a possible invasion by a Soviet Union run by hardliners. Instead, Poland said that it was more concerned to have NATO help guarantee its borders from millions of potential refugees.

The limit of toleration of those who would accept a reformed but still intact and Communist Soviet Union was reached in August 1991, so they attempted a coup. The prospects for another Communist coup, successful or otherwise, seem to be close to nil, because all the institutions which might support such a coup are being dismantled or overhauled, although there is a possibility of non-Communist authoritarian rule. The leaders of the various post-Soviet states have abandoned military competition with other countries, are generally trying to avoid getting into military competition with each other, are using their armed forces in some cases against their own secessionists and political opposition, and are trying to concentrate on dealing with their crippling economic problems. They will probably move rapidly towards small, relatively well-paid all-volunteer armed forces as opposed to enormous, poorly-paid conscript forces. They are also unlikely to invest much in inevitably costly high-technology weapons.

## IV. Economic Reform: How Radical? How Effective?

In order to deal with the problems facing the Soviet economy, *perestroika* was aimed at a switch from growth in output without regard for quality of competitiveness (extensive growth) to higher quality output (intensive growth). The hope was to provide material incentives not just in terms of higher wages but also in goods worth buying which do not have to be ordered years in advance. Earning more is not enough, as the high rate of Soviet savings indicated (around 500 billion roubles in 1990, which exceeded the total value of retail trade for the year): the consumer also has to be able to buy things worth buying.[16] The problems of the inefficiency of collective agriculture, increasing labour and energy shortages, and weak performance in the high-technology sector can only be overcome by dismantling bureaucratic controls and allowing private agriculture, more free movement of ideas, and wider access to computers, printing facilities, and communications technology.[17] Even if resources are freed through arms reductions, those resources must be deployed correctly in order to improve the economy.

In practice, Soviet economic reforms were very half-hearted. *Perestroika* was characterized by the legalization of many black-market activities, very limited reductions in state ownership of industry, and the establishment of small co-operatives. By early 1990, 80 per cent of Soviet enterprises were still being run from Moscow; in mid-1990, co-operatives accounted for less than 7 per cent of Soviet Gross National Product (GNP); and 160 out of 180 machine-building enterprises were the sole producers of their goods in the whole of the Soviet Union.[18] The proponents of radical economic reform were in the minority: most top politicians (including Gorbachev), planners, and managers were trying to reform Communism, not dismantle it. The relatively conservative majority shared a preference for central planning, opposition to the vagaries and rigours of the market, and a strong tendency, in spite of *glasnost* (openness), towards secrecy and information control.

Inequalities and uncertainties existed in the Soviet Union anyway, as skilled workers earned more, and much was decided by *blat* (connections) and *na levo* (the black market).[19] However, the removal of subsidies and a shift to payment based on performance requires painful transitional costs. In September 1990, Gorbachev rejected the radical Shatalin plan for a transition to a market economy in 500 days in favour of a more limited shift to a 'regulated market'.[20] As a result of this failure to reform, the Soviet economy went into steep decline, with great uncertainty over the exact dimensions of the chaos. In 1990, its GNP fell by around 7 per cent; 996 out of 1,000 goods monitored by the state were not available regularly in shops; rationing for basic goods became widespread; inflation ran at anything up to 80 per cent; and the budget deficit was anywhere between 90 billion and 200 billion roubles. In the first six months of 1991 alone, GNP fell 10 per cent and exports fell by 23.4 per cent.[21] It was this economic chaos combined with the rebelliousness of the republics which provoked the coup. The post-Soviet states seem to be willing to make radical changes, but are in desperate need of outside economic assistance and are not at all sure what changes are needed or how to make them.

To assist *perestroika*, the Soviet Union made limited efforts to end its isolation from the world trading and financial system. It began to negotiate membership of the most important international economic institutions, namely, the International Monetary Fund (IMF), the World Bank, and the General Agreement on Tariffs and Trade (GATT). Although it wanted to attract foreign investment, the rouble was not convertible into other currencies, which meant that foreign companies could only take profits out of the country in the form of goods such as Soviet cotton which they could then sell or use abroad. Post-Soviet Russia has reaffirmed its desire for a convertible rouble,[22] but it may be some time before the rouble is strong enough for such a move. The other states, some of which are reinstating their pre-Soviet currencies, will probably also move towards convertibility.

With a population roughly equal to that of the United States and double that of Japan, the Soviet economy was half the size of the US economy and only two-thirds the size of the Japanese economy in 1988. It accounted for a mere 4 per cent of world trade, which put it behind countries such as Belgium.[23] What little trade the Soviet Union engaged in expanded most rapidly with the West and Japan, as the Soviet Union was interested in trade primarily as a means of promoting its own economic development rather than as a way of exercising political influence.[24] Being isolated from the rest of the world economy had the benefit of giving other states virtually no economic leverage over the Soviet Union but equally put limits on Soviet leverage.

Any perceptions that a shift to a market economy might mean prosperity without effort have dissipated. A Soviet survey published in December 1990 asked respondents which standard of living they expected to exist in the Soviet Union in the year 2000 in comparison to other types of country: 20 per cent replied least developed like Asia and Africa, 38 per cent said developing countries, 15 per cent said moderately developed capitalist countries, and 1 per cent said most-developed capitalist countries. 44 per cent expected the disintegration of the USSR within six months, and only 34 per cent did not.[25] Whatever economic arrangement the post-Soviet states develop, it will not be a model for other states: instead, they will be looking to other states in order to follow their lead.

## V. How United are the Post-Soviet States?

Any successful economic reform is crucially dependent upon the relationship between the republics. The slide towards the disintegration of the Soviet Union started in response to the liberation of Eastern Europe at the end of 1989. Even before the Yeltsin revolution, all fifteen Soviet republics declared their sovereignty, and in particular that their laws should take precedence over Soviet laws. They reaffirmed their declarations of sovereignty in the wake of the failed coup. They also symbolically killed off the Soviet Union by abolishing Gorbachev's post of Soviet President. It is likely that all of the states will decide in the end that nothing less than complete secession involving the establishment of a separate constitution, foreign policy, and military capability is enough for them.

The Baltic states of Lithuania (3.7 m), Latvia (2.7 m.), and Estonia (1.6 m.) have been recognized as independent states and have refused to join the CIS. The fact that most of the Russian minority in Lithuania who voted in the republic's referendum in February 1991 voted in favour of full independence suggests that some Russians preferred to be part of the minority in an independent democratic state than part of the majority nationality in an empire. Georgia (5.4 m.) has also declared itself to be an independent state, but the West was reluctant to recognize it, mainly due to its dictatorial and repressive President, Zviad Gamsakhurdia, who backed the August coup, and who did not last long in power.[26] In September 1990, South Ossetia declared its sovereignty from Georgia, and said it would break away from Georgia to join the Russian Federation (which contains North Ossetia) and sporadic fighting has broken out. The Abkhazian minority has also opposed Georgian secession.[27]

In the west, in the Ukraine (population 51.7 m), there has been great dissatisfaction with the way Moscow dealt with the Chernobyl nuclear disaster of 1986. By a quirk of history, both already have seats alongside the Soviet Union in the UN.[28] In Moldavia (4.3 m.)—also known as Moldova or Bessarabia—the ethnic Moldavians want to form a larger republic with other Moldavians in territory which is now part of Romania. However, there have been counter-declarations of independence within the republic by the Trans-Dniestrian region dominated by ethnic Russians and Ukrainians, and the Gagauz region population mostly by Turkish speakers.[29]

In the south, in Turkmenistan (3.5 m.) Uzbekistan (19.9 m.), Tadjikistan (5.1 m.), and Kirghizia (4.2 m.), the independence movements are anti-Russian and anti-Communist. Kazakhstan (16.6 m.) is perhaps the third most important of the states after Russia and the Ukraine. Russians constitute 41 per cent of the population and Kazakhs only 36 per cent, and there have been violent anti-Russian riots. Moscow sent troops to Azerbaijan (7.0 m.) in order to try to prevent the persecution of Armenians and end the economic blockade of Armenia (3.3 m.) by the Azerbaijanis. Azerbaijan is Shiite Muslim dominated and some people within it are seeking a larger independent state with Iranian territory where more Azerbaijanis live. One of the catalysts of the conflict was the vote in 1988 by the Armeniandominated region of Nagorno-Karabakh to secede from Azerbaijan. In spite of Moscow's military assistance in dealing with the Azerbaijani threat, Armenia declared its complete secession from the Soviet Union in August 1990.[30] Armenia decided in September 1991 that it wanted no part in the new confederation and has been converting tractors supplied by Moscow into armoured personnel carriers to use against Nagorno-Karabakh. Nagorno-Karabakh responded by declaring itself to be a separate republic within the post-Soviet commonwealth and laid claim to the territory of the Shaumyan district of Azerbaijan.[31]

Even if all the other republics seceded, the Russian Federation would still be a crucial trading partner for them. Russia has a population of 147 million (51 per cent of the Soviet total) which is 83 per cent Russian, with no minority making up more than 4 per cent of the population. Although the Russian heartland is primarily in the west, Russia also includes Siberia so that it constitutes 75 per cent of Soviet territory and produces nearly 75 per cent of Soviet raw materials, 63 per cent of the electricity, 91 per cent of the oil, 75 per cent of the natural gas, 55 per cent of the coal, 58 per cent of the steel, 50 per cent of the meat, 48 per cent of the wheat, 85 per cent of the paper, and 60 per cent of the cement.[32] There are also a growing number of nationalist threats to the Russian Federation itself as well as to the other republics from the assertiveness of autonomous regions. In August 1990, Tataria (also known as Tatarstan) and Komi declared themselves to be separate republics, and have continued to press their claims on the CIS. They cite their economic dependence on the centre as an argument for sovereignty so that they can have the power to reduce that dependence. Kalmykia, Yamal-Nenets, Karelia, Mariskaya, Udmurtia, Bashkiria, Buryatia, and in Siberia Yakutia and Chukota among others have followed suit.[33]

The idea behind the confederation is that each republic could decide separately which powers it would give to the centre, such as aspects of defence, foreign policy, and economic co-ordination. Initially, the states interested in confederation agreed to co-operate in a State Council as an executive body, a Council of Representatives of People's Deputies composed of twenty representatives from each republic as a parliamentary body to draft the constitution, and an Inter-republican Economic Committee.[34] The worry of many is that Russia will dominate any confederation. To some extent this will be an inevitable product of its sheer size. However, the further worry, that it will try to establish a new Russian empire, will to a great extent depend on the political values of Russia—that is, whether or not it will take a democratic course.

## VI. Is the Ideological Struggle Over?

Through the bloody civil war of 1917–21, the Soviet Union as we knew it until recently was established. Its basic ideology was revolutionary socialism, and Communism was to be achieved through the abolition of private property, profit, and the market by means of the class struggle, with the Communist Party to help the process along. A succession of leaders left their imprint on how these ideological issues were approached. However, the changes introduced since Gorbachev came to power raise the question of whether or not the ideological struggle is over.

### The First Phase of the Gorbachev Reforms

The Soviet reforms before the Yeltsin revolution went through two distinct phases. In the first, between 1985 and late 1989, Gorbachev was trying to coax the Eastern European states into adopting reforms. His ideal was lots of little Gorbachevs—Communist reformers still loyal to the Communist Party of the Soviet Union (CPSU)—in Eastern Europe. The policy of *perestroika* initiated in April 1985 was intended to result in *uskorenie*, that is, the acceleration of Soviet economic performance. Then, owing to bureaucratic and popular resistance, Gorbachev turned to *glasnost* in order to mobilize the people and generate policy alternatives from the intelligentsia to counter the power of the party functionaries.

### The End of History?

Although Europe was still divided, the Cold War had ended, in that to a great extent the Soviet Union had given up trying to compete with the West in terms of conventional global war capability, competing for the diplomatic allegiance of other states, and getting involved in Third World conflicts. Gorbachev argued for the 'de-ideologizing' of international relations: 'Ideological differences should not be transferred to the sphere of interstate relations, nor should foreign policy be subordinate to them, for ideologies may be poles apart, whereas the interest of survival and prevention of war stand[s] universal and supreme.'[35] He did argue that there is an ideological and class struggle going on in the world, but he said that whether the outcome will favour capitalism or socialism will depend on the force of example, on peaceful competition, and on the conditions internal to each country rather than external intervention.[36] Alexander Yakovlev, a close adviser to Gorbachev, went even further in June 1990 when he stated that convergence of the socialist and capitalist systems was occurring as 'an objective process' and that 'We must rediscover social democracy for ourselves.' This viewpoint had previously been a heresy to Soviet ideologists, for it involves the denial of any serious ideological differences between the West and the Soviet Union.

As the cracks in the Communist system began to appear, Francis Fukuyama, then Deputy Director of the Policy Planning Staff of the United States State Department, created a stir by hailing the developments in the Soviet Union provocatively as the 'end of history', that is 'the end point of mankind's ideological evolution and the universalization of Western liberal democracy as the final form of human government'.[37] To Fukuyama there appears to be no serious ideological challenger: fascism is defunct, Communism is melting away, and Islamic fundamentalism has no appeal outside already Islamic societies. Nationalism is important, but it is always linked to some other ideology and is compatible with liberalism. He does not mean that all societies will become democratic, but he does claim that liberalism will be the most influential ideology of all.

Although the challenge from Soviet Communism has disappeared and liberal democracy is in the ascendant, there are a number of limitations to Fukuyama's thesis. He underplays the struggles and great diversity within liberalism. For example, there are many differences between the political parties within Britain, and between countries like Britain and the United States. Nor does he consider just how tenuous a hold democracy has in many officially democratic countries. In addition, he does not deal with the fact that a number of states such as South Korea, Taiwan, and Singapore have shown that economic success is possible even with rather authoritarian governments, and this may turn out to be the model for the post-Soviet states and many Third World countries.[38] Finally, in the long run to which Fukuyama refers, a new but as yet not conceived ideological challenger may emerge.

## The Second Phase of the Gorbachev Reforms

The second phase of the Gorbachev reforms was brought about by the rapid, real democratization which took place in most of Eastern Europe in the second half of 1990. Partially free elections in Poland in June were followed by the conversion of the Hungarian Communist Party into the Socialist Party in October. Anti-Communist revolutions followed in East Germany (which included the tearing down of the Berlin Wall), Bulgaria, and Czechoslovakia in November, and Romania in December. Gorbachev suddenly found himself transformed from being the most radical to the most conservative leader of any of what had once been the Soviet-bloc countries. For example, Gorbachev found himself arguing unsuccessfully that it was 'expedient to retain' Article 6 of the 1977 Soviet constitution which asserts the 'leading and guiding role' of the CPSU, at a time when similar clauses had already been dropped in East Germany, Czechoslovakia, Lithuania, and Estonia.

Gorbachev tried to continue his reforms while balancing between the conservatives and the radicals. In March 1990, ultimate power in the Soviet Union was transferred from the Politburo of the party to a presidential system of government, with the Soviet President elected every five years by a Congress of People's Deputies. He stayed on as General Secretary of the party (until forced to resign from the post before the banning of the Communist Party after the August 1991 coup), but no government ministers were in the Politburo, which was expected to restrict itself to party matters only. In practice, this system was paralysed. The republics insisted that their laws took precedence over laws passed at the centre, while conservative party and local government officials ignored laws such as those promoting private agriculture on collective farm land in order to sabotage *perestroika*.

Gorbachev was hoping that Soviet Communism and limited democratization would be compatible. As the trouble with the republics and in Eastern Europe made it clear that they were incompatible, he gradually sided with the forces of repression to try to save the Soviet state. Censorship was increased and democratic political organizations were denied access to printing presses and paper. After Gorbachev replaced the liberal Interior Minister Vadim Bakatin with Boris Pugo, a former KGB chief and Communist Party leader in Latvia, a number of top reformers resigned from the government in December 1990, including Foreign Minister Eduard Shevardnadze, who warned prophetically that 'Dictatorship is coming'.[39] It is ironic that Gorbachev had hand-picked all of the people who led the coup against him—Vice-President Gennady Yanayev, Prime Minister Valentin Pavlov, Defence Minister Dmitri Yazov, KGB chief Vladimir Kryuchkov, and Pugo, among others.

## The Ideological Implications of the Yeltsin Revolution

The basic totalitarian institutions of the party-state with a monopoly of power (the 'leading role'), the central plan, political police, the dual system of administration whereby the party shadows all bureaucratic activity, collectivized agriculture, and *nomenklatura* (the lists of posts and candidates for those posts almost exclusively from the party) controlled by the party's 150,000 full-time or part-time paid functionaries (*apparatchiks*) have been, or are in the process of being, demolished in the Yeltsin revolution. In referring to the Yeltsin revolution, it is not being suggested that the changes we have seen were created entirely by him, but that he has been the main leader, shaper, and embodiment of those developments. In his autobiography published in 1990, he showed an explicit awareness of the value of the spread of democratic values in Soviet society in producing people-power to undermine the power of the hardliners. In considering the possibility of a coup, he also seemed to share the prescience of Shevardnadze: 'I shall fight for Gorbachev . . . Yes, I shall fight for him—my perpetual opponent, the lover of half-measures and half-steps. These, his preferred tactics, will also eventually be his downfall, unless of course he realises his chief failing in time.'[40]

As it turned out, Yeltsin led the fightback while Gorbachev was held incommunicado in his Crimean *dacha*.

There is still an ideological struggle under way in the post-Soviet states, between those who want to use freedom from central control to establish democracy and those who want to establish new dictatorships. Within the democratic camp, there are tensions between the advocates of social democracy and the advocates of individualist free marketism. Although manifestations of democracy within the post-Soviet states are widespread, there is no deeply rooted democratic political culture. The fact that there are hundreds of political parties without the party discipline necessary for stable democracy is not a good sign, and when conflicts of interest are great, democracy is liable to be pushed aside. The chaotic lack of clarity of the relations between the centre and the republics and between the republics themselves may remain unresolved for some time. This disorder and the related economic dislocations may lead many to become disillusioned with democratic processes and to welcome a return to authoritarian if non-Communist government.

Some argue that a coherent CIS would still be a challenge even if it was democratic because of its economic potential. This is the neo-realist perspective in which the primary actors in the international system are states which are functionally undifferentiated (that is, states whether capitalist, socialist, or whatever act in basically the same ways according to the distribution of power) and which seek to maximize their power.[41] Nevertheless, the form of competition between states does matter: a trade war is better than a shooting war, at least from a liberal democratic perspective.

Up to this point, the analysis has concentrated on the themes of military, economic, and ideological power. To provide a more complete understanding of the demise of the Soviet Union, this chapter will now consider the role of the Soviet Union in Europe, the Pacific, and the Third World (which overlaps the Pacific).

## VII. What did the Soviet Union Achieve in Europe?

Until the Gorbachev revolution, Soviet post-war medium-term (that is, ten- to fifteen-year range) objectives in Europe could be listed as follows: minimize the US military presence in Europe, minimize West German military capabilities, minimize West European military and economic integration, gain Western acceptance of Communist control in Eastern Europe and ensure the viability of that control, and promote and lead Communist movements in Western Europe.[42] There were real trade-offs and dilemmas in the pursuit of these objectives. For example, US military withdrawals might have freed those forces for use elsewhere and have resulted in increased West European integration and West German force levels to compensate. Alternatively, the success of Eurocommunism in Western Europe could have been a powerful magnet to Eastern Europe so that the Soviet Union would have found its leadership challenged in the west by Eurocommunists as well as in the east by China.

As it turned out, the United States has been substantially involved in Western Europe, West Germany remilitarized as part of NATO, the Eurocommunists did not attain power, and Western Europe developed a degree of military identity and substantial economic integration through the European Communities (EC). Fear of the Soviet Union was important in shaping West European politics, but that fear was not translated into either subservience or into a positive support for and belief in Soviet-led Communism.

The Soviet Union was only able to impose its preferences in Eastern Europe, and this was only temporary. On the most important question—establishing systems which were both pro-Soviet and viable—the Soviet Union failed miserably. To try to achieve its objectives in Eastern Europe, the Soviet Union directed the bulk of its economic assistance to that region, composed 60 per cent of trade subsidies with the rest in interest-free long-term loans. This assistance excluded independently minded Yugoslavia (which is now in the process of disintegration) and isolationist Albania (which has had a legal non-Communist opposition since December 1990 and a non-Communist coalition government since June 1991).[43] The experiment in Eastern Europe failed and these countries are now turning to liberal democracy to greater or lesser degrees. Poland, Czechoslovakia, Hungary, and what used to be East Germany have been the most committed to democratization, whereas the hold of democracy is more tenuous in Romania, Bulgaria, Yugoslavia, and Albania.

*'A Common European Home' or 'The European Common Interest'?*

Sergei Karaganov, deputy director of the Soviet Institute on Europe, stated in early 1990 that the Soviet Union is a European regional power and had given up its ambitions to be a Superpower. He indicated that he wanted the United States to continue to have a presence in Europe to help manage change through NATO and the Warsaw Pact.[44] Even that was beyond the Soviet Union, as the states of Eastern Europe forced the Soviet Union to agree to disband Comecon (designed to promote economic co-operation between them) and the Warsaw Pact by April 1991. In the CFE agreement mentioned earlier, no single country is permitted to have more than 30 per cent of the total forces in the region as a whole. As the Soviet Union lost all its allies in the region and had to begin the removal of all of its forces from Eastern Europe, in effect it agreed to a treaty which would reduce it to a position of more than 2:1 *inferiority* in the Atlantic to Urals (ATTU) area.

Before the CFE treaty was signed, the Soviet Union (legally) moved large amounts of military equipment east of the Urals, to keep the best of it and to avoid the cost of having to dismantle it under the treaty's verification procedures. In addition, the Soviet Union seemed to have been dishonest about how much equipment it had and even reassigned three divisions with 1,000 tanks to the navy's coastal defence forces to prevent them from being counted in the treaty. It appears that the armed forces, who were unhappy with the treaty, were acting at least partly independently.[45] The evasions mattered more for what they said about the balance of political forces within the Soviet Union than for their military significance. The leaders of the new CIS have made it clear that they will abide by all previous Soviet treaty obligations such as the CFE treaty. Cheating on arms control treaties is unlikely— indeed, unilateral reductions by the post-Soviet states are likely to exceed those required by existing treaties.

The main concern of the Soviet Union in recent years was not the European military balance, but the nature of its role in a Europe which was (and is) both broadening and deepening its integration. In 1987, Gorbachev noted that 'Some in the West are trying to "exclude" the Soviet Union from Europe.'[46] His emphasis on a 'common European home' was founded on the hope that his political reforms would prevent this exclusion. His aim was for NATO and the Warsaw Pact to be dissolved and all European security issues to be dealt with primarily through the thirty-five-member Conference on Security and Co-operation in Europe (CSCE) process which includes the United States and Canada.

The alternative view was summarized by the US Secretary of State James Baker who talked of the 'European common interest' based upon the political legitimacy of free elections, free market economic prosperity integrated into the international economy, and European security guaranteed by NATO and a US military presence.[47] He saw the CSCE process as only supplementary to this structure and not a substitute for it. For many, the integration of the Soviet Union into the legitimate circle of international actors was not acceptable, in spite of the end of the Cold War. It was seen as undemocratic and unstable and thus a potential enemy which may have needed to be deterred.[48] However, in response to the revolution of 1991, British Prime Minister John Major began to use the previously shunned phrase 'common European home', which implies that he thinks that the post-Soviet states are not a threat to Europe, even if they are unstable.


# VIII. What did the Soviet Union Achieve in the Pacific?

## The Overshadowing of the Soviet Union by Japan

The Pacific region's importance springs from the economic vitality of Japan, the Newly-Industrialized Countries (NICs)—South Korea, Taiwan, Hong Kong, and Singapore—and the proto-NICs—Thailand, Indonesia, Malaysia, and the Philippines. When they are combined with the poorer (Communist) countries of the region—China, Vietnam, Laos, Cambodia, and North Korea—they account for 17 per cent of the world's GNP compared with 20 per cent to 25 per cent each for North America and Europe. The Pacific's share of world trade is 14 per cent (with Japan alone responsible for 8 per cent), compared to 14 per cent for the United States, and 32 per cent for the EC.[49] Some excitement is being caused by Japan's increasing military expenditure. Japan's defence budget in 1990 was $28 billion. For comparison's sake, the defence budget for the United Kingdom was $33 billion, West Germany $31 billion, the United States $290 billion, the Soviet Union at least $117 billion (and possibly double that), and China $6 billion.[50] The Japanese military expenditure is an expression of an intention to be more politically assertive rather than a response to perceived external military threats or opportunities.

In this region of economic dynamism, the Soviet Union tried to find a role through economic aid and a military presence. Soviet-bloc aid accounted for 20 per cent of Vietnam's GNP before the Gorbachev era.[51] Vietnam, which dominates Laos and Cambodia, showed its gratitude by providing the Soviet Union with naval facilities in Camh Ranh Bay. However, the CIS is likely to withdraw from the base as it shows no interest in maintaining a capability for global war. Vietnam has introduced limited reform in response to aid cuts and is seeking economic relations with capitalist states, but has also stepped up internal repression in order to maintain the Communist system.[52] Tortuous negotiations are under way in Cambodia to establish a coalition government, while poverty-stricken Laos is also reforming in the hope of attracting foreign investment.[53] The regime in North Korea is currently Stalinist but desperate for outside economic assistance from the capitalist states due to the fact that it can no longer play China and the Soviet Union off against each other. Should reunification occur between North Korea and industrialized, semi-democratic South Korea after the death of North Korean leader Kim Il Sung, it will probably involve the rejection of socialism.

Although the Soviet Union had substantial military deployments in the region since the 1970s, there is no good evidence that they were used for political intimidation, and they have been cut back significantly. Japan was the Soviet Union's third-biggest trading partner after West Germany and Finland. Although the Soviet Union wanted to expand this trade and encourage Japan to help it exploit Siberia, its military presence in the region was a liability, as was the Soviet unwillingness to make concessions on the Japanese islands they have occupied since the Second World War. Yeltsin, as President of Russia, has indicated that he is interested in a rapid territorial settlement in order to secure Japanese investment. Even with military cuts and territorial concessions, the Russian Federation will find it difficult to make exploitation of Siberia financially attractive to outside investors owing to political instability combined with the great difficulties and high costs of operating in such a hostile and remote region. Investment takes the path of least resistance in the direction of reliable profit, so that Japanese money is much more likely to go to countries such as the NICs.[54]

## IX. What did the Soviet Union Achieve in the Third World?

*Global Access, Not Global Success*

Before Gorbachev came to power, Soviet-bloc aid accounted for 40 per cent of Cuba's GNP.[55] Drastic cuts in that aid have resulted in Cuban austerity and hints of political pluralism in return for reduced US hostility,[56] while the CIS has indicated that it will pull its troops out of Cuba. The left-wing Sandinista government of Nicaragua was voted out of office in early 1990, so Soviet assistance was replaced with US backing for the new government of Violetta Chamorra. Soviet economic assistance to non-Communist Third World states went mainly to the following, in order of greatest beneficiary downwards: Turkey (a member of NATO), India, Afghanistan, Morocco, Egypt, Iran, Algeria, Pakistan, Syria, and Iraq.[57] Egypt, Syria, Iran, and Iraq have all shown that the Soviet Union could not influence key decisions such as whether or not they would go to war. The same may be said of India and Pakistan. The Soviet Union at least maintained reasonable relations with India, but there was much Soviet hostility towards Pakistan due to its support for the rebels in Afghanistan. Mongolia, which was Communist controlled and heavily dependent on Soviet aid, moved quickly towards democratization of a kind with multi-party elections late in 1990 as the Soviets pulled out their armed forces.

Under General Secretary Leonid Brezhnev, the Soviet Union invested heavily in conventional forces. It could only hope to exercise significant influence abroad when there was a prospect of military conflict, and even then success was by no means assured because of the dynamics of local politics and because of external, often indirect and non-military, counter-intervention, especially by regional powers and the United States. The limited gains made in Angola and Ethiopia were exceptional and were not consolidated. The incursion into Afghanistan was not a complete failure, as pro-Soviet President Najibullah managed to stay in power, but the country is still racked by civil war and the cost to the Soviet Union of its intervention was enormous. In September 1991, the United States and post-Soviet states agreed not to supply the two sides with further arms.

The Soviet Union relied heavily on arms sales and arms aid in its relations with the Third World, as it did not have the economic resources to provide much economic assistance to more than a few states. Gorbachev supplied some twenty-seven states world-wide with arms, partly to buy influence but mainly to earn hard currency, although his major arms sales were much more limited.[58] In October 1990, the Soviet Union decided to reduce further aid to foreign countries,[59] and in September 1991, the Foreign Minister of the confederation, Boris Pankin indicated that the trend will accelerate.[60] The post-Soviet states can be expected to concentrate on their own economic problems and compete for aid and investment themselves.

The Middle East had been seen for many years as the most likely location for another world war to start owing to its proximity to the Soviet Union, the importance of its oil for Western Europe and Japan (and, by extension, the United States), and the political volatility caused by the Arab–Israeli conflict. This did not come to pass. The Soviet Union made no move to take control in the region and looked incapable of doing so. The Soviet Union found that inter-Arab rivalries were beyond its control in spite of its high level of arms-sales diplomacy. Cuts in Soviet military and economic aid, a devastating civil war, Islamic and tribal opposition supported by Saudi Arabia, and the collapse of the Communist parties of Eastern Europe impelled Marxist South Yemen to agree in May 1990 to its reunification with pro-Western North Yemen, with free elections planned for late 1992. As the prospect of an East–West world war fades and as the oil glut and protective measures take the sting out of any potential future oil embargo like that of the 1970s, so the economic importance of the Middle East declines. Now that the Iran–Iraq war has fizzled out and Israel looks fairly secure militarily, the United States is shifting its aid and political priorities to Eastern Europe and the post-Soviet states.

This underlying trend was obscured by the war waged in the first two months of 1991 by a very broad coalition of states led by the United States under the UN flag to expel Iraq from Kuwait which it had invaded and occupied in August 1990. The Soviet Union voted in favour of all the UN resolutions for action to be taken against its erstwhile ally but did not send any forces to the Gulf. Instead, it tried to find a diplomatic solution before and during the fighting. In the end, the United States and the rest of the coalition destroyed up to 80 per cent of Iraq's military hardware, which had been supplied primarily by the Soviet Union, and damaged its economy so much that it may take thirty years for it to recover.

The hardliners in the Soviet Union believed that the war showed that the Soviet Union needed to put more effort into high-technology weaponry and that the United States was exploiting the end of the Cold War to support conservative Arab oil states and show its willingness to use force. These suspicions were hardened by the fact that some in the United States opposed the Soviet Union's peace initiatives at least partly on the grounds that the Soviet Union should be kept on the margins of the Middle East political process. New thinking in Soviet foreign policy has been characterized by the promotion of negotiated solutions in places such as Namibia (which was occupied illegally by South Africa), Angola, Afghanistan, and Cambodia. This allowed the Soviet Union to retain a degree of status and influence in the Third World. The fact that the Soviet Union was being shouldered aside increased its incentives to act unilaterally and in competition with the United States.

Overall, the Soviet Union had global access rather than global success. The states it tried to woo were often successful at manipulating it in order to further their own agendas. The likelihood is that the CIS will not attempt to rival the international leadership of the United States for many years to come, if ever. This is exemplified by Gorbachev's extrication of the Soviet Union from Afghanistan. He realized that the stakes in the Third World had been exaggerated greatly, that there had been an expensive and pointless pursuit of prestige, that it was very costly to prop up weak governments, and that successes were easily reversed.

## X.  What are the Implications of the Collapse of the Soviet Union?

It might seem a little premature to be writing about the implications of the collapse of the Soviet Union before the dust has settled. After all, when the North Vietnamese leader Ho Chi Minh was asked for his opinion on the implications of the French revolution, he replied 'It is a little too early to tell.' Rather than offer a single interpretation, this concluding section will offer both pessimistic and optimistic perspectives. As far as possible, the analysis will be organized around the topics of this volume's various chapters. While readers can make their own choices, the view of the author is that on most counts the optimistic perspective has the better of the argument.

### The Perspective of the Pessimist

The operation of the security dilemma between the republics is likely to be intense, as they begin to arm competitively to safeguard their territory or prosecute their territorial and ethnic disputes. Interminable feuding will be punctuated by wars, for example, between Armenia and Azerbaijan, or between Georgians and South Ossetians. All these conflicts will make effective economic reform impossible, resulting in hyper-inflation, widespread famine, and the reduction of economic activity to barter. The international economy may be disrupted if the various republics repudiate all or part of the many billions of dollars of debt inherited from the Soviet state. Indeed, the republics may be unable to agree on their relative share of that debt. Russia, faced with the need to impose order on chaos, will have no choice but to try to re-establish a Russian empire, and this will cause a civil war. After all, civil war took place between these peoples within living memory—it lasted the five years of 1917 to 1921 and cost millions of lives. Yeltsin, with his charismatic populism, will make him an ideal imperial leader.

These terrible consequences are made more likely by the authoritarian political culture of the post-Soviet states. Even if civil war is averted, this political culture will be indifferent to terrorism, abuses of human rights, or degradation of the environment. Environmental disasters will result from the attempted commercial exploitation of Siberia and from more nuclear reactor meltdowns in republics lacking expertise and money. Nuclear weapons will fall into the hands of ruthless leaders willing or desperate enough to use them in war or for nuclear blackmail. Owing to the unwillingness of the rest of the international community to step into this quagmire, international organizations will not have the backing they need to respond. Worst of all, there is little the world could do because of the scale and interlocking nature of these problems which will spill over to affect others. Just because effective action is necessary does it not mean that it is possible.

## The Perspective of the Optimist

The implicit assumption of the pessimistic scenario is that everyone involved will pursue their narrowly perceived interests regardless of cost. It entirely misses the basic cause of the demise of the Soviet Union—the desire of ordinary people to have a decent standard of living and to live in spiritual and political freedom. Most of what we know about what is happening in the post-Soviet states is good news. Yeltsin is a committed democrat without imperial ambitions, and undemocratic republican leaders such as Gamsakhurdia in Georgia are likely to be toppled by popular democratic opposition. The republics are taking responsibility for their collective debt and are fulfilling their international obligations in order to induce other countries to invest. While there already are some violent intra- and inter-republican conflicts, these will be limited in scope. They will not turn into general civil war as they are not closely interlinked, unlike, for example, the rivalries in Europe in the days before the First World War. On the question of nuclear weapons, Russia is in a hurry to reduce its arsenal dramatically and the other republics have no nuclear ambitions of their own. The international community has a valuable part to play, and in some respects is beginning to act accordingly—just because it cannot do everything does not mean that it can do nothing. For example, crucial emergency food aid to avoid winter famine is being organized for humanitarian reasons and to help avoid political instability. On environmental issues, it is in the interests of the rest of the world to provide the technology and finance to make the dangerous nuclear reactors safe.

More than anything, the collapse of the Soviet Union has created a truly historic opportunity for the liberal democracies to reassess their self-images and priorities. Until recently, the West existed in opposition to the East, and the Third World existed to be competed for by the capitalist First World and Communist Second World. Increasingly, these terms are anachronisms. Many have mourned the loss of the psychologically comforting certainties of the Cold War, such as the existence of a clearly defined primary enemy. Those certainties always were false and distorting, but even those who do not accept this proposition are having to accept that the Cold War is over for good. Belief in those supposed certainties often resulted in the subordination of democracy to anti-Communism in the competition for the diplomatic allegiance of the leaders of other countries.

The wrong lesson to draw from the demise of the Soviet Union is that the United States is the sole Superpower with a chance to establish its dominance and pre-empt a possible 'Pacific century'. In a world of complex interdependence, the idea of a Superpower is drained of much of its analytical value.[61] Furthermore, the term is associated with concerns of the status and prestige of states—too much has been sacrificed in the pursuit of such delusions of Superpower. The people in what was the Soviet Union realized this, and it is to be hoped that the people of the other 'Superpower' recognize this before too long.

## Notes

The author would like to thank Ken Booth, Martin Crouch, Nick Rengger, Gerald Segal, and Rebecca Woodley for their valuable comments on earlier drafts of this chapter.

1. Zbigniew Brzezinski, 'The Soviet Union: Her Aims, Problems and Challenges to the West', in *The Conduct of East–West Relations in the 1980s*, Adelphi Papers, No. 189 (London: Brassey's for the International Institute for ɔtrategic Studies (IISS), 1984), 3–12, and Paul Dibb, *The Incomplete Superpower*, 2nd edn. (London: Macmillan, 1988).

2. William T. R. Fox, *The Super-Powers: The United States, Britain, and the Soviet Union: Their Responsibility for Peace* (New York: Harcourt, Brace, 1944). On the concept of 'world powers', see Martin Wight, *Power Politics* (Harmondsworth: Pelican, 1979), chap. 4.

3. Gerald Segal, *The World Affairs Companion*, new edn. (London: Simon and Schuster, 1991), 7.

4. David A. Baldwin, 'Analysis and World Politics: New Trends Versus Old Tendencies', *World Politics*, 31/2 (1979), 161–94, and id., *Economic Statecraft* (Princeton, NJ: Princeton University Press, 1985).

5. Id., *Economic Statecraft*, passim.

6. The leading work on popular non-violent power in the face of potential or actual violence is Gene Sharp's *The Politics of Nonviolent Action*. On the strong tendency of states to balance against a powerful opponent instead of trying to jump on its bandwagon, see Robert Jervis and Jack Snyder (eds.), *Dominoes and Bandwagons: Strategic Beliefs and Great Power Competition on the Eurasian Rimland* (Oxford: Oxford University Press, 1991).

7. IISS, *The Military Balance 1989–1990* (London: Brassey's for the IISS, 1989). The increase in French nuclear forces was trimmed in July 1991. *Guardian* (23 July 1991).

8. See Robert Jervis, *The Meaning of the Nuclear Revolution: Statecraft and the Prospect of Armageddon* (London: Cornell University Press, 1989).

9. See McGeorge Bundy, *Danger and Survival: Choices About the Bomb in the First Fifty Years* (New York: Random, 1990), and Richard K. Betts, *Nuclear Blackmail and Nuclear Balance* (Washington, DC: Brookings Institution, 1987).

10. For the importance of the symbolic role of nuclear weapons, see Jervis, *The Meaning of the Nuclear Revolution*, Chap. 6.

11. *Guardian* (11 Sept. 1991).

12. Ibid. (4 Sept. 1991).

13. Mikhail S. Gorbachev, *Perestroika: New Thinking for Our Country and the World* (New York: Harper and Row, 1987). For an excellent joint exploration by United States and Soviet academics of the theoretical and practical implications of mutual security, see Richard Smoke and Andrei Kortunov (eds.), *Mutual Security: A New Approach to Soviet–American Relations* (London: Macmillan, 1991).

14. Jack L. Snyder, 'The Gorbachev Revolution: A Waning of Soviet Expansionism?', *International Security*, 12/3 (1987–8), 93–131.

15. Dibb, *The Incomplete Superpower*, 228.

16. *The Economist* (6 Oct. 1990), 114. One rouble was roughly equivalent to one pound sterling in 1990 but only six pence in January 1992.

17. A. Hewett (ed.), *Reforming the Soviet Economy* (Washington, DC: Brookings Institution, 1988).
18. *The Economist* (15 Sept. 1990 and 20 Oct. 1990).
19. Martin Crouch, *Revolution and Evolution: Gorbachev and Soviet Politics* (London: Philip Allan, 1989).
20. *The Economist* (15 Sept. 1990), 11.
21. Ibid. (20 Oct. 1990), 114; *Observer* (15 Sept. 1991).
22. *Guardian* (9 Sept. 1991).
23. Dibb, *The Incomplete Superpower*, 219–20.
24. Ibid. 230–1. See also Segal, *The Soviet Union and the Pacific* (London: Unwin Hyman, 1990).
25. *The Current Digest of the Soviet Press* [*CDSP*], 42/59 (1990), 25.
26. *Observer* (15 Sept. 1991).
27. *Guardian* (4 Sept. 1991).
28. The details of this bizarre episode are contained in Adam B. Ulam, *Expansion and Coexistence: Soviet Foreign Policy 1917–73*, 2nd edn. (New York: Praeger, 1974), 372–4.
29. *International Herald Tribune* (16 Oct. 1990); *Guardian* (26 Oct. 1990; 8 Nov. 1990; and 4 Sept. 1991).
30. *CDSP*, 42/34 (1990), 115.
31. *Guardian* (4 Sept. 1991).
32. *Time* (12 Mar. 1990).
33. *CDSP*, 42/35 (1990), 28; 42/39 (1990), 21; and 42/42 (1990), 26; *The Economist* (29 Sept. 1990), 55–6; *International Herald Tribune* (16 Oct. 1990); *Guardian* (27 Aug. 1991).
34. *Guardian* (3 Sept. 1991).
35. Gorbachev, *Perestroika*, 143.
36. Ibid. 148.
37. Francis Fukuyama, 'The End of History?', *National Interest* (summer 1989), 4.
38. Segal, *Rethinking the Pacific* (Oxford: Oxford University Press, 1990).
39. *Guardian* (21 Dec. 1990); *Independent on Sunday* (23 Dec. 1990).
40. Boris Yeltsin, *Against the Grain: An Autobiography*, trans. Michael Glenny, fully updated (London: Pan, 1990), 204. On his understanding of people power, see pp. 48, 139, and 196.
41. The two key contributions are Kenneth N. Waltz, *Theory of International Politics* (New York: Random 1979), and Robert O. Keohane (ed.), *Neorealism and its Critics* (New York: Columbia University Press, 1986).
42. Coit Dennis Blacker, 'The Soviet Perception of European Security', in Derek Leebaert (ed.), *European Security: Prospects for the 1980s* (Lexington, Mass.: Lexington Press, 1979). For a very useful method of analysing a state's foreign policy objectives, see K. J. Holsti,

*International Politics: A Framework for Analysis*, 5th edn. (Englewood Cliffs, NJ: Prentice-Hall, 1988, Chap. 5.

43. The other main recipients of Soviet foreign economic assistance were Cuba, Vietnam, Nicaragua, Mongolia, Laos, and Kampuchea. Dibb, *The Incomplete Superpower*, 232–8.
44. *Guardian* (22 Nov. 1989).
45. *The Economist* (9 Feb. 1991), 60–1.
46. Gorbachev, *Perestroika*, 191.
47. *Guardian* (17 May 1990).
48. See Colin S. Gray, *War, Peace and Victory: Strategy and Statecraft for the Next Century* (New York: Simon and Schuster, 1990), esp. chap. 7.
49. See Segal, *The World Affairs Companion*; id., *The Soviet Union and the Pacific*; and id., *Rethinking the Pacific*.
50. IISS, *Military Balance 1990–1991*.
51. *Time* (15 Apr. 1985), 33.
52. *Guardian* (14 Aug. 1991).
53. Ibid.
54. The two best overviews of Soviet policy in this region are Segal, *The Soviet Union and the Pacific*, and Myles L. C. Robertson, *Soviet Policy Towards Japan: An Analysis of Trends in the 1970s and 1980s* (Cambridge: Cambridge University Press, 1988).
55. *Time* (15 Apr. 1985), 33.
56. *Guardian* (13 Aug. 1991).
57. Dibb, *The Incomplete Superpower*, 233–4.
58. Stockholm International Peace Research Institute (SIPRI), *SIPRI Yearbook 1989: World Armaments and Disarmament* (Oxford: Oxford University Press, 1989).
59. *Guardian* (17 Oct. 1990). For an exceptionally valuable analysis of economic aid as a foreign policy instrument, see Baldwin, *Economic Statecraft*.
60. *Guardian* (6 Sept. 1991).
61. For an explanation of the idea of complex interdependence, see Robert O. Keohane and Joseph S. Nye, *Power and Interdependence: World Politics in Transition*, 2nd edn. (Boston: Little Brown, 1989). For an application of the idea to the Soviet Union, see Walter C. Clemens, Jr., *Can Russia Change? The USSR Confronts Global Interdependence* (London: Unwin Hyman, 1990).

# FIFTEEN

# Europe Beyond the Cold War

*John Baylis*

At the Malta summit in December 1989 between President Bush and President Gorbachev the leaders of the Superpowers declared that the Cold War was finally over. This verdict was officially endorsed at the meeting of thirty-four CSCE states in Paris in November 1990. After more than forty years of periodic hostility and tension, the improved relationship between the United States and the Soviet Union which had developed since 1985, opened up the prospect that the 1990s would usher in a new European order. The post-war bipolar European structure, which emerged in the late 1940s following the collapse of the traditional balance of power system in the Second World War, had itself been significantly undermined by the welter of events of the late 1980s. These events were taken a stage further by the failure of the coup in the Soviet Union in the summer of 1991 and the collapse of Communism that followed. The key questions facing statesmen from both East and West were whether a new more-stable system of security could be developed and what form a new European order might take.

In order to understand the significance of these events it is important to set them in the broader historical context of the changes which have taken place in the European state system in the modern era. This will provide the setting for a discussion of the European system which emerged from the Cold War period and which prevailed until 1989. Attention will then be focused on four main questions: what were the main characteristics of the post-war European state system? what were the main challenges to that system? what was the significance of the events of 1989? and what are the prospects for a new European order?

## I.  What were the Strengths and Weaknesses of the Classical European Security System?

The European state system which prevailed from the late 1940s until 1989 emerged following the collapse of the classical European order which had been in place from the end of the Middle Ages. From 1500 onwards, for over four centuries, Europe was characterized by a constant process of diplomatic manœuvring and frequent conflicts between states. During this period, despite the wars which occurred, almost all of the European states managed to maintain their existence. This was largely the result of the successful working of a continuously shifting, but generally maintained, balance of power amongst the main European states. The patterns of power altered ceaselessly but the fundamental structure of the relations between the European states persisted. Periodic attempts by Spain, Austria, and France to achieve hegemony in Europe were effectively contained by other states in the system.

During most of the sixteenth century the two Habsburg monarchies led by Spain attempted to dominate Western Europe. Their power, however, proved inadequate to overcome the combined resistance of France, England, and other European states. They tried again after 1618, this time led by Austria. Once again they failed. Next it was the turn of France. After building up a successful coalition to check the Habsburgs, Louis XIV made his own bid for European hegemony. By 1714 this attempt had also been thwarted. At the end of the eighteenth century France tried again and almost succeeded for a time. By 1815, however, Napoleon's drive for supremacy had also been checked.

The balance of power system succeeded because of its ability to adapt to changing patterns of power. There were no rigid alignments and the distribution of power shifted from one generation to another reflecting changes in population economic strength, and the quality of political leadership and military organization. In the sixteenth century Spain, Austria, France, and England were the leading states. By the seventeenth century they had been joined by Holland and Sweden. Holland, Sweden, and Spain declined in power in the eighteenth century and Prussia and Russia took their places. By the time of the Seven Years War in

1756 there were five great powers dominating the stage in Europe with a variety of lesser powers. The balance of power system worked because the important states were reasonably well matched in power terms. If any one state appeared to be getting too powerful and ambitious the others sooner or later combined together to deal with the threat.

The system also worked for two further reasons. First, because the participating states came to believe that it would. As a result their ambitions and calculations were adjusted to the working of the system. The recognition that alignments were temporary and today's enemies might be tomorrow's allies helped to limit the scale of violence which occurred. And secondly, it is possible to discern 'a kind of international ethic of self-restraint which grew up in the eighteenth and early nineteenth centuries. This ethic condemned any drive to European hegemony or any threat to the very existence of the established state, as an improper challenge to a satisfactory system'.[1] This is illustrated by the widespread condemnation of the partition of Poland which took place in the eighteenth century.

Although the balance of power remained the key feature of the European system up until the First World War it was increasingly challenged by the emergence of a unified Germany after 1870. Initially German unification was sanctioned by European opinion as a legitimate right of national self-determination. Bismarck also achieved respect for his circumspect policies designed to keep Europe quiet and maintain the status quo. Before long, however, the development of German industrial power outstripped that of its neighbours and created the foundations for more expansive policies by Bismarck's successors after 1890. By 1914 German power was organized on such a scale compared to its neighbours that it would have been able to win the world war which broke out and establish its dominance in Europe had it not been for the intervention of a non-European country, the United States. German power could not be contained by any other European state or even by a coalition of European states. It took the superior resources of the United States to shift the balance and bring about the defeat of Germany.

The First World War therefore fundamentally undermined the traditional balance of power system. This fact, however, was obscured for a further twenty years by the Versailles Treaty which attempted to restore the old European System. With the return of the United States to isolationism the artificial, unnatural, and transitory nature of this attempt to turn the clock back was revealed. By 1940 Germany was once again on the verge of achieving European hegemony and no combination of European states was capable of preventing it. Only the combined resources of the United States and the Soviet Union in conjunction with Great Britain could bring about the defeat of Germany in 1945.

The Second World War finally revealed the failure of the old European state system to perform its most essential task of maintaining an internal balance and the independence of its member states. With Germany defeated, France devastated by occupation, and Great Britain severely weakened by the effects of the war, the classical European balance of power system had been swept away. For a time, however, it remained unclear what system of European order would take its place.

The war had left the United States and the Soviet Union, the two Superpowers, as the dominant states in Europe. It was not long before a series of disagreements over Poland, the future of Germany, and events in Eastern Europe together with major ideological differences undermined the aspirations for a European and world order based on great power co-operation. The coup in Czechoslovakia in March 1948 and the Berlin Blockade from June 1948 to May 1949 ushered in the Cold War and each side institutionalized its presence in Europe. The establishment of NATO in April 1949 and the incorporation of the new West German state into the alliance in 1955 was followed by the rearming of East Germany and the formation of the Warsaw Pact in the same year.

The year 1955 was in many respects a milestone in the development of a new European security system. As a by-product of the Cold War the two Superpowers had by this time managed to establish a new system of relationships with and among the states of Europe. In his book *Europe Between the Superpowers*, A. W. DePorte provides an interesting discussion of the break-up of the balance of power system and the ironic emergence of a new European system from the hostility and tensions of the Cold War. He argues that:

Germany's victory in 1940 swept away the shadowy remnants of the old European system; its defeat in 1945 opened the continent to an American-

Soviet occupation and rivalry; their competition, in turn, resolved the German problem in an unintended way and at the same time brought into existence a bipolar set of relationships which taken as a whole constituted a state system encompassing not only the superpowers whose actions created it but the European states as well.[2]

Much the same point has been made by Paul Seabury in his study *The Rise and Decline of the Cold War*.[3] While pursuing their Cold War, he argues, the Superpowers stumbled on a solution to the problem which the states of Europe had wrestled with unsuccessfully since 1890—the position of a too-powerful German state in a European system which was not capable of preserving the independence of its members in the face of overwhelming German power.

Having dealt with the collapse of the classical balance of power system and the emergence of a new European state system in 1955 we now turn to a number of key questions about the nature and challenges to that system culminating in the historic events of 1989.

## II.  What were the Main Characteristics of the Post-War European State System?

In many respects the European state system which emerged from the late 1940s was completely unlike the system which had prevailed for the previous four centuries. Six distinguishing characteristics in particular were discernable.

First, it was essentially a bipolar system in which the United States and the Soviet Union predominated. Both Superpowers maintained a balance of power with respect to each other in Europe. The United States with its nuclear superiority for many years and its dominant economic position balanced the vast conventional forces of the Soviet Union and its burgeoning nuclear capability. And vice versa. Both were immeasurably stronger than any of the other European states or indeed any combination of European states. Inevitably as a result the nature of Superpower relations, whether co-operative or hostile, was bound to have a profound influence on the working of the European state system.

Linked to this was the second characteristic feature of the post-war system. Unlike the essentially fluid nature of the old multipolar balance of power arrangements in which alignments were constantly changing in a kaleidoscope manner, the bipolar structure of power was much more static. This brought advantages and disadvantages for European security. On the positive side it overcame the uncertainties of constantly shifting coalitions of power and helped maintain stability in Europe. On the negative side it institutionalized the Cold War tensions and hostilities which made the search for accommodation and co-operation between the two blocs in Europe very difficult to achieve.

A third characteristic of the bipolar system has been the way the European states have been linked to one or other of the dominant Superpowers through a wide range of security, political, and economic ties. One of the consequences of this has been to give the system more durability than seemed possible in the aftermath of the Second World War. With the absence of a peace treaty and the continent divided, peace in Europe appeared precarious in the early days of the Cold War. The consolidation of both halves of Europe helped to provide a framework which did not resolve the underlying problems but prevented them from erupting into violence.

A fourth characteristic has been the asymmetrical nature of the western and eastern subsystems. In the western part the United States has held a dominant position but the NATO alliance has involved voluntary commitments between independent sovereign states. The western alliance has involved a community of interests in which security relationships have been supplemented and reinforced by a web of economic and political ties. In contrast the eastern subsystem was based on a much more coercive relationship between the Soviet Union and the Eastern European states. The Warsaw Pact and Comecon were not voluntary associations but organizations established primarily for the military, economic, and political benefit of the Soviet Union.

The fifth characteristic feature of the post-war European order has been the division of Germany. The traditional problem of a Germany which has been either too weak or too strong was resolved through the division of the country into two German states, each integrated into the opposing alliance systems. This provided a satisfactory solution for Germany's neighbours and an acceptable arrangement for German leaders in both eastern and western parts of the country, at least until 1989.

The final characteristic feature of the European state system has been the emphasis given to nuclear deterrence. Both sides built up a formidable array of nuclear capabilities designed to deter the other from aggression. Through the threat of escalation and the fear of the devastating consequences of nuclear conflagration a balance of terror was established which became the central feature of European security arrangements. Peace and stability were sought through the threat of nuclear annihilation.

## III. What were the Main Challenges to the Post-War European Security System?

In the thirty years after the emergence of the bipolar European state system in the mid-1950s there were numerous challenges which at times threatened to undermine the whole structure. These challenges resulted from severe tensions between the two blocs; periods of *détente* between east and west; major strains resulting from the Soviet Union's coercion of Eastern European states; and periodic divisions between the members of the Western alliance.

At the beginning of the period a short-lived improvement in East–West relations following Stalin's death in 1953 soon gave way to a crisis over Soviet intervention in Hungary in 1956. In its brutal suppression of the Hungarian revolution the Soviet Union demonstrated that it was not prepared to allow its dominant position in Eastern Europe to unravel. Attempts by the Eastern European states to break away from the Soviet sphere of influence would ultimately be met by force. Despite their harsh condemnation of Soviet policies, the Western powers, preoccupied with their own divisions over the Suez crisis, were not prepared to intervene. Through their inaction the West tacitly accepted Soviet hegemony in the Eastern European subsystem. Hungary was a challenge to the system. The manner in which the crisis was resolved, however, helped to reinforce and consolidate the system as a whole.

Hungary was followed by a series of further challenges as Cold War tensions increased in the late 1950s and early 1960s. During the Berlin crises which continued off and on from 1958 to 1961 the Soviet Union attempted to use its apparent military superiority which stemmed from its surprise launching of Sputnik in 1957, to change the status quo in its own favour by forcing the West out of Berlin. Despite their differences the Western powers stood firm and in August 1961 the Berlin wall was built. This 'ultimate symbol of the status quo' dramatically highlighted not only the division of Berlin, Germany, and Europe but also the essential bipolar structure of power between the blocs. The Soviet attempt to ease the West out of Berlin had been a challenge to the system but the building of the wall had once again consolidated that system.

Shortly after the confrontation over Berlin, the Cuban missile crisis erupted. Although the attempt by Khrushchev to install missiles in Cuba was not directly a European crisis it was an attempt by the Russian leader to change the balance of power (including the balance of power in Europe) in his favour. Success would have improved Khrushchev's bargaining-position in resolving a wide range of outstanding difficulties with the west, including the problems of Berlin and West German rearmament. The crisis took the world to the brink of nuclear war but was finally resolved by tough but flexible diplomacy by President Kennedy. Khrushchev backed down and Soviet missiles were withdrawn from Cuba.

An important outcome of the Cuban missile crisis was that it helped usher in a new era of improved relations between East and West. The threat of nuclear war brought a renewed determination to seek arms control agreements. With the essential ingredient of 'political will' present the Superpowers concluded the Hot Line Agreement and the Partial Test-Ban Treaty in 1963.

*Détente*, however, brought new challenges to the European state system. In particular it provided an opportunity for centrifugal forces to emerge in both the Eastern and Western subsystems. In the Eastern bloc the growing conflict between the two dominant Communist states, China and the Soviet Union, encouraged some of the satellite states to adopt more independent policies. This was especially true of Romania under Ceauşescu. The Romanians used the Sino-Soviet rift to steer a much more independent line in foreign policy from Moscow. This more-permissive environment, also encouraged a process of liberalization in Czechoslovakia where Dubcek introduced reforms designed to create 'Communism with a human face'.

The Eastern bloc was not alone in this challenge to the cohesion of the subsystem. In Western Europe tensions emerged as President de Gaulle attempted to pursue a more independent French policy. He attempted to detach West Germany from its dependence on the United States and to open up better relations with the Soviet Union as part of his grand vision of establishing a new system of Europe from the 'Atlantic to the Urals'. The French President criticized American hegemony in Europe and withdrew France from the military integrated structure of NATO in 1966 as part of his overture to the Soviet Union to join France in creating a 'Europe of the states'.

Attractive as French independence was to the Soviet Union de Gaulle's radical challenge to the European status quo involved too many risks for the Soviet leaders, Brezhnev and Kosygin—especially as the liberalizing forces in Eastern Europe were taking a number of states in the region in an uncomfortable direction. The Soviet Union responded in 1968 by forcefully suppressing the process of economic and political experimentation taking place by the Dubcek regime. In so doing the Soviet Union once again consolidated its position in Eastern Europe and reinforced its adherence to the prevailing European bipolar system. The invasion of Czechoslovakia also had a sobering effect in Western Europe. Once again the West refused to become involved but the crisis did lead to a modification of French independence and a return to a more monolithic western position.

In many respects this consolidation and discipline in the two alliances was a prerequisite for a new round of *détente* which emerged in the 1970s. Without Soviet and American confidence in the stability and cohesion of their respective alliances it is doubtful that Chancellor Brandt of West Germany would have been able to pursue his policy of Ostopolitik in the early 1970s. This attempt by the West German government to open up ties with the East brought a series of treaties with the Soviet Union and Poland in 1970, and the East German government in 1972. The rather anomalous Western enclave of Berlin deep in the heart of East Germany had been a source of bitter friction between East and West in the 1940s, 1950s, and 1960s. With the Quadripartite Agreement, although major differences continued to exist, from 1972 Berlin ceased to be a major focus of unrest and potential source of conflict.

Ostpolitik was largely a bilateral process of diplomacy between West Germany and her neighbours. It laid the foundations, however, for a broader multilateral framework of negotiations which began in 1973. The Conference on Security and Cooperation in Europe (CSCE) between thirty-three European states together with the United States and Canada resulted in the Helsinki agreement in 1975. This involved an attempt to lay down a series of rules to guide the behaviour of states in Europe and build confidence between the two military alliances. In the Helsinki Final Act emphasis was placed on such things as the importance of human rights, the inviolability of frontiers, and the need to refrain from the use of force or threat of force in settling disputes. Provision was also made for economic and scientific co-operation between the states of eastern and western Europe.

In some ways the improvement in relations associated with Ostpolitik and the CSCE process represented a significant challenge to the bipolar system of European security, built on Cold War confrontation. Attempts were being made to break down the barriers of mutual hostility and much of the initiative was coming from the European states themselves (including the neutral European countries) rather than the Superpowers. These were challenges which, in the longer run, were to prove more significant than they seemed at the time. In the shorter run, however, Ostpolitik and the CSCE process once again served to reinforce the status quo and consolidate the prevailing European order rather than to undermine it. The treaty between East Germany and West Germany helped to overcome some of the residual insecurity which stemmed from the absence of a peace treaty after the Second World War. The tacit acceptance by the government in Bonn of the East German state and the treaty with Poland, served to dampen down Soviet anxiety over West German ambitions to change the status quo. The Helsinki Final Act also helped to reinforce the existing framework of security by providing the Soviet Union with Western recognition of Eastern Europe as a Soviet sphere of influence. As such it helped to ratify the two-bloc structure of European security. The *détente* of the early-to-mid 1970s proved to be short-lived (although its effects were to be felt later). In the second half of the 1970s East–West relations deteriorated once again as major disputes arose over Soviet activities in various parts of the Third World. With the Soviet intervention in Afghanistan in 1979 and the election in the United States of a resolutely anti-Communist President, Ronald Reagan, a 'new Cold War' erupted. For the new American President the Soviet Union was 'an evil empire' which had to be contained through a major build-up military capabilities.

In Europe this renewned hostility was reflected in two challenges to the system. The first centred on Poland where the rise of the free trade union movement, 'Solidarity', in 1980, threatened to undermine the leading role of the Communist party. Unlike Hungary in 1956 and Czechoslovakia in 1968 the threat to Communist rule came not from the hierarchy within the party but from a broad workers' movement. This represented a serious ideological problem for Moscow. The traditional Soviet–Polish hostility also made the task of military intervention more difficult to contemplate. The situation was only resolved (temporarily) by the installation of a military government under General Jaruzelski and the imposition of martial law in 1981. Once again the Soviet Union had been able through a 'Polish solution' to maintain its dominant position in Eastern Europe.

The renewed Superpower tensions also created difficulties within the Western alliance over how to respond to Soviet activities and the build-up of Soviet military capabilities. The most serious of these disputes centred on NATO's twin-track decision in 1979. Faced with the deployment of a new generation of Soviet missiles (SS-20s) targeted on Western Europe, the alliance decided to deploy its own Pershing and Cruise missiles unless an arms control agreement could be negotiated with the Soviet Union. Although the decision was prompted initially by Chancellor Schmidt's anxiety over the decoupling of American and European security it soon became the source of massive public demonstrations in Western Europe. This in turn led to recriminations in West European–American relations as some European governments had second thoughts over the deployment of the missiles and the conduct of negotiations with the Soviet Union. For many Americans it appeared that the Europeans were going soft on Communism. For many Europeans, on the other hand, the belligerent policies of the United States threatened to lead to nuclear war with the Soviet Union which they feared would be fought out in Europe. As a result of this growing antipathy a great deal of speculation emerged in articles and books that European–

American relations were in a state of terminal crisis.[4] Many felt that the 'widening Atlantic' would lead to a gradual process of American disengagement and the disintegration of the Western alliance. For many in the European Peace Movement and the isolationist camp in the United States these were developments which were long overdue.

The tensions of the 1979 to 1985 period, however, were soon replaced by a new era of improved East–West relations. After a succession of short-lived leaders in the Soviet Union Mikhail Gorbachev came to power in March 1985. Faced with enormous economic difficulties, a crippling defence budget, a deadlocked war in Afghanistan, and stagnation in Eastern Europe the new Soviet leader set about the task of radical reform. Through a combination of *perestroika* (economic restructuring) and *glasnost* (openness) at home and 'new thinking' in foreign policy Gorbachev attempted to reverse the decline and confrontation of the latter Brezhnev years. He recognized that if the deep-seated structural problems of Soviet society were to be contained let alone reversed a transformation of relations with the West would be necessary. Over the next four years, therefore, as he wrestled with economic and political reforms, he sought to dampen down the most serious areas of tension and build a new framework for peaceful relations with the Western countries. Soviet troops were withdrawn from Afghanistan, the defence budget was reduced, and unilateral cuts were made in Soviet forces, including those in Eastern Europe. The Soviet leader also showed himself to be more flexible than any of his predecessors in arms control negotiations with the United States. In Washington in December 1987 Gorbachev signed an Intermediate-range Nuclear Forces (INF) Agreement which was unprecedented. For the first time it was agreed to cut the numbers of nuclear weapons. Land-based INF were to be reduced to zero. This involved asymmetrical reductions with the Soviet Union dismantling significantly more weapons than the United States. Gorbachev also accepted for the first time intrusive verification techniques which none of his predecessors had been prepared to permit.

The INF Treaty proved to be just one part of a much broader *rapprochement* between East and West which characterized the late 1980s. Significant progress was made in the Strategic Arms Reduction Talks (START) designed to reduce strategic nuclear weapons by 50 per cent and in the Conventional Force Reductions in Europe Talks (CFE). In both cases agreements were to be signed in the early 1990s. Regular Superpower summits initially between Gorbachev and Reagan and later between Gorbachev and Bush also helped to recreate a new atmosphere in which war seemed less likely than at any time since 1945. It was in this greatly improved international environment that the dramatic events of 1989 occurred.

## IV. What was the Significance of Events in Eastern Europe in 1989?

Michael Howard has described 1989 as an *annus mirabilis*.[5] Although the upheaval which occurred had its roots in the previous forty-five years of Soviet hegemony in Eastern Europe, it was the specific interrelationship of events from January to December 1989 which was of crucial importance. In particular it was the events in Poland and Hungary which sparked off the 'people's revolutions'.

In Poland despite the banning of 'Solidarity' in 1981, the movement which was 'more than a trade union and less than an organised political party' retained its position as the legitimate voice of the Polish people. Without 'Solidarity', it had become clear, there could be no solution to Poland's chronic economic difficulties. In January 1989 therefore 'Solidarity' was once again legalized by the Communist regime of General Jaruzelski and in February it was brought into direct consultation with the government. By April a new representative constitution had been agreed and in June in limited democratic elections, 'Solidarity' demonstrated its widespread popular appeal by taking virtually all the contested seats. In a worsening economic climate, 'Solidarity' became the dominant partner in a coalition government in August with its own man, Tadensz Mazowiecki as Prime Minister. For the first time in Eastern Europe since 1945 a largely non-Communist government was in power. Just as significantly the process of reform had been accepted (perhaps even encouraged) by the Soviet Union without military intervention or the threat of force.

While these events were taking place in Poland far-reaching reforms were also under way in Hungary. The regime in Hungary had been recognized for some time as the most liberal in Eastern Europe. After some limited economic success, however, by the late 1980s the economy was little better off than others in Eastern Europe. New measures were needed to prevent economic crisis and stagnation. The powerful reformist wing of the Communist party recognized that economic reform could only be brought about through major political changes. As a result Hungary became the first Communist country to grant freedom of political association and to announce that multi-party elections would take place. Moves were also made to open the frontiers with Austria and to drop the title 'Workers' Republic' from the name of the state. The leaders of the party even went as far as to stop calling themselves 'Communists'.

For most of 1989 these liberalizing tendencies in Poland and Hungary were condemned by the hard-line regimes in Czechoslovakia and East Germany. In both countries, the old leaders installed during the Brezhnev era resisted the 'heresies' which were emerging elsewhere and adamantly refused to march down the road to reform. Without support from Moscow, however, both regimes had been swept away by the autumn. In August thousands of East Germans went on holiday to Hungary and never returned home. They made use of the recently opened Hungarian–Austrian border to travel on to West Germany.

Attempts by the East German leader Erich Honecker to halt the emigration brought huge crowds on to the streets. In October Honecker was forced to resign as the party made a belated attempt to introduce reform before it was too late. Egon Krenz, Honecker's successor, tried to control the exodus of East Germans by opening the Berlin Wall on 9 November and promising free elections. As a representative of the old regime, he too, however, was forced to resign in December as public demonstrations continued all over East Germany. With the end of the Communist rule and the promise of free elections German reunification was once again firmly back on the international agenda.

Much the same sequence of events took place in Czechoslovakia. After attempts were made to break up the growing demonstrations with riot police, the Jakes government collapsed on 17 November. As a result the Communist party disintegrated and Vaclav Havel, a leading playwright and dissident, was elected President, as Czechoslovakia returned to democracy. It had been just over forty years since the Communist coup which had extinguished Czech democracy and ushered in the Cold War.

With these events in Poland, Hungary, East Germany, and Czechoslovakia it was not long before the fire of liberalization spread to Bulgaria and Romania. In all cases, with the exception of Romania, the revolutions were remarkably peaceful. In December the Romanian dictator, Ceauşescu, desperately attempted to retain power by ordering the secret police to open fire on the crowds. The army revolted and joined the demonstrators and on Christmas Day 1989 Ceauşescu and his wife were executed. By the end of the year all the Communist regimes in Eastern Europe, apart from isolated Albania, had been swept away, in revolutions which future historians will see as one of the major milestones of the modern era. Nineteen eighty-nine will take its place alongside the momentous events of 1789, 1848, 1919, and 1945 as an important turning-point in history.

Taken in conjunction with the momentous changes in East–West relations, the events in Eastern Europe in 1989 are of profound significance for the European state system which has prevailed since the 1950s. Almost every aspect of the Cold War system was under challenge. That system, it will be remembered, was characterized by a bipolar confrontation between the two Superpowers and their heavily-armed alliances facing each other across a divided Europe and divided Germany. By the early 1990s the hostility between the Superpowers had given way to a new era of more cordial relations.

It was also evident that a relative decline was taking place in the traditional dominant positions of the Superpowers in Europe. This was particularly true of the Soviet Union. The attempts by President Gorbachev to modernize the Communist system eventually failed. In the aftermath of the failed coup by a hard-line conservative group in the summer of 1991, Communism, and with it the highly centralized political system that had governed the Soviet Union since 1917, was swept away. As Eric Herring has shown in his chapter above, the events of 1991 represented a collapse of Soviet power and the beginning of a process of disintegration which had profound implications for European security.

Although this left the United States as the sole Superpower, the dramatic changes in Eastern Europe and the Soviet Union also signalled a weakening of American involvement in Europe. Arms control agreements like the CFE and the end of the Cold War provided the opportunity for the Bush administration to withdraw military forces from Europe and reduce military expenditure to help resolve its own budgetary problems.

This decline in the role of the Superpowers had a major impact on the alliances which had institutionalized the conflict between East and West since the 1950s. The Warsaw Pact ceased to exist in 1991 and Soviet forces began to withdraw from the countries of Eastern Europe. NATO was faced with increasing pressure to transform itself from a military alliance into a more political organization to reflect the changes that were taking place. At the same time the long-standing division of Germany which had symbolized the confrontation between East and West ended with the unification of the Federal Republic of Germany and the German Democratic Republic. The old European System had been shaken to its foundations. But what was to replace it?

## V. What are the Prospects for a New European Order?

The image of the future which struck the imaginations of most Europeans in the early 1990s was President Gorbachev's conception of a 'Common European Home'. The Soviet leader explained what he meant by the notion in a speech to the Council of Europe on 6 July 1989.

The philosophy of the 'Common European Home' concept rules out the probability of an armed clash and the very possibility of the use of force or the threat of force—alliance against alliance, inside the alliances, wherever. This philosophy suggests that a doctrine of restraint should take the place of the doctrine of deterrence. This is not just a play on words but the logic of European development prompted by life itself.[6]

It was this restraint which Gorbachev used in providing the green light to the process of reform in Eastern Europe. Without this new approach the dramatic events from 1989 to 1991 would not have occurred.

Gorbachev saw this doctrine of restraint as the key to a less militarized and more co-operative Europe. His vision owed something to General de Gaulle's 'Europe from the Atlantic to the Urals'. For the Soviet President the aim should be to try and achieve an increasingly interdependent commonwealth of sovereign states in Europe which pursue greater economic and political collaboration and resolve outstanding differences without the resort to force.

President Bush also put forward a similar idea for a Europe 'whole and free'. As with the Soviet leader's vision the emphasis was on breaking down the barriers between East and West and establishing a more co-operative framework for the mutual benefit of all. The American President, however, argued that 'There cannot be a "Common European Home" until all within it are free to move from room to room . . . The path of freedom leads to a larger home, a home where West meets East, a democratic home—the commonwealth of free nations.'[7] In President Bush's vision an important prerequisite for the creation of the 'new Europe' was the successful completion of the movement towards democracy by all the states of Eastern Europe.

The architectural structure most favoured by proponents of a new European peace order has been the CSCE process. Despite its limited early achievements the CSCE proved remarkably success-ful in the late 1980s 'in fostering a greater sense of common European identity, and an emerging consensus on humanitarian values, including human rights.'[8] The institutionalization of the Helsinki process, agreed at the CSCE summit meeting in Paris in November 1990, was designed to pave the way for the transition from the old system of European security to a new pan-European security order. Moves were also initiated to transform the Cold War military alliances into essentially political organizations designed to help maintain stability and lay the foundations of a CSCE-based European peace order embracing the principles of 'common security' and non-provocative defence. Building on the major cuts in conventional forces agreed in November 1990 (the CFE Agreement) it was envisaged that further radical cuts in military forces would take place together with the restructuring of defensive forces so that they were structurally incapable of attack and the extension of confidence-building measures in Europe. Overall the aim was to create a largely demilitarized Europe in which security would be based on collective security arrangements.

These security structures would then be reinforced, proponents of a new European order argued, by a more co-operative and integrated European economic space which stretched across the continent. On the economic plane the EC would act as a framework for economic regeneration in Eastern Europe and an expansion of prosperity in the West. The evolution of democratic governments in Eastern Europe, the Baltic, and perhaps eventually the former Soviet Republics, embracing market-economics would open up the opportunity for a broadening of the community and the breaking down of economic as well as ideological and military barriers at the heart of Europe.

In this process the reunited Germany will play a key role. It is hoped that the new democratic Germany will be a source of both prosperity and stability. Deeply embedded in the EC and the new security arrangements, Germany is seen as the economic power-house for European economic development without being a major threat to the other states of Europe as it has been in the past.

This model of a new European peace order built around the CSCE and EC is based on what Jack Snyder has described as 'neo-liberal institutionalism'.[9] This approach assumes that the Hobbesian tendencies which are likely to arise in Europe as the old order breaks up can be 'mitigated by an institutional structure that provides legitimate and effective channels for reconciling conflicting interests'.[10]

This approach is very attractive in many ways. Such institutions, based on pan-European principles, would be radically different from either the classical balance of power system or the bipolar European security system which prevailed from the mid-1950s onwards. The new system would involve much greater inter-dependence between states, a broader consensus of normative security and humanitarian values, and a degree of demilitarization which has rarely been seen in European history. (The system developed during thirty years after the Treaty of Westphalia from 1815 to 1845 when the Concert of Europe prevailed would be the only comparable framework.)

Questions arise, however, over whether such a European order is realistic and if it was introduced whether it would be capable of bearing the heavy traffic of European security on 'bad days as well as good'.

John Mearsheimer is one writer who has been rather pessimistic about the prospect of European security in the post-Cold War era.[11] Basing his ideas on the philosophy of political realism he argues that the Cold War imposed stability and discipline in

Europe. The confrontation between East and West, together with the development of nuclear weapons, produced a bipolar configuration of power, he argues, which has encouraged predictability and helped prevent war. For Mearsheimer the end of the Cold War was likely to usher in a more multipolar structure of power which would bring greater uncertainty and increase the chances of miscalculation leading to conflict between European states. He entitled his article 'Back to the Future' as a warning that Europe could return to the rivalries and conflicts which had scarred its history.

There are other interesting criticisms which have been levelled at the more optimistic views about a new European security order.[12] In particular there are those who argue that it is naïve, idealistic, Utopian, and impractical. According to this view such a concept of a 'European peace order' ignores the prevalence of national self-interest and of deep-seated ethnic and national rivalries in Europe; it overlooks the dismal failure of the League of Nations in the inter-war years; and it fails to consider the internal tensions that regional inequalities and uneven development are likely to generate in Europe over the next twenty years.[13]

In other words critics argue that those who advocate these ideas are guilty of wishful thinking. Such a system, to work effectively, would require a transformation of international politics and of human nature, they suggest, which is unlikely to occur in a world which still exhibits deep-seated and intractable tensions.

There are also those who argue that many of the terms used to describe the European peace order remain ill-defined. Concepts such as a 'Common-European Home' and a 'Europe whole and free' have a superficial appeal. But what precisely do they mean? The attempts to clarify such concepts have so far been little more than high-minded generalities.

Another criticism is that such ideas are 'dangerous, seductive and delusory'.[14] By promising so much they might encourage statesmen in both East and West to give up 'the tried and tested security structures of the post-war period . . . in order to adopt some ill-defined and untested concept of "collective security" '?[15] According to this argument, NATO in particular, has to remain the primary focus for western security until a new and effective alternative structure can be developed. The implication of arguments such as these is that, attractive as moving towards a

European peace order may appear, it is important to be prudent and cautious about discarding a system of security which, despite its limitations has helped to keep the peace since the end of the Second World War.

Deciding between these two sets of optimistic and pessimistic arguments is extremely difficult. Those who argue that the 1990s provide a unique opportunity to build a more legitimate European and international order have a case.[16] The speed of events since 1989 has been breathtaking and their significance has been far-reaching. As a result of the collapse of Communist power in Eastern Europe and the Soviet Union the main foundations of the post-war era have been swept away. International relations in the future are unlikely to be dominated by the same kind of ideological confrontation between East and West as it has been in the past. Neither is Europe likely to be divided in the same way into two heavily armed camps. At the same time the growth of 'people's power' and a new pan-European consciousness together with the relentless march of interdependence appears to herald important changes in domestic politics and international relationships within Europe. We may not be witnessing 'the end of history', as Fukuyama has argued, but a new era of international relations which is less militarized and more interdependent than in the past.[17]

Writers like Hyde-Price, however, are right to emphasize the need for caution and prudence. Despite the euphoria over the events of 1989 it is important to remember the reactions which followed in the wake of past revolutions. After 1789 there was the 'Great Terror' and after 1848 the 'forces of reaction' were back in power by the end of 1849. Already the end of Stalinist discipline and totalitarian control in the Soviet Union and Eastern Europe has led to an upsurge of bitter ethnic disputes and nationalist rivalries. The problems of Azerbaijan, Armenia, Moldavia, Georgia, and especially the clashes between Serbs and Croats in Yugoslavia provide a timely warning of the enormous potential for instability which lies smouldering beneath the surface on the European continent. It remains to be seen whether the Eastern European states and the former Soviet Union make the peaceful transition to democratic government given their severe economic problems and fragile political systems. The invasion of Kuwait by Iraq in August 1990 and the Civil War in Yugoslavia in 1991 also provided a reminder that military force remains an important feature of international relations in the post-Cold-War world. Despite the vast political, economic, and social changes of the late twentieth century it is still too early to predict that the future is going to be wholly unlike the past. Equally it would overly deterministic to argue that Europe is condemned to relive the violent conflicts of previous generations.

The 1990s is an era of transition in some ways similar to the period from 1945 to 1955. During that period a new system of European security was gradually—almost inadvertently—built on the ruins of the old classical balance of power system. That system, however, emerged from the hostility of the Cold War. This time, despite the undoubted tensions which remain, the atmosphere of international relations in Europe is, in some ways, more auspicious. In the place of ideological and military confrontation between the Superpowers a new more co-operative relationship is being forged. There will undoubtedly be set-backs and the form the new European order takes will depend as much on unpredictable events as 'grand designs'. Nevertheless, the postwar bipolar system dominated by the Superpowers is now over. With the collapse of Soviet power, the partial withdrawal of the United States, and the more permissive atmosphere of co-operation, the Europeans are faced with an unprecedented opportunity to build a new European order based on a healthy mixture of realist and utopian values. The debate between optimism and pessimism, however, is evenly balance.[18]

## Notes

1. A. W. Deporte, *Europe Between the Superpowers: The Enduring Balance* (New Haven, Conn.: Yale University Press, 1986), 3.
2. Ibid. 116.
3. P. Seabury, *The Rise and Decline of the Cold War* (New York: Basic Books, 1967).
4. See L. Freedman, *The Troubled Alliance* (London: Heinemann, 1983) and S. Lunn, *Burden-sharing in NATO* (London: Routledge & Kegan Paul, 1983).
5. M. Howard, 'The Springtime of Nations', *Foreign Affairs*, 69/1 (1989/90), 32.

6. Quoted in J. Hoagland, 'Europe's Destiny', *Foreign Affairs*, 69/1 (1989/90), 38.

7. Ibid. 45.

8. A. Hyde-Price, *European Security Beyond the Cold War* (London: RIIA, 1990).

9. J. Snyder, 'Averting Anarchy in the New Europe', *International Security*, 14/4 (Spring 1990), 15.

10. Ibid.

11. John Mearsheimer, 'Back to the Future: Instability in Europe after the Cold War', *International Security*, 15/1 (Summer 1990). For the interesting debate which followed the publication of this article, see Stanley Hoffman, Robert O. Keohane, and John Mearsheimer, 'Back to the Future, Part II: International Relations Theory and Post-Cold War Europe', ibid. 15/2 (Fall 1990), and Bruce Russet, Thomas Risse-Kappen, and John Mearsheimer, 'Back to the Future, Part III: Realism and the Realities of European Security', ibid. 15/3 (Winter 1990/1). For another view of the implications of the end of the Cold War, see Stephen von Evera, 'Prime for Peace: Europe after the Cold War', ibid.

12. For some of these criticisms see A. Hyde-Price, *European Security Beyond the Cold War*.

13. Ibid. 214–15 and 232–58.

14. Ibid.

15. Ibid.

16. See K. Booth, 'Redefining East-West Security', *International Affairs*, 6/1 (1990).

17. F. Fukyama, 'The End of History?', *National Interest* (Summer 1989).

18. C. McInnes, 'European Security: Pessimism, Optimism or Post-Modernism', unpublished paper delivered at the Conference of the Political Studies Association in April 1991 (1991). This article discusses both optimistic and pessimistic arguments and comes down in favour of a more optimistic assessment. See also B. Buzan, M. Kelstrup, P. Lemaitre, E. Tromer, and O. Waever, *The European Security Order Recast: Scenarios for the Post-Cold War Era* (London: Pinter 1990).

# SIXTEEN

# A Pacific Century?

*Gerald Segal*

It was Karl Marx and Friedrich Engels who noted in 1850 that 'the Pacific Ocean will [soon] play the same role as the Atlantic Ocean does now and as the Mediterranean did in the antiquity of the Middle Ages—the role of a great water highway of world commerce—and the Atlantic Ocean will decline to the level of an inland sea, as the Mediterranean is now.'[1] Marx and Engels were wrong about a number of matters, and this is another one.

Is it less than ten years to go to the Atlantic Century or the Pacific Century? At a time when the strategic balance seems to be shifting in Europe and in East Asia, the short answer is that both the Atlantic and Pacific will be areas of vital change. But while much has been, and is being written about the new European security, very little thought has been given to the shape and importance of the new Pacific. Both the problems and the possibilities in the Pacific are ignored at our peril. Even for those primarily interested in the fate of the new Europe, the lessons from the Pacific are vital.

Yet if 'thinking Pacific' means thinking of the geographic region as a coherent cultural, political, military, or economic bloc, then 'thinking Pacific' is obsolete. The true importance of the changes taking place in the Pacific concerns the new trends in ideology, military security, and economic relations, none of which depends on there being some coherence to the region commonly known as the Pacific.

## I. What is the Pacific?

Let us begin with the basics—geography. The Pacific is an ocean, in fact it is by far the largest ocean, stretching across 200 degrees of longitude. Apart from a scattering of sparsely populated islands, it is only populated around the rim. Properly speaking, the Pacific Century refers to the prospects of those people who live by the waters of the Pacific Ocean. Yet most writers on the subject are not concerned with Latin America—80 per cent of which lies east of Boston anyway, and most are also not concerned with the largest Asian country (by territory), Russia.

In fact, apart from the neo-Europeans in North America and Australia and New Zealand, most people talk of the Pacific Century and think of East Asia. What is more, they really only think of the prosperous parts of East Asia, and therefore exclude the three Indochinese states, the Philippines, and even Indonesia. Needless to say, there is much ambiguity about the meaning of the Pacific, and any definition will appear arbitrary.[2] But the way in which lines are drawn when thinking Pacific says a great deal about what is expected from the region.

Indeed, it may seem strange to say it, but the Pacific is a European idea. The first person to cross it deliberately was Ferdinand Magellan, sailing under a Spanish flag: curiously, none of the great civilizations of the Americas or East Asia had ever thought of traversing it. It is to Magellan that we owe the name of the ocean, which for centuries was better known as the South Seas. The Spanish were the first to think of the Pacific in commercial terms, using its waters as a transport route linking their colonies in Asia and the Americas.

The British were the most regular mappers of the islands and coasts, which is why so many English names are scattered around the area.[3] Britain did more than any other country to reshape the demography of the Pacific, by settling millions of people in the Americas and Australasia, and moving Chinese and Indians around its colonies. The Russians came in smaller numbers, but, by the mid-twentieth century, after nearly every other empire had retreated, the Russians retained their foothold on the shores of the ocean.

Russia, Britain, and most of the other imperial powers which had coveted the Pacific saw it as a region of huge potential and challenge. As we have already noted, Karl Marx and some nineteenth-century American Presidents thought that the twentieth century would be the age of the Pacific. But they have been proved wrong, largely because the diverse inhabitants of the Pacific rim have had more interest in rivalry than in a regional vision.

Apart from the tenuous cross-Pacific links of European empires and the United States, the first real attempt to think of the Pacific as a coherent whole came from the Japanese. But even that part of the Second World War which took place in the Pacific was focused on a continental objective, the 'Greater Asian Co-Prosperity Sphere' (much as the Chinese empires traditionally thought of expansion by land rather than of taking to the high seas). Yet as a result of the war, the United States emerged as the first country with Pacific-wide reach. Americans came to think of the Pacific as an 'American lake' because during the war American soldiers had slogged their way across it from island to island. By 1945 it was American power that spanned Pacific waters to reach allies around the western rim of the ocean.

With the retreat of most of the old European empires, the local states in East Asia gained their independence more or less within the same boundaries as the states that existed before the Europeans first came. The United States was left as the predominant military and economic power in the region and, in the atmosphere of the Cold War, it tried to organize its friends into coalitions against the Communist regimes of China and the Soviet Union.

Thus any definition of the Pacific, either in geographic or historic terms, depends on where you sit. Despite all the uncertainty in Europe about where its borders are to be found and the nature of the links across the Atlantic,[4] the problems of defining the Pacific, like the ocean itself, are far more vast. Let us then turn to the major contemporary dimensions of the Pacific for some insight about the importance and nature of the Pacific Century.


## II. How Many Ideologies and Cultures?

To a large extent, the idea of the 'Pacific' was fostered by those accustomed to thinking about an Atlantic community. The transfer of tens of millions of Europeans and Africans to the 'neo-Europes' of the Americas extended powerful bands of common culture. Although the new world nurtured new ideas, it also retained close links with the original European cultures and ways of thought. In later years, the traffic was often reversed, with the expansion of North American cultural, economic, and military influence. The Atlantic community is built on a shared culture and ideology; no such structure is apparent in the Pacific.

There are many reasons for the absence of a key cultural base of 'Pacific' consciousness, the most obvious being the lack of a large flow of settlers. To be sure, millions of Chinese, Japanese, Filipinos, and Vietnamese are scattered throughout the Americas, but they constitute a tiny fraction of the immigrant population. The great civilizations of East Asia, most notably the Chinese and Japanese, have been reluctant to export either their people or their culture. Chinese communities play an important role in part of South-east Asia, but in most cases their minority status exacerbates regional differences. The Sinic world is distinct from South-east Asia, as are the proud cultures of Korea and Japan, not to mention the 'neo-Europes' of Russia, Australasia, and the Americas.

If there are reasons to think of the Pacific in terms of cultural or ideological unity, these are perhaps to be found in the universal images of a 'global village' or 'Coca-Cola-i-zation'. Hollywood may be in California, but the culture it represents is more international than Pacific. Mao Tse-tung's portrait looks out over Tiananmen Square in Peking at the world's largest Kentucky Fried Chicken outlet, part of the planetary spread of American 'fast food' culture. What is more, the much-discussed shrinking of the world because of better communications has also meant that American culture has been diluted and distorted by other Western cultures, which filter through it to East Asia. Trendy young Japanese wear clothes influenced by European couture, they eat in French restaurants as interpreted by Japanese tastes, and watch Italian films.

In any case, this global popular culture differs greatly according to local traditions. The richer and less related to the English language the culture is, the more distinctive it appears. The new Australian cinema and literature flourish because they are different from those of the United States. In Japan, the distinctiveness of the local arts is even more obvious, and greater prosperity and strength in the global economy have only enhanced Japanese self-confidence. Hong Kong, Taiwan, and now even China have film industries that may pander to the Kung-fu-loving masses, but their morality and style owe far more to Sinic traditions.

The habit of quoting the commissar in the five Communist States of the Pacific has added yet another layer to local culture, one owing (at least initially) more to European socialism than to American influence. The diversity of the political ideologies of the Pacific stands in sharp contrast to the relatively unified character of the North Atlantic world. Few states of the Pacific are liberal market-economy democracies as understood by mid-Atlantic political culture. Besides Australia and New Zealand, only the North Americans really fit the mould.

Even before the collapse of Communism in Europe in 1989, by virtue of China and Vietnam, there were always far more Communists in the Pacific than in Europe. Now, with Communists hard to find in Europe, students of comparative Communism need to become East Asia specialists. It is in the Pacific, too, that Communists have fought their bloodiest and most dangerous internecine wars.

It was China's split from the Soviet Union in the 1960s that destroyed the credibility of Communism as a world movement. It was the death of reform Communism in Europe that left the Asia Communists virtually on their own as believers in the true creed. But their beliefs seem likely to survive if only because many of their revolutions were home-grown and managed to modify pre-Communist political culture to suit Communist ends. Peasant Communism was always a different version of the European namesake, but it is only now that Europeans appreciate the extent to which Asian Communism may survive as a result of its distinctive qualities.

Another distinctive ideology of the Pacific is what Chalmers Johnson has called the 'capitalist development state'—the idea of mixing a command economy with elements of a market economy, all guided by authoritarian rule in the pursuit of prosperity.[5] Japan, then Singapore, South Korea, Hong Kong, and Taiwan have demonstrated this route to development. Some of the aspiring recent additions to the 'club' of Newly Industrialized Countries

(NICs), including Thailand and Malaysia, are experimenting with a similar mix of ideas. Just as Communism in East Asia evolved into a different pattern from its European predecessors, so capitalism in East Asia has taken on special characteristics.

The greater role for authoritarian government and management of market forces makes the CDS distinctive. It also suggests a middle ground between the old Communism in Europe and the more unrestrained market economies of Western Europe. Whether this serves as a possible middle option for the recently liberated states of Eastern Europe is impossible to tell. But it seems true that the East Asian CDS' experience with managing the transition to a market economy and opening up to the international market economy may have application for those in Eastern Europe seeking ways to cushion the process of democratic transition.

In sum, political culture in the Pacific remains a complex pattern of universal trends and sub-regional traditions. The new technologies of communication make possible the simultaneous spread of global ideas and the 'narrowcasting' of local concepts. If 'thinking Pacific' means thinking in a comprehensive way about the region, then it will always be suspect. A much more fruitful and realistic approach is to study local cultures as part of the global, rather than regional, pattern, each making its own distinctive contribution. In such a world, even the Europeans will have something to learn about ideology and political culture.

## III. Military Security: How Much and for Whom?

Students of military strategy rarely appreciate the cultural and ideological roots of military security. Little heed has been paid to the variegated nature of political culture in the Pacific and fruitless attempts to plan a region-wide strategy for security have been made. The European and Atlantic experience led many to believe that multilateral alliances, based on division into Communist and non-Communist blocs, was the inevitable way of the post-war world.

In the Pacific, the outcome of this erroneous analogy has been wars and human tragedies on a scale not equalled elsewhere since 1945. Between the periods of the Korean war and the various phases of conflict in Indo-China, millions have died believing that one side or the other in the Cold War was worth fighting for. But China detached itself from the Soviet Union and, in 1969, both sides rattled nuclear sabres in an East Asian version of the Cuban Missile crisis. The single greatest strategic loss suffered by the Soviet Union between 1945 and 1989 was the split with China and the need to plan for a two-front war. By the late 1970s, Cambodians were being killed by the million in the cause of one definition of true Communism. Subsequently, Soviet-supported Vietnam attacked Chinese-supported Cambodia and then China and Vietnam had their own war in 1979. It gradually dawned on the combatants that security in the Pacific was no longer a question of Cold War allegiances, but a far more complex matter.

The United States dimly recognized the fact of East Asian political diversity when it withdrew from Vietnam in the early 1970s. Initially Henry Kissinger and Richard Nixon thought they could play off one Communist regime against another in order to minimize the impact of the American strategic retreat from the area. The new focus for America was on the kind of power it knows best—naval strength and economic prosperity. By the 1980s the United States was the principal Pacific power, though it was barely a land power in East Asia. Nearly all of its fragile multilateral alliances in the Pacific had disintegrated in the face of regional diversity.

Conservative Americans tried to reconstruct some new version of Pacific security, but the realistic among them understood that security in the region would have to be sought through further sub-regional arrangements. The Soviet Union was slower to realize that grandiose theorizing about Pacific and East Asian security was not likely to be fruitful. However, with the general revolution in foreign policy that came with the Gorbachev administration, the Soviets finally developed a more sophisticated appreciation of the Pacific.[6]

A new, Asian balance of power is emerging as the Superpower overlay is lifted. Indeed it can be argued that the revelations that came to Europeans in 1989 when they too saw the Superpower overlay raised, were first apparent in East Asia. The Superpowers were always far less important in East Asia and there were always more powers waiting in the wings to take up the challenge of multipolarity.

Of course it was true that the Europeans were the first to appreciate the relative uselessness of military power in the age of nuclear deterrence. The result was the peaceful transition in Europe in 1989, that in other ages might have ended in major war. But in East Asia, wars had been far more prevalent. This was in part due to the fact that the Superpowers had less direct clashes of interest and therefore were, like in other parts of the developing world, more prepared to allow allies to go to war. But in East Asia, before any other part of the developing world, the risks of war were appreciated and the region settled down to more Cold Wars or controlled conflict. Nuclear deterrence played a part in this calming of conflicts, but it was not the primary factor.

Indeed, the relative unimportance of nuclear issues was apparent in the evolution of a more multipolar balance of power. The rise of China, Japan, and even Vietnam made pre-1989 European-type calculations of deterrence impossible. Thus it can still be said that the East Asians came to multipolarity before the Europeans. The East Asian experience also suggests that such multipolarity can be safely managed, but it will never be as neat as a bipolar world.

The relative decline of the Superpowers, growing multipolarity, and the declining utility of force, are evident around the globe, but best seen and studied in the Pacific, where the world's two most powerful candidates for Superpower status are adjusting their arsenals. According to prevailing rates of currency exchange, Japan now spends more on its defence than any other country except the superpowers, and China, like Japan, is searching for a new definition of independence in an increasingly interdependent world. China, Japan, the United States, and Russia all come frigate-to-frigate in the crowded waters of North-east Asia. In an era of great power *détente*, with both Russia and China courting South Korea, the basis of an uneasy stability is growing even though there are serious concerns about North Korea's nuclear potential and the problems of Korean unification.[7]

Yet it is remarkable how this limitation on conflict has so far been achieved without formal arms control. While the Europeans, even in the relatively simple calculations before 1989 of a bipolar balance, were often fruitlessly engaged in negotiating the minutiae of arms control agreements, the East Asians never became involved. To be sure, the East Asians benefited from such treaties as the NPT or the 1987 INF agreement. But they never saw the need to negotiate formal accords of their own.

This is not to suggest that the East Asians did not reduce military tension, for they seemed to prefer tacit arms control as being easier and more quickly successful. Arms reductions along the Sino-Soviet frontier or in Indochina were examples of such successful tacit arms control.[8] Only in 1990, after the major cuts had already started, did China and the Soviet Union agree on formal confidence-building measures. By 1989, and the new multipolarity in Europe, some in the Atlantic world were beginning to look at the advantages of tacit arms control in times of rapid political change. Legalistic negotiators simply could not keep up with the desire of the European people for a 'peace dividend'. Once again, there seemed to be something important that might be learned by the experience in the Pacific.

## IV. Economic Growth: Why and for Whom?

As the American attempts to organize Pacific security became less plausible, the Japanese took up the theme of Pacific co-operation in a way that played to their own strengths—economics and trade. The rise of the Japanese economy from the devastation of war has been truly phoenix-like. Until it assisted its neighbouring NICs in East Asia to repeat its success, Japan was the only non-white state to make the transition from developing to developed economy. It now has the world's second largest economy, and is the second largest creditor nation (Taiwan took the top spot in 1990). Japan's economic relationship with the United States is so close that much of the American budget deficit is financed by Japan. In return, the openness of the American market has made Japan's economic miracle possible. The relationship between the two nations is aptly described as one of Mutual Assured Destruction (MAD)—in the event of an economic war, either country could destroy the other's economy.

Thus the Japanese–American link is the strongest across the Pacific and, indeed, supports much of the latest talk of a Pacific Community. As Japan has gradually replaced the United States as the major trading partner of many States in the region, it has become increasingly easy to see the attraction of regional economic co-operation. Australia joined in, forming a three-way 'think-tank' partnership.[9] Twenty years ago, the ideal of a Pacific Community, like the troubled European Economic Community, seemed slightly premature but still plausible. The result was a number of informal groups of regional leaders—the most successful of which is the combination of government, business, and academia in the Pacific Economic Co-operation Conference. The rise of the NICs as major trading nations reinforced the belief that there was real potential for multilateral economic co-operation.[10] The failure of the Association of South-east Asian Nations to improve the level of their 'internal' trade supported the argument that co-operation had to be broader.

But today, in an era when the European Community seems finally to have got its act together for 1992 and beyond, the idea of a Pacific Community has begun to lose its lustre for some. The fear of EC and North American trade zones with barriers to external States is encouraging many in East Asia to think of the Western Pacific in self-defence. But such a thought, like that of a wider Pacific security, is probably also out of date.

The idea of a Pacific economic community depends on an obsolete idea of the importance of the State in the global economy.[11] Much of world trade, over 50 per cent according to recent work at the Royal Institute of International Affairs, is within companies.[12] States are not often the main actors. Multinational corporations are everywhere, and the NICs have recognized that by setting up their own so they can compete on a global basis.[13] The level of interdependence is quite staggering. More than 30 per cent of Taiwan's, and 40 per cent of Japan's trade imbalance with the United States is due to American-owned companies buying or making things in Taiwan and Japan, then exporting them back to the United States. Some 60 per cent of United States imports from both Singapore and Malaysia come from American-owned firms. And American-owned companies in Japan sold more goods in Japan than the total of the American trade deficit with Japan in 1985. Forty per cent of all Japanese exports and imports in 1986 were to and from affiliated companies. Japanese firms are able to weather currency revaluations because of their heavy investment elsewhere around the region.[14]

To some extent, this interdependence encourages some economists to 'think Pacific'. But the percentages of Pacific states' trade within the basin are not clearly on the increase.[15] What is on the rise is sub-regional trade, which leads some to argue that we will see the formation of a Yen bloc.[16] Certainly in North-east Asia, Japan's trade with the sub-region has gone up from 13 per cent to 18 per cent in the past six years. But few states have actually seen the percentage of their trade within the wider Pacific rise, largely because Japan has replaced the United States as the major trade partner.

Americans make much of the fact that their trade with the Pacific is worth more than their trade with Europe. But West Europeans are also finding that their trade with East Asia is increasing faster than their trade with the Americans.[17] Japanese investment in, and trade with, Europe is growing faster than its equivalents with the United States. Similar trends are already becoming evident for South Korea and the NICs, and Japan may well find the lure of the new Europe more appealing than the difficulties of dealing with a grumpy United States.

The implication is clear. We are once again watching the growth of a global rather than a regional economy. As a recent advertisement by the *Financial Times* suggests, it will be the Japanese who benefit first from the Single European Act, because they will be inside the European market producing for the world's largest capitalist economy. Along with Japanese factories and finance, come university chairs and Japanese schools in leafy London suburbs. This is the interdependence of the global economy at work and it is transforming the way in which we think about international relations and prosperity.

## V.  What Kind of Pacific Century?

Of course there is usually more fashion than fact in proclaiming that one region or state is on the rise and others are falling. It is one thing to suggest that the percentage of military and economic power at the disposal of Russia or the United States is declining in relative terms—true enough. But it is far more important to note how much power is left and whether the declining states are still in leading or even dominant positions. Far too much fruitless word processing has gone on about the relativity of Superpower decline. But it remains true that the Soviet Union has fallen faster than the

United States and, if anything, the United States is far better off forty-five years on from the end of the Second World War. In the Pacific at least, the United States remains the only plausible guarantor of the interests of the global market economy and hence the prosperity of the region.

Yet it is also true that major parts of the reason for the decline of Soviet power had to do with the rise of American allies rather than the United States itself. The growth rates in Western Europe and parts of East Asia have clearly outpaced those in the United States and have brought us back to something like the balance of world GDP seen in the late 1930s. All the indications are that the Europeans and the select East Asians will continue to outgrow the United States. What is more, neither East Asians nor Europeans need American military power as much as they did in the post-war era, and thus American leverage is reduced.

As accurate as such geopolitical thinking might be, it leaves out one crucial fact. The power of the United States as well as those of its friends in Asia and Europe depends on continued co-operation in the global market economy. The realities of complex, sub-state economic interdependence suggests that it is far too difficult and painful to contemplate undoing the ties that bind. In military security, the notion of interdependence is also well established, with the United States playing a vital role in maintaining the system. Thus if we talk of either a Pacific or Atlantic Century in terms that suggest regional coherence, it is unlikely to be accurate. Yes there is more regional interdependence, but there is also far more global interdependence. The regional variety depends on the success of the global interconnections.

Yet it is fair to talk of both a Pacific and Atlantic Century in the sense that both regions will be vital parts of the global process. In relative terms, growth in the Pacific is likely to be faster than that in Europe. It also seems likely that Europe will be a less secure place than it has been in the days of bipolarity and therefore the gap between the relative securities of the Atlantic and Pacific worlds may not be as great as once thought. Certainly arms control, in all its different varieties, will not be so much more successful in Europe as many had thought. The Pacific Century may not be based on a coherent region, but it will be part of the prosperity of Europeans and Americans alike.

## Notes

1. Karl Marx and Friedrich Engels, 'The Global Consequences of the Discovery of Gold in California', in Saul K. Padover (ed.), *On America and the Civil War: The Karl Marx Library*, ii (New York: McGraw Hill, 1972), 14–15.
2. This is discussed in Gerald Segal, *Rethinking the Pacific* (Oxford: Clarendon Press, 1990).
3. Adrian Room, 'Naming the Pacific', *Pacific Review*, 3 (1988).
4. These points are best developed in William Wallace, *Remaking Western Europe* (London: Frances Pinter for the RIIA, 1990).
5. Chalmers Johnson, 'South Korean Democratisation', *Pacific Review*, 1 (1989), and Gordon White (ed.), *Developmental States in East Asia* (London: Macmillan, 1988).
6. Segal, *The Soviet Union and the Pacific* (London: Unwin Hyman for the RIIA, 1990).
7. Id., 'East Asia: The New Balances of Power', *World Policy Journal* (Fall 1989).
8. Id. (ed.), *Arms Control in Asia* (London: Macmillan, 1987), and id., 'The Asian Road to Arms Control', *Arms Control Today* (May 1989).
9. David Arase, 'Pacific Cooperation', *Pacific Review*, 2 (1988).
10. Peter Drysdale, *International Economic Pluralism* (London: George Allen & Unwin, 1988).
11. Segal, 'Japan and the New International Relations', *Japan Forum* (Apr. 1990).
12. DeAnne Julius, *Global Companies and Public Policy* (London: Frances Pinter, 1990).
13. Peter Buckley and Hafiz Mirza, 'The Strategy of Pacific Asian Multi-Nationals', *Pacific Review*, 1 (1988).
14. Segal, 'Thinking Pacific', *Times Literary Supplement* (28 Apr. 1989), and 'Rethinking the Pacific', *Review of International Studies* (Summer 1990).
15. Kate Grosser and Brian Bridges, 'Economic Interdependence in East Asia', *Pacific Review*, 1 (1990).
16. Bill Emmot, *The Sun Also Sets* (London: Simon and Schuster, 1989).
17. Segal, 'East Asia', in Peter Byrd (ed.), *British Foreign Policy under Thatcher* (London: Philip Allen, 1988). See also Segal, *Rethinking the Pacific*.

# GUIDE TO FURTHER READING

N. J. Rengger

As will now be obvious, the literatures on all of the subjects covered in this book are enormous. Much of what is relevant is covered in the notes to the various chapters. However, it seemed sensible to prepare a short bibliographical guide to each of the sections in addition to this in order to facilitate further reading or study by those who are so minded.

## INTRODUCTION AND PART I

There is no complete account of the history of international thought. However, excerpts from the writings of well-known theorists and philosophers who have considered the questions of relations between as well as within political communities are included in H. M. A. Keens-Soper, Murray Forsyth, and Peter Savigear (eds.), *The Theory of International Relations* (London: George Allen & Unwin, 1970) and discussed in: Martin Wight, 'Western Values in International Relations', in H. Butterfield and Martin Wight (eds.), *Diplomatic Investigations* (London: George Allen & Unwin, 1966); Hedley Bull, *The Anarchical Society* (London: Macmillan, 1977); E. B. F. Midgely, *The Natural Law Tradition and the Theory of International Relations* (London: Elek, 1975); Chris Brown, *New Normative Theory in International Relations* (forthcoming); and N. J. Rengger, *Tradition, Transition and International Society* (forthcoming). An entertaining, if somewhat eccentric view is also sketched in Michael Donelan, *Elements of International Political Theory* (Oxford: Clarendon Press, 1991).

Books of articles that survey the course of twentieth-century writing on international politics include: Hedley Bull, 'The Theory of International Politics 1919–1969', in B. Porter (ed.), *The Aberystwyth Papers* (Oxford: Oxford University Press, 1972); Michael Banks, 'The Evolution of International Relations Theory', in id. (ed.), *Conflict in World Society* (Brighton: Harvester Wheatsheaf, 1984); A. J. R. Groom and William C. Olson, *International Relations Then and Now* (London: Harper Collins, 1991); Brown, *New Normative Theory in International Relations* (forthcoming); and N. J. Rengger, *Traditional, Transition and International Society* (forthcoming).

For accounts of the methodological questions at stake in international relations theory and debates about its future course see, amongst others: R. O. Keohane (ed.), *Neo-Realism and its Critics* (New York: Columbia University Press, 1984); Martin Hollis and Steve Smith, *Explaining and Understanding International Relations* (Oxford: Clarendon Press, 1990); James N. Rosenau, *Turbulence in World Politics: A Theory of Change and Continuity* (Hemel Hempstead: Harvester, 1990); James Der Derian and Michael Shapiro (eds.), *International/Intertextual Relations: Postmodern Readings of World Politics* (Lexington, Mass.: Lexington Books, 1989); and N. J. Rengger and Mark Hoffman (eds.), *Critical Theory and International Relations* (Hemel Hempstead: Harvester, 1992).

Most of the major works relevant to our three issues of this section are referred to in the notes. The two classic statements of the security dilemma are: John Herz, 'Idealist Internationalism and the Security Dilemma', *World Politics*, 2/2 (1950) and Herbert Butterfield, *History and Human Relations* (London: Collins, 1951). The classic statement of interdependence theory is Keohane and Joseph S. Nye, *Power and Interdependence: World Politics in Transition*, 2nd edn. (Boston: Little Brown, 1989).

Those interested in the political culture debate relevant to these issues and especially to the questions of international society and order should note that it is not usually considered part of the literature of 'international relations'—a view we believe is far too narrow and restrictive. Relevant work here includes Michael Gibbons, *Interpreting Politics* (Oxford: Basil Blackwell, 1989) as well as classic essays such as Peter Winch, *The Idea of A Social Science* (London: Routledge and Kegan Paul, 1956) and Clifford Geertz, *The Interpretation of Cultures* (New York: Basic Books, 1973). A useful modern edited collection is John Gibbins (ed.), *Contemporary Political Culture: Politics for a Postmodern Age* (London: Sage, 1989). For the implications of the debates for international politics, see especially Rengger's chapter, 'Incommensurability, International Theory and the Fragmentation of Western Political Culture', ibid.

PART II

On international policy economy the two best general texts are Robert Gilpin's magisterial *The Political Economy of International Relations* (Princeton, NJ: Princeton University Press, 1987), and Steven Gill and David Law, *The Global Political Economy* (Hemel Hempstead: Harvester, 1988). Other books covering different aspects of the literature include:

Roger Tooze and Craig Murphy (eds.), *The New International Political Economy* and Stephen Krasner (ed.), *International Regimes* (New York: Cornell University Press, 1982).

Of the writing of books on war, of course, there is virtually no end. Notable recent contributions that focus on the impact of modern technology include: Barry Buzan, *An Introduction to Strategic Studies* (London: Macmillan, 1987); Mathew Evangelista, *Innovation and the Arms Race* (Ithaca, NY: Cornell University Press, 1988); and Barry Posen, *The Sources of Military Doctrine* (Ithaca, NY: Cornell University Press, 1986). Two recent books that have both made a big impact and whose arguments should be pondered are: John Mueller, *Retreat From Doomsday: The Obsolescence of Major War* (New York: Basic Books, 1989), and Robert Jervis, *The Meaning of the Nuclear Revolution: Statecraft and the Prospect of Armageddon* (Ithaca, NY: Cornell University Press, 1990).

Diplomacy has not been as well served in recent years as some other areas of international politics. The best general treatment is still Adam Watson, *Diplomacy: The Dialogue between States* (London: Methuen, 1982). Other useful books of note include: Ronald Barston, *Modern Diplomacy* (London: Longmans, 1988), and, a classic of its kind, Harold Nicholson, *The Evolution of Diplomatic Method* (London: 1954).

International organizations, in contrast, have been the recipients of a positive explosion of interest and scholarship in recent years. A classic treatment is Inis Claude, Jr., *Swords into Ploughshares* (New York: Random House, 1971). Among useful recent books on this subject are: Paul Taylor and A. J. R. Groom (eds.), *International Institutions At Work* (London: Francis Pinter, 1988); Adam Roberts and Benedict Kingsbury (eds.), *United Nations, Divided World* (Oxford: Clarendon Press, 1989); Clive Archer, *International Organisation* (London: George Allen & Unwin, 1983); David Armstrong, *The Rise of International Organisation* (London: Macmillan, 1982). N. J. Rengger, *Treaties and Alliances of the World* (Harlow: Longmans, 1990) contains much useful documentary material and a general discussion of the role and function of aspects of international organizations in Chapter 1.

## PART III

For the ten issues in our last section we will give just two or three general books for each with one or two additions if warranted. The bibliographies of each of these will be a useful guide to further reading as, of course, will the notes in the relevant chapters. On Nuclear weapons and arms control, see: Jervis, *The Meaning of the Nuclear Revolution: Statecraft and the Prospect of Armageddon*; McGeorge Bundy, *Danger and Survival: Choices about the Bomb in the First Fifty Years* (New York: Random House,

1988); Richard Betts, *Nuclear Blackmail and Nuclear Balance* (Washington, DC: Brookings Institution, 1987); Lawrence Freedman, *The Evolution of Nuclear Strategy*, 2nd edn. (London: Macmillan, 1990); J. Baylis and J. Garnett, eds., *The Makers of Nuclear Strategy* (London: Pinters, 1991). See also Nye, 'Arms Control After the Cold War', *Foreign Affairs* (Winter 1989/90).

On terrorism, a standard general book is Paul Wilkinson, *Terrorism and the Liberal State*, 2nd edn. (London: Macmillan, 1987). Other recent works include: Charles W. Kedley, Jr. (ed.), *International Terrorism: Characteristics, Causes, Controls* (New York: St Martin's Press, 1990); Grant Wardlaw, *Political Terrorism: Theory, Tactics and Counter-measures*, 2nd edn. (Cambridge: Cambridge University Press, 1989).

On mediation and conflict resolution, see: C. R. Mitchell, *The Structure of International Conflict* (London: Macmillan, 1981); Banks (ed.), *Conflict in World Society*; and John Burton, *Global Conflict* (Brighton: Harvester Wheatsheaf, 1984).

Environmental issues have been another growth area of late, of course. An excellent background to the thinking can be found in Andrew Dobson, *Green Political Thought* (London: Harper Collins, 1990) and a first-rate survey of the contemporary issues is Frances Cairncross, *Costing the Earth* (London: Economist Books, 1991). Other good general treatments of this are D. Adamson, *Defending the World* (New York: St Martin's Press, 1990), and S. Schneider, *Global Warming* (San Francisco: Sierra Book Clubs, 1989).

The role of Islam in world politics is best explored in James P. Piscatori, *Islam in a World of Nation States* (Cambridge: Cambridge University Press, 1986) but interesting and perceptive analyses are also found in: Edward Mortimer, *Faith and Power: The Politics of Islam* (London: Faber, 1982); Albert Hourani, *A History of The Arab Peoples* (London: Faber, 1991); and Ira M. Lapidus *A History of Islamic Societies* (Cambridge: Cambridge University Press, 1990). Other relevant books include: Adeed Dawisha (ed.), *Islam in Foreign Policy* (Cambridge: Cambridge University Press, 1983); Patrick Bannerman, *Islam in Perspective* (London: Routledge, 1988); and Dilip Hiro, *Islamic Fundamentalism* (London: Collins, 1988).

The Debate on US decline was sent into overdrive by Paul Kennedy's *The Rise and Fall of the Great Powers* (London: George Allen & Unwin, 1988). The claim is also made, in a different form, in Peter Savigear, *Cold War or Détente: The International Politics of American Soviet Relations* (Brighton: Harvester Wheatsheaf, 1986), and analysed in Michael Pugh and Phil Williams (eds.), *Superpower Politics: Change in the United States and The Soviet Union* (Manchester: Manchester University Press, 1990). The best response to Kennedy's book, and indeed to the 'declinist' thesis in general, has been Nye, *Bound to Lead: The Changing Nature of American Power* (New York: Basic Books, 1990).

The current state of the Commonwealth of Independent States (which is the latest designation of the old USSR) is so indeterminate and changing so fast that books detailing what is going on are often out of date before they are published. However, recent books that are eminently worth reading, concentrating mainly on the significance of the changes both for the state itself and for its role in world politics, include: Michael MccGwire, *Perestroika and Soviet National Security* (Washington DC: Brookings Institution, 1991); Raymond L. Garthoff, *Détente and the Revolution in Soviet Military Doctrine* (Washington DC: Brookings Institution, 1990); and Pugh and Williams (eds.), *Superpower Politics: Change in the United States and the Soviet Union* (Manchester: Manchester University Press, 1990).

The changes in Europe since 1989 have also given rise to an explosion of books and articles on the subject. Among the most stimulating and provocative are: Ole Waever, *et al.* (eds.), *European Polyphony: Perspectives Beyond East–West Confrontation* (London: Macmillan, 1989); Barry Buzan, *et al.*, *The European Security Order Re-cast: Scenarios for the Post Cold War Era* (London: Frances Pinter, 1990); Richard Ullman, *Securing Europe* (New York: Adamantine Press, 1990); Adrian Hyde-Price, *European Security Beyond the Cold War: Four Scenarios for the Year 2010* (London: Sage, 1991); and Ralf Dahrendorf, *Reflections on the Revolutions in Europe* (London: Chatto and Windus, 1990).

The debate over the rise of the so-called 'Pacific century' has had a rather longer lead-time than many of the other issues in this section. Good discussions can be found in: Gerald Segal, *Rethinking the Pacific* (Oxford: Clarendon Press, 1990); Simon Winchester, *The Pacific* (London: Hutchinson, 1991); Robert Elegant, *Pacific Destiny* (New York: Viking, 1990); and S. B. Linder, *The Pacific Century* (Stanford, Calif.: Stanford University Press, 1986).

# INDEX